EYES TO SEE, EARS TO HEAR

A Journey Out of Fear
Into the Light

Grace
Faith
Peace

Robin Beth Saget

ISBN 978-1-63885-801-0 (Paperback)
ISBN 978-1-63885-802-7 (Digital)

Covenant Books
11661 Hwy 707
Murrells Inlet, SC 29576
www.covenantbooks.com

This book is dedicated to
Evan Parker Stewart
and
Betty "Buddy" Jazowski.

CONTENTS

Introduction..7
A Simple Prayer (St. Francis of Assisi)...................................9

1. Aloneness 11
2. Connections 18
3. Contradictions...31
4. Control—Burdens..48
5. Empty 57
6. Expectations 136
7. Faith and Trust 164
8. Forgiveness 277
9. I Am 290
10. Judgment..319
11. Masks 326
12. Outcomes..333
13. Reactions 373
14. Silence—Stillness...463
15. Wandering, Wondering 515
16. A Few Thoughts 554
17. My Testimony..570

Bibliography..573

INTRODUCTION

When making a decision, I tend to weigh the pros and cons of the results, and then I have to deal with the combative voice in my head that asks, "Is this the right direction, or will I fail?" Once I silence that voice from my thoughts, I can clearly determine if I can live with the rewards or consequences of my decision. I stop and retreat from the combat within me and listen to hear God's wisdom and the guidance I've been given to live with what decision I choose.

After spending decades listening to opinions, judgments, and interpretations, I was guided to seek the truth. I became a truth seeker. I asked questions, researched references, and read anything I could find to help me make sense of the life I was living. This was not an easy task, because I had to question what I believed was my truth and whom I trusted to deliver the truth. I asked how I would really know what the truth was.

I lived my life in the shadow of others' interpretations of the truth. I always feared doubting their word, because when I sought an alternative to what they offered, I was threatened with banishment, so consequently, to my own detriment, I stayed in bondage in my own self-inflicted prison and doubted my own truth. I knew that love was the opposite of fear, light the opposite of darkness, and truth the opposite of a lie. I knew a lie was still a lie even if one hundred people said it was the truth.

I just wanted to know the truth so I could continue to live in the light and love of God and have faith so when I asked for the truth, I would get the truth. I spent decades searching for the truth, writing letters to God and meditating on the messages that I received from Him. I learned to become still enough to silence the combative voices, ultimately being guided by His truth.

This is a book of all my meditations and letters to God. It is my hope that you know you are not alone on your journey and that these words will inspire you to seek your truth and live in peace, joy, hope, and faith with God's voice guiding you, as I have allowed Him to guide me.

> May the Lord bless you and keep you; may the Lord make His face to shine upon you and be gracious to you; may the Lord lift up His countenance upon you and give you peace. (Numbers 6:22)

A SIMPLE PRAYER
(ST. FRANCIS OF ASSISI)

Lord, make me an instrument of your peace.
Where there's hatred, let me sow love.
Where there's injury, let me sow pardon.
Where there's doubt, let me sow faith.
Where there's despair, let me sow hope.
Where there's darkness, let me sow light.
Where there's sadness, let me sow, joy.
O Divine Master,
Grant that I may not so much seek
To be consoled as to console,
To be understood as to understand,
To be loved as to love.
For it is in the giving that we receive,
It is in the pardoning that we are pardoned.
It is in the dying that we are born to eternal life.
Amen!

CHAPTER 1

Aloneness

GET MY ANSWERS

When I am alone and I reflect on where I was and where I've arrived, I realize that being alone is sometimes necessary to hear the still small voice. When trying to understand a situation, it is sometimes necessary to get another's point of view, but only if it's a suggestion. Taking someone's opinion as only a suggestion, not making it my solution, is part of my life's journey. So it is best, at times, to have a deep conversation with God to figure out what to do next.

When I depend too much on someone else and not on God, I find myself doing what's best for them but not for myself. When I am confronted with a future situation, I can find myself so absorbed in the future dialogue that I lose sight of my present situation; this is fear of the unknown. The simple prayer, "Thy will be done!" helps me regroup back into faith. I will concentrate on my positive reactions and faith. It is all meant to be as God intends, and I trust that. I have faith that in my aloneness, I will get my answers.

PROMISE OF SPRING

After I remove the burdens of carrying that which is not mine to carry, I am emptied. I can be alone knowing I am never alone. I can have relationships that complement rather than engulf. In their leaving, which left me empty and alone, I was able to give back to them that which was not mine to hold. I can now connect knowing I am okay if I am alone. My need to be filled was a diversion of my wanting to be loved and cherished. I had to fill the need so I would notice and accept His gift. In my aloneness, it is time to pull the weeds and fertilize the garden again for the promise of spring.

What Path?

In my time alone, I can ask myself, "Is where I am where I want to be? Is what I'm doing good for me? Is what I'm doing really what I want to do? Does this direction feel right for me, or am I following in another's footsteps?" My choices may not please others if they are good for me. I am being true to myself if I listen to the answers to my questions, which guide me on my own path to make footprints of my own.

I can accept and trust that all my struggles to fix things only caused detours and pain. Whether they are meant to be with me or I am meant to be alone, I no longer detour off my path. Being with me is more important than detours. I am never truly alone. I am in the best company with God and myself. In my aloneness, I know that someone gave me a gift because He planned to fill it. It was God, so I am never really alone.

Choices

I am a product of all my experiences and of all the opportunities for me to become who I am and to evolve my spirit. I am surrounded by another's life lessons, and when I am hurt by their choices, I struggle with letting it go. I know it's not about me, but I take it so personally. I know I am not their target, but my faith in them is compromised. I am able to get through the pain that I feel when others make choices that hurt me.

I used to be surrounded by the loud drama of others. I surrounded myself with those who kept affirming the negative. Being alone and emptied are better than being filled with negative drama.

The questions I ask are, "Why do I let their choices hurt me? Why am I giving them so much of me that I suffer? They have moved on with their lives, so why won't I? I know it can't be changed, so why do I struggle to let go of what is if it can't be changed? Even God can't erase the past, so what is my goal by holding on to something I can't control or change?"

I have faith and trust in God's plan because I know He is in control. I know we are put in one another's lives for a reason—to learn or teach. I am learning to learn and teach without losing myself in another's lessons and to be as good to myself as I am to others.

No Sacrifice

No one's prejudice, judgment, or fear defines me. I define myself through my voice, my truth, and my faith. I was always losing myself in the image of everything I experienced by making me into who they defined me to be. I was others' lightning rods and their problem solver, rescuer, and caretaker. I lost me to those I loved.

I am more than how others define me. I am embracing everything clearly, and I am now learning not to impose who I am and not to lose who I am meant to be. I struggled with keeping me real in the turbulence of others and lost me to their needs. If a life lesson is hurtful, I clearly take care of me by saying no. I no longer sacrifice myself for another and no longer accommodate them at the risk of compromising myself. I am grateful for all my life lessons knowing that all helped me become who I am evolving to become. By letting go of what was for what I want and at the risk of being alone, I can trust I am where I am meant to be today. I no longer sacrifice me for another.

Not Always about Me

I have surrounded myself with people who have similar issues to mine. Now that I am changing my behavior and healing, I am beginning to say no to those I have always said yes to, and that is not acceptable to someone who has always been allowed to control me.

I always gave them what they wanted so they would accept me even if it meant I was sacrificing my own truth. Now that I am no longer engaged, they have chosen to leave.

In my aloneness, I am finding my worth and seeing how special I am. No one could have done this for me, so I am emptying them and accepting the void that once housed them. I am filling myself with me. I know not all life lessons are about me, and if I am touched by another's life lesson, I can say, "No, this is not mine. I no longer enable, sacrifice, rescue, or problem-solve at my expense." I bless them, love them, and pray they find their way. I no longer detour for them. I learn what is needed, and I'm grateful. I have faith and trust in God's plan. If I've learned anything, it is that it always works out as God intends; and it may not necessarily be what I want, but it is His plan.

QUESTIONING

Membership card—when one becomes a member of an organization, a card-carrying rite of passage ensues. When one is born into a family, their membership becomes purposeful, and the responsibility of donation begins. Yet when the purpose is interrupted by estrangement, it can take longer to arrive at the destination due to an unwilling participant. During this wait, learning about life and growth will continue.

An adult's lie becomes a child's truth, and the product is misleading. I believed what they said was my worth. I believed because I wanted to be accepted. Now that I have questioned their truth and I have found my voice, whether alone or not, I know who I am. I have journeyed alone for many years, willing to continue to fulfill my purpose.

SKIPPING STONES

When we leave one painful situation without resolution, it's like skipping stones. We keep hitting the water, causing rings of discontent. We can only wait until the water becomes still again. In the aloneness, we can only learn the lesson within the pain so we can heal and move on.

I used to be so afraid to be alone that I would knock on any door to open, exchanging one painful situation for another so that I would feel full. I skipped, like a stone, from relationship to relationship, not dealing with what was the core of my fear. It was only when I became empty and still, like water, that I could hold my own heart in my hands and saw my soul in my own eyes. That was when I truly felt and saw love.

WANT, NEED, RELEASE

We all have basic needs—food, shelter, and clothing—yet when they turn into a deep-seated desire, wants can replace needs, and the journey of being lost arises. I wanted to be loved and accepted by others, but I needed to love and accept myself first and have them complement me, not complete me. When I come to a decision that will only have an impact on me, I will investigate if it will enhance or deter my spiritual journey. In relationships, we are all stakeholders in decisions and must all have a voice unless it only has an impact on ourselves. When I gave away my voice to be accepted, I sacrificed myself to meet their agenda. Now being on a parallel or perpendicular road with others, I need to be emptied and alone in order to travel alongside them without losing me.

A WALK IN THE LIGHT

I had to learn to be alone with myself. Having allowed myself to be defined by others, I had to shed and let go of their burden that I became responsible for carrying. This learned behavior helped me see whom I didn't want to be, so I had to be alone in order to see myself. My awareness began when I started saying no. Even though I did not honor my own word and even when I questioned my own truth, I slowly began to release that which was not mine, again leaving me alone. Yet at times, the silence became so loud that I wanted to fill the empty space of loneliness with drama to feel alive. I had to relearn what it meant to be alone in order to relearn what it meant to say, "Hello. This is who I am." I now no longer walk in their shadow but in my own light.

Nourishment

When I find myself reacting over someone's choice that differs from mine, what really matters? Does it matter that I am right and he/she is wrong? Does it matter if I focus my energy into making them think as I do? Why do I get so irritated if their behavior does not align with mine? In these uncomfortable moments of disconnection, what really matters? Why am I feeling this way, and what is it that I need to do to make myself comfortable? What matters is what lesson I am supposed to learn from this situation for my life's journey. Where does my true nourishment lie?

Seek

I used to get my validation and shame from the responses of others. Now no longer attached to their approval or disapproval, I find myself alone in my thoughts and actions. Would I rather be surrounded by angry souls and assimilate myself and allow them to define me, or would I rather be alone? I guess that question is answered by my present status. At times, I want someone to hold me or to engage in a conversation, but now is not that time. I refuse to go back to my old behavior—making my uncomfortable silence loud with their drama. So in this alone time, I will continue to seek and learn the truth and will continue on my life's path to fulfill my destiny.

Help Me One More Time

How many more times do I need to give a piece of myself away to be seen or loved? How many more times do I have to show up wearing a mask so that no one will see the true, needy, broken me? How many more times do I allow myself to hear words of self-loathing and unworthiness? How many more times do I have to look to someone else to fill me and deny God's love for me? How many more times? One more time: Help!

Let's Meet for Coffee

I used to hold on to relationships because that was where I defined myself. I saw myself in the eyes of another, believed the words spoken about me as my truth, and accepted actions toward me as justified. I feared that if they left or if I changed, then who would I be? I danced their steps, sang their songs, and answered their requests, only to be tossed aside when I began to dance my own steps and sing my own song.

When this was done to me, I thought it was unjust and unfair, and I felt abandoned. In my aloneness, I found that the words to my own song defined my truth and that the steps to my own dance protected me from stumbling. That was their greatest gift to me, that in their goodbye, I finally said hello to me. So let's meet for coffee, and we can get to know each other as our authentic, true self.

CHAPTER 2

Connections

OWNING

When we purchase something, we own it; it is ours for the duration. But when another soul crosses our path, that soul and that soul's choices are not ours to own or control. That soul is there to complement or contradict; either way, it will bring a life lesson to share. It is when one's behavior causes distress that conflict arises. Unless we can truly and honestly own our own behaviors and choices, the union is futile. The back-and-forth banter of right or wrong ensues, leaving the soul's purpose unseen, unheard, and unlearned. So I am to own my own no matter how unpleasant it may be; unless I can see myself, I will never see anyone else.

WILLING TO SHARE

My first experience with truth and ownership is when someone asks me to share. As this rite of passage unfolds, I am asked to find comfort in allowing someone else to share what is mine. It is the expectation that this moment will be reciprocal and that what is mine is yours and what is yours is mine. This can draw us into the abyss of confusion, ultimately asking this question: "What is mine?" My soul, my body, my spirit, my choices, my behavior, my truth, my word, my actions, my beliefs, and my life can only be shared but never relinquished to another to be controlled. So when we are asked to share and make connections, remember, "What is mine is me, and what is theirs is them."

AUTHORITY

In the word *authority* is the word *author*. We write our own stories as we encounter others on our journey. The words, "You're not the boss of me!" are spoken in desperation to keep my identity to be seen, heard, and cherished for the gift that I am. I am willing to communicate and collaborate, but not to be controlled. My need to push back from the control is to keep my own voice and live in my own truth even if it means I will be abandoned.

CONNECT

There comes a time in one's life when materialistic things don't matter as much, when money is only celebrated by affording what's needed, and when love is the only song the heart wants to sing. The busyness of the day deadens the joy and the blessing of the smallest miracles, the oneness we all want to share. We no longer stop and gaze into another's eyes and bring a smile, which, in turn, can voice kindness into warmth, even for the coldest heart. This is one ultimate connection, yet we battle to connect. When we all look at our similarities, we all see that we want and need the same things: to be seen, to be heard, and to be loved.

BARTERING

In history, the major way of trading was to barter; someone had what someone else wanted or needed, and the trading would begin. Trying to offer less than the original worth became the cornerstone of not showing its true value or its real worth. This has been taken into our relationships. By not honoring, cherishing, blessing, and showing value to one another, we have learned to chisel away at someone's true worth by bartering them down to what will fit our needs. This dismissal has caused many a heartbreak. There is no bartering truth, worth, or love. There is no room for minimizing what truly matters. The only real thing that we should accept to its fullest potential is knowing we are all the love and light in God's eyes.

Separate and Equal

Our origin is not only physical; we all come into the world through the same channels, and we all die. The spiritual origin is that we all are children of God and are here for a spiritual evolution of our soul. With that equal, what separates us are the life lessons, experiences, and opportunities for our soul to evolve. Yet add into that the equation of marriage, children, siblings, or friendships and the journey then becomes more separate and equal. Whose journey is most like or unlike ours? Whom can we identify with the most? Who is open or closed to our love and support? There comes a time in our life when saying yes or no is the only response. The rest is up to God and us to evolve. Whom can we help, and who will embrace it?

Sharing Is Not Losing

When we finally learn equity of voice, our silence can become deafening if taken away. When we finally learn how to share our physical and emotional being, we can become a ghost if we lose sight of our shadow. When taught how to share, there is a fine line between what is mine and what is yours and what is ours. How many times have our vision become blurred by the request of, "Can you?" It is in the pivotal moment of enlightenment, when one has to take a step back, that with a compassionate heart and in a loving whisper, we say no. So when asked to share what is mine, the caution is always going to be assessed. How much do I give of me before I am lost in you?

In God Company

I must be careful whom I call friend and be careful with the company I keep. Despite having put my negative experiences in the rearview mirror, there are times when glancing at the past, they will appear as a trigger in my now. In these moments, I assess what is mine and what is theirs. When in the company of manipulation, how much will I choose to own or engage? Although I will not treat others this way, others will still engage in this activity in my presence. It is then that I have to decide to set a boundary not to change their behavior but to protect my energy. So when I encounter energy that is not positive, I will continue on my journey toward good company.

Engage

When asked to engage, it is an invitation into a scenario, a story, or a dance with another. Yet if not aware, the pull into another's drama cannot be foreseen, and the hook will pierce the heart. Careful footing when contemplating engaging in another story takes careful thought. How much do I want to give so that I still see me? I can love and show compassion and empathy without losing my truth or my voice. It comes with compromise and with the boundary of how far I can bend before I break.

No more willing to be a ghost in someone else's story, I choose to love without forgetting who I am. Sharing is giving, but giving is not relinquishing myself to the point where I become invisible and where when we stand together in the sunlight, there is only one shadow. Love and accept whatever gets in the way until it ceases to be an obstacle, and engage in the act of living out what is.

Share My Story

Fear of being vulnerable is a big issue. When I was vulnerable, trusting, and innocent, I was abused, and my good nature was taken advantage of. This began my defense system—the walls I built and how I responded with sarcasm. I found it easier to deal with the pain of feeling taken for granted by becoming defensive than to talk about the pain. I see now that, that was not productive. It prolonged things and usually caused damage. Things that were said in anger and defense to protect myself may have hurt the other person.

Communicating my wants, needs, desires, and fears may not change the other person's behavior, but it will help me get back to myself. It may not get me what I want, but it may uncover this to the other person. By communicating my feelings, it may make the other person aware of these feelings, but I can't expect to change the person's actions to make me happy. Expressing my fears to another may help them be aware of inappropriate behavior they may choose to address.

By relating my feelings, I may be at risk of disappointments; but if I don't share my feelings, I will always lose. No one can read my mind. I have to remain vulnerable knowing I can protect myself from being taken for granted or abused. I have a voice.

Reflection

How many times have I looked in a mirror and stared into my own soul through life's eyes only to see the true me? How many times have I judged another and tried to control or manipulate an outcome only to see me? It is in my silence and my listening that I hear the subtle, kind, gentle whisper that reminds me that what I judge in others, I judge in myself and that which I do not like in another is my true reflection in my life's mirror. We are all souls on an evolutionary journey. This union with others, myself, and God is a reflection of my truth. See the beauty in all our reflections.

Standstill

The more I move into someone else, the more I move away from me. There is a crossroad into someone's story, yet with compassion, empathy, understanding, acceptance, patience, and love, I can support another without losing balance. When I stand still in the midst of being confronted by drama, I remain steadfast in my footing, not stumble or fall into another's drama. I can show support without stepping into their story, becoming another player. By showing my positive gifts and attributes, I am able to be me while I help them find who they are meant to be. My burden is when I venture into another's footprint. I need to remember to stand still when my feet have already made an imprint.

MY ENERGY

What do I focus on and what do I devote most of my energy toward that will benefit my spiritual growth? It is one thing to be kind, loving, considerate, compassionate, and giving, but crossing that fine line between you and me is how I can lose me in you. I may be tempted to make what's yours mine, but this may result in me trying to control outcomes, which results in disappointments, resentments, and judgments. All my energy is then drained in these negative reactions, so when you show up in my life, I am aware of what separates us, what draws us together, and the wisdom to know who I am.

GOODBYE AGAIN

On my new adventures, I see what I need to take along and what I need to leave behind. Each time I have one more encounter with someone from my past who has helped me evolve, it is one more goodbye. Each time I can gently bless someone with a thank-you for a memory that no longer serves me, it is one more goodbye. I may never know anyone's purpose in anyone's life, but I am grateful for those who have crossed my path or those who have remained. As I repack my luggage for my new journey, I reflect and purge that which is no longer needed. It is with one more goodbye that I move toward my new adventures. I now say hello and welcome.

Whole and Parts

It is said that no one can complete another and that we must enter a relationship with our completeness to complement another. We are all parts of another's experience that makes us who we are, yet one of our parts may be misplaced. So we may replace our missing part with their part, which ultimately brings sorrow and pain. We need to be complete with our own parts to make us whole, so consequently, no one's parts can make our wholeness. We are complements of choices from another's experiences; we decide what fits and what doesn't. We need to celebrate our parts of diversity and commonality. That's what makes us whole.

Our Triggers' Goal Is Peace

When I am in the presence of someone who is in pain, his or her issues may mirror a memory, which may trigger some pain. If not careful, sharing can develop into a competition. All our pain is important, but instead of revisiting my trigger, I can move from that into joy and validate how I have moved into peace. It will help me focus on the goal of recovery rather than the pain that motivated me into it. Mark Nepo wrote, "I had to be less than I was intended in order to be loved so I shelved my light. Now there is no more room for worthlessness."

Show Up to Share Instead of Disappearing

I used to show up for a visit as my true self, only to quickly assimilate into my visitor. I used to condemn a breaker of promises, only to later question trusting my own promise to myself. Sharing experiences is an opportunity to present my story with another. This story is not shared so that I can feel good about myself or to seek pity for an adversity I have survived. It is through sharing and showing up that I begin to see me in you and understand that as vast as the universe truly is, we are all connected by sharing our stories and not allowing one another to disappear in another's drama. We make connections by sharing and updating our souls' core, only to evolve and grow into one another, ourselves. We are one, just different puzzle pieces.

What Lies Beneath

A quote from *The Help* from one of the maids to a little white girl is, "You is smart, you is important, you is good." This very telling affirmation from one soul to another depicts the very essence of what lies beneath. It diminishes gender, race, and status. It alleviates prejudice and control. There is no social status connected to a sentence that validates and that is filled with pure love, joy, compassion, acceptance, approval, patience, and peace. So as I continue to move through my journey, I thank everyone I meet who offers a smile of kindness or a piece of his or her energy, whether it be positive or negative. It teaches me who I aspire to be and exactly who I don't want to be. I bless everyone who shows me who they are beneath.

Share a Memory

If I were to truly separate myself from all my experiences, life lessons, and opportunities, who would I be? If I were to purge all my pain, sorrow, joy, and pleasure, what would be left to share? In my intimate connections with my soul, I am the keeper of these life lessons and experiences to share. I am holding them, flipping the negative into positive to share the ultimate love and light that we all have inside. We are not our memories, yet through our experiences, we get to share wisdom. We are all a special delivery for all the lives we touch. Our stories do not define who we are; they are merely opportunities to say, "I see you in me."

Belonging

Friendships come and go, and families remain connected through blood, yet they may become estranged. Children are connected, and then they leave, and partners remain and grow together or apart. But ultimately, we belong to ourselves. Despite going through all these scenarios, I am still longing to belong. It's different now that I no longer accommodate everyone. Those whom I love and want close are not interested. This need to belong sometimes becomes so big that I give pause to what I need to do and whom I need to be, and then I come back to me in this moment, cherishing all that brought me back to myself. I will compromise but not sacrifice. I know where I do belong, and I am home in me.

MENTOR

Wanting to mentor someone is a responsibility that requires the knowledge they seek. Knowing what works for me may not align with your journey and may cause a disruption, which, in turn, develops guilt, regret, and shame. How can I teach you something without the knowledge that is required for you to learn? If we are not destined to continue our journey, this is when I will humble myself and affirm that I don't have all the answers to the questions that you ask. I will let go of you and pray that God will bring someone into your life who will lead you to the knowledge you seek, to the answers to your questions. This is love, and I love you.

FEET ON THE GROUND

Keeping someone on a pedestal can be painstaking for me and for them. My expectations of them will far outweigh their ability to meet my needs. Their participation may lead them to feel they need to be in control. Either way this plays out, we're all better off at eye level with our feet on the ground, looking into one another's eyes, extending our hands out. When I look up, I see God.

I SEE BOTH OF US

I always thought I was alone in my shame and despair, that I was the only one who had suffered such pain. In my own self-inflicted bondage, I hid so that no one would see me, like I was a leper with all my scars. I humbly know that we all have our stories and our pasts and that we all have scars that we hide in fear of judgment and retaliation. So my promise is, I will come to you and invite you to come to me so we can share our stories and see our similarities, and we will know that you are no better or worse than I, and I am no better or worse than you. I see you in me.

THE GOLDEN RULE

In times of fear, when my faith is blocked by the darkness, I pray and ask God to help me feel His light, and I am reminded that He is my provider and protector. Then I am able to feel the love that He gives to me, and I pass it along. We are all His children, so I want to let you know, I am available to help any of you, my brothers and sisters, even from a far. I can pray for you!

LANGUAGE BARRIER

Finding a way to live in peace amid turmoil needs my conscious effort so I'll remain positive even if I feel as if I need to be combative. I don't always understand the things I'm told, so I will continue to ask questions. This may lead to the frustration of the other person as they try to learn a new language that I will understand. I know this is cumbersome, and having been a teacher, I know we all learn differently. So please help me find patience when I am faced with a combative person as they learn to communicate with me so I'll understand.

AN INVITATION

It's one thing to choose something for ourselves and quite another for that something to be chosen for us. This action can cause fear and rebellion if that something is not what we want or request. So in this time of uncertainty and distance, what do we really need to do to accept the unacceptable? As the illness of our nation continues to wreak havoc on our daily lives, what we really need to see is God's light in these dark times. The sun is still shining, the birds are still singing, our children are still laughing, and God is still providing. What I need to do is stay in that light and stay in faith as my hopes and dreams come to fruition. Would you join me in this humble request?

Discussion

Discussions can harbor resentment if judgment enters the mix. Information can be viewed as opinions or facts, but the discussion can become heated if one person is trying to change the mind of the other as they present their information into the forum. Points of view can enlighten a discussion as new information is presented, but if I am told what to believe or who I should be, then the discussion will come to an abrupt halt as I walk away. Don't tell me what to believe or who I should be, but tell me what you believe and who you are by respecting who we are in the discussion. I'm not better than you. I'm just better than I used to be.

My Calling Card

What is the first thing I notice when I meet someone? Is it how they are dressed, their height, their race, or their gender? What is it that I want people to see in me when they first meet me? I will greet them with my calling card: my smile. I will show them how God lives in my heart by displaying my joy and gratitude by using my calling card: my smile. They may not remember my name, but they will remember how I made them feel when they received my calling card: my smile.

New Relationship

Learning to live drama free in a dramatic world can be cumbersome. It can lead to stress and anxiety in fear of being chastised or scrutinized by someone with an opinion different from ours. When we stop listening to one another with an open heart and an open mind with a closed mouth, we cease to have a relationship that is full of opportunities to learn, grow, and deepen one another with exciting new possibilities. So let's learn how to communicate with a kind, open heart and mind so we can have the relationship we both want.

Encouragement

The word *encouragement* refers to the act of giving someone support and hope. I've watched a mother bird encourage her baby to take his first flight by gently nudging him to the edge of the nest. I've watched a young child crawl up onto the lap of her grandfather and hand him her favorite book, which he has read to her so many times to the point that he has memorized the words, but her reaction is still so precious that he is willing to encourage her to read. I've watched tears flow from a broken heart that has to learn to let go before they are ready to say goodbye.

I may not know everything, but if I can encourage someone to ask questions, then they can seek the knowledge they need to encourage another. We learn what we live, and if we live with hope and faith, then those whom we are meant to encourage will become hopeful and faithful. What am I teaching others to see?

Show, Not Tell

Having fostered many opinions in my lifetime, I've realized I am not responsible for anyone else's opinions, judgments, or interpretations. We are all on our own timeline and journey, and to promote my viewpoint onto another without solicitation is no better than someone else telling me how to feel when I lose a loved one. I can offer advice and encouragement without telling the person who to be or how to act. I will show them, not tell them, because they will be able to see God in me by my word and deed.

Reaction

It's so easy to be in a good mood when those I love are happy. But the minute someone becomes agitated or unhappy, I feel an unrest, and my old behavior whispers in my ear to go fix it for them because I was the one who caused the unrest. This serves no purpose, because there is absolutely no truth behind that thought. So I will check in with the person, and then I will ask God to keep my heart soft as their heart remains hardened. I will look for the joy from my own eyes even if their eyes see darkness. I will find blessings in each moment as they complain about everything. I will pray they find peace, joy, love, and healing in their despair as I continue to live in love, faith, and hope.

Show Up as Me

I've watched relationships crumble to dust, those passionate love stories withering away like a dried leaf. I've watched families spew cruel accusations with lies and judgment, resulting in a closed, hardened heart, all for the need to control. I've watched a child's smile turn into a painful expression of loathing and despair. To what end is all this behavior forging toward? Knowing no one is any more responsible for anyone else's choices, how will all this result in a positive, loving relationship of diversity? I will continue to show up and be my best self, accepting you as I hope you'll accept me.

CHAPTER 3

Contradictions

Hater of Haters Is Still a Hater

I know that the closer I get to you, the more negativity pulls on me. I continue to struggle with remaining in my light when all I want to do is defend myself for not going into the darkness. I have to remember that I am a soul in a human experience. We all are. What is my goal—to be right or to be happy? When I judge another, call it negative, am I not being negative about their negativity? Hating a hater is a hater. I am a blessing, so I should act like it.

Detachment

Detachment, setting boundaries, and letting go—these recovery words have been the forefront of my healing. As I can come back to healing, I will forever be trusting, I will forever be forgiving, and I will forever be my own light. Those who want to face toward the light hold accountability. Again, the burden of encouraging is not my ultimate responsibility. We all do what we choose; we all believe our own truth. If our truths collide, I will bless them, walk away, and stay true to myself. This is all I can do to be in my light for today.

Flip-Flop

As I flip-flop through my contradictions and as I heal my broken dreams and accept all that is, I know too well that sorrow often breaks the crust of a superficial life, only to uncover its deepest realities. Through the darkness, I know I have always arrived where I intend to be. What is my struggle?

Contradictions

Negative or positive, one thing I know for sure is how I can drill my negative trigger to its origin. One thing I am perfecting is flipping a negative thought to a positive thought. I choose to believe, trust, and have faith. I choose to be comfortable in not knowing. I've chosen to bless those who still suffer in the darkness. I choose to show compassion and empathy without sacrificing who I am and who I have become.

Dissipate

How many times have I survived a fall, broken promises, inappropriate responses, abandonment, bullying, or shattered dreams? How many times have I gotten up after a fall? And although bruised and perhaps a bit broken, in spite of all of it, I've survived many times, and I've forgiven, found compassion, and moved forward into the days and moments of my being. This is life in spite of the hurt, the joy, and the humble moments of clarity; this is what it is. So dance, plant a garden, take a walk, and notice everything. This is the evolutionary journey of the soul.

Opposites

Opposites; contradictions; unsymmetrical experiences; judgments of good, bad, happy, sad, dark, or light; and the struggle of always trying to make it right are defined by standards, and to what end? We are born into this world to evolve. We are souls on a journey to experience all opposites so that we can always know that light is love. Yet in my struggle, I continue to emerge from the darkness of the abyss. I know the abyss has not always been a foe; it's shown me refuge when the fear has become too real, and it has helped me take back the energy and the power given to the darkness. So I welcome all experiences of opposites, contradictions, and unsymmetrical faces to assist in my journey.

A Cloudy Day

One may think that with clouds come sadness or that I can only be happy if the sun is shining. Having survived and gotten up off the floor many times, I've realized the falling down does not bring the fear it once held. Always searching for that feel-good moment has left me missing many opportunities—truth and honesty; understanding and peace in knowing; climbing offering new sites; and kindness offering, giving, breathing, and knowing the air of God's breath. Even if the sun is not shining, there is always an inner light that illuminates who we are.

Anxiousness versus Acceptance

How many times have I been so anxious or so impatient that I took matters into my hands? How many years have I spent not looking at all the answered prayers and at how I've always found the silver lining on the dark cloud? As I reflect on my years of recovering, I am reminded that all my worry and anxiousness never amounted to anything but feeding the fear and making me unhappy. So after I dry my tears and rid myself of the self-inflicted pain, I can say that I do have faith in God's timing and His plan for His grace. When fear knocks at the door, let faith answer.

Soften

A stone wall with no cracks or no light shining through makes me wonder how to penetrate that which has been hardened. God only enters through the cracks, and that is where the light comes in. Having hardened and softened my heart for years, the contradictions have left me wondering, will there ever be a time when I will remain soft and open? My contradictions are trust versus mistrust, abandonment versus fulfillment, and fear versus love. Yet by having faith, trusting in God, and believing His grace, I can soften.

PURPOSEFUL

The word *purpose* has a goal in mind: to use whatever to get to the destination. That whatever then becomes purposeful to teach that goal. Yet it is when trying to use the old to attain the new that the journey becomes difficult. Carrying the old that has helped me survive and attempting to fit it into the new to assist moving me along to fulfill my purpose are contradictions that cause pain. I can't make the old fit into the new any more than I can fit a square peg into a round hole. So it is with a gentle push goodbye and an acknowledgment of grace that I humbly thank all who have helped me get here. All that is purposeful is temporary, as the more I empty, the more I receive.

FORCE

When I push when I should pull, I waste valuable energy. When I hold on to that which I should let go, that is infringing my energy into and onto that which is not mine. This force can be used for or against; it is either helpful or a hindrance. Clutching my fist will not make it mine any more than if I take it without permission. Yet how many times have I put this into practice only to bellow the pain of my noncompliance with the truth? When I open my hand, my mind, and my heart, the light shines in me so that I am illuminated and my path is clear. When I can bless that which does not complement my soul and when I let go of that which is not mine to hold, my emptiness is filled with what is.

Forward, Sidestep, Stumble, Fall, Get Up

Forward, sidestep, stumble, fall, get up—this dance of life can be as exciting and joyful as it can be painful and debilitating. The changes and movements in the dance of life are all about evolution. Everyone enjoys the first lick of ice cream on a hot day, but for it to remain in that moment, it will melt into sadness. With every painful and joyful experience and with every contradiction, there is a life lesson to be drawn from this evolutionary dance. This requires a recalculation of the movements and steps. The algorithm of two steps forward, sidestepping, stumbling, falling, then getting up and repeating makes for one exciting, beautiful journey when viewed through the eyes of a child. So I will dance on in my life.

I Exist

Even if I disappear from another's life, that does not mean I'm invisible. Even if I'm abandoned by another's heart, it doesn't mean I am unworthy of being loved. Even if another walks away from me, it does not mean I am not approachable.

Say No

I have watched so many messages that tell about selling the soul to be loved and accepted. I have compromised my values, my morals, and myself just because I was told to do so in order to be accepted. This action was a clear contradiction of who I really was. My words and deeds were negotiable with the stipulation that I would receive love. Until I was willing to lose all that I allowed to define me, I realized I was only betraying myself, and I finally said no.

Glimmer

I see that I am a product of all my experiences. I can accept the negative and the positive. I have learned to be as kind to myself as I am to others. Just because a relationship has ended doesn't mean they have stopped loving each other. Sometimes, they have just stopped hurting each other. So one of the easiest ways to be happy is to let go of that which does not define me, the things that make me sad. I can find a glimmer of light and hope in all the little annoyances that may rob me of my joy.

Not to Settle

Settling for what another has to offer or accepting the status quo or seeing this as all I deserve to receive is me selling myself short. This gives my power to another as if they know what's better for me than I do for myself. Only God and I know what's best for me.

Abundance is not determined by race, gender, social status, or religion; but by the grace of God, all are deserving and entitled to receive unconditional love, financial security, emotional stability, and good health. So if I can think it, I can believe it. If I can strive forward, then I can achieve it. Whatever it is, I deserve what God has to offer.

Do unto Others

Living in a world and being a part of a family of contradictions, the old adage, "Do as I say, not as I do," comes to mind all too often as I have certain encounters. Giving advice, a compliment, or a helping hand is clothed in kindness, consideration, and compassion. Yet when control and manipulation are added into the recipe, it causes defensive behavior housed in fear, an ingredient that makes the relationship toxic. So while the others are choosing to live in fear, I am choosing to "do unto others." This simple statement allows you to be you and me to be me so we can continue our journey together.

When the Shoe Doesn't Fit

We can spend a lifetime looking for love, happiness, and the just right fit. When I encountered that which did not complement my soul's purposeful journey, instead of a simple, "No, thank you!"

my chameleon assimilated me into fitting into a shoe that did not fit. Yet it was when I began with my simple, "No, thank you," even though others left me that I remained true to myself. I will not judge them if we don't fit, but I will thank them for teaching me exactly the person I don't want to be and for the blessing of being true to myself as I strive to be the person I am meant to be.

Let Go to Find Me

When one says goodbye, the sadness may take a while to melt into gratitude. When I said goodbye to those I thought would join me on my journey, I held an empty space in my heart for a new experience. Despite dealing with knowing that this end was only going to bring a new beginning, I still grieved for what I thought it should have been. The familiar and predictable, even though painful, was a comfort. Knowing what to expect was easier to live with than the unknown. They were there to merely teach me what love wasn't supposed to be. Now I can say goodbye to the loved ones who have taught me how to love myself by not loving me.

Now with new relationships forming, the triggers of the past may cause sadness of what could have been, but now I can stand on my own, welcoming a new experience. With their goodbye, I let go of the need for them to fill me and learn to stand alone and accept God's love and forgiveness. Now open to the possibilities of greatness and new relationships, I can welcome them without getting lost in them or looking for them to complete me. I melt into my own heart. I had to let go to find me.

Participation

Interesting how I came to depend on the other shoe to drop when all was well and quiet. I used to live in the drama that others drummed up for me, and even though I was a willing participant, I always had the choice to walk out of the storm and into the peace of not knowing yet believing. It was as if I was a member of the drama clan and only felt alive if someone was in crisis. Then I showed up in my role as caretaker.

I have learned to find compassion and care without compromising who I am. I have learned to give solicited support and not lose my reflection in their mirror. I have learned to find my worth even if they do not feel worthy. On any level I choose, I can participate and be a part of their story but not have their story be mine.

YOUR TRUTH, MY TRUTH

When trying to resolve a conflict, recalling a memory can be used as a reference point. We all speak what we think is our truth. Since communication did not occur, all we had to follow was our interpretations and reactions to our experiences. Believing someone whom you trust and with whom you have a deep-seated relationship will override someone whom you barely know and who has been labeled by others' interpretations.

So what are you more likely to believe, what you're told or what you have yet to unfold? Recollections will always be different, as we share our interpretations of what we believe to be true. The only way toward resolution is if you share yours and I share mine. Then we'll begin to understand why!

WHAT AND WHY

Forgiveness melts resentment and disappointment so that healing can begin. I pray to understand so I can forgive. I accept what happened knowing I cannot change it, and I'll find the origin of the pain to figure out why it happened. Knowing that my story is not the only one to be told or heard, if I hold on to ill feelings, it will block my compassion and deafen me to their story. If my story is the only one to be told or heard, then judgment, disappointment, and resentment will not melt into compassion, empathy, and forgiveness. I may not trust the relationship, but I can trust myself when I choose to forgive knowing we are all attempting to find love, peace, and joy in this life.

As I Melt Into

Sometimes, when the voices get too loud though I've tried everything to silence them, I allow them to rant, and then I can get in touch with their needs. In the contradiction of them trying to sabotage my happiness with their drama and me trying to stay with God, I can hear them banter back and forth for attention. When I do not fight them, I can ask God to release my need to control, and I give it to Him to help me find peace. This is when empathy and compassion enter my mind and melt into my heart. I can let go and let God handle all that I am not meant to handle and find my peace in knowing that He's got me. His will, not my will, will be done.

Look for Happiness

Each day is a blessing to live a fruitful, abundant life with unconditional love, financial security, emotional stability, and good health. Each precious moment gives us an opportunity to grow and evolve, and each moment can be deemed good or bad if it turns out different from an expectation. Disappointment can cancel joy, resentment can cancel celebration, and judgment can hide the gift of an experience or a life lesson that holds growth. It is only through the cracks of a broken dream that the light can enter and heal and reveal its promise. This wonderful gift of life will not hold the promise of being pain-free but the promise of amazing opportunities for joy. Looking for the happiness in spite of all the negativity can bring peace.

One

When making a choice, I can decide if it's in my best interest without infringing on another. But if it's best for me and not for you, I am then to decide how to present my true self in the midst of your rebellion. A compromise is acceptable if I can still remain in my truth. Yet there may come a time when I may be asked to compromise my truth to present myself other than being trustworthy. This may get me the result of acceptance but will ultimately compromise who I truly am and want to be. If I am willing to sacrifice my truth for the mass, how might I engage when I am alone with my own reflection? Is it worth risking the acceptance of ten to sacrifice the truth and love of one?

I Am Always Being Seen—Humble

When I look at myself in the mirror to ask for forgiveness and affirm self-love, I can see that I, too, am guilty of the very behavior that I judge and condemn. How arrogant to believe that I know better for anyone or that my way is the right way. I am quick to judge when I should be still and compassionate. I am quick to act when I should breathe and turn my fear into faith. When I need to move is when I need to sit and be still; when I feel an urgency to resolve an issue or a conflict is when I need to stop and tap into my faith that all will work out without my intrusion. A hater of haters is a hater, bullying a bully makes one a bully, and condemning someone else is playing judge and jury and God. I need to love and show myself the kindness that I show others. I need to act in kind knowing I am always being seen.

The Light in the Darkness

In the stillness, I am stirring and remaining in peace; at the same time, I am dealing with contradictions. During letting go and holding on or during the struggle of suffering over my suffering is when I need God's help to be aware to think and act from a place of love and not fear, a place of security and not insecurity, and a place of faith and trust instead of fear and doubt. When I act in fear and weakness, I regress and suffer, because this is when I am holding on too tight and won't let go. So I release all that is not mine, and I live with the contradictions, appreciating the light in the darkness.

Battles

I experienced my life in the love of God. I lived my life in the depths of pain. In this contradiction, I ventured toward where I could be filled. In the drama, I felt alive; so even though it was painful, I felt connected. It was in this very drama that I allowed my light to dim. It was this turmoil, which I called aliveness, that prevented God's light to shine in me. So when the silence got too loud, I needed noise; when the contentment got too comfortable, I stirred up the drama; and if the threat of past drama crossed my path, I drummed up enough vengeance so I could put on my armor, ready for battle. In the letting go of that which was not mine, I was released from these burdens. No longer in battle, I now live in the light and love of God.

TINY POKES

Here on earth, the goal is not to be free from pain, which will always be present, but to live with pain differently: in faith and trusting that all will work out as per God's plan. Avoidance and denial will prolong healing. The contradictions are part of life, but they are not all of life. The fear of contradiction is the crisis with an unexpected jarring that brings me into contact with God. It is only in crisis that I seek answers. It's God's tiny pokes that I need to feel to look for His guidance and wisdom when broken by an experience.

LESSONS LEARNED

Recovery is about healing and cleaning up the old debris by facing it and by searching for what I learned from that experience. What wisdom can I learn and gain from that pain or that joy? How has this experience helped me evolve? I thank all who have helped me move forward into forgiveness and learn to live in the light. In the stillness of my soul, in the coming home to me, I am now void of the drama. I have now let go and live my life in peace, having conquered the fear of not knowing. In this emptiness I am once again filled with God's love and light.

FLIP THE SWITCH

When things become so automatic for me that before I know it, I am lost in a negative thought or I have reacted in a defensive way, the first thing I strive to do is flip the switch. I want to turn my negative into positive and want my mouth and mind to think before I react. This may be an automatic behavior for some, but I am forever struggling with the inner battle of dealing with unkindness and injustice. I feel that if I don't say something, then I am condoning the behavior. "Evil prevails when good men do nothing." I diligently look for the positive switch when I encounter a negative behavior. I know that if I react with the same behavior, fight fire with fire, it will cause more fire. A hater of haters is still a hater. I am so much more aware now that I need to flip the switch when a negative emotion crosses my path.

STONE

When I am confronted with an intentional, deliberate, painful act, I can choose how much energy I am going to give my pain. I can't change the outcome, and living in disappointment and resentment will only harm me, giving my power to something that is set in stone. The only stone that can crack is my hardened heart. We all deal with fear in different ways. So instead of cursing, condemning, and criticizing, I will find compassion and pray that they will become accountable for how they have hurt others with their fear. This is between them and God. As for myself, I will pray that my heart stays open and that I will find compassion to help me understand that their fear is no different from mine.

COMPETITION

There is an underlying competition in society—that someone has to be right and someone has to be wrong. The times when we are given opportunities to share have become a challenge of assimilation. When trying to explain a position or when asked an opinion, it can welcome peace in sharing a voice or wreak discourse. When I find myself in competition with another, I may choose to engage to a point where the other person has to hear me and validate my truth. Other times, I can merely choose to say what I need to say with an open heart and an open mind and walk away from any potential conflict. I don't need to compete with anyone to know my truth and live in peace.

SELF-LOVE AND CARE

After spending my life as a caretaker, I have now included myself on the list of those who are important to love and care for. Now that the house is empty and quiet of others' drama, I am focusing on me. I am listening to myself. What do I want, need, and have a passion for? What brings me joy, peace, love, and comfort? I am able to love with compassion and empathy. Intimacy no longer means sacrifice. It is now an exchange between two or more souls who are learning to dance and sing with joy and love.

STOP THE WAR

I have been exposed to labels my entire life—the good, the bad, the beautiful, the ugly, the kind, the mean, the love, the hate, and all the contradictions that go on and on. Always striving for positivity, I am constantly reminded of that which I've tried to erase or conquer to be my best. I take a deep breath, and with an exhale, I am reminded that we are all the sum of our parts and of our experiences and that with my struggles, I always find clarity. So this war of push-and-pull that I have tried to control has left me unsettled and unhappy. When I become aware of the fog that has lifted to expose a blue sky again, I will live with the contradictions and stop the war. I will just be, flaws and all.

WHAT TO DO

I find it so easy to know what's best for me and, when given the opportunity, to tell someone what's best for him or her. But now after many years of thinking I did know what was best for others and me, I can humble myself enough to realize I was wrong. This practice was done to me, so that was where I learned it, but despite knowing how much I resented it, instead of purging it from my repertoire, I embarked on the same behavior. Humbled once again, I will ask for guidance, not knowing what to do, and I will also help someone seek his or her guidance. This is what I know for sure to do.

High Road

When I find myself getting caught up in the behavioral choices of another and find that they don't align with mine, I strive to communicate so it doesn't result in defensive behavior. If we are unable to come to a crossroad, all I can do is say a prayer for them and for myself. I pray that I remain true to myself and don't engage in inappropriate behavior that will only make me feel bad about myself. I will take the high road.

Day by Day

Day after day, I strive to live my best life and to be my best self. I'm aware of how I allow others and situations to interrupt my peace. I am reminded that without confusion and disorder, there would be no peace. Without sorrow, there would be no joy. Without laughter, there would be no tears. Without fear, there would be no love. So as I go about my day with this daily reminder, I have free will to choose how long I will remain in any situation and how I will choose for it to affect my peace.

Move Toward

Within my sadness, I will move toward joy. Within my darkness, I will move toward light. Within my despair, I will move toward hope. Within my anxiousness, I will move toward calmness. Within my loneliness, I will move toward companionship. Within my grief, I will move toward comfort. Within my turmoil, I will move toward peace. Within my fear, I will move toward faith. Within my unmet dreams, I will move toward hope. Within my faith, I will be with

God. I will continue to move from negative fear toward positive, hopeful light.

Willing to Hear

No one likes to be criticized, and it's a known fact that when an imperfection is revealed, the first course of action is to cover it up as quickly as possible so that more criticism will be abated. But if our imperfections are brought to light in love, then the results will be constructive instead of disastrous and defensive. Covering up grays, trying to remove wrinkles, or not presenting oneself in truth are all signs of fear of judgment. But if the spoken words are done out of love and good intentions, then criticism will only enhance the soul instead of breaking it. What advice do I need to hear that will help me move forward and enhance my soul? What am I willing to hear?

God's Gifts

As my heart beats, so do the hearts of others. As my mind thinks, so do the minds of others. As my eyes see and my ears hear, so do the eyes and ears of others. When used in faith, my heart beats with love, my mind thinks of joy, my eyes see blessings, and my ears hear the truth. I don't need to write about the contradiction of all these gifts, but I am aware of their presence. I will remain in faith and hope that every time a contradiction of God comes to mind or to sight, I will thank God for His gifts and His presence in my life. I pray this for all of us!

Remove and Move On

At times, it is required to review the negative choices that have brought me where I am today. Sometimes, I can get caught up in one memory because it's unfinished. Looking for an affirmation or an apology to finish it and move on may be futile. So I review what happened, take responsibility for what is mine to make an appropriate, healthy change, and move on. I can live with contradictions with appropriate boundaries. When I review my day, I look at all the potential drama that could draw me back into a memory or a trigger that is unresolved. I tend to attach today's drama into yesterday's pain. Now that I am aware of this potential danger that gets me stuck in the past, I can review the life lesson and then move on.

God's Way

Everyone has encountered a disappointment—a broken promise from another's lips, a broken heart from unreciprocated love, or an unmet expectation that what was wanted would be delivered. However, going around and trying to get vindication from unfulfilled dreams is a futile waste of time and energy. It's as if I have accumulated a list of anyone who has ever let me down, and I spend countless hours planning with retribution as my goal. What a waste! I've learned that if I didn't receive it, I was not meant to have it or it just wasn't my time. So instead of wasting my time on trying to make things work out my way, I will trust that God's way is what's best for me.

Rubble

I sometimes begin thinking about something and a memory will ease its way into my thought. It can cause me to go down a path that has caused pain, but I am learning to seek the lesson in the memory of the pain. Knowing that all is meant to be, I can search for the good within the rubble of the pain. I look at homes that have been destroyed after a storm. Even if my house no longer stands, I have a strong foundation and will build again. There is always hope in the pain.

Support versus Enable

When a child is learning to take their first step or speak their first words, we are there as a support system to assure them of their potential success. Yet it is quite another story when that support crosses over into enabling. No one will ever learn to walk unless they fall. No one will ever smile unless they've known sorrow. Contradictions come with a very fine line that can be easily blurred when crossed. Helping with compassion and empathy is one thing. Showing us and losing ourselves are quite the opposite. In the end, it's between us and God. You can do it.

FLIP THE COIN

Heads or tails, dark or light, happy or sad, good or evil, or up or down—the list of opposites and contradictions is endless. How else does one know one without the other? Yet it is through our own judgment that what we deem uncomfortable should be negative and bad. It is through our own fear that what does not align with our security and comfort is where we miss the opportunity to see and learn exactly where we are giving our power of security.

Perhaps we aren't comfortable in the situation because of a lack of self-worth to accept its goodness, or perhaps we don't like the person we just met because his or her behavior mirrors a character trait that we are trying to change. Whatever makes us uncomfortable is a gift toward our evolution and self-authenticity, so flip the coin; heads or tails, you are a winner.

CHAPTER 4

Control—Burdens

What Is Mine, What Is Yours, and What Is Ours

It is sometimes very apparent and other times very confusing what is mine, what is yours, and what is ours. When I'm simply not focused, negative energy can engulf me so quickly that before I realize it, the boundaries that separate us and the lines that join us become so misguided and blurred that my vision is blinded. It is when I settle into my true, best, positive, authentic self that all is clear and I know. Control of what is mine can be as debilitating as trying to control what is not, so when the thought of control comes to pass, I humbly pray and ask for guidance knowing I am not in control of what is yours, and I am guided by what is mine and ours. I pray to remain positive when I am seeking an alternative route and stay with God and peace.

Changing Seasons

In the anxiousness of impatience and not having faith, I was led to many hours of pain. I allowed others to control me as I tried to control the situation, and this was futile. I used to think that if did the right thing, then I would be accepted, that there would be no more pain or abuse, and that I would find my self-worth. My pain was holding on and trying to make it happen, and this was my burden.

It has now been removed. I have been awakened; the confusion has melted into the newness of spring. Now all that is new and awakening from the darkness of the winter of my life has brought me home. As I continue to empty more of that which is not mine to hold, I release the effort to try to make things different from what they are. This is where I find peace, hope, trust, and faith. Pain is in the effort to control, but peace is in the surrender. No matter what detour I take, there is only one road home.

MY OWN HEART

Looking at what no longer defines me, labeled by others or myself, the acceptance of quiet and drama-free measurements can be uncomfortable. I lived with loud, dramatic experiences, and now I choose to move into what I can control. So as the void gets smaller and as I let go of what I can't control, I am learning to see me and feel my own heart.

THE GLUE

In letting go of that which is not mine, the burden of needing to control outcomes to save others and promote and restore peace has left me drained. The pain comes with the disappointment of dreams and tasks unfulfilled. Having faith in God's plan eases the pain, and though I want it now, God's got this in control. He knows better for me than I know for myself. Born broken with a lifetime to mend, God is the glue.

NOT MINE TO CONTROL

By releasing that which is not mine, I remember that life lessons are sometimes painful. What is the pain telling me about what can I take away from this experience? That which is not mine to control will not give me the results I want, so I need to let go, trusting my own word and deed. This is where my faith lies, because my word and deed are from God, telling me who to be and what to do. My choice to allow others' behavior to affect me will always bring me back to the emptying of this burden and allowing my faith to be strengthened. I am okay with not knowing. I trust, and I have faith.

CONTROL

What truly is in my control? Thoughts, words, actions, and feelings are; yet the need to be loved, accepted, cherished, and blessed gets so strong at times that I give up my control to get something that only I can give myself. Believing in someone else's word can set in motion an abandonment so wide that it takes a lifetime to retrieve. My way is good for me, how I choose to live my life in word and deed. I do not impose my will on another, but I show up to be my best, true, positive, spiritual, authentic self for God and me. I am blessed to know what I can control and who I am.

SETTLE IN

I remember the comforting memory of a snowfall that I knew would silence the hectic world, so I settled into the knowing of just being. But when the threat of the storm was illuminating over my serenity, I panicked and preplanned what to do next and next and next as if I had any control over the outcome. I gave all my energy into the outcome that I hoped for. It was when I let go and trusted in the not knowing and used my faith that I settled into the peace, joy, and contentment of my life. Disappointment is inevitable, but misery is optional, so I have learned to trust and have faith that all is as meant to be.

WHAT IS CONTROL?

There is a difference between self-control and trying to control another. Self-control brings all my choices into my vision with what is truly mine. Yet in a split second, I think I know better for another than they know for themselves or vice versa, and the control battle begins—who is stronger or more versed in language or demeanor? When I truly drill to my core, I find that my need to control is from my lack of control; therefore, trying to control just shows how much I lack it. This tornado of what is mine is my biggest fear, and it drives my need to be perfect and causes my imperfection. So when I come home to my soul, what is left is the acceptance that with God's help, I can evolve when I know what's mine, let go of everyone else, bless them, and know God has them too. I have my voice and my choice just for me, as they do.

HURRICANE AND WHIRLWIND

In the midst of the chaos of the storm, the very center is the core, and this is where the silence is. Yet in the middle of everything, what the storm chooses to pick up becomes a burden. Yet when I stop in the midst of my own storm and I go within, I feel my truth in all the turmoil, and I know what is mine and what is not. I can then let go and give back the burden of carrying that which is not mine and find compassion as I let God take over. I can sift through the rubble of all that is left after the storm and rebuild.

I SEE YOU, AND I SEE ME

When I look at pictures of myself from over the years, I can recall that specific stage in my life. I can see myself amid my pain and see my soul's light still illuminating through my pain's darkness. When I see someone else in the midst of their darkness, I still struggle seeing them as just another soul on an evolutionary, spiritual journey. It is then that I decide to move away from their darkness knowing my old pattern of losing myself in their pain. At times, I struggle and suffer over their suffering. This is then the time to focus on myself and get out of God's way by handing them and their burdens over to Him.

When Saying When Is Now

It is spoken that when one has had enough, they say when. In seeking approval, acceptance, and love, I had to have these needs fulfilled by my efforts to please, yet I gave all of me and lost touch with my true self. The approval I got was never truly satisfying when I had to give myself away to get it. It left me wanting more, so I gave more to get more to feel full. I kept looking for my when in them. Now I have let go of my need to be accepted by them, to seek their approval, or to expect their words and behavior to match what I need. I do have to remember that they, too, are wearing a mask and searching for their own when. I am watchful and not judgmental, as we all journey into our when.

Just Feel

When I work on trying to be happy yet I still feel my sadness, I spend so much energy on trying to be happy and trying to keep the sadness at bay that I ultimately waste energy and time. What we resist persists; therefore, I have chosen to face and feel the sadness, guilt, resentment, disappointment, anger, and fear instead of masking it. Instead of the negative controlling my energy as I try to control the negative, I have now chosen to love, forgive, heal, and live in peace. Having thought that all will be healed, my life journey has been to make peace from within and learn to forgive trust and have faith.

Present

In an instant, I can flip from a positive experience to a negative emotion. I can be so caught up in the joy of the moment that I may lose sight of the darkness that lurks in the shadows of my fear. This is when I can be swept away from joy into darkness without realizing that I have been caught up in the abyss. I am not saying to look for the doom and gloom or that I need to be armed and ready for battle, for that would be negating the positive moments that I can encounter. I am merely suggesting that being vulnerable has its risks, so I will be aware without giving it my power. I am learning to be present in the moments of my life.

Not Always My Pain

I know we are in this world to love one another and receive love from relationships. I know that our experiences are meant to help one another. The pain I have experienced and healed can assist another, as they also experience the trials and tribulations of life. At times, I have to be careful of my reactions, because although I may think I know the origin of the pain and how to deal with it, I may be so off base that my judgment will blur the true meaning behind the pain. I may know what's best for me, but I am careful to offer solicited assistance without knowing how to heal others' pain; that's God's job.

Catch and Release

When we catch a ball in a game, we can choose to hold on to it or engage by releasing it. This metaphor is associated with any conflicts or confrontations we may have that may or may not enhance our dance with life. Resentment comes from my expectations not being fulfilled as I desired, so holding on to resentment is holding on to disappointment and expectations of a broken dream. It serves no purpose but to hold me in bondage with the pain being the bars of my prison cell.

If an expectation has not been fulfilled to my desired outcome, then retaliating with resentment, judgment, and disappointment will not change the outcome or another's choice. My faith lies in the fact that I can catch their decisions and release it to God and look for the life lessons in the experience. When I can let go of my desired outcomes, I can avoid any negative feelings and learn to accept that what I have and where I am are as God intends for me.

Conditional Faith

I can say I have faith when I pray for something and it's delivered, yet in the in-between moments when I have to trust that all will be as God intends it to be is when my anxiousness may turn into an expectation. In this expectation, I harbor my happiness, that if I get what I want, then all will be well. But this is not faith; this is a conditional outcome that, if not fulfilled to my specifications, comes with disappointment, judgment, and resentment. After I accomplish my responsibilities, my true faith must lie in receiving what is best for me. When I relinquish my control and know I cannot accomplish this on my own, I can live in joy and peace.

CONTROL MY REACTIONS

When I react in a negative way due to someone's negative choices, I feel I'm caught up in a whirlwind of toxicity, and I allow it to steal my joy. Their reactions are not in my control, but mine are, so I have to remain aware of how their behavior affects me and choose a behavior that does not make me feel unhappy or angry. I spend time in thought about why their behavior is so uncomfortable for me to witness. This allows me to change my discomfort and judgment into compassion. I am learning to set boundaries and shield myself from their behavior. I may not be able to change their reactions, but I am in control of mine.

MY WORD

How many times have I gone through the same situation and the results don't change? I hold the other person accountable for their word, but what about my word? I ask someone to walk their talk, but what about me doing the same? This is not about exonerating the other person so they don't have to be responsible. That's up to them. What this is about is that I keep my word, I walk my talk, I honor my boundaries, and I treat others the way I want to be treated. I won't expect another to do something that I don't want to do myself. I'm not giving up and letting them walk all over me. I am letting go of my need to assure that they are responsible and honorable. I can only control myself. I'm not giving up on myself, just letting go of my need to control outcomes that involve someone else.

What Controls Me?

It's so easy to blame my mood on the weather, the financial market, my body aches, or on another's behavior. While all these situations may have an impact on how I feel, it is my choice whether I allow the situation to control me or how, if I can, control the situation. I do not need to be anyone's target, and I gradually detach from allowing this to happen. I can own what is mine, ask for forgiveness, change my behavior, and refuse to take responsibility for what's not mine to own. My reaction is the key to how I will process my pain. Ultimately, my own happiness and inner peace will not come from anyone or any situation. If I want to be happy, find peace, and live in the light of joy, I need to look at how my own perception is enhancing or impeding that goal.

My Child

Ask any parent, and they will all agree that letting go of a child is the hardest thing they'll ever have do. They give birth to him, nurture him, love him, and guide him with the knowledge that they have; and then they have to let him go. So wish him well, pray for his safety, bless him on his journey, and love him forever. But when it's time to let go, it's time to let go. If anyone knows how that feels, it's me. If anyone knows how that feels it's God. If God can give His son to us, I can give my son to God.

Reclaim

Taking back control that has been relinquished can run smoothly if it's done with care and a kind, positive reaction. The smooth transition for regaining power is in the kindness of the affirmation that what has transpired assists the journey. Even though the transfer of power, however temporary, may meet with resistance, the behavior of the person reclaiming the power comes into play. So I will thank you for teaching me, once again, that you do not complete me, and I

55

will regain my power and transfer it back to where it belongs—with me and God.

Leaving It to God

The dictionary defines *sin* as "an immoral act considered to be a transgression against divine law, an act regarded as a serious or regrettable fault, offense, or omission." What are the criteria in judging a transgression, trespass, or sin? Who says what is worse—murder or lethal injection, a liar or a thief? How can I say that my sin is more forgivable? When an intentional behavior, words, or actions hurt another, is that a sin? It's time to stop judging others and look at my own behavior. I'll leave the rest of you to yourself and God.

All the Children

I thought that if I loved them enough, I could save them from pain. I thought that if I did what they asked or even demanded of me, then that would ease their pain. I was willing to do anything to make them happy and content, even at my own expense. I can care about you and wish you well, but I am not responsible for your choices or your happiness with the choices I make. We are separate and equal. So if you're hurting, I will pray for your healing; but during those painful times, I will not own your pain or try to heal it by sacrificing myself. I wish you well and pray for your peace.

And then He said to me, "You cannot save them, and it is not your job to save them. It is Mine. That was why I was born, to save all my children." And so in accepting God's love for me and Him being born and dying to save me, I wish you well, and I'll pray you allow Him to save you.

CHAPTER 5

Empty

Honor My No

Why is it so difficult for me to convince someone of my no? When I hear no from someone, I do check to make sure that I have received their message correctly and, ultimately, honor their request. Yet when I say no, I am pushed, questioned, and ignored to the point where I get so frustrated that I retreat into my pain. Perhaps I have to question what message I am sending them for me to be treated this way. I will continue to explore the reason I am not honored when I say no, but until then, no is no.

What's Mine to Hold

It's amazing to me how when I finally let go of my burdens, I am at peace. When I find myself holding on to a situation that isn't even mine to hold, I become agitated that it's not working out according to my timetable with my results, and it's not even mine to hold. This is when I become my most humble and ask for forgiveness for thinking I know better for another or myself. In this humble mode, I become enlightened about what's mine to hold. My solutions for my own hurdles may be just right for me, but when I offer unsolicited advice to help another, their burdens become overwhelming, and I feel lost in my own abyss of fear. I am aware what's mine to hold, yet

I need to remember to also become aware of where I am placing my energy. I can offer support without losing sight of my own reflection. I choose to hold on to me.

Believe It or Not

Holding on to past information that was never mine became a common practice for a member of our clan. I was defined by their truth and fed with their knowledge and was asked to accept it without regard for other information. But going out on my own, finding my own truth to define myself, and handing back their truth to live in my own light are now more common than not. We are on a spiritual journey so that we may evolve to fulfill our purpose, but I may get wrapped up in another's drama and truth. This leaves me confused and asking deep-seated questions about God and myself. In my fear, I still remain in their arena and feel that if I do pursue other avenues, it is betrayal.

Now I know that I was betraying myself and not seeing the whole picture, that I was living in the middle instead of looking at what was being presented in its entirety. I am now at peace knowing what I've always known to be my truth. I am as precious, purposeful, needed, loved, cherished, accepted, appreciated, and forgiven as everyone is. I know God's voice in my soul and that He loves me so much that He chose to come to earth in human form to die for my sins, to forgive me, and to restore my soul. It's a choice to believe it or not, and I believe.

My Peace Within

When I am feeling my best, I know that I am truly humble enough to trust that God will protect me. When I am feeling lost, lonely, and fearful, I then remember that the burdens that are weighing me down are not mine to hold. When I get caught up in another's drama or negative energy, I feel so heavy with sadness and pain, so I try to make them comfortable. But all the while, I am sacrificing my own happiness. So in my release, I can exhale the negative darkness and inhale the positive light. They are not mine to own or fix. That's God's job. I will walk away from their shadow and back into my light to keep my peace within.

DEFENSIVE VOICE VERSUS VOICE OF DISCUSSION

Learning how to have a discussion with someone takes on a new connection when feelings of defensiveness melt away the ability to discuss or even debate an issue. When someone has a different vantage point on a topic that may not agree with mine, the need to be heard may turn a discussion or a debate into a defensive stance where someone has to be right. I engaged in this practice for most of my life as someone tried to impose his or her views of who I should be. Not feeing accepted for who I was or trying to become only caused a rift between us because I was feeling that they did not have the right to define who I should be. When I can engage in a conversation that may turn into a discussion or debate, I can share my voice and my stance to participate. If the other person is only there to control or manipulate the outcome, I will choose to walk away and not engage.

HEALTHIER SPACE

Moving forward has had its challenges. Although familiar, leaving behind the dysfunction of manipulation and abuse has been one difficult aspect of letting go as I grow accustomed to the emptiness and the void. Even though it was predictable, holding on to the familiar had been an unhealthy practice because it was harmful, but that was better than being alone. Holding on to that which was toxic so that I didn't feel empty only burdened me because I was ready to move on and felt stuck. Now as my faith strengthens and I know I am in a healthier space, physically and emotionally, I can live with the uncertainty, the unknown, and the emptiness as I continue on my journey to fulfill my purpose.

Engagement

This thing that's called reaction is so powerful that it can make or break a relationship in one small word or deed. When I am confronted with a negative reaction, whether it is my issue or not, I show up in full armor for battle to defend my honor even if I am not being threatened. I look at the subtleness of sarcasm or of passive-aggressive messages that can easily swallow up my light when I choose to engage. The difficulty that comes with letting it go and not reacting may be construed as an acknowledgment of weakness if I don't defend and engage. Yet what I am learning is that their negativity is not about me, and if it is, they have a responsibility to engage in a productive way. I no longer want to feel on edge or in a defensive mode because someone else is unhappy. I will choose to engage in a positive, productive manner or not at all.

Wish Them Well

Being around negative energy can cause me to respond in a negative way. Having mastered the art of caretaking, I can now take on anyone's pain and harbor it in my heart until it breaks for them, and all I want to do is help. I am learning that this old behavior has become very detrimental to my own well-being. So I will offer solicited advice, say a prayer, send a blessing, and move on with my life. Their choices may be detrimental to them, but it is their journey and their life lesson. All I can do is wish them well. I think this is what getting a life looks like.

The Alternative

I have been in the midst of the storm of life, and I have been tossed around in the whirlwind of indecision and the fear of the unknown. Having been there, I have seen the alternative to unrest, and it is peace. It's so astounding to me that I chose to live in fear for so long, not trusting that the results of my needs would come to fruition. I totally understand this mindset, having trusted and believed in the lies of others. But now that I understand more than I did then, I am beginning to open my heart, mind, and soul to an unconditional love, which dissolves fear into trust of the unknown.

I do know that my inquisitive nature, my need to understand, may have to become acceptant of the just is. This letting go of my need to control an outcome or to be a part of someone's drama or to sway another into love has set me free to just be as I am meant to be. Although I am not yet proficient in this thinking, I would rather strive for this goal than the alternative. I like peace over drama, joy over pain, and love over fear. This is a good place to explore.

OF MY CHOOSING

I spent most of my life defined by the stories that I was told to be true. When I questioned this truth, my voice was silenced, and I assimilated toward acceptance. No longer in the light of another to become their second shadow, I am in my light, and all is well. I review what stresses I react to; my children's choices, my husband's needs and opinions, and chasing the friendships that have blown away in the wind are all things that I have chosen to place my energy on. But as I review what is mine and what is not, I feel peace. None of this defines me, none of this is in my control, and none of this can cause unrest or stress unless I choose. So the question is, why choose that if I can choose peace?

I AM AWARE

After spending a lifetime of pleading my case of who I am and why I have worth, I have finally let go of my need for approval. I no longer need to impress or seek approval from another because I have learned what I desperately want them to know about me. No longer having anything to lose, I can do what's in my best interest to evolve without retribution or retaliation because I do not meet the needs of another. I am careful not to dismiss compassion and empathy with a self-serving destination. I am aware of letting go of my thoughts to hear God's truth so that I make a decision that won't inflict harm on others or on myself. I am aware.

HOLDING ON TO WHAT'S DONE

I used to think that if I held on to a hurt, then the trespasser would be holding on too. I used to think that if I prayed hard enough, then the hurt would disappear as if it never occurred. I've seen myself hold on to a hurt long after the event has blown away in the wind. I've seen myself drag up past hurts when a new hurt occurs, combining the pain and searching for similarities that justify my negativity. Letting bygones be bygones has been one area in my life that I have struggled with. If I let go of the pain and forgive, then what message does that send to the person who have hurt me, that's it's okay or that I don't matter enough?

In this scenario, I am the only one who is preventing me from healing and letting go. The other person has moved on and does not give their behavior against me a second thought, yet I hold on to what's done. The question is, is holding on and revisiting or dwelling in what's done in my best interest to find peace, joy, and fulfillment?

I HAD TO CHANGE

It's been said that the definition of insanity is doing the same thing over and over again and expecting a different result. I lived most of my life with hope for a better today when I realized that my behavior and thinking had to change. I had to change my acceptance of that which was by letting it go knowing I was not in control. I had to change my belief that we all wanted peace, joy, and love and accept that some people just like drama and being a victim. I had to change my mindset, believing instead that no one made me feel anything I didn't want to feel or do anything that I didn't want to do.

I had to change from believing that I wasn't a blessing and wasn't meant to be loved into knowing how wrong and damaging that thinking was. I had to change my acceptance of mediocrity into accepting only the extraordinary knowing I deserve all the comforts, blessings, and love that everyone else deserves. I had to change my thinking of deprivation to abundance, from fear to faith, and from pain to joy. This change only happened when I let go and emptied myself of all the negative messages that I held as my truth. I am changing.

WHERE I CHOOSE TO SETTLE

We are all worthy of blessings and comforts. We all have life lessons to learn, which can sometimes feel as if our blessings are not comfortable enough to be celebrated. Not all life lessons will bring joy, but in the end, the experiences and opportunities that come with surviving a fall can outweigh the discomfort along the way. Sometimes, the discomfort can be interpreted as the status quo. I can sabotage my own happiness and talk myself into believing that the pain is all that will come from the experience and that it is all I deserve. This trigger can take root if I ease into negative decisions and pitch a tent there. This is when I give the pain a voice, look for the deep-seated reason why, and move through it instead of settling into it. Having already engaged in this self-sabotaging dance and allowed the negative to control me, I have decided that I am worthy of the blessings and comforts of life. This is where I choose to settle.

CAPABLE HANDS

One of the most difficult feelings I have had to endure is letting go of those I hold so deeply in my soul that I ache and have a deep-seated pain in the hole that is left after emptying them into the hands of God. It was not like they were not in the hands of God, but having thought I knew better for them than they knew for themselves was a learned behavior, as I was controlled by others who said they loved me.

This total faith and trust in someone that I have never met but who is a part of my soul and who I know loves me more than I have ever loved myself is the pure essence and definition of unconditional love. So I will always ache for them, but I know they are on their own journey, as I am on mine. Perhaps we may meet again or for the first time, but whatever. "Thy will be done," and I know that they are in the most capable hands, as am I. With an exhale of acceptance, I am at peace and filled with grace and gratitude.

TIME'S UP

When I find that I've dwelled on something long enough, I say, "Time's up." This is not a sign of defeat but a sign of strength, a sign that I've given it my best effort and that now I am going to walk away, leave it to God, and move on with my life. With this heroic behavior comes grief and sadness, because although I want a different outcome and I've done all that I can to try to resolve the issue, it is what it is meant to be.

It's an acceptance that maybe I am not meant to have what I have so desperately put all my thoughts and energy into. It's an acceptance that I am where I am meant to be and that perhaps I am being sheltered from the continuous drama that I have left. It's an awakening that what is in front of me now holds more joy, passion, and comfort than what is in my rearview mirror.

It's time to enjoy the fruits of my labor and leave the rest in the hands of God. Time's up in giving energy to the past and time to dwell in the present. I am blessed with unconditional love, financial security, emotional stability, and good health. What a great place to dwell and place my energy.

WHAT THEN?

When all the obstacles on my path have been removed, what then? When all my problems have been resolved, what then? When all my relationships have been mended, what then? When all my pain has stopped and has been healed, what then? When all that is not mine to have has been emptied, what then? When all has been forgiven and behavior has changed to enhance the journey, what then? When all my prayers have been answered, what then?

I am no longer waiting for the obstacles to be removed from my path, for my problems to be resolved, for my relationships to mend, and for my pain to stop; to fill myself while I am in the process of being emptied; and for the apology that may never come, the behavior to change, or all my prayers to be answered. My "What then?" is my now!

FILLING WITHIN, EMPTYING WITHOUT

It is written in Tao, "Living in contentment and having nothing to lose creates the space for joy. If you spend your time longing for things you don't have, you are likely to miss the treasures you carry." Such as in a relationship where two become united yet still separate, a partnership is formed. Yet in the constant search for that which is not present, we may lose the essence of the gifts that are already present and that can be cherished. The emptying of that which no longer defines us and becoming authentic so that the treasures within are real, true, and can be shared can be a painstaking journey. Cherish the treasures within so that you can welcome the treasures of another to form a partnership in truth and love.

LIFE'S FLUIDITY

When a river is flowing, it carries all its welcomed guests toward their destination. Such is the river of life—ever flowing and can be ever changing if the flow is interrupted. I spent many years getting in God's way because I thought I knew when I didn't and I thought I could when I couldn't. Until I remained still and silent enough to hear, feel, and see His miracles did I then let God have a place in my heart, and my river began to flow again. I needed to empty all that was cluttering up the flow of my life's river in order for me to continue on the path that I was destined to take and to fulfill the purpose of my life. There is only room for positive love and light in my heart.

Lifted Burdens

It's so interesting that once burdens have been lifted, life seems brighter and lighter. Not making light of the conflicts in the world, but when I come into my quiet silence and listen to my heartbeat and to the birds sing, I know what is in my control. I can't solve the problems and conflicts in the world, in my community, or in my own family; but what I can control is how I am going to react to the situation.

When something is not going my way or someone has acted in a hurtful way toward me, my anxiousness and fear can kick in, and I can react defensively. This will get me nowhere but toward frustration. I can no more make them change than I can solve their problems. That is not in my power, and it is not about me. What I do is I express my displeasure and set a boundary. This will not assure that the behavior will change, but it sure gives me back the power and energy I have spent in reacting to anxiety and fear. I can learn to live with discomfort, and even if the situation has not come to a resolution, I can lift the burdens to God and listen to my heartbeat and to the birds sing.

Completed, Not Depleted

Expectations caused me disappointments and resentment, because I believed that if I gave, I would receive. This mindset left me in a state of deprivation, because my emptiness was a result of giving all of me. When I expected to be replenished by the very source that I allowed to drain me, I was left depleted. So now living with this contradiction, I have learned to empty myself of all expectations so that I will be filled by another. Again, I am empty by releasing the burdens I feel I need to carry to complete another, which results in waiting. I am now completed, not depleted, because I fill myself with the love of God.

Accessorizing

Putting on a new hat or a new outfit and then finding the just right shoes or finding a throw pillow that will accent an earth-toned couch can bring a new outlook to things and bring them all together. When a blank canvas is presented, the landscape of a life unfolds. The experiences and opportunities begin to paint a portrait of a life. When a new relationship unfolds or a new experience shows the depth of a conviction, this becomes the snapshots that truly matter.

When I was told the words I needed to hear in order to feel fulfilled, I then allowed another to decide what picture to take or how to paint my portrait of life. I allowed them to define me instead of accessorize who I already was. Having emptied their thoughts and beliefs and replacing them with my own, I now know that disappointments may occur when I place my hopes and dreams into another's words and deed. They can only accessorize the masterpiece that I am becoming.

Take a Number

While waiting in line to be served, it is customary to take a number and wait your turn. So many times in my life, I was unable to be patient in the silence of the emptiness, so I filled it with someone or something else. This prolonged my pain, because instead of waiting for the new to arrive in its proper time, I filled it with a person, place, or thing that was not part of the plan. In my haste to not be uncomfortable, I detoured; but it only made me reevaluate, revisit, recalculate, and review my need to be filled with anything or anyone. So now I will sit in the silence, I will embrace being emptied, and I will celebrate all that I have become. I will take a number and wait for what's next.

I Am Home

In my stillness and my emptiness, I let me down, and I disappointed me. My resentment was displaced onto those who left while all along, I was the one who left me. I abandoned my true self because I thought they knew better for me than I knew for myself. I now trust myself that I won't leave me. I love, support, accept, appreciate, and approve of myself. I want me. I am home in me. I forgive me. I am my own blessing.

In my stillness, I am finally hearing my heartbeat. I see myself in the eyes of my inner children, and I am acceptant of who I was, who I am, and who I am meant to be. I am where I am meant to be. I am with whom I am meant to be. They pushed me away so that I could be pushed toward me! Thank you for all your assistance in helping me come home to myself. I am home in my heart and my soul and with God.

What Truly Is

When I am in a place of unrest, I connect to that which is not mine. Even as the others return in my life with their stories and drama, I'm aware of triggers, burdens, and the connection I have with God. I've reached the point in my life where I see the truth and hear the truth. What lessons am I to learn in their presence? What is mine? Then I remember God's timing, to be patient knowing He's got this.

What truly matters is that I've found my light again. I've found my soul's core again. I know God's truth as mine. This is what truly matters. I pray and hope for resolutions and to let them go. I am home with all that is meant to be. I am at peace in knowing God and trusting Him. We are all evolving, teaching one another, learning from one another, and just being kind and showing love. This is what matters.

Priorities

I no longer call on that which no longer fits, that which has made me feel unworthy. I now know I am worthy of kindness, love, appreciation, and patience toward myself and toward others. There are no more masks to fit the glow of my energy. Priorities of my spirit outweigh the needs of my physical existence. New fulfillment waits to fill the emptying of that which is not mine.

MEANT TO BE

As I reflect on all that I am and what has helped me arrive, I know that through all my experiences, all was meant to be. All that matters is, I know myself. I've worn masks, assimilated myself, approved of inappropriate behavior, ignored my intuition, silenced my voice, acted out in fear, allowed abuse, and been abandoned. Emptying myself and no longer taking responsibility to fix things, I am now living alone in my new healing, forgiving my own trespasses, and accepting without judgment the choices of others. Although I cannot control another's thoughts or actions, I know I can control my reactions. All is as God intends, and I accept without resistance.

YOU IN ME

Having had relationships my entire life, I was always confused where you were in me and where I was in you. In these blurred lines in my life, I rarely understood how kindness and helpfulness could cross into a loss of me. Always excited to meet new faces, I rarely understood the meaning of unconditional give-and-take. Now emptied of those burdens that used to define me, I am slowly allowing new relationships to develop, all the while watching how much of you I allow into me and how much of me I allow into you. Even though I am always giving, kind, loving, understanding, and forgiving, my lines are no longer blurred. I know where I begin and end. Now I can say, "Hello. It's nice to meet you."

FIND WHAT'S IN THE EMPTINESS

I became what I knew from the knowledge I learned and from those I encountered. I took bits and pieces of everyone else to become who I was. I learned that not everything I read was applicable to me, nor was everyone's word I heard my truth. Yet this was whom I became in spite of my own truth. I spent decades taking what was given, whether willingly or not. Now in this season of my life, I shift through all that I have packed for my journey and donate, dismiss, or discard that which does not fit. I am now experiencing life for myself. My own experiences will be colored with my own joy, passion, and truth, filling the emptiness I find in myself.

Tunnel through the Darkness

As I reflect on my memories, I recall being a child and being dressed layer upon layer to keep me warm from the bitter cold as I played in the snow. Even though I could barely move, my determination to roll the snow into a snowman's head far surpassed how my body couldn't maneuver itself to actually manipulate the snow. I knew that beneath the layers, I was still there. The same has applied for my journey. I tunnel through the darkest of my hurtful memories and surface knowing that I am still here. Even with all the layers piled on top of me, I'm able to tunnel, shed, and empty all that is no longer needed to define me. I have tunneled through the darkness and into the light of my heart and soul.

Making Progress

When I start a task or project, I look at the destination and its completion, yet I tend to ignore my life's journey to empty myself and to help myself heal as I make progress. When I stop and take the time to breathe and just be, I find myself in awe of my possibilities and of the steps I've made on this journey to learn how to live with the full sense of who I am. Having identified what is mine, I have let go of past transgressions and trespasses against others, melting them into compassion, love, and myself, seeing who I am. What's taken decades to accumulate has now taken time to empty. It took a brave decision to walk from the life I knew and into my new life to make progress. With one deep inhale, I start my day.

Where I Land

When making plane reservations for a trip, the destination is known, but not so much in life, though. We can wish, hope, pray, manipulate, and sacrifice for a desired outcome; but in all reality, where we land is where it's planned. Actions, words, and thoughts all drive us to an outcome, yet desired or not, we are meant to learn something from every experience. Whether we are the lead actor in our life's play or a walk in someone else's life, we are meant to be there. Now that the dust has settled, the boxes of my life's journey have been unpacked, and I have emptied all that is not mine to carry, where I have landed is where God has planned for me. Welcome home!

Living in Another's Reaction

Very early in life, we are taught the meaning of experiences, and then we understand these experiences when we add language and feelings. How many decades did I live my life in the reaction of another, allowing their reaction to dictate my life? But this never negated my purposeful journey. My emotions and feelings became reactions to others rather than reflections of my positive light. I just wanted to get past the pain.

Now I am living in my happiness, blessing those who choose negative behaviors. I wish them well and pray that they, like me, can become enlightened about the newness of the positive reactions we can all achieve. Worry robs me of my faith and of the blessings in front of me, so I savor these moments of living in the positive light and love that is being offered. React to that!

Stripped to the Light

We are born in pure love and light. Even our skin is a bit transparent to see our soul illuminate through to the beholder of our wonder. We then start on our soul's journey, meeting, greeting, saying goodbye, thanking, and at times, shedding tears of joy and of sadness. We begin to carry memories, life lessons, experiences, and opportunities to enhance or detour our soul's journey. All the while, we become sponges, soaking in all that is meant to help us evolve. Yet there comes a time when we have to stop, when we have to look into that which we have carried and begin the painful extraction of that which we want to hold on to but that no longer assists us. We begin to strip and empty ourselves so we can once again see our pure light of love.

THE SPIN CYCLE

Having watched clothes in the washing machine, I have discovered that the spin cycle can cause wrinkles. When I am plagued with conflicting, contradictory thoughts, I feel as if I am in that spin cycle. The positive and negative chatter can get so loud that I need to detach and isolate myself so that I can reflect on what the deep-seated lesson is. Removing myself from a potential conflict is my first course of action. As I hold my tongue, I can breathe through the need to defend myself before I add to the conflict. Usually, I can find a safe place to have my conversation with God. It is in these quiet, silent, emptying moments of my mind that I can find my answers. I have learned that removing myself from the spin cycle before the wrinkles set in brings me more peace than having to iron out the wrinkles.

EMPTY TO MAKE ROOM

From the time we are born, we begin to fill ourselves with another's love, knowledge, wisdom, and blessings. Unfortunately, in this world of contradictions, we are also filled with another's negative energy. Yet when we hold on tightly enough to our soul's truth, we can protect and even dismiss what negativity has infiltrated our pureness. One of my greatest attributes is that I give everyone the benefit of the doubt. I trust their word and deed until I realize that I am replacing my truth with theirs.

Having believed in another's message about me for decades, I am now in the painful process of what recovery calls letting go. I have had to examine what is my truth in the mix of what I've come to believe. I've had to revisit, let go, forgive, and try to understand this entire process of having to empty to make room for something new, to let go of that which is no longer needed, and to seek to know what truly is.

CONFRONTATION

Confrontation can be construed as a negative encounter; it means to confront or to have a conversation for clarity. Yet sometimes, assertive behavior is replaced with aggression, and the lesson is lost in the battle of self-preservation. Masks and armors are put on, and the battle to defend the truth for one's self-interpretation then becomes a manipulative ploy to bully another into submission. This conflict is not necessary but has become the norm for these disagreements.

What's the worst that can happen, that they will gang up on me, leave me, lie about me, bully and abuse me, or leave me all alone? This has all been done, and I am still standing. I continue my journey with or without them, as either way, I have the knowledge and truth of who I am. Having emptied all that I thought completed me now gives me the room for who I am meant to be with and journey on.

TIME ALONE

I spent most of my life in the company of others through work and play with family and with other relationships. I had very little time alone. At first, I thought being alone was terrifying, that it was as if I was being abandoned. After having to find myself in the image of others, I thought that if they went away, it would be permanent and they would never return. So I hung on as tightly as I could, reconfiguring myself to meet their needs, redesigning a new mask to meet their approval, and filling me with them until there was no me to see. Finally emptying that which was not mine, which was the burden of my pain, I developed a deep-seated soul relationship with

73

myself. They can now come and go, and I am quite satisfied with just an occasional visit. I savor my time alone.

EXAMINE WHAT THE STORM LEAVES BEHIND

Once something stirs up dust that disturbs my silence, it's difficult to breathe and see and engage. It tends to paralyze my mere existence, of just being in the moment. At times, protecting myself from the dust can be effortless, or it can drain me if I allow myself to participate in its dance. When the dust settles, I can evaluate the damage, if the storm has left a trail. I can remove the negative debris that's been left in my path and begin to move forward as I make my way through the settled dust. It may take moments or hours or days, but I am tenacious and willing enough to clear my path to make for a cleaner journey for tomorrow.

I ACCEPT WHAT IS NOT ME

When wanting to please someone, the natural tendency is to compromise to accommodate so all will find comfort. It is the consistent asking and demanding that will draw me to the boundary line of saying no. I may be in the presence of someone who over-accessorizes my comfort level or who will bling beyond my fashion level, and I can always appreciate their need to step it up. But when it comes down to joining in, I accept what is not about me. Having to learn to say no and to honor that boundary has brought me to the edge of anxiousness. I will wait for a response that will honor my no, or I may encounter a manipulation that will try and change my mind. I would rather be alone and be true to myself than be surrounded by those who require a mask. I know what is about me.

HUMBLED WHEN OFFERED CRITICISM

When I was called on my behavior, my initial reaction, like most others, was to justify and defend myself and to try to explain so that I would be accepted and, hopefully, be seen as I saw myself.

That used to be my reaction. What I've noticed about myself is that when I have truly emptied myself of others' opinions and judgments, I can see myself and appreciate the views of others without having to own it or feel as if I need to defend myself. Although there may be some truth, instead of reverting to my old behavior, I will welcome a dialogue about why they see me in that light. Knowing my truth, my own history, and who I truly am, I can listen to their point of view and can try to visualize what they see and how much is valid. I am the me I see myself to be, and I welcome what others can add or delete.

How Worthy I Am

I used to be a chameleon and would be whatever I was told to be for fear of abandonment. I realized I was only abandoning myself when I decided that being a contortionist with everyone I met made me lose who I was truly meant to be. But being fear driven because of threats of being left, I dabbled in learning boundaries and learned to honor my own no. I realized I was more important to me than they were, so I learned that I could live without them. Now that I am learning to honor myself enough to live in my truth as my authentic self, they are coming back.

I was given the most amazing gift in the form of them leaving, the gift to see myself and relearn to love myself. I have learned I can live a purposeful life, I have learned that being alone with myself is good company, I have learned to empty myself of their burdens, and I have learned to heal my fear of abandonment and have learned to trust my own word. I no longer need them to complete me or show me how worthy I am.

What Lies Within

I strip away materialistic items that bring me joy and comfort. I strip away the bling I decorate my body with. I strip away the belief system that has held me hostage. I strip away all the negative messages I play in my head that drown out my truth and my fear of not being loved, of always being judged, and I strip off the mask, which I refuse to wear again. I strip away all that is not in my own best interest and that takes me away from my light, and what lies within is my soul. What truly matters is not what I choose to believe is my truth but what lies within my soul. That is my truth.

I Know that I Don't Know

Being a culmination of all the experiences and opportunities I've encountered does not define me if I have borrowed from others. In emptying that which is not mine, I begin to know that I know that I don't know unless I begin to experience it, whatever it may be, for myself. I can gather information, then sift through what I can to find the answers to my questions. I now resist what is not mine to have and continue to grow and evolve in that which is mine to have. Being one who needs to understand, I will continue to uncover, unmask, and unveil that which I am supposed to know, become, and just be.

Fear toward Faith

I used to watch all that was driven by fear turn into a behavior of manipulation and control. I watched as all the unsung prayers and screams in the dark gave way to the light of hope. I used to listen to dialogues of defense that were never spoken yet that always seemed to end up speaking the words of love. It was in the moment when I succumbed to the darkness that I made my way to the light. It was when I realized that I needed to empty the burdens of others that I was carrying in order to find peace. It was when I began to empty myself of that which was not mine that I became full. It was when I stopped being afraid and full of fear that I found love and faith.

Remove One More Layer

Exfoliation helps remove impurities on the skin. When we are born, we are already pure, and then we spend a lifetime accumulating layers upon layers of information that help develop our character. If all this is an asset to our spiritual evolution, then what we choose using our own free will can only enhance our purpose. It is when we are caught in the whirlwind of life that we may collect something that is not ours to have, which makes us feel as if we are in bondage. It is then that we need to be clear of our intentions, to be still, and to make no hasty decisions as we contemplate removing one more layer to be empty. We can reconsider what we have to integrate with the new by being still, gradually removing, and then emptying.

THE STORM

The chore of cleaning up after a storm results in the sifting through of the debris left behind. It is through this sifting that what we find left behind what's meant to be. All that has been stripped away from the storm has served its purpose. Celebrating what is found and grieving for what is lost leaves the way to rebuild, relocate, remember, and redefine what today will hold. This letting go of the old to make way for what's here and will be can result in a hardship to accept the empty space ready to be filled. Refill what is now needed, then say goodbye to what's gone, and let's start cleaning.

A PART

It has been said that we can be in a situation but not have the situation in us. This is a very fine boundary line that we tend to cross when the feeling of compassion turns into caretaking. Our responsibilities to our self are our first line of defense so that we may carry that to be a part of a family, a relationship, and a community but not have any of them stay a part of us to define us. Just because everyone says it's true doesn't make it true. The confusion of the truth will come to light only to truly know our truth. This may take a lifetime to uncover, but there will always be three sides—yours, the unknown truth, and mine. I can help you through the storm, but the storm will not penetrate me, for I am a part of and remain apart from.

Be My Guest

When I first learned to forgive, I chose not to forget, so I had an inventory of past transgressions. If I saw them repeating, I would pull away. Patterns of behavior toward another are difficult to sever, especially when a yes becomes a no. But it is in the releasing of the old and then being comfortable in the emptiness that we are then filled with the new. Inviting an estranged soul back into my life takes this very action, but I will trust again until I am given reason to pause. If my guest has made the effort to begin anew, then there is hope for a future with them. However, if my guest continues with the old, I will bless them and become cautious. I am worthy of respect.

My Journey

Having lived on the spiritual journey, I have seen so many blessings, so much joy, and so much good health, financial security, and emotional stability that I feel blessed to be living in God's backyard. All the choices or how I have reacted to others' choices have caused harm and pain or joy and peace. Yet each choice has its blessing—to learn to let go, empty, engage, and trust and to be thankful and to just be. I do not need to be engaged in drama or negative energy to feel alive or to define my worth. I can thank the life lessons, opportunities, and experiences and see what is in front of me now. Then I watch my footing, giving thanks and praise, having faith that I am where I am meant to be.

U-Haul

In any split moment, I can be in my past, present, or future. I used to grieve over my past, spending a lot of time packing a U-Haul and bringing it with me everywhere I went. I used to dream of hopes of a happy future, making plans on how I was going to live. And all the while, I was lugging around my U-Haul of pain and living in moments of the future that never were to be. I neglected to see me in the present.

In this moment, this is where I am. Although I am the product of my past and hopes for a future me, this is who I am now. So as I unpack and purge the contents of the U-Haul, I bless and pray for myself that I fulfill my purpose where I am now and who I am now.

SHRED AND BURN

When we come to the end of the year, we gather pertinent information for our taxes, then shred and burn anything that we don't need. I have spent years filing all my emotional information without sifting through to inspect what I truly need to keep. Now I am in the process of shredding and burning all that I no longer need to survive—my victim, poor health, anger, armor, fear, and anything else I carry to protect me or to shift blame. I am emptying all that I believe I need and have found I need very little. So as I continue to empty, shred, and burn that which I no longer need to survive, I see who I truly am and what I do need. I need my truth, my voice, and my faith in God.

EMPTY MYSELF (INSPIRED BY TAO)

Feeling responsible for putting the comfort of others first left me with disappointment, judgment, and resentment for unfulfilled expectations. So as I learned to gradually let go of my need to assure that everyone was happy, I was left with my feelings and me. Now that I've let go of their burdens, which I chose to carry, I am now seeing that I have to empty myself of opinions and judgments that destroy my true self. "I lean on them because they give substance to my personality." There is no room for positivity if I keep holding on to the past, and no light can enter a hardened heart, yet it is through the risk of breaking and emptying that we can be whole and full. I am reprograming my thinking, and I live to contradict my contradictions.

Showing Up

I used to fill my days with school, work, children, and chores. I used to fill my heart with the needs of others, and amid their requests, I neglected to save some for myself. In my years of service, I gave and always waited for a return, for that was where I got my validation and worth. I now know that I am worthy and that I was mistaken in thinking I was supposed to be who they defined me to be and in agreeing with them. I am working on emptying myself of others' drama and am now beginning to stop misrepresenting myself to the world. Who am I? I am love.

Owning What's Mine

During my period of unrest, I teetered back and forth on what led up to what I allowed to steal my peace. I would rewind and replay what they said, how I responded, how I felt, and how I would resolve the issue. In my past, I would not allow myself to sit with the unknown and unresolved for too long, for it was uncomfortable. So I owned all of it, compromised myself, tried to make nice, and ultimately, took on all of the unrest as if I was responsible for everything. Then I realized I couldn't always be wrong, that this unrest couldn't always be about me. So now I sift through the drama of relationships and see what is truly mine. That is all I can control and change, and even if they show up with the same behavior, I know who I am and what is mine.

Shedding Layers

We are products of our experiences and how we can assimilate ourselves into another's belief system. Now is the time to shed that which I truly know is not mine. I pride myself in digging deep to understand what fits, and I am letting go of the rest. In my cycles of ups and downs, I release that which does not compliment who I am. I am continuing to shed that which does not fit to make room for all the blessings that I am destined to receive. I have now begun the journey to see who has been under the mask. I see me.

May I Introduce Myself?

When placed in a new situation, we always want to make a good, lasting first impression. Sometimes, this presentation may come with falseness—acting a certain way or looking a certain way to be accepted. Wanting to be loved and accepted was my lifelong struggle. With it came a false presentation for fear of not being accepted. I wore masks and uttered the right words to impress. Yet as I was receiving what I thought were accolades, I realized they were merely acts to control and manipulate. So as I smothered myself under one more mask, I finally heard my own cries of enslavement. Having shed and emptied myself, I can now present myself in truth.

I Know That I Already Know

Having lived a life of fullness and emptiness, it's difficult at times to decide what to keep and what to discard. Things that I needed in the past and that helped me arrive to my now may no longer be acceptable or applicable to where I am. That which I believed to be true may now have a deeper meaning or may have led me to a contradiction that I have then decided to drill down further. Either way, I know what I already know. There is light and darkness. All that is helpful, true, positive, and real is in my life. When I question what I know, I deal with new information that may challenge a belief system or a contradiction. So I breathe, I hear, I listen, and then I know that I already know.

What's Left When the Dust Settles

I spent most of my life trying to assimilate myself to meet the needs of others and to assimilate them into believing I had the answers to their problems since I was their caretaker, but I have given up this burden. I no longer show up as anyone other than me. I no longer engage in another's drama or try to fix someone or something that is not mine. I've decided to forgive and have deep-seated relationships with authenticity, not wearing a mask or acting in any other way but in the light of the truth of God. Even if it means I will be on my own, I can trust my word. I know I will love myself without conditions. We are all on a journey to find our voice and to live our truth. When the dust settles, I see me.

Hold and Release

There is a saying that if it's meant to be yours, let it go; and if it returns, it is yours. What I've held in my heart has practiced this behavior. There was a time when my grip was so strong that nothing could penetrate what I was holding in my fist. But once I opened my hand to release, I was able to receive what was meant to be. Holding on to the predictable and comfortable mindset will always get me more of the same. It is only the release that will bring what is meant to be. As I relinquish that which is not mine to control, I can now hold in my heart, my mind, and my soul all that is mine and all I am meant to carry.

Release

I used to hold on so tightly for fear that if I let go, I would fall or someone I loved would leave. That death grip of fear only smothered that which I wanted, because my grip suffocated those whom I held in my heart. The fear was not so much in the release and not receiving; it was in how I was supposed to live in the emptiness of that void that was left when I let go. Yet I decided to trust myself enough and love myself enough and to have faith that when I did, in fact, release it, it would make room for all my exciting new adventures and opportunities to fulfill my purposeful life. Now I have defined myself in my eyes, and my heart is open enough to see the blessings of all who enter and leave.

Paralyzed

I used to feel like it was the end of my happiness if there was discontentment or any unrest between me and those I loved. I was paralyzed in those very moments of fear when I thought all could be lost if I deviated from their plan. I would tiptoe around an issue and become subservient to any request even if it defiled my truth. Yet living paralyzed was not living; it was merely existing. It took a leap of faith, an act of trust, and a purging and emptying of that which shadowed my light. Even though it might not have resulted in an outcome that I hoped for, I knew my truth, I sang my song, and I danced my life into the endless possibilities of what is and yet to come.

The River Will Flow Again

When someone hurt me, I would stay with the pain, reliving and rewinding the transgressions, as if staying in the pain would help me learn how to live with it. And when I made a transgression, I would relive and rewind the pain as if in making my decision, I would find justification on why I chose the behaviors I did. But neither behavior ever healed the pain. It was always in my best interest to assess the situation to find a life lesson, whether it be mine or not. Yet hashing up old hurts and reopening old wounds did not serve any purpose other than keeping the pain alive and justifying being a victim with a getting even mentality. This served no purpose. What was done was done.

I now get to choose where to go from here. Apologies have been made, behaviors have been changed, and life lessons have been learned, allowing the damned river to flow again. When a thought comes to mind, I find gratitude for how I was able to get through and heal the pain; it is done!

The River

When the river of life flows, it carries new experiences in and removes that which is no longer needed. When unrest ensues, the river of life becomes damned up with that which is trying to be removed and with that which is trying to be replaced. Consequently, there is no room for anything but chaos, and a flood wreaks havoc on what already is. Neither good nor bad, this is the very essence of growth—that which would still fit and that which wouldn't. Whether it's a materialistic purge or a spiritual cleansing that is needed, the river of life's water can wash away the old so that the new can settle in once the water recedes. But cautiously, I am reminded to let go of that which needs to be cleansed or washed away so that I can float through life instead of drown.

I'll Remain

With one touch, one promise, or one smile, I was sucked into someone else who would complete me. I did whatever it took to feel complete through them, so I ended up settling for the crumbs left for me as if those were enough to sustain me, and I filled in the gaps. I paid the bills, cleaned the house, and went beyond the giving of myself to fill the void for which others did not contribute. I called this acceptance, and I settled. I settled until I decided I was worthy. Then I started to see me, hear me, and know my own soul void of them. I emptied what I felt I was responsible for to sustain a relationship until I was indeed empty and left with me. Now on this next part of my journey, they can come and visit, but I am the only one who will stay to complete me.

This Is Me

I have worn many hats over the decades of this life. Some were chosen for me, and some were of my own choosing. As a child, I would wear something or do something; and if I were challenged, I would begin to doubt myself. After years of questioning whether others knew better for me than I knew for myself, I realized that this was me. Having been labeled and wearing those labels even when I knew they didn't fit, I shamed myself for not advocating enough to hear my own voice or to be seen. Yet when I tried, I allowed the shame to continue. I finally removed myself from the box that contained me, and I began to see my worth and to honor myself enough to melt the shame that blocked me; now I am moving into the sunlight of my life. Now I live in the light of my truth with my voice, and I say, "This is me!"

That Which I Am Meant to Hold

I have been blessed with the gift of holding others in my life. I am blessed with holding my sons in my body and in my heart. I am blessed with the possibility of looking into the eyes of my grandchildren. I am blessed with holding the hopes and dreams of restoring my family and my marriage. I am blessed with the aspiring publications of my books. I am blessed with holding the security of being financially secure to take care of my needs. I am now looking to become hopeful enough that through prayer and faith, I will have that which I am meant to hold. I'm learning to release that which is not mine. Letting go of that which is not mine to hold allows room for that which I am meant to receive. I continue to keep my heart, my mind, and my hands open and empty for the endless possibilities of all that I am meant to have and hold.

Release and Empty

I used to be convinced that if I held on to resentment, it would guilt someone into owning their behavior, as if holding on would make them change. But I've come to realize that I was the only one holding on and that they went on without me, leaving me with my own disappointments, judgments, bitterness, and resentments. So I am learning to release their behavior that hurt me, and I am emptying myself to allow joy and peace into my life.

Worry, obsession, coercion, anger, and manipulation cannot change what was. Only releasing, keeping my voice, and living in my truth can help me heal from any transgressions. And whether they own their behavior or not, it is not about me! What is about me is how much of me I am giving while waiting for them. If they change, I will be happy; if all is restored, I will find peace. I can be happy and live in peace while we all find our way. How much I release and empty to make room for joy and peace is up to me.

With One More No

I spent my life allowing my behavior to close my soul, whether it was someone's word or actions that hurt me or hurting myself with choices I had to own and forgive. I learned to say no to myself when I knew I was capable of a behavior that would cause me or someone else harm or if another's actions continued to hurt me. I used to believe that if I gave just one more chance, tried a little harder, or talked myself out of the pain, telling myself, "It's not that bad," then all would be peaceful.

I learned that light cannot be seen in the dark if it was smothered by negative energy and that healing could not occur if behaviors weren't questioned, challenged, or changed. So with one more no, I became the person whom I was intended to be, I set boundaries with those who kept showing up the way they always showed up, and I learned I could say, "No, thanks."

Release and Exhale

I inhale the positive and exhale the negative, and with one more step, I move into the light while I step away from the darkness. This simple ritual of releasing, removing, and replacing can be as healing as a prayer of hope and restoration. In letting go and moving forward, I can release that which I used to think I need and move into that which is now applicable for where I am. Making sure I am coming from a positive place and not from one of revenge, I can slowly inhale the new knowing that even if I am breathing alone, I am breathing. If done in faith, change can be an exciting adventure. With one more goodbye and one more tear, I can welcome the new and thank my past for its lessons of love.

For You, For Me

For years, I showed up for you and not for me. At any request, I could become a contortionist, bending and stretching for you, but not for me. Instead of presenting me to you, I presented you in me. Denying, excusing, and becoming accountable for you, there was no me left to see in the reflection of my soul. As I began to see you in me, I made the humble decision to step away from that drama and back into my life. There will always be you, as there will always be me. But no longer in you, I am willing to remove myself from any behavior that does not complement the soul I am meant to be. So for you, I bless and wish you well; and for me, I honor the many life lessons learned from you today.

Settle Down

In my youth, when I became so loud that my voice was heard or became too big because of my dance, I was told to settle down. This direct order caused me to withdraw into my shell so as not to be seen or heard. Struggling with the need to be a part of something, when requested, I sang their song and danced their steps. After moving toward my life, shedding their song and dance steps along the way, I settled into my own.

Settling down has taken on a more positive lifestyle. I have settled into and settled down in the comfort and blessings of my journey. I sing the verses of my own song, and I dance the steps of my own journey—not following another's but placing my own foot-prints on the sand of my beaches. I've learned that someone else's dance or someone else's song is not the place that fits me. I have settled down in my own life.

What Matters Now

When I started my recovery, I thought that if I said the right words or thought the right thoughts or chose the right behavior, all would be well. I thought that pain would melt into this huge meadow of flowers and trees and that apologies would come and tears would flow, then all would be as it should be—happy, content, and drama free. But that's not how the journey of life flows.

What I learned was, as I drilled into the depths of my soul to clean out that which I thought was mine, there was pain. There were tears that flowed like a river that cleansed the debris that dammed up my spirit. There were hopes and dreams that faded into the reality of what was and what was meant to be. There were goodbyes and moving forward without apologies that I thought I needed to exonerate myself from their drama. So what matters now? All that I am and all that I have removed to see me again matter.

Purposeful Packing

On the journey of life, we encounter people, places, and things that remain for a moment or forever. Every person, place, or thing holds a special lesson, whether it is to sit and enjoy a thunderstorm or to hold the hand of a loved one in pain. Sometimes, we can become confused by the longevity of these gifts. "Just how long will I be able to stand in front of the ocean at sunset? How long do I get to hold my favorite childhood toy? How long will you be in my life so that I see you in me and you see me in you?"

Being on this journey, packing becomes very purposeful; and having to carry your own luggage, only packing what is essential can make the journey lighter and easier. What I choose to pack now is quite different from my past journey. Now having emptied another's baggage, I can enjoy the snowfall as I send out a blessing and hold on to the picture of a loved one and say a prayer.

My Responsibility

Having been a caretaker for most of my life, I am still learning to enforce and honor that fine line between kindness and confusion. What is mine to be responsible for are attributes that help me be my best, true self. To follow rules and laws assists my attentiveness to be honorable. When someone is not being responsible, then it becomes a heartfelt feeling in me to rescue and make it all better. This is the exact behavior that has kept me a prisoner in my own self-inflicted victimization. I pray that they will find clarity and pray they listen to guidance. I am no longer on the floor as anyone's doormat. I am responsible for my own word and deed, as others should be for theirs.

Live within Me

When I am asked to help someone, I have an amazing capability of taking over so that his or her burden becomes lighter. In taking on someone else's burden, it can then become my burden. When I try to hand it back, guilt and manipulation may enter this kind act, which, in turn, may result in me feeling taken for granted. Resentment may replace kindness, so I am now cautious to help without carrying others' burden.

I won't enter another's life without leaving mine. This behavior causes me to question how much of me I can give to you before I disappear and can't tell the difference between you and me. I have vowed never to lose myself in another's drama, making me assess what I can give away and still see me. I will live with but not within anyone else but me. I will offer to walk hand in hand, but when finished, please return my hand to me.

Scattered Pieces

I've learned through many painful moments of my life that the harder I hold on to something, the chances of it breaking are even more inevitable. I spent my life wishing for something and then receiving it, and this only kept me wishing for more or for a different outcome. I neglected the journey to keep the need to be filled alive. I ran around picking up the scattered, shattered, broken pieces of my life and keeping them locked away. Occasionally, I tried to glue them back together, but I was always distracted by the next best wish. When I finally stopped running and remained in the silence of my emptiness, I brought all my scattered pieces out into the light and began to reassemble those pieces that still fitted and said goodbye to those pieces that no longer belonged. Knowing this is my life's journey, I am carefully holding each piece of my life as a gift; and as I am reassembling my life's pieces, I find gratitude and peace in the journey knowing that all is well.

LET'S TRY AGAIN

When I stumble or fall, I get up and try again. When I attempt something new and I am not yet proficient, I try again. Such as in a relationship, when I choose to be surrounded by people with similar situations, it is a gift that they offer help or need support. This exchange assists in the evolutionary journey of the soul, yet I have been known to take on more than my own share and not get replenished. Due to a lack of communication, the relationship suffers; but with diligence and faith, I try again.

There is a point where the relationship must end because the similar situations have changed. Not wanting the unhealthy drama of others, of those I call friends, I am now open and empty to try again. I am seeing how selective I am because I want to react in a positive way when I am confronted with a negative situation. So leaving my judgments and expectations that cause resentment and disappointment behind, I try again, and life goes on.

IN BETWEEN (INSPIRED BY TAO)

What is the use of acquiring what I don't
need? Contemplate what I will hold in my hands
as I die and I will know what really matters. Alive
I hanker, yearn and crave, I have only the chal-

lenge of letting go. Somewhere in the middle I must achieve balance, knowing what is enough. I must find balance between satisfaction and dissatisfaction, between need and want, between that which serves me and that which distracts me from enjoying the life I've been given to live.

The emptying, purging, and mask removal are helping me reveal the true, authentic me. All these burdens have distracted me. Living in the in between means accepting not knowing and releasing the control of an outcome I want but may never receive, and having faith in the void is the total relinquishing of the soul to an energy greater than me. In this humbling experience, I am becoming more comfortable in finding my balance in the in between. I am giving this one day to live in joy and peace and in the acceptance that I don't know.

Begin Again

I used to need the validation of another to tell me that what I was saying was correct, what I was doing was acceptable, and how I was feeling was justified. If I got a thumbs-up, I felt complete, but one snarl or one more disapproving word drained all my self-worth, turning it into a deep pool of doubt. I needed so badly to have others agree with me. I needed my answers and opinions to matter to them. I needed all of us to be on the same page for me to feel worthy and complete. I needed my voice to matter to them and for our truth to align.

And then I stopped needing them to complete me, and I started purging them to see me, and I questioned my truth to see how much of their truth was mine. I began to see all of us, and I began to forgive and to stop judging and tried to be seen and heard. I started living my life, defining myself in my truth. I took one more breath and began again. How blessed I was to start a new with one more chance.

Taking Me Along

Change is one true, inevitable rite of passage. We all come into ourselves, as we have learned in a world of positive and negative energy. As change occurs, we shed that which no longer aligns with our true self yet take that along the attributes that will align with our destiny. Even when I was unsure of who I was looking at in my own reflection, I knew who I was within, just waiting to be seen and heard. I'm grateful for that which I've kept and that which I've emptied. I see me in my reflection from within as I continue on my journey, taking me along for the ride.

The Grip

The grip is a tight hold in fear of letting go. Within this tight hold, the hand can become tired, so the grip is released inch by inch. What am I holding on to so tightly that it is causing me to clench my fists to the point of pain? Having been filled with the perceptions of history, the news, teachers, family, and peers, what I have chosen to believe has become my truth. Do I still need to hold on to their truths to be loved, or is it now time to release the grip of everything I hold true, that I have allowed to define me, and to actually know what is true, what is real, and what is authentic to me? This is a leap of faith, to live in the not knowing, to live in the without-ness in order to be void and empty to make room for the truth. I have been gripping fear, so I open my hand, release it, and let go; and there is faith.

Empty Canvas

We are a portrait of all our life experiences, a tapestry of each carefully woven thread that signifies a specific event or experience in our lives. If an experience has outlived its welcome or the life lesson has been learned yet the situation still flutters in and out of my life, my canvas can still hold that which is no longer needed. I've chosen not to erase anything from my canvas of life or remove any thread from my tapestry knowing all will unravel. I have chosen to look at my canvas and fill it with my truth, to add more of my own threads to my life's tapestry, and to stay and live in my truth. This process takes time, and when I become anxious or uncomfortable in the not knowing or feel the need to put something on my blank canvas, I pause, breathe, pray, listen, wait, trust, and have faith. I am a masterpiece in the making. We all are.

FOR ME, NOT TO ME

Having to learn to forgive myself and to discount all the misinformation and lies I once believed, I am coming into this new phase of my journey. I am becoming more intuitive. I am listening and becoming more silent to hear, emptying myself of that which is not mine or no longer defines me. I am continuing my quest to find out what is true and what I can believe. I am learning to walk my talk, honor my boundaries, and see my worth.

For too long, I ignored who I was meant to be so that I would fit another's mold. No longer surrounded by that energy, I find peace in the simplicity of my life. It does not have to be so difficult, this journey of mine, yet I stood in my way for too many decades so that I could parade wearing the mask of shame. Now I know that what happened to me was what happened for me. With one more inhale, I can thank God for my journey, love Him and love others, and know that all is well.

TAILOR-MADE

As a fine suit is tailor-made, so are our life lessons and experiences and the opportunities for our souls to evolve. We have been blessed by being surrounded by people who have similar experiences. They have been carefully placed in our lives to teach us something or for us to teach them. Once the lesson is learned, we tend to find ourselves holding on to that community that we've outgrown. Moving on can hold a time of sorrow, as we will leave them to continue on our journey. Getting stuck in the in between can cause anxiousness and uncertainty and can even rob us of our joy.

We can learn to be supportive of their journey without sacrificing our own. We can offer guidance, love, compassion, and even empathy without having to disappear into their drama. Prayer is a powerful energy, and what we think is our responsibility can be handed to God. This is where our life continues as we bless their journey and continue on our own. Each life lesson is tailor-made to fit us. We can participate in another's journey without losing sight of our own. I will lend a helping hand, and I will leave with both hands in my pocket.

THE GREAT SHIFT

In the stillness of the new chapter of my life, I am aware of the great shift in my soul. I am very aware of my contradictions and triggers and my ability to stumble when I allow fear to rule my thoughts. I have learned this in my life's story. I once thought, "If I only…, then…" But now I know that when I am in my light, I am forgiving, compassionate, kind, empathetic, and patient. I'm able to hand my burdens and all that needs to be fixed over to God to be in peace. This helps me move into the acceptance of what is and to be comfortable living in the not knowing. It is here in the emptiness that I find my peace and connect with my soul, knowing, trusting, and having faith that God is and always has been.

A JOURNEY WITH MY OWN LUGGAGE

The luggage for my life's journey holds the direct connections to my soul's evolution, yet unless the luggage is opened and unpacked, the use of that which is not mine may substitute what truly and deeply is mine. I have traveled the roads in my lifetime, occasionally opening my luggage to go within for help, and that occasional visit has now become a daily ritual. Going within my own luggage can help me let go and hand back that which I have borrowed along the way. With a gracious heart, I can live from my own luggage and know that all is well. This journey is not about conquest; it is about living in love and light, showing the world what a blessing I am, and for them to see the blessing that they are.

EMPTY WITH COMPASSION

In my emptying of that which is not mine, I make it clear that compassion and empathy are all I want to give. No longer will I settle or accept anything but love, accountability, honesty, consideration, respect, and truth. No longer will I assimilate for another. I have a clear vision of who I am. If the connections come, I will be my best self for the both of us; I have nothing more to lose or empty. I am in God's light, and whether others are, I am and will forever remain there.

IN THE VOID

After emptying that which was not mine and handing back the burdens that did not define me, I noticed that those who judged and found me guilty were engulfed in their own pain, the pain that I thought was mine to heal. My old behavior dictated that I fix it, change their minds of what they thought about me, and wear the mask of their choice. Now having let go of the burden to control their mindset about me, I've realized that it really doesn't matter. It doesn't matter how I am perceived, if they love me or not, or if I am accepted. What does matter is that I perceive myself in God's goodness, only to be forgiven time and time again for my trespasses. What does matter is I accept and love myself. I am a blessing of God—we all are—whether they know me or not.

So in my emptying of that which is not mine, there is a void. Amid the uncomfortable and unfamiliar feelings of being able to fill it with me, the question then becomes, "What do I fill this void with?" So as I wait and ponder the possibilities, the familiar old anxiousness starts creeping back. Being uncomfortable but real is better than being uncomfortable and wearing a mask. I am real. What do I fill my emptiness with now that all is empty?

Substitution

The emptying of that which is not mine only to replace or substitute it with something or someone else is not emptying. Words can only have meaning with actions, so all the words about letting go or not knowing or of faith or trust are just printed symbols on the page until letting go, emptying, not knowing, trusting, and having faith take action. I spent years substituting one behavior for another, never really letting go, emptying, or trusting in the not knowing or truly having faith that God got this. So even in my solitude, in the emptiness and silence, who I am has already been established. Now it's time to get going and become who I am meant to be as God's blessing.

Time to Say Goodbye

Saying goodbye or holding on to something that no longer fits can be as painful as feeling an emptiness inside that won't be filled. There is no room for the new if the old is still harboring its space. Saying goodbye is admitting completion, and even if what I am saying goodbye to is something or someone I love, when it's time, I have to let go and move on. Remaining stagnant will not change the outcome. Setting my sights on the light will help me acknowledge and thank those lessons learned that have assisted in helping me be my best, true self for God. It's time to say goodbye.

Emptiness

It is said that in order to receive what you want, you have to let go of all you desire. It is said that in order to have yourself full, you must be empty. The undoing and redoing with a different agenda can be painstaking. Relearning the truth after living in another's lie stretches one toward pain, but it ultimately moves into joy. Trusting the inner voice of the truth requires faith in the not knowing. I have lived my life this way. I am redoing, relearning, letting go, emptying, and changing my attention toward God's love, and this has brought me fulfillment. It's time to live again.

How Much More?

Where do I draw the line before I say enough? How much more of myself am I willing to give? It is one thing to be compassionate, empathetic, patient, and forgiving; but at what cost do I relinquish all the pieces that leave me invisible, that will make me become just another you? So before I ask myself how much more before I lose myself in you, I will ask, when is enough? Before I empty myself into you, I have to be emptied of you so I can be full of who I am to enable an exchange without depletion. The prefix co- means "together," so I am still who I am while I am sharing with you.

Exchange

In the emptying of that which is not mine, I am removing the old that no longer serves me to make room for the new. Holding on will not change it, but letting go will heal it. Knowing the origin, I can now say goodbye to that which has caused pain and allow the new to fill me and to bring me joy. It may not be what I expect to get, but it will be what I am destined to have. May we all find God's love and light so that we can replace the sword with a handshake and replace the armor with love.

Release the Grip

In my emptiness, even where I am no longer attached to the negative and to the masks, lies, and inappropriate behavior that block my light, I may still experience triggers. I look back on what is familiar, which calls me to contradict who I am. Now knowing there are no do-overs, I don't need the acceptance or approval from others to fill me. Getting to know myself after the dust has settled and the masks are taken off and discarded is when I question, who am I?

97

Getting to know myself will take effort. The effort entails letting go of expectations, disappointments, resentments, denial, and the darkness. It entails coming into the light, seeing myself in the truest, purest light, feeling my feelings, and owning what is mine to forgive. In my aloneness, grasping at unsung dreams and reviewing memories, I will heal. When I hold on too tightly, I can't feel the wind between my fingers. When my heart is closed, I can't feel the love that's there. So I will release the grip and have an open hand and open heart.

BROKEN PIECES

When I looked at what was preventing my happiness, I came up with a list of what other people were doing or not doing. I found myself looking for them to be responsible to make me happy and to find peace. I was giving my power and energy to them, and looking for my happiness was contingent on what they could do for me. I found myself falling to pieces. It was then that I decided to pick up my broken pieces and put myself back together knowing I could live and find happiness and peace with or without them. God is the glue of my life.

FEAST OR CRUMBS

Keeping my focus on me is the most important part of my recovery. This is a daily ritual so that I don't lose myself again or relinquish my control to others. I have allowed others to dictate what's appropriate, and this has relinquished my control to them. I can make productive, healthy choices for myself. I can agree to disagree, be comfortable or uncomfortable, take crumbs that are offered, or set my own table for a feast.

Learning new behavior takes time. I have to empty all that I have deemed comfortable and predictable, which may leave me empty and uncomfortable for a while. I need to internalize what is being presented and then find a way to apply it for my best interest. I deserve the best, and that's what God has intended for me. I am learning patience, and I am learning to listen and hear my God's voice. This new normal will become a given, and all will work out as it is intended, in God's time, for me.

DETACH IN LOVE

I have had many relationships with family and friends. When any of these people had a bad day or just needed to withdraw, my immediate reaction was to ask if I did something wrong or if they were angry with me. I took it so personally and thought I was the reason for their unhappiness. Their validation was so important and was the root of my self-worth. I have now learned that no one can make anyone feel or do anything unless they give the other person permission. I realized I was giving my power away and giving them permission to treat me in a way that was not worthy of my goodness. Then I learned to detach in love.

I've learned to listen, ask questions, be compassionate and empathetic, and offer solicited advice; and now I take nothing personally unless it is about me. Detachment in love means to support the person in need yet step aside so they may continue their agenda and work it out to get their answers. No longer feeling the need to rescue or be accountable to fix everyone's problems, I now allow myself to focus on my own life, no longer defining mine as theirs.

THE LEAKY SHOWER

My shower was leaking into the drywall, causing the walls to rot with mold. I had to demolish the shower before it leaked into the foundation of the house to prevent structural damage. This scenario is parallel to my recovery. If I had not taken care of my emotional foundation, I would have crumbled. I have been tearing down the walls to my deep core to remove and replace the rotted old walls of my life. One-half of the shower walls are gone, and I look at the foundation, which has holes, mildew, and rot, just as I look at my own life.

The old still remain as I wait for the new. It's temporarily left with holes that will soon be filled. I can't rush this, for if it's rushed, how solid will the new walls be? Rushing may cause future leaks. It will be a slow process, and I can't rush rebuilding. It's in a transitional state, half torn away, half remaining, just like me. As the emptying and replacing process goes on, all will be ripped away to be replaced with the new. This is a slow journey, but after, I will be more solid than ever.

THE RIGHT DIRECTION

Sometimes, I feel the need to crawl back into my old behavior. It was so predictable and so safe. I knew what to expect. At the end, there was only pain, but that was okay, because I believed I was not worthy of anything but the pain that followed. Things are different now. I no longer need the pain, and I am only worthy of good. I deserve the best, and I don't need to act inappropriately or control or manipulate to get attention. I can feel good about myself because I now believe I am worthy.

The old behavior is no longer comfortable. I no longer need it to survive. I accepted this way of life because it was all I knew. Now I know different, and I know more about myself. I now ignore what I knew and what I believe is my old behavior. I'm not comfortable with that anymore. Having emptied the old, even though I have no idea what to do next, there is a peace and tranquility about the unknown. I feel safe because I know God is helping me. He's given me gifts of intuition to help guide me. Ignoring this gift would be like ignoring God and myself, so I choose not to crawl back into the darkness anymore. I am headed in the right direction.

THE PAIN OF RESISTANCE IS NOW
THE PEACE OF ACCEPTANCE

In the letting go of that which is not mine to control, I am emptied. The anxiousness and impatience due to my lack of faith have caused me to live in pain. The pain of holding on to that which was not mine but was God's was my tug-of-war, and this was my burden. I lived as if I could control others, as I had allowed them to control me. The fear of being emptied drove me to fill myself with everyone and everything that wasn't me. In letting go and surrendering, God took my burdens from me. The emptiness of what used to be there now made room for God to fill me. The pain in resistance was now the peace of acceptance.

I've replaced my sword with a handshake, replaced my armor with a hug, and replaced anger with love. I have moved into the acceptance of and faith and trust in God's plan. He is filling my emptiness with His promise that He's got this. I have let go of the fear of not knowing by knowing He is love. Now there is room for me. I have my light, which once was dim but now shines. The fear has now melted into the spring of my life. All is new and awakening from the darkness of the winter of my life. Trying to make it happen because I knew what was best has evolved into faith that all is meant to be in God's plan.

Release

When I work on trying to be happy yet still feel my sadness, I spend a lot of energy on trying to not feel sad in order to be happy. I try to keep my sadness hidden, so I ultimately waste time and energy in keeping this sadness at bay. What you resist persists; therefore, I have chosen to face and feel the sadness, guilt, resentment, disappointment, anger, and fear instead of masking and stuffing my feelings. Now instead of negativity controlling my energy, I've chosen to feel and now love, forgive, heal, and live in peace. I release the burdens to control or heal others.

Relearn

How many times do I trust the word of someone who has promised to change their behavior but remains the same? How many times do I need to step into a revolving door, only to stop and walk another path? Learning how to be a friend requires being true to myself, saying no, and being able to trust another and myself. I get to relearn.

Pack Light for the Trip

I had a visual of dragging everything I ever owned, everything I ever felt, and everyone I ever met along with me on this journey. Everything was tied up, and I held fast to that rope, not letting one thing fall off the enormous mountain of stuff I dragged behind me. I grasped the rope over my head and faced my load, pulling and tugging every step of the way. I rarely stopped to regroup unless something fell off this mountain of stuff. I spent years dragging these stuff until I finally understood letting go and giving my burdens to God.

Mark Nepo wrote, "There is no point in holding on to the deepest things that matter for they have already shaped us." Feeling the need to be noticed and believed made me pack all that I thought I needed to defend my honor, yet I have already arrived, so I need to hold on to that which I already am and release what has hurt me. In this release of that which is already imprinted and can never go away, I am giving myself permission to shed, release, and empty that which is no longer needed to prove to myself I am loved and worthy of all the blessings I wish on others. Now I pack light for the rest of my journey and pack only what I truly need.

One More Goodbye

There comes a time in one's life when purging is necessary. Discarding the old is to make way for the new. It is also profound to realize how very little one really needs to be fulfilled. Others' hats, various masks, and an abundance of other people's stuff make for a very heavy, tiresome journey. It is the sifting through, the letting go, and the saying goodbye that has helped me realize that when I am once again empty, what is left is what truly matters. So with one more goodbye and one more layer that is shed, my true authenticity finally has room to celebrate the abundance I have always had.

One More Chance

As long as I have breath in my lungs and as long as my heart beats, I have one more chance. It's never over; it's only peeling away layers into the depth of my core to see that which really is. It is the drilling down to the very depths that truly allows the light to penetrate. In this emptying out, all may seem tedious and a repetition of the same issue, yet it is allowing that which is new to replace that which is being emptied. So I will continue to make a clean, holy space for all the blessings waiting to make a home in my soul.

Release

When I hold on too tightly, I tend to put all my energy into something or someone that I ultimately have to release. Putting energy into that which is not mine to have has led me to compromise my true self in order to be a part of a puzzle where my pieces don't even fit. Releasing, letting go, forgiving, moving on, and getting through are words that ultimately leave me empty. This void needs not be filled so quickly. Ultimately, if I don't slow down, I will refill it with the same information, judgments, and opinions that I just emptied. Being still, silent, and in the void help me trust God and myself. I would rather be alone than with those who want me to wear a mask.

Satisfaction

Trying to fill something that does not need to be filled is in vain. Don't think that one more sweater, a pair of shoes, showing kindness, validation, a hug, a kiss, or a smile to fill the emptiness can be a life's journey. Yet when realizing that nothing is needed, there is a satisfaction and contentment, so look at what's already there, not what you think needs to be there. Come home. Stop chasing what is not there and be complete and comfortable with what is. Relationships don't define us; they assist us on our journey to be our true self. Every yes and no has helped me become who I already am. I conquered the fear of not knowing.

The Juggle

An interesting concept is throwing many objects in the air and beginning a dance to assure all remain airborne. How many times in our busy lives had something so precious shattered as it hit the floor? As I continued my journey, I noticed how many times that precious something that shattered as it hit the floor was me. How many times did I bite off more than I could chew or nibble at something that was not even mine, only to add it to my juggling repertoire? Learning that I can show up for others without leaving myself out of the equation has brought me to a point where I have fewer objects to juggle. I am worthy of being airborne.

Alone and Empty

If I were to choose between wearing a mask and being surrounded by those who are wearing masks, would I choose that over being alone? If I were asked to harbor another's drama and be available to clean up their mess and sacrifice my own truth, would I choose that over being empty? With those choices come pain, but the alternative is being alone and empty. I am living my truth and living in faith. In the stillness at the end of my life, I matter, who I am matters, how I served mattered, and that I am a blessing and worthy of love and respect matters.

And Now

I used to think that if I met everyone's needs to make them happy, then I would be happy. I used to think that if I could take away their pain and harbor their burden for them, then they would find peace, and so would I. Yet now I know I am only responsible for my own needs, my own pain, and my own burden. Most of my pain and burden had been because I carried theirs and felt responsible for making them happy. My happiness depended on their happiness. But now I know I cannot labor for them. I will not own their behavior or take their consequences as my own. I am responsible for me, and they are responsible for themselves. I choose me.

Grasp the Lesson

I have always had to reread and ask probing questions to understand, yet when asking God my whys, it took silence and faith to hear. So in my silence, I heard Him tell me to empty that which was not mine and hand over burdens that were His to own and forgive. I learned that we were all souls on a journey and that with each painful experience came a lesson of understanding. So now I don't live in someone else's drama but share stories. I don't wear masks to be loved but present my authentic self. I own what is mine, and I am defined by my own choices.

Become a Diver

When a huge wave is coming toward me, instead of hitting it head-on, I become a diver. Drilling down deeper can cause a rupture in that which has hardened; it is through the cracks that the light can enter. Having started a new geographical journey, the illusions of what-ifs and unresolved pain came along with me. I thought a new address would change what I had yet to confront, so settling into my new address, thinking all the pain would disappear became my new mask.

As I now remove more debris and dive deeper into my soul's core, I am reminded that the changes I am making on this journey require me to stop behaviors that are causing me pain and replace them with becoming still, silent, and emptied. I came here and repeated the same behavior, consequently living the same life. Now it's time to find the new. Who am I now, and who do I want to be?

Stripped Away

In learning and striving to rekindle a relationship with myself, it can be easier to say what I am not than what I am. Yet when it comes to affirmations of who I am, I tend to have to pause and dig deep. I know how to please others; but when it comes to fulfilling my dreams, living in joy, and exploring my passions, I realize I have to empty and strip away all the parts that are not mine. Having been a member of various groups, one can assimilate into that which is accepted. But once one moves into the realm of relationship with their true self, the question then becomes, "Who am I without you?" It's time to explore the possibilities.

What Is Mine

We go around in our lives being collectors of materialistic items and others' knowledge and wisdom to see what fits and what should be returned. In our gathering, we may encounter another who thinks we should take what they are offering. At times, it will be a choice; at other times, it will be forced. I am now going around and returning all that is not mine to keep, whether it was my choice to borrow or it was forced. I am now in control of what happens to me, how I am treated, and what wisdom and knowledge is mine to keep and share. I've gathered knowledge, and it may take some time to sift through all of it to see what is mine.

Getting Comfortable with the Emptiness

When all is said and done, change happens. Whether we embrace it or not, it's inevitable; so hesitating, denying, or rebelling only causes pain. Letting go of that which is comfortable and familiar, even if it's negative, can bring an emptiness that brings fear. What do I do while I am in transition between emptying the old while waiting for the new? When moving to a new home, the faith that the moving van will arrive is real and powerful. It will come; it's on its way. I have faith. When the new arrives, it can only be embraced to its fullest if the old has been dismissed. How do I have faith it will come? How do I become comfortable when it arrives? This depends on how I want to feel and live my life.

SETTLING IN

I can lend an ear for the turmoil of others' drama, complete a task or project, or visit with a friend, then come back to settle in. The routine of my everyday life is prayer, meditation, journaling, exercising, writing, and reading. I find comfort in knowing I am showing up for me and living in and with my joys, passions, and blessings. When I allow the drama of another to filter into my quiet, my emptying must stay intact. I am very aware of what is mine and what is not, and I am very aware that there is a very fine line between compassion and caretaking. I am willing to support but not willing to forget me. I have settled into my life, willing to change, grow, and find peace.

LIVING WITHIN, LIVING WITHOUT

Once I've emptied myself of that which is not mine or which no longer fits, there is a very uncomfortable waiting time. In releasing the drama, there is quiet; and in halting the confrontations, there is silence. Now without the stimulation that used to drive me to show up and rescue another, I am alone, quiet, and in a waiting mode, asking myself, "What now?" So I am continuing to fulfill my destiny. Having served and loved God's children, I am learning to love me. I am writing to help another, as I have walked in that experience. I love nature and am rediscovering my passions and what brings me joy. What I am waiting for is already here.

RULE OF LIFE (INSPIRED BY TAO)

"Man's untutored tendency is to love himself and to consider his own conduct in the proper role of life. If you keep longing for things you don't have, you are likely to miss the treasures you carry." I am safer in the hands of God than under the rule of my or another's will. These words remind me of God's determination to help me evolve. He has given me all I need to assist me in my journey. When I allow others' or my will to control a situation that may be uncomfortable, it only ends up on my checklist of lessons learned that have led to fear. So I listen and feel the emptiness of what I once accepted to be filled with what is needed to assist my journey.

GUIDED

When lost, it is wise to stop and ask for directions. At times, I think I have figured it out, only to get turned around again, sometimes more lost than when I first realized I was lost. But in the quiet, still, silent emptiness of echoes past that used to show me the way, I am guided by all that is love and true. I have had a good life of life lessons. Mine have not been any more difficult than anybody else's, and I know that these were handpicked lessons for my spiritual growth. Now in this season of my life, I am learning to be content with listening and allowing all my emptiness to be filled with love, joy, peace, and God.

BE SILENT TO LISTEN

I will admit, I've spent a lifetime defending my truth, almost forcing or trying to control others to believe me. In turn, that has made people leave. Those who choose not to believe me will have to live with their truth. When the truth is revealed, they will have to reexamine the choices they've made to see themselves in the light of truth. I no longer sing a song to defend myself, and I have emptied myself of the need to be believed. In this emptiness, I am silent, and I now listen to how I am to show up for life. I find it humbling to now watch them struggle as I did, only to accept the light of the truth, not to be their judge but to be silent and offer a loving hand and heart and words of comfort and to listen to their story.

EMPTY TO BE FILLED (INSPIRED BY TAO)

"With a lack, I am compensated, with a weakness, a strength arises, when I fall, I am lifted up." After filling myself with another's story, I now know and live my own. Filling myself with me takes time as I release one more aspect of someone else. I am filling the emptiness with that which fits me. I am not harboring resentment. I am allowing my pain a voice, yet I am no longer consumed by that pain. For too long, I have lived with the pain, not in the pain. I am celebrating my abundance, allowing myself to live with my passions, joy, and faith.

Broken to Whole (Inspired by William Paul Young)

"When the way of my being matches the truth of my being, I am whole." I forgive trespasses of expectations and let go of resentment, disappointment, and judgment as my last resolution to clear away the old and heal my brokenness. Knowing from the depths of my soul that we are all souls on a journey helps me release the unwanted influences that have broken me. Having survived what I have, I am continuing to gather my pieces and make what is broken whole. So I will continue to praise God for the remarkable life that I have led, be grateful and humbled by my abundance of material and spiritual gifts, and release the resentment, disappointment, and judgment of that to which I thought I was entitled. Now the pieces of life that have broken me help me move toward my wholeness.

Giving Me Away

It is one thing to be compassionate and empathetic. These are wonderful attributes that not only show another kindness but also help to make sense of pain once suffered. Yet it is quite another when I give all of me to engage in another's drama. For so much of my life, I put aside my joy, passions, and happiness when another decided to bring their drama into my peace. I once saw myself allowing this to drain me of my peace, but now I can acknowledge that this is not my burden. I wish them well; pray for their peace, healing, and enlightenment; and step back into my peace.

Hold On or Let Go

Holding on to that which is predictable can be paralyzing. Even with the knowledge that it is not in my best interest, I still feel the need for drama to feel alive and be a part of something other than me. Yet it is in the wake of letting go of others' drama where my real life truly is. I am alive in spite of their drama, and I am loved in spite of their dismissal. To make that empty-handed leap into the void requires faith that God has always been in control of my journey, and even though I have been given free will, I have now believed in me. So every time I question myself if I still need the drama to feel as if I am a part of something, I will ask what is standing in my way to let go and move on.

FILL, EMPTY, REPEAT

It is said that when the bucket is ready to overflow, it is time to empty it. Filling my soul with what now matters to help me fulfill my purpose requires the emptying of that which no longer fits. This procedure is fluid, yet when I try to hold on to that which I think matters through a want or a need, I am burdened with the fullness of that which I am not intended to have or feel. So one more time, I am full, then I am empty, then I repeat. What I am intended to have through this life's journey is my soul and God. Everything else will come, stay, or go. I am loved by merely being me.

COME TO AN END

With each goodbye comes sadness over what was, could have been, or I hope of being. When I look at the blessings of all those who have said goodbye, I thank them for all my life lessons, experiences, and opportunities to evolve. I may not understand this closure through a physical or emotional death, but I am certain it is in my best interest. Along the way, I have struggled to let go—one of my biggest burdens is holding on to that which is not mine to have—so I say one more goodbye to the relationships I hoped to have that have come to an end.

ACCEPTANCE

Acceptance is a tricky growth experience that requires total forgiveness of self or others for a transgression that has brought negative energy into a relationship. The results can be the beginning of a new experience or the end of the status quo. Yet I relied on my old behavior to mask my fear of abandonment. I was apprehensive of the feelings of being emptied of the old to make room for the new. My thinking was that holding on to that which I needed to release only brought on the pain of becoming a chameleon while choosing behavior that only made me feel shame because I was not my authentic self. This was a huge conflict. I was living with should-have-beens and what-ifs. Now having faith and trust in God, I accept, forgive, and live my journey in peace.

ON HOLD

I have spent a great deal of my time postponing my happiness and joy, waiting for the ones I love to be at peace. This is the root of my codependency, the sacrifice of having spent most of my days making others comfortable instead of living in my comfort. This has drawn out resentment, disappointment, and judgment due to my expectations for them to show up and do the same for me. Having no control over anyone's reaction or choices has freed me to live my life with joy, happiness, and peace in who I am. I am a blessing, and we all have been given this blessing to let go of that which we hold on to that has put our life on hold. Now I get to be who I am.

MAKE ROOM FOR THE NEW

When I seek help, it means I have emptied that which I no longer need for my journey; therefore, in this emptying, I have made room for the new. If I seek quiet and peace, I have emptied that which I cannot control and that which is not mine. Do I want to move forward? Do I need drama in my life to feel alive and purposeful? What I seek requires an open emptiness waiting to be filled. I am only emptied with enough room for my own, and if I burden myself by carrying that which is not mine, I will be stuck with too much, and there will be no more room. So I am still, silent, and empty to be filled with the new.

Rise Above and Dance with the Trees in the Wind

I know there is no promise for a pain-free life, so now what? What lessons are there to be learned in pain? What will really matter at the end of it? Why is it? Where is its origin? What is the message? These deep-seated, reflective questions don't have any beginning or end; they just are. So instead of trying to end it only to begin again, why not just be empty and be willing to explore and learn all there is to know? If I fall, I will always rise above and dance with the trees in the wind.

Already Have Abundance

I dream for more and wish for another result, but I am already where I am meant to be today, with whom I am meant to be, and with everything I am meant to have. Yet it is when I fail to find gratitude in my present and celebrate my journey that I lose sight of my blessings of abundance. I humbly believe in my truth and that we are souls on an evolutionary journey in human form. When control and manipulation take over, fear seeps in. I can detour from my abundance back into my what-ifs. It is then I am pulled back to what is.

Resolution: Needs versus Wants

I am recalling how sad, lonely, and desperate I felt. I wanted to belong, to be included, and to feel loved. Yet the more I grew in my faith, learned to forgive myself, and emptied myself of the toxicity of the dynamics I called family, the more present I felt in peace. I need air to breathe, I need the sun to rise in my soul, I need to eat a healthy diet and exercise to sustain my body, which houses my soul, I need to love myself, and I need God and faith in my life. The wants I now have are no longer desperate to fill the voids I used to have. Now empty, what I thought was best for me has dissolved into a compassionate, empathetic understanding that I complete me. All are welcome as I bless their journey, yet the difference is, I no longer need them to feel loved, worthy, and cherished. I was able, along with God, to accomplish that myself. Emptied of them, I am now filled with God and me.

Don't Ask Unless...

How often have I prayed for a burden to be removed from my life when I thought it wasn't mine? How often have I asked for a relationship to mend instead of searching for the life lesson or message that severed the connection? Too often, I have tried to rush into a new with the old in tow. Where can I put the new if I am still holding on to the old? Not only does this leave me frustrated, but then doubt also seeps in, and faith starts to dim. When I am feeling the blessings of the abundance I already have, then I will know what to hold on to or what to let go of to make room for the new. I will and have always had all I need.

The Second Helping

At times, I may, as my mother used to say, have big eyes and bite off more than I can chew. In unhealthy relationships, going back for more has always been a dance, whose steps I've learned well. Even when I had too much, I still went back for a second helping. There was no more room for anything else, whether it was more of the same or something new. Going back for a second helping became a habit that was predictable even if the outcome was pain. I am now comfortable with filling my plate with that which complements and satisfies my growth.

Living My Truth

In a world filled with opinions of right and wrong, good and bad, or happy and sad, it tends to be, at times, a challenge to live in my own truth. I have always known my truth yet have chosen to deviate from it to be accepted and loved and to align with another's opinion. Never in the course of my life has this ever worked for me. I could forever be a chameleon and never please everyone, only betray myself, which can never result in happiness or peace. So right or wrong, good or bad, or happy or sad, I will live my truth.

Strength (Inspired by a Jewish Prayer Book)

"Assured that yesterday's reverses have not broken me, they have only given me added knowledge, where with to grasp my problems more firmly." Knowing that change is inevitable, I am confident and assured that I am exactly where I am supposed to be, doing what I am supposed to do, and in the company of those who are assisting me to move toward my soul's goal. My pain comes from holding on to burdens that are not mine or remaining with those who are living in the past. All the times I remain with these losses only bring more pain, because I know that all is meant to be and that I am meant to thank them and move on. So I continue to empty that which is not mine and release the need to fix them. This is God's job.

Life after This

When filled with the words of another's story, it can be cumbersome to remove and empty that which does not compliment who I am and want to be. Dancing in the footsteps of another can lead me to wonder where my feet belong. Then the wandering begins, and the anxiousness to fill the void of the emptiness of another's footprints leaves me lonely. Yet at times, it is only in that quiet, lonely silence where I truly find where I am going and who I am. Removing that which does not fit does leave room for the new. Although I may be lonely, I am never alone; that is when I come to know where I truly am and who I am.

I'm Ready, Willing, and Able (Inspired by Mark Nepo)

"I had to be less than I am in order to be loved. I shelved my light. There is no room in my life for worthlessness." Why waste time in conflicts that don't matter? There will always be critics, and I will always be falsely accused. Joel Osteen said, "Others don't define me; they cannot keep me from living my purposeful life. God is my defender." I accept this change, the emptying of the burden that I carry for others. I have faith that God will fill me with what I need to live my true, purposeful life. I am releasing that which is in my way and that which is not mine to carry. I have faith that all will come to me when I am ready to receive it. First, I release, then I believe, then I receive; and now I'm ready, willing, and able.

Guests Should Leave

Just like how a welcome guest should stay and visit, so should our feelings. What we resist persists. Denying this will only prolong what wants a voice. Whether it is solicited or unwelcome, a guest has a shelf life, as do my feelings. When all my energy is placed in one area, I tend to focus on it to the point where I get lost in them while the rest of me still wants to breathe. All visits are purposeful and have a special message to give or receive, so it is in that acceptance and embrace that we should visit, but after a while, guests should leave.

Empty to Fill

We all know that when something is full, there is no room for anything else. This is when purging takes place, What is needed is salvaged, and what is not needed is discarded. So it was when I began looking for my truth. Having believed in how I was defined by the truth of others, I began to question all that was said about me or done to me. What I needed to salvage and what I needed to discard became my awakening toward my truth. Needing to empty the lies, manipulations, and control left me empty. Knowing my pattern of discomfort in not knowing, I found myself holding on to that which needed purging because it was predictable. This was where I learned to depend on my faith and began to trust my own intuition and voice. Emptying that which no longer defines me has now made room for the truth and light I deserve. This is how we evolve; we must empty to be full.

115

Safe within My Own Skin

It has taken me a lifetime to feel safe within my own skin. This body, which houses my soul, has been a wonderful suitcase, for it has always made room for that which I think I need to pack for my journey. So in my lifetime of gathering and purging, I now have what I need for my journey. I have a kind and caring soul, I have an acceptance of what I have left behind in order to arrive where I am, and I have a deep-seated faith in the promise that I will always have unconditional love, financial security, emotional stability, and good health. Although my suitcase is no longer a U-Haul, I know I have what I need and the ability to carry it throughout the rest of this lifetime. I am blessed.

It's Okay

It's a hard challenge to stay true to ourselves in the face of indifference. Rejection and opposition are painful, especially if we are misunderstood, judged or ignored but being treated as if I don't exist is quietly devastating. Somehow our need for love gives tremendous power to the opinions of others, and so, we are required to guard against turning our lives over to the expectations of others. No one can really know what you are capable of but you. Even if no on sees or understands, you are irreplaceable.

This speaks volumes about my life journey. I feel as if he and I and you and I have walked this road together, but only in silence for fear of judgment, ridicule, and rejection. Yet I stand here today in the light of my own truth to tell you that it's okay to be who you are and it's okay to be who we are. With this affirmation, I am okay!

His Grand Plan

When I see the smiles of a new grandparent, recall the memories of my own children as I look through old photos, see a friend grieve at the passing of an elderly parent, or witness a young couple planning their future, I feel an overwhelming sadness for times gone by and dreams that never came to pass. Even in my humbleness to accept God's will, I still feel an emptiness for what I thought was going to be, and I attempt to keep faith in what is. I have so many blessings and comforts, yet I still feel the void left by my children, parents, and grandchildren as I welcome another birthday. I will keep reminding myself that God's will is bigger than mine and that His plan is grander than I can ever imagine.

The Answer to the Whys

I find it difficult at times to live 100 percent in faith that all is meant to be and that His will, will be done, especially if it's a long-time prayer request. So when there is a ray of hope that the prayer is beginning to be answered, all I want to do is hurry along the process so I can resolve the turmoil and be released from the bondage I have held myself in for so long even if I say I have given it to God. But my true testimony of faith is that I have moved on with my life and have learned to live with the pain without the pain defining me. So now that I see God's hand in this resolution, I am also beginning to understand the whys of what He has allowed to happen. If I had stayed, then I would have postponed, if not met, my destiny to release others' burdens, to find my voice, and to live in my truth in peace.

In the Light of My Mind

Thinking before I speak, act, and react is one of the life lessons that I still struggle to master. If I am not receiving a positive affirmation, then I find myself reacting in a defensive mindset, because I get my worth from what is said. Keeping my mind in a positive light can

117

be easily achieved if I give as much energy to the positive that I give to the negative. Admitting that they are all wrong about me and that they think I am less than what I am and for me to believe them have been one of my biggest life lessons. When I stay in the light, then I can achieve what I am meant to do and become who I strive to be.

ALONE

I had to learn to be alone with myself. Having allowed myself to be defined by others, I had to shed their definition of me and let go of their burden, which I became responsible for carrying. I did not blame anyone, because I chose this for myself in order to be loved and accepted. This learned behavior helped me see the person I did not want to be, so I had to be alone in order to see myself. My awareness began when I started saying no to those whom I always accommodated.

Even though I did not honor my own word and questioned my truth, I slowly began to release that which was not mine to hold, again leaving me alone. At times, the silence got so loud, and I wanted to fill the loneliness with drama so I could be a part of something to feel alive. I had to relearn what it meant to say, "Hello. This is who I am," without wearing a mask of who they wanted me to be. This risk no longer burns, because I have been reacquainted with who I am. I can now walk with another without walking in their shadow but in my own light.

THEN IS THEN, AND NOW IS NOW

I was led to believe that I was worthless and unwanted. Then I believed I was worthless and unwanted and acted as if this was my truth. I was asked why everyone had an issue with me. They all couldn't be wrong, so it must be me, I thought. I surrounded myself with people who complimented my issues, and when I finally began to heal and take back my life, I began to say no. So the reason they took issue was because the person I used to be, who always said yes, had now learned to honor herself enough to say no. Now I believe I am worthy of love, abundance, joy, happiness, contentment, knowledge, kindness, and forgiveness. Then is then, and now is now!

My Forgiveness

I used to think that forgiveness was giving the other person a free pass, exonerating them from their trespass, and giving them permission to continue their behavior. Now I know it's a nonjudgmental view of how we are a part of a painful life lesson and how we each become a part of one another's dance and story. I can now walk away, forgiving and doing better, setting boundaries, trusting myself, and knowing that I, too, am not perfect. Judgment will only make someone more right or wrong rather than make them look at the lessons life has to teach. Forgiveness does not condone or condemn but leads to opening the lines of communication toward understanding the behaviors that have been chosen.

I have now emptied those burdens that are not mine to hold. I have stopped enabling hurtful behavior and have learned to set healthy boundaries by saying and honoring my no. I have silenced the adults' lies that are my truth to unveil. What I now know is information that has been left out of my learning. I have taken my education further by reading, listening, and living the truth. In the pain, I can now see the gifts; in the words, I can now begin to understand and see God's greater hand in this for me. I am gratefully blessed.

I Will Even If They Don't!

If all was calm in the lives of others, would I then be calm? If all had peace, joy, and love in their hearts, could I then keep my heart soft and open? If all treated one another with kindness, respect, compassion, and love, could I then reciprocate this behavior? If all were trustworthy and forthcoming in love and let go of judgment, resentment, and disappointment, could I then have a relationship? If all walked their talk and kept their word, could I then honor my own word and fulfill my deeds? If all lived up to my expectations, could I then trust them? Would this bring peace to my world?

119

I've come to know that this contingency plan has been my life's burden. I am always waiting to react in kind—"If they did, then I would." I have led my life by reacting and mirroring their behavior so that I will be accepted and loved, but all this effort has only led to me being invisible in their shadow.

I asked myself, "Could these burdens that I keep holding while expecting their behavior to fulfill me be released so I could breathe and be happy?" Then my answer came, and I now live my life knowing that even if they decide to leave, I will keep an open heart and treat others with respect, compassion, kindness, and love. I will be trustworthy, I will walk my talk, and I will release judgments for unmet expectations. I will even if they don't!

Who I Am before You

Our physical, emotional, and spiritual development is a life journey. We mirror those who are our caretakers and become minimes until we are able to understand our first feeling of pain and judgment. This is when your decision for me becomes more right than my own self-exploration. I am in no way advocating for a non-parenting involvement; however, I know that dismissing who I am to become who is in front of me can lead to a life of self-deprivation and to being a lost soul. It's important to learn from the masters who are present in our lives, but learning and doing have to be experienced by the receiver. We all become products of all those who pass through our lives. We are taught whom we want to emulate and whom we never want to be like, but this is our own choice. Knowing who I am before I meet you will only enhance our encounter.

With One More Smile

Expecting someone to complete me is a life battle. When someone is kind, I immediately let down my guard to allow them to take my heart, and I become so vulnerable with that one smile that I allow old behaviors to replace my inner peace. I know that my true nourishment only lies within myself and is a gift from God, so when

I allow that one smile to melt my heart into losing my own reflection in his eyes, I will remember that we are all souls on a journey and that only I can complete me. Being kind when he is going through his own battles does not mean I tolerate any inappropriate words or behavior. It means I will take a deep breath, set a boundary with kind words by explaining how the behavior is offensive and will not be tolerated, and then walk toward my own heart to know I am safe and complete. With one more smile, I can walk alongside him without losing my own shadow.

Moving On

When did I take the time to feel, deal, and heal from one disappointment? I only hurried up and moved into the next situation without really dealing with the pain. By not taking the time, I acted as if but really did not, so I harbored resentment. I wrapped myself up in the new but did not deal with the fallout of what just happened. I was not finished before I started filling myself up with the new. There were still echoes of the pain that resonated in my heart. How could God possibly give me what He wanted me to have if I was still dealing with what I was holding on to and fearful of what I was about to lose? So I'm taking the time to move on to be empty.

My Thoughts

Being dismissed or ignored is a painful lesson to learn if I am looking for love and relationship. When hurt, my immediate reaction is to react in kind, but resentment and retribution have no place in my soul if I am searching for peace. I can understand with my heart and seek compassion and empathy if I am to forgive and understand their story. Yet if my head is on a mission to be a victim, this closes down the very fabric of my relationships, and there will be no communication or resolution.

Having always been the seeker of peace, my anxiousness hurried the process along too quickly, so vital life lessons were missed, because I was too busy cleaning up everyone's mess and taking on all the responsibility. I can acknowledge the hurt and decide how much responsibility is mine and hand the rest back to them. I continue to strive to enter from my heart and listen to the dialogue in my head to hear how valid my thoughts are to decide if those thoughts are here to continue my suffering or to heal my soul.

LIVE IN THE UNREST

After a confrontation, it was my pattern to check in with the other person to find out how they were doing. But in this kind act, I allowed myself to be sucked into their pain; and ultimately, I owned all the strife, which, in turn, exonerated them from their accountability and responsibility for their part in the conflict. Harboring all the misgivings always left me depleted, because not only did I want to assure their happiness but I also doubted myself and my own integrity, thinking it was merely my fault. Now I own what is mine and have become patient in the unrest, believing that all will be as it is meant to be. I can live with not knowing.

MIRROR OF MY LIFE

I've made my life's journey a quest for truth and understanding. I've tried to empty that which is not mine to hold and flip the lies into truth and heal the sadness of my broken dreams. There comes a time when the emptying is complete and the sadness of broken dreams melts into the acceptance that all is meant to be. When the blame-shifting ends and the victim heals, the next layer is what is exactly mine.

What responsibilities do I have in the schemata of my own life? If I judge a bully, am I not that bully's judge who thinks her way is the right way? If I talk over another, am I not taking their voice? If I spew past transgressions into another's face, am I not being accountable for also being a trespasser? "Do unto others" are words that are not suggestions but words that are essential guidelines. When the mirror of my life shows the reflection of who I am, who do I really want to see?

Never Truly Alone

In my emptiness, there is a calm and comfortable acceptance that I need not hold on to that which is not mine, that there is no need to fix that which is broken if it is not mine, and that I must accept the stillness of that which just is. My journey has crossed many paths, and whether the remainder of my journey is to be with others or alone, I know I am never truly alone.

Where Do I Go from Here?

When all the cards have been played, all that need to be said has been spoken, all that need to be seen has been seen, and all that is needed to be heard has been heard, where do I go from there? Despite knowing in my head that the past cannot be replayed or changed, I still struggle to tell it to my broken heart. The dreams of all that I thought was meant to be or that I was entitled to have, have melted into disappointment. As I struggle to understand that which may never be meant to be understood, I discipline myself to melt the resentment that is growing and hardening my broken heart so that it will melt into forgiveness.

In my uncomfortable grief, I have learned to wait, to be still, and to empty the pain I am carrying. So as I wait for spring to melt the frozen winter of my life, I can listen to His quiet, loving small voice as He tells me where I go from here.

Joy Stealers

Life is a journey through pain and joy and through learning not to stay in the pain. At the end of my life, will I reflect on how I fulfilled my purpose, or will I look at the struggles and pain that I had to feel? Will I ever acknowledge the joy? As I continue on my journey, I explore what causes my pain. It used to come from the burden of needing to be accepted, to feel worthy of being loved, and to control an outcome to my specifications to make me feel secure and wanted. Then I started to ask myself, if I got what I wanted, would I be content, or would I move through that success to the next challenge? Am I still stuck between contentment and conquest? Will I ever settle in the joy?

My Residence

There are too many times in my life when I failed myself. Even when I knew my truth, I ignored it to live in another's. I lost trust in myself due to what another told me. I wore different masks, never feeling safe or worthy to reveal the true me. I said yes when I meant no and said no when I meant yes, all to be accepted and loved, and with one more compromise, I sank deeper and deeper into the darkness until I couldn't even see a glimmer of light.

When I decided I no longer needed or wanted to be this way, I started to journey into the light and risked being abandoned by those who wanted to keep me in bondage. I realized that it was I who was keeping myself imprisoned in a life that was not meant for me. At times, I get lonely and scared that no one will be there for me or that I may be alone, but then I know I am never truly alone. No longer blame-shifting my situations, I now own what is mine and live in the truth and the light. This is where I dwell.

Release

I pray and pray for things to work out the way I would like them to. When I am asked to be patient, in my impatience, I may help things along, thinking I know what's best. This only prolongs the inevitable, that when it's time, I will receive. God can't give me what He wants me to have if I am still dealing with what I have lost; there would be no room. There is no room for the new if I am crowded with the old. The light cannot penetrate a hardened heart unless it's cracked. I cannot feel deeply if I live in shallowness. In my humbleness, is what I am harboring more important than what I am to receive? Knowing what is blocking the light, is staying negative and bitter going to heal anything? Do I need to get even or stay angry in order to feel vindicated? It's only when I am willing to be open-minded and openhearted that I will receive. Time to release!

Not Right, Just Happy

Packing up the old that no longer serves me is a painstaking task. For it, I need to decide what to keep and what to discard. Old clothes that are out of style, worn out, or too big can be donated to another. Books and crafts that I no longer use can be donated to another. But when I come to discarding feelings that no longer suit me, where do they go? Holding on to my resentment kept me ready for battle. I needed to exonerate myself because they lied about me. Feeling disappointed by unmet expectations gave me permission to judge and harbor anger. I thought that if I kept this negative energy alive, then I could make sure they got hurt the way they hurt me. But when I decided that I was giving away my energy and power to those who didn't care about how I felt or how their behavior hurt me, I decided to care for myself. I began to see my worth and that they did not define me.

Now that this behavior is no longer useful, where does it go, and who do I become? When I finally get all my questions answered and when all my exaggerations are put to rest, I can then release the burden that I no longer wish to carry. I remove myself from the tangled mess to get even. Not wanting to be right but wanting to live in peace, I make amends for past hurts, acknowledge the pain, and move forward. I don't need to be right, just happy!

Moving Slowly

I can't continue to choose the same behavior and expect a different result. That's the definition of insanity. Yet when it comes to change, I have learned that I have to change from within. Giving up all my hopes and dreams has caused me pain, so I continue to gradually release that pain in order to have it replaced with something new. I know from past experiences that it will take as long as it takes, and I won't rush through it. That which no longer serves me is being purged, but if I keep holding on and living with resentment for those unfulfilled dreams, then there is no room for something new. I have to continue to explore the concept of giving up my right for renewal to ease the anxiety of those around me. It's during the waiting time and in the emptiness that I sometimes become impatient or so anxious that I hold fast to that which no longer fits or I try to rush into something else to fill the void. I will move slowly and wait for God knowing I am safe and all is well.

Move or Remain

Fear of moving on because of feeling that no one will join me has left me teetering between my future and my past. This leaves me feeling that sometimes, I am unable to be true to myself as I continue to purge the lies that have been my truth. If I continue as if nothing is a trespass and the behaviors don't change, I am still giving them and myself permission to live in a lie. I am giving up my right for renewal to keep the peace, and consequently, I am wearing a mask. So as I continue to believe enough in myself in order to walk into the light, I may be leaving them behind in the darkness. I am not responsible for dragging them along or waiting for them to join me because they choose to remain and not move forward. I love them but not at my expense, and I no longer sacrifice me to accommodate them.

Intimacy

Intimacy is the meeting of souls through touch, a glance, or some other energy connection. I have always received intimacy this way, and yet a few times, my own boundaries have been crossed. I have confused the soft touch or a glance as completion, but it is in the emptying of needing another to complete me that I find true intimacy. Resentment comes when my expectations are not met, yet when I drill down and come back to me, the only boundary I need to make is how much of me I choose to give away to fill a void that only I am responsible for filling. Only I can complete me.

THE LAST BOX

Anyone who has ever moved knows what it feels like to open that last box and review its contents. The secrets it may hold may still be needed or desired, or it may not be wanted anymore, so it will be discarded. This is a new adventure. But what happens when the fear sets in and you think that the box may not have what you're looking for or that it just may be empty? Opening the box takes a leap of faith that what is held inside is exactly what you are meant to have and what will make things complete. Open the last box!

NOT TO RUSH

After I decide what is mine and what is not, the painstaking result of this epiphany will be to let go. Having made room for others' issues or drama, which have helped define my role in life, I am now letting go and leaping into faith. The void that is left will soon be full with something better. Replacing the emptiness right away to fill the void can lead me to revert to that which I have just purged, so I am learning to remain calm in the void as things begin to trickle in to fill the emptiness with something better than what I have left behind. This faith in not knowing is helping me stay in the stillness and silence of the blessings that each moment may bring. When fear creeps in, I can replace it with love.

LIVE WITH IT OR IN IT?

Growth and change are inevitable. It is only painful when that which needs to be shed is held on to so tightly for fear that it is needed to move forward. Living with memories is a paradox. Holding on to that which causes pain can make us continue life in that pain, reliving it over and over. There is no room for healing or for learning to live with the pain. This behavior will paralyze and prevent growth, prevent learning what the pain has to teach rather than what it has destroyed. So as I continue to change and grow into my authenticity,

I will bless the life lessons and those who have taken part and who continue to live in God's love and light with or without.

Connect the Dots

My life has been a mass number of dots floating around and trying to connect. I have been in constant turmoil against connecting my own dots while trying to purge those dots that are not mine. I had to empty myself of how I was defined by others. I was led to believe certain things about myself that were not true but spoken in order to control me. I had to seek the truth about what I was told and what was not revealed in order to get the full picture. I had to dig deep into the origin of what I knew to be true, purge that which was false, and connect with the truth. I have my dots, and I am connecting them to get the full picture of who I am.

What Is Mine

We are all a culmination of our experiences and opportunities. We take a little piece from everyone we meet, integrate it, and make it our own. There may come a time when self-doubt takes a front seat and we need someone to fill our emptiness. These are dangerous waters, for they may then become us. So as I continue to purge their truth to seek my own, I am very selective in what I will call my truth as I sift through what is being presented to me. We are on our own journey and seek our own truth.

My Shadow

As I continue my journey, I am exploring what it means to have a relationship. Knowing what I know about dysfunctional affiliations, I am exploring what I do want as I purge what I don't want. This painstaking process can lead me to voicing my opinions and needs louder than I need to, because in my past experiences, silence meant submission and insubordination led to pain. Now I am emptying my own belief system about the definition of relationship as I wait patiently to be filled with a new ability to relate. We can only complement one another by being nearby as we move through our day. I am learning to be close to someone without losing my shadow.

SLOW STEPS

While trying to adjust to the uncomfortable situation of purging and emptying, I may hold on to something that I need to release so that I won't feel the void. I need to be aware of what exactly is replacing that which I am purging in order to not settle for anything just to feel full. Learning new information may come with the anxious awakening of wanting to put things in motion before I can assimilate it into my knowledge base. This is when I need to become silent and still and think about my thinking (metacognition). If I hurry, then I may miss a vital lesson or I may cling to something that is not going to enhance my journey. I can step slowly into my new normal.

TAKE IT SLOW

Determining what should remain and what to let go of can be a painstaking task when purging what is no longer needed. Being in the right mindset is a requirement so that no regrets are felt, but this may require a deep-seated assessment of what is truly still required to survive and to live in joy and peace, so I will take my time as I sift through the collections of my life so I will live with no regrets and enhance the fullness of the days that remain ahead of me. It's time to look at the experiences and opportunities of my past that have helped me arrive to where I am today. It's time to let go of painful memories in order to make room for new ones. So I ask this question: "How much longer do I need to hold on to those feelings of disappointment that those whom I love no longer want me in their life?"

One More Challenge

When I decide that the battles I have been fighting have never been mine to fight and are no longer worth my energy, I can lay down my sword and move forward. Countless decades have been spent looking for validation and helping another heal and gaining self-worth, but when actions come with these conditions, they are fruitless. I have learned to send blessings and prayers to others without any outcome or payback in mind. Knowing what is in my control has brought me peace, but staying with this new knowledge is the challenge. Help me know what is mine and what is not.

In Front of Me

As I continue to struggle to empty that which no longer fits in my life, I still desperately hold on to the hope that those who have left me will return. But if they do return, things will not be as they were when they left, because I am different, and they might be as well. I am reminded that what I have in my life is all that I need now, and those who are present with me are those who are here to help me evolve. Anything else or anyone else will only be a detriment and may postpone my destiny. So I will say a prayer that they are well, and I will let them go knowing what I have in front of me is what I am supposed to focus on.

Seeking the Truth

We have the amazing responsibility of filling our young with the goodness and promise of life. As I watch a child imitate their parents, I am astonished by how the mini-me is a perfect replica of their every move. I have watched myself as I filled my mini-me with all the knowledge my elders offered, even at the expense of me being wrong. If we are going to be surrounded by the darkness and the light, we need to make sure, by trusting our own word and deed through our intuition or God's voice, that what we are filling ourselves with is accurate and true. Even though I am still in the process of emptying that which no longer serves me, I can now, albeit cautiously, begin to see the truth as it is revealed to me one word and deed at a time. I am taking the time to seek the truth.

CHANGE

I want to embrace change with the wonder of a child in God's love and light and not give my fear of the darkness any power. Change can be difficult when one is set in the ways of the old and familiar, but it is the stretching of the heart, mind, and soul muscles that bring a new awareness. Putting on a fresh new coat of paint will require scraping of the old in order for the new color to be illuminated to its fullest potential. Emptying that which no longer fits or letting go of the comfortableness of an old behavior will only keep joy at arm's length, so I choose to dabble in the new with the fresh perspective that I will be successful, and I will enjoy the wonders of new experiences, knowledge, and peace. I embrace the wonders that await me as I begin to change.

MEETING MY NEEDS

When I needed someone to show up for me and they didn't, my first thought was of abandonment, and my notion was that I didn't deserve to have my needs met. The resentment festered, and bitterness grew as I showed up for them and they only took and not gave. Surrounding myself with these people only affirmed that I was asking them to give what they didn't have to give. Knowing I am worthy of requests, I will no longer knock on a door that will not be answered and will move forward knowing that in time, my needs will be met.

WHAT TO DISCARD AND WHAT TO KEEP

Learning a new behavior or changing a lifestyle can be so confusing, because what do I keep and what do I discard? I keep searching for the truth in all that I have been told and discard that which is not. I hold on to words and deeds that define my character and discard that which does not. I examine relationships that are healthy and pray for those that are not. So how do I learn new behaviors or change a lifestyle one moment at a time? When I know, I'll know what to discard and what to keep.

Clipped Wings

We may have been born pure, but life experiences can taint what is clean. A lifetime of choices, some appropriate and others that need to be changed, can bring us to a point in our lives where we acknowledge that we may not have always made the best decisions for ourselves, but now we can make those decisions right. Whatever changing an inappropriate behavior looks like, it must come with the conviction to live with a new behavior, and that may be challenging after habitual behaviors have driven decisions. Living with clipped wings does not mean permanent impairment; it means there is always time to heal what is broken and restore what is clipped. We can still soar with clipped wings.

Release

When a behavior is required to change, a release is inevitable in order for the old to be replaced with the new. This can be a painstaking endeavor, as the question, "What to keep and what to release?" is posed. This may require an investigation of how deep my pride drives me to make my decisions. If I am aiming for self-gratification rather than living to be my best, true self, then I must ask myself, "What do I keep, and what do I release?" It's time to see my motive— to punish or to heal, to control or to assist, or to help or to enable? Time to release!

Clean the Closet

My closet can be a time capsule of past fashions. Going through my closet to see what I still wear or what I need to discard is a painstaking experience. Will I choose to keep clothes that I no longer wear or that no longer fit? Such is so with past experiences and revisiting what I have brought along from the past in order the assist me in my present. An unresolved issue may need to be examined because I still harbor resentment from a past hurt or I may still be reacting in a defensive manner and want to know what transpired in my past that I still need to defend myself. I may need to revisit why these behaviors are still here with me so I can understand my reaction today. I continue to work through my past so that I can decide what is still needed now and what I can discard. As I discard old clothing that no longer fit or that I no longer wear, so I do with my old behavior. What do I want to keep?

BORROWED EXPERIENCES/KNOWLEDGE (INSPIRED BY TAO)

When we begin to recognize that we have borrowed our experiences from others and have not had them for ourselves, we begin to see the trouble with knowledge. We pass information around and pretend we know things when we really don't. Borrowed wisdom is not wisdom this at all.

Assimilating myself in the words of others left me to only become a parrot and a robotic image of them, but when I emptied myself of their drama that I allowed to define me and when I stopped knowing one of us was more right or more wrong than the other, I became who I was born to be. A part of self-acceptance is releasing other people's opinions. I have God's knowledge to guide me. He is my road map.

WAITING FOR A FLOWER TO BLOOM

Waiting to be refilled from that which has been emptied is an expression of anticipation and faith, and holding on to that which no longer serves is a sign of expectations and fear. In my humbleness, I used to believe in my own faith. I thought that I knew better for myself so I did not need to find patience and acceptance. I attempted to fix problems and go after what I thought would be in my best interest.

Of course, it has taken many lessons to learn that God knows better for me than I do for myself, His timing is better than mine, and it's okay to be empty knowing I will be filled with that which I am destined to have. In my emptiness, I am secure in the anticipation of being filled. In not knowing, I am filled with the anticipation that all will be revealed. In my silence, I know I will hear, feel, and see what I already know as mine. We are all flowers destined to bloom.

When Silence Got Too Loud, I Needed Noise

I have lived my life in the love of God. I have lived my life in the depths of pain. In this contradiction, I have ventured toward that which can fill me. In the drama, I felt alive and connected. It was in this very drama that I allowed my light to dim. When the silence got too loud, I needed noise. When the contentment got too comfortable, I stirred up drama. And if the threat of past drama crossed my path, I drummed up enough so I could put on my armor, ready for battle.

Now I am living my life in peace, having conquered the fear of not knowing. I live with the emptiness of just being. It is this turmoil, which I call aliveness, that has prevented God's light to shine in me. In the stillness of my soul, in the coming home to me, I am now void of drama. I have now let go, and I live my life in the peace of having conquered the fear of not knowing. In this emptiness, I am once again filled with God's love and light. I no longer need drama to feel alive or to feel that I belong to someone or somewhere. In the stillness, I find peace, joy, and contentment; in silence is the entire joy of being.

Give to Get

At times, we are given the choice to receive something, but we must relinquish something else to make room for it. This was not such a difficult task when I bought a new pair of shoes to replace a worn-out pair, but this did become a crossroad when I was asked to give up my old way of thinking to embrace a new one. It required me to seriously consider what my belief system was and what I was going to trust. There is no room for everything, so we all must give to get. What do I believe in?

CHAPTER 6

Expectations

LIFE SIMPLY GOES ON

"Endurance is not a quality that prefers life over death or strong over weak; rather it is a continuous unfolding in the present moment. Life simply goes on." I have endured many joys and heartbreaks. Life simply goes on. In a moment when a passion comes to fruition to bring joy, life simply goes on. In a moment when a loved one dies or a new one is born, life simply goes on. Even in moments when a memory is made and forgiveness melts into restoration, life does simply go on. What, then, matters?

VALIDATION

When I offer myself to assist another, it is not my decision to accept or deny. I spent decades trying to convince others to accept my offers. If it was accepted, it validated my worth; and unfortunately, I expected a kindness in return. If it wasn't accepted, I took it as a personal offense, making me think that I was not good enough. Now I will offer without conditions or expectations of receiving anything but the grace in knowing that I am fulfilling my need to be kind. I will no longer take their acceptance or denial as a personal validation of my goodness. I know who I am. I am kind, considerate, trustworthy, respectful, and responsible. It is not for them to see me in this light but for me to know I already am with or without their validation.

GIVING FREELY

When offering a kindness, the only thing that will make it unconditional is that there is "no need to seek credit for the accomplishment or to focus on the result. Contentment comes from doing the task for the task's sake." If I try to control the outcome of the kindness, then I am only giving with the expectation of something in return. Even if I am uncertain or unclear about the recipient's goal or agenda, I have to give freely in faith. Regardless of the outcome, I trust that God is in complete control of every situation. Living in fear of a negative outcome will only bring the unsettling feeling that I will be hurt and that my kindness will be taken for granted. If it is, that is not about me! My responsibility is to share my kind soul in His grace and leave the rest to Him.

HOLDING ON

If I could only remember five things, what would those be? If I could only keep five things, what would they be? Is what I am holding on to purposeful for my journey? Is what I put my energy toward purposeful for my well-being? Is how I'm feeling benefiting my health? Am I spending more time feeling resentment, disappointment, and judgment than joy? Am I spending more time with what has happened in my past instead of what is happening now? Am I living each day as if it's my last in God's positive love and light and in faith and peace? Am I thinking before I speak, act, and react? What am I holding on to that it's now time to let go? Perhaps it's time to seek the answers.

PERSEVERANCE

"Doing the same thing and expecting a different outcome is the definition of insanity." Waiting, finding patience, and being still are attributes that I find difficult at times when I am looking for a resolution. In previous times, I knew what I wanted; and of course, thinking that I knew what was best for me, I manipulated and controlled the situation in order to have the outcome match my desired goal. Needless to say, not knowing what was in my best interest, manipulating and trying to control only set me back to the first steps of wanting, waiting, being still, and finding patience. Even though it is uncomfortable, I am choosing a new reaction and behavior that can only bring growth. Although it may be an uncomfortable journey with another, I know that I am where I need to be and that all is well. I am dedicated and believe in God's grace that He knows what is in my best interest.

Control or Release

Self-conquest or domination of another is an issue I have struggled with. Having allowed myself to be defined by another's truth, I have been given the message that this is the way of the world. But knowing better and always striving to do better, when I get disappointed because someone else does not walk their talk or keeps sending me mixed messages, it all comes down to me and what exactly I choose to believe and why I allow this behavior to affect me. I cannot change the other person, but I can control how it affects me, and I can release that behavior back to them.

Compassion without Caretaking

"Old habits are hard to break" is a saying that rings true in my life, especially if that habit has become my way of life. Always taking care of others, even by sacrificing myself, has always led to disappointment, resentment, and judgment when I do not receive what I have given. Growing up not loved without conditions or ever feeling unconditional love, I am now in the later season of my life to learn. I am seeing my worth and know I am lovable, yet when confronted with the same behaviors from others, I find it difficult to live with my new behavior as I encounter their old behavior. So how do I let go of old behaviors when they are still present? With compassion for others knowing we are all souls on an evolutionary journey, I can say no and pray that they find their way. I am not responsible for being their caretaker. That's God's job. I am responsible for taking care of myself in the midst of their storm.

WALK THE TALK

I hold on to what is not mine, but I am learning to let go for God. I find that I struggle with others' accountabilities, for them to walk their talk. The expectations of one walking their talk have left me empty and looking to only trust actions. In holding on to what is mine and letting go of what no longer serves me, I struggle with my need to expect that others will honor the golden rule, but all that matters is that I will. So I am learning to go within and heal my soul of disappointments and possible resentments when someone does not keep their word.

OF MY CHOOSING

"Disappointment is inevitable. Misery is optional." Who would think that one would choose to be miserable? How many times have I been disappointment with someone who does not walk his or her talk? How many times have I allowed someone else's actions to steal my joy? I have free will, and I can choose to be joyful. It is not the circumstances of life or the behavior of another that bring me joy. Joy comes from my own choosing! I am willing to forgive another's behavior that could lead to disappointment, judgment, and possible resentment. It is of my choosing if I want someone's word and deed to dictate my day. I can set a boundary, honor my word, and find joy in my day. This is of my choosing!

AFTER THE FOG

How long have I waited for my ship to come in? How many times have I prayed for resolution for something that has been left unfinished? How many tears have I shed from a broken heart because what I think is a rite of passage and an entitlement is not mine to have and hold? After the fog lifts and after the tears have dried, my faith in God's plan, although different from mine, is now my plan. It has required faith and letting go of that which has not been received and honoring that which has been. He has a reason, known or unknown to me, and knows what is in my best interest. So the next time I question why, I will have already known that after the fog has lifted and the sun shines through the clouds, God's answer will always be, "Because I love you."

What Is Real

I thought that if I became spiritual and free, the pain would not be there anymore. I didn't realize that an important step on my road to freedom was releasing my belief that I owed people something, that the world owed me something, and that I could control my destiny. I know that what I can't let go of has a permanent hold on me. Life is a journey, and spiritual unfolding is its purpose. Illusion of control keeps me from my truth and my purpose. I want the second half of my life to be as good as the first half was miserable. Help me work as hard at accepting what's good as I have worked in the past at accepting the painful and the difficult. Negative thoughts pass through me but are not a part of me. I can control my thoughts. Help me believe in the midst of my unbelief.

Predictability

What can I truly predict that will come to fruition? What can I truly rely on that will never disappoint me or let me down? Expectations are dangerous when put upon another or myself, because if not careful, the outcome may outweigh the lessons hidden in the journey. So if I predict an outcome and it doesn't turn out as I plan, then a hardening of the heart may ensue, where no light or love can penetrate. Now I know that I will always receive what I am intended to receive. I will always have enough at the exact time God knows I am ready to receive it. If I am cluttered with expectations, there is no room for God's gifts.

The Truth Be Told

It is said that the universe hears all thoughts. I strive to walk my talk and have made this the cornerstone of my life since my truth is my core. Due to my trespasses that stemmed from expecting others to feel and act the same, I suffered disappointments and resentments since I depended on their word and deed to complete me. Since I was showing up for them, even at times wearing the mask they requested, I expected that they would complete me. So my heart broke, and my dreams shattered, and the universe heard my sorrow and knew my truth. And until I could hear my own thoughts, feel my own heartbeat, and depend on God and my own words and deeds to complete me, I was incomplete. That's my truth.

My Own Accountability

There is always a risk of disappointment and resentment, which comes with expecting another to walk the talk. Resentment and trust issues may develop if the word is not matched with the deed. Apologizing for an inability to fulfill a request may become habit if the behavior continues. That behavior is not about me unless I let it hurt me. I trust, I believe, and I forgive; yet my own accountability comes from allowing others' words to define my happiness. I find happiness and peace in walking my own talk. I am complete and blessed in knowing, trusting, and having faith in God and myself.

How Many?

How many times have I heard the words letting go and moving on? How many years have I struggled to hold on, waiting to be exonerated by another's acknowledgment of guilt? How many years have I struggled, trying to crawl out of the abyss I have put myself in due to another's definition of who I am supposed to be? How many years have I worn a mask to receive an empty word of acknowledgment? In the depth of my soul, I know my worth, my joy, my passions, and my heart; and I know my truth. How many? As long as it takes to come home to me.

Words and Acts

Expecting another to walk their talk before I can breathe or trust myself has been one more burden to release. No one's definition of me makes me that person. I know who I am. What they think is of no value unless it comes from a place of love and light. Their judgments are only there to control. Their origin is one of fear, not love. So labels, judgments, and words drawn from the breath of fear do not sustain love; they wreak havoc in one's identity. So I choose to speak words of love and do acts of kindness.

Expecting Others

Setting myself up by expecting others to walk their talk is one of the biggest struggles that has caused me harm. I have reverted to my darkness and struggle with what I am making my truth. If I trust in someone's word and deed and they turn out false, then what does that say about how I trust? It doesn't compromise my truth, only how I see the world. Not putting my heart and soul into another's words will assure that the masks that are being worn are not mine.

To Thine Own Self Be True

"Do unto others as you would have them do unto you"—these are inspirational words of love and compassion. So as I spoke, I did; and as I promised, I delivered. The burden came with thinking that everyone was like this—walk your talk or you were not honorable and were not worthy of trust. It became my mission to not only show up for others but to also hold others accountable, so I became the judge and jury, and disappointment and resentment were my results. Now knowing we are all responsible for our own actions, I no longer police anyone but myself. Words are just words unless they are matched with actions. I will continue to be true to others and myself. This is what I can control.

POWER IN A WORD

A promise can hold so much hope, and if broken, it will turn into disappointment. I always lived on the promise of the word from another's lips to plan my day, and when I was left with disappointments that turned into resentment, I hardened so that my light became dim. Now I live my life by walking my talk and by only being responsible for me. My happiness exists in my own words. Not feeling responsible for another's choices leaves me with being responsible for who I am meant to be, how I react, how I evolve, and how I show up for me. If others join me, then I will be positive, yet I now know I am complete with or without them.

I KNOW WHO I AM

I am grateful when I forgive trespasses that cause me to feel resentful, disappointed, and judgmental because I expect someone to walk their talk. When they don't, I felt betrayed, unworthy, unloved, invalidated, unimportant, and invisible. Yet when someone says something and doesn't follow through, I take it personally. When they don't honor their word, it is not about me. What is about me is that I will walk my talk even if they don't, and I will stop looking for validation within their word and deed. Letting go of expecting that others will honor their word leads me to this: that I am worthy, loved, important, and validated. I see me, hear me, and feel me even if I am alone.

THIS IS THE LAST TIME

How many times have these words passed my lips or have flown through my mind? How many tears have been shed as the boundary of honoring these words was violated? How many years were spent in self-doubt while these words held my power and I watched it wash away with the rain? Trusting myself, my heart, my words, and my truth was the most humbling of all life lessons. For all the while, I complained about them not honoring me when in fact, it was me who didn't show up for myself. It was I who needed to forgive myself. How could I ever expect anyone to honor my voice if I am not respecting my own soul? Now that I have emptied myself of their expectations, I am humbled, gracious, and honored to know me as God does.

Be Me, Not Thee

"Disappointment is inevitable. Misery is optional." When someone does not walk their talk, I am disappointed because I expect they will. Consequently, I become miserable, judgmental, and resentful due to another's behavior. I give up my peace and allow my energy to dissolve into judging them for not honoring their word to me. I lose my peace and become a part of their drama. All it does is bring me out of my peace and into their misery. Now my question is, why do I engage in this behavior if it causes me misery? What is my true goal?

Giving versus Sacrificing

"Do unto others" is the golden rule and the main stepping stone in my life. I was always taught to give that which I wanted to receive, yet the outcome was not always as I expected. Giving unconditionally results in inner peace, which does not require anything in return. A simple thank-you and a smile are payment enough. Disappointment arrives when the giving has an expectation attached, that when I give, I will receive the same in return. I realized it didn't work that way, so I continued to give until I crossed my own boundary and moved into sacrificing. It was where disappointment, judgment, and resentment were born. So when I give and say yes, I must mean it, and the same goes when I choose to say no. Not being true to myself may disappoint me, but I always have one more opportunity to try.

I Thought

I am grateful that I have learned to forgive myself for my expectations. I thought that if someone said they would do something, words would be followed with actions. I thought that if I did a kindness, I would receive the same. I thought that if I followed the golden rule, everyone else would too. I thought that if I fulfilled someone's expectations, then they would fill mine. I have lived on the promises of others' words, whether they complemented me or not. I thought that if I sacrificed myself to comply and fit into their world, I would be completed by their acceptance. I betrayed myself by expecting them to follow through, so now I no longer wait for their words of apology or acceptance. I can forgive myself for not seeing my own worth.

Accept Outcomes

When a plan is made, certain expectations and outcomes are desired. It is when the desired outcome does not turn out as expected that the time for disappointment sets in. Initial reactions are fear based—anger, denial, sadness, and then acceptance. After I effortlessly try to knock on doors that are closed, I come to a point in time, with raw knuckles, when I know enough is enough. I start to honor myself knowing that I have tired, and if it is God's will, then it will come to fruition. I will continue to evolve with or without what I desire. This is the time when I find peace and live in faith and allow my knuckles to heal.

Compassion versus Caretaking

When I hear of one's suffering or disappointment, I immediately feel sadness for them, yet there is a very fine line that can easily be crossed between compassion and caretaking. I tend to have the need to rescue and ease their pain, and this can become detrimental if I give more of me away than I keep for myself. Volunteering and kindness do not have to deplete me, yet my compassionate heart

145

sometimes goes too far, and that is when my expectations of receiving the same kindness leave me disappointed and resentful. So I am learning that giving does not equal depletion and that compassion does not equal losing myself in another. I am blessed with a kind, caring, and forgiving heart, and I can share it without losing me.

THINK OUT LOUD

Thinking is the gift we've been given to process and act upon any situation and feeling. It can overload the brain if one is thinking about too many things at once. I've learned to think out loud to help me process and make a decision from all the information I have to sift through. When someone else does this and I am within earshot, I tend to take their words and attach them to an expectation of action. This has gotten me into situations where I then became disappointed, resentful, and judgmental, thinking that they didn't walk their talk when they were in the act of thinking out loud. I now engage in probing questions and no longer look at situations like this as a broken promise.

INSECURE DAYS

On my insecure, triggered days, I look to others to help me through. I may go to the extreme by blaming someone for this trigger. Their behavior may have triggered a feeling, but what to do with it after it's triggered is my responsibility. If I don't get my way, I may condemn someone because my needs aren't met. I will put fault on someone so I can justify my right to ask, and they then become wrong for not fulfilling it for me. This gives me a false sense of strength and power and does not lift my self-esteem. All that this does is prolong my responsibility to take care of myself.

If I am insecure, I can ask for support. If I don't get it, it's because God expects me to help myself, or perhaps I have asked the wrong person. It's not about right or wrong. I have the right to ask, but not everyone is going to give me what I want and need at the exact time I request it. This downtime is usually time to put my hands in my pockets and look at other resources. They are not wrong to say no. I have to take care of me as they do knowing we all have that right.

I Have Learned

I spent so much time focused on what I lost and what I wanted to receive that I neglected what I already had. I would see beauty in others, but not in myself. I would see what others had but never took the time to see it in myself. I was too busy honoring them that I neglected to honor myself. I thought that if only I could give more of me, then I would get more of them. I learned that giving more of me left a void that no one could fill but me. When I needed them, they were not available. I looked at this as being abandoned, but they did me a favor by not honoring my request. This left me depleted, but I learned that the only ones who could fill my void were me and God.

I have learned to give without the expectation of receiving. I have learned to love without the expectation of any reciprocation. I have learned to accept others without the need to get acceptance. I have learned to give attention without the expectation of being seen. I have learned to approve of others without the expectation of approval and knowing that I may be judged. I have learned appreciation without the expectation of being thanked or acknowledged. I have learned to validate my own work without the expectation of ever feeling worthy, except from God and myself. I have learned that I am worthy of love and forgiveness and that we all are!

Life Lesson in the Pain

When a baby cries, it is usually a sign of discomfort, a need to be changed, held, or fed. When language develops, the uncomfortable has meaning. When an expectation or a promise is broken, there is pain. Then the reaction to the pain is disappointment, which can result in resentment or judgment. These are feelings from the pain, but what is the lesson in the pain? Perhaps it is giving too much power to another. Perhaps it is not honoring that God-voice called intuition or consciousness. When asked what the life lesson in the pain is, the answer will come when the dust settles, the tears are dried, stillness fills the air, and the small, sweet voice says, "I never left you. Let's come together and learn." This is faith.

What I Deserve

There is an air of entitlement, of being deserving of what one wants. There is a fine line between wants and needs that sometimes becomes blurred. We all need to be responsible members of society when it comes to give-and-take, being cautious that one does not override the other. We have all been created in love, and if I find fault in things, I find it easier to fight for what I think I deserve. Fighting keeps me separated, and it gives me a temporary power that fades into loneliness. So as I continue my journey to fulfill my purpose, I keep forgiving myself and keep believing that I am worthy of being loved even if I am the only one I need to convince. I will keep showing up for myself and strive to forgive and strive to feel worthy.

Bells and Whistles

As a child, I put so much energy into the future—planning a vacation, visiting a friend, or receiving presents on special occasions. But the energy that I gave away to the future soon fizzled into disappointment because no one or nothing could ever live up to my expectations for when the moment arrived with bells and whistles, so I learned to give to myself, and I learned not to deplete or deprive myself. Although I may not have exactly what I have planned to receive, I am grateful and blessed. For the bells I hear are from the churches in my small town, and the whistle I hear is from my local train. So I am filled every day with gratitude, and I am blessed with what I have in this moment.

Prepare for Battle

I have always prided myself on having a forgiving, openhearted, rose-colored-glasses view of the world. So many times, when confronted with a pending confrontation or a trigger that brought me to my knees, I would prepare for battle by closing down my body and heart and scripting my verbiage as if the conversation in my head was preparing my pending defeat. This was the burden of needing and wanting to be seen and heard. Now I know my worth, my voice has returned, and I live in my truth. What others may bring to the table is not about my engagement with them. I will send them a prayer and follow the golden rule.

Step Back to Me

We all need people in our lives, but when the lines get blurred and crossed, then it's time that I step back to me. I have an amazing capacity to forgive, trust, and seek knowledge to enhance my growth. When I forgive, I open my heart again, only to see the old behavior; so again, I step back to me. When my sadness brings me to my knees and my scream penetrates my soul, I step back to me. When I depend and trust another's word and deed and get disappointed, my judgment and resentment surface, and it is then that I step back to me. When I try to fill my emptiness with another's promise, I step back to me.

Flexible with Change

Planning my day or a trip can be effortless; all I have to do is show up, thinking that what I have planned with care will come to fruition. Yet the old saying, "We make plans and God laughs," can ring its song in my ear with an illness, a stumble, or any type of delay. I used to give the delays so much of my power, feeling anxious with any amount of change that deviated from what I planned. Learning to embrace this has taught me to become flexible and look for an opportunity in the experience. Perhaps it's a quiet time that has presented itself to reflect on an obstacle or just to be in the moment. Whatever the reason is, it will always outweigh inflexibility, stress, and manipulation. Learning to be flexible with change can bring a surprise and an opportunity that I may not receive if I rush to fill my plans.

Love Thyself

When we are born, we are totally immersed in ourselves; our food schedule, diaper change, and sleep pattern all hinder self-satisfaction by bellowing a mere scream. We are then taught to do unto others and to love our neighbor, yet in the hustle of our daily lives, we forget about ourselves. While loving our neighbor, we wonder why our neighbor does not love us. We start to react in resentment and disappointment, and then chaos ensues, and no one gets loved. Loving thyself in today's society does not mean making it all about you. It means a soft, gentle self-discipline to show up in the way we can be a person of integrity. The mindset, "I don't get mad; I get even," will never allow us to rise to be our best self, so let us honor and respect ourselves and others even if we're the only ones engaging in that behavior.

Offering versus Sacrifice

From a very early age, we are taught to share and that what's mine is yours. I can offer to share, but there is a fine line that may be crossed if I am asked to give more than I have or that takes me out of a giving mode and into an obligatory mode. The giving of a soul or emotions is a very intimate layer of an offering. When it is taken and then manipulated, a lifetime of healing ensues. Learn to listen to your intuition and to not overreach or exceed your own boundaries. Be aware of why you are offering and assure yourself that you are safe. This is a way to be honored. What are you offering?

Gang Up

It's one thing to choose a side in a political arena, but it is quite another when one family member takes a side against another. Ganging up to control a soul is one of the most manipulative, hurtful experiences that can occur in a family or a relationship. Learning to agree to disagree is a way to keep the lines of communication open. Taking sides when it's not about anyone else but the people involved can wreak havoc in a family's dynamics and may cause separation in a relationship. Clarifying conversations are needed to assure that communication will remain intact. Miscommunication because of a lack of clarity will cause pain and hurt feelings. All that is needed is a question, an open heart, an open mind, and a willingness to see, hear, and love one another.

THREADS LEFT UNWOVEN

"If I should die before I wake..." is a phrase I utter in my nightly prayer. The what-ifs, should-haves, or buts that I live with are all the unfinished business of my life. At times, I feel that these words become threads woven into the tapestry of my life so I feel incomplete. This question pushes me into the place that needs to be finished and complete. The incompleteness won't keep me from my happiness of today. Thy will be done to finish what's been started.

THE MENU

When ordering something from a restaurant or a catalog, there is a menu in which to choose a desired outcome. Whether it's a food item, clothing, or any other choice from the menu of life, it is our choice. Having been given free will, we have the ability to make the choices that bring us joy and also bring us pain. With self-gratification comes the consequence of only doing something to oneself, leaving out everyone else who may be influenced or touched by that very choice. Therefore, even in our world of desire, there is still a moral, ethical, and spiritual responsibility that what we choose will not make anyone doubt himself or herself. This is not a conquest or contest. We can agree to disagree and show respect and kindness for the choices we make from the menu that may differ from another. We need to strive to do what's right for ourselves and for one another.

My Own Expectations

I thought that if I wanted or needed or prayed enough, I would receive it. That which I desired was not always in my best interest, and when denied, I took that as a sign that I was not worthy and shamed myself into believing what I was told. Because of my expectations on what others should be and do, I did things for them, but it left me disappointed, judgmental, and resentful. The more I pushed, pulled, assimilated, and sacrificed, the less I was filled with me. Now emptying their needs and replacing it with mine, I can bless them from afar, I can honor my own journey without getting lost in theirs, I can see all of us and not lose sight of my own reflection, and I can hear my own voice. We can move apart and come together with no expectations, always fluid and changing.

Share

We are taught, at a very early age, that to share is kindness. There is a specific boundary between the receiver and the giver: that only when comfortable can the request to share be honored. Too many times, that boundary can be crossed when the giver does not give unconditionally or when the receiver may not look at the gift of sharing as a humbleness to connect. When we uncover the knowledge of our true connection, what is mine is yours, and what is yours is mine. If this energy can be honored, then all the negative reactions will cease to exist. By the mere exchange of a "Please" and a "Thank you," we can exchange the many gifts we've each been given. There's no gift better than the other, just a friendly exchange of love.

Cosign

When someone becomes a cosigner, it becomes a partnership. It says, "I trust that you will do right by me as I will do right by you." It is a joining together of two or more to become a family knowing that if one of them stumbles, the other is there to lend a helping hand. This partnership does not mean one completes the other; it is a dual commitment—"I will show up for you, as I hope you will show up for me." There is a fine line that, if not careful, can be crossed where one shows up more than the other. This may come to feel like a burden if all do not participate in an equitable, responsible way. Any relationship can have a *co-*, which means "together." But if not careful, two can become one, and one can become two. Having someone as a partner, friend, or companion will always assure me that there is someone there. All I have to remember is to be present as my true, authentic self.

Not the Boss of Me

I recall how as a child, when I tried to control my younger brother or cousin, they would tell me that I was not the boss of them. But I was given a message very early on that I was to be the caretaker, so I translated this as an assurance that not only were the others safe and their needs met but also that I knew better for them because I was told to take care of them. So I took this job very seriously, assuring not only their happiness but also that my way was the safe and successful way if they were to achieve peace, but I was mistaken. Although my intentions came from a place of love, their defiance and defensive reactions confused me, so a battle ensued. All I wanted to do was protect and love them, but what transpired was control, manipulation, bullying, and pain. So now I will offer solicited advice, and if I see that their choice is not aligned with mine, I will walk away, send a prayer, and release them. I will focus on my need to be safe and happy and at peace.

Not a Problem

The phrase "No worries" can hold its weight in gold if taken seriously. The words "Not a problem" would hold so much for me if, in fact, they are true. So many times, I have been put in a situation that may be uncomfortable or that simply does not align with my greater goal, which is to be a person of character. If I say, "No worries," or, "Not a problem," I am creating the exact chaos that I am trying to avoid. By trying to convince myself that the pain is not real, I can become hardened to that which does matter. Living too long in the shadows of expectations that have resulted in disappointments and, sometimes, resentment has only hurt me.

A mean word or deed from another can be as significant as blowing out a candle, but if I linger in the smoke that is left behind, I am the only one who suffers. What's done is done. How I choose to live in the pain or with the pain can speak volumes about how I spend my day. I can make it my worry or not, or I can see it as a problem for me or not. Either way, what is about me is what I can control, how I react, and how I can be proactive. I can bless them, pray for them, and hand it over to God; for He is my greatest problem fixer, so I'll let Him do that job.

The Last Word

When there are words spoken in frustration and pain, they can cause a tsunami from which no one can recover. After the debris has settled, what's left can mean rebuilding or discarding; but either way, it will never be the same as it has been. What is the ultimate goal of hurtful words and actions? Is it to control and manipulate another into the assimilation of what is a status quo? In the views of another, their right or wrong is not the last word, yet the power that is given away toward acceptance can leave a void in the soul so deep that one can no longer see their own reflection or know their own truth. So the last word belongs in our souls and with God knowing that all He ever wants is a relationship where we give and receive love. The last words are, "It is done."

Finding Gratitude in the Pain

When my expectations are not met, disappointment, judgment, and resentment can set in and take my light into darkness. In these painful times, I may not be able to see the blessing and find gratitude if I settle in the expectation. When I can see the blessing and feel the gratitude in the pain, I am able to be enlightened into the life lesson that may be presenting itself and understand the experience that will lead me on a path different from what I think I should take. Call this faith or enlightenment or whatever label you feel comfortable with. All does work out as it is meant to be. Finding gratitude in the pain will shed light in the darkness and will lead me to where I am meant to be.

A Few More Steps

With every expectation, there is a chance for disappointment. As I continue to reach further into my journey, I encounter resistance and fluidity. With each blessing comes an outcome that may or may not coincide with my expectations. But either way, I am receiving exactly what I am required to receive for this part of my journey. I look back on my education. I was expected to learn addition before I mastered multiplication, yet I was immature in my processing, so I struggled to grasp what was expected. I became hardened and disappointed to the point where I deemed myself a failure. Now I can look into the eyes of that struggling child, and now I know that in each lesson, there may come a few steps where I may stumble. Even if I fall, I know I am safe, as I choose to catch myself and know that God's also there to lend a hand. This lesson is a blessing, as it reroutes my journey to a better road ahead. As I take my next steps, I am safe with the potholes or a newly paved road.

Release Yesterday

For many decades, I harbored resentment, judgment, and disappointment from many unmet expectations. This caused harm on my soul, because as I chose to hold on to all that I thought I needed, consequently, there was no room for the many gifts that were to come my way. I can now choose to make a conscious effort to either bring the fears and disappointments of the day with me into my tomorrow or say goodbye and awake with new ones. What I am meant to have for this day, I will have. What I am not meant to have from yesterday is not meant to be. Remembering the positive experiences will out-

155

weigh the negative disappointments of my yesterdays. I can choose to release my yesterday and live in my today with hopes and faith for my tomorrows.

I Am as You Are

How many times have we all tried to get someone to see our point of view? How many times have we tried to make them not only see our point of view but also become a believer of our truth? Based on my experiences with doing this to others and having them do this to me, ultimately, there is an "I give up" mentality that hits the soul and an awakening of acceptance and not defeat that I am as you are. There are very distinct lines of right and wrong, as religious and governmental laws have scripted, but in our everyday encounters with opportunities to show kindness, the only laws are to love God and love our neighbor. So why do we make this such a difficult gift to accept? I'm not sure about your excuse, but for me, I have no excuse. So I will continue to strive to be my best, true, authentic self to see you as you are and become a better me.

Define Me

For much of my life, I looked for perfection the way it was defined for me. I hung on to so many hopes and dreams that were placed in my heart from others' definitions of what happiness was. So many times, I became disappointed in myself because I did not fulfill what was required. This inadequacy, not living up to their expectations, resulted in a hardened heart. I closed myself off to everything that ridiculed my effort and became so afraid of judgment that I deemed myself a failure before another could label me. This self-inflicted shame was my foundation, which could only crumble into dust, leaving me open and empty. It was then that I began to fill myself with light and replaced the negative self-loathing with positive self-acceptance. I am worthy of greatness, and this is how I choose to define myself.

With No More

I used to think that if I could make everyone love me and approve of me, then I would be full of the love I so needed to feel worthy of breathing and my deprivation would disappear. I used to think that if I had one more piece of jewelry, then I would be happy; or if I had a bigger house and designer clothes and handbags, then I would feel pretty and accepted into their clan. I used to think that if I just had more... But now I know that with the simplicity of just being where I am and who I have become, I don't need any more than what I have. I am complete, loved, blessed, content, happy, and joyful. I don't need any more than that.

Connection, Not Competition

When we share our story with one another and we find a common experience, those connections between our lives may become a competition of who has suffered more or who has made more growth in their spiritual journey. In these missed opportunities, we can disconnect over a rivalry that is never meant to occur. Yet when we can look in one another's eyes without losing ourselves, then I can see me in you and you can see you in me, and we can then make that connection and a bond by saying, "I have walked on your path, and I can empathize with how you feel. Tell me what you need."

With One More Time

It is said that others will treat us the way we allow them to treat us. Sometimes, in my own wishful expectations, I get caught up in someone else's drama, and I allow their fear to inflict pain. This is in my control; however, being blindsided, I will still show up and be my best, true, authentic God-self even when negative energy falls on my path. In this shadow, with one more time, I will always strive to stay in the light.

Time to Move Forward

I was asked why everyone took issue with me. I thought they all couldn't be wrong, so it must have been me. I surrounded myself with people who complimented my issues, and when I finally began to heal and take back my life, I began to say no. So the reason they took issue was because the person I used to be, who always said yes, had now learned to honor herself enough to say no. Now I look at all that I feared—abandonment, judgment, being called a liar, and people who I thought loved me leaving me. All this did happen, but I'm still alive, and now it's time to honor my life and fulfill my destiny. It's time for me to move forward.

He Knows Best

Sometimes, I may become impatient because something is not happening according to my time frame. I think I've grown enough, I think I've emptied enough, I think I've let go enough, and I think I'm ready; but it still doesn't come. It is during these times of impatience and not knowing that God gathers all the puzzle pieces of my life to make sure they fit perfectly. When I intervene, I can cause a tornado and blow all my puzzle pieces away. Then I have to gather them again and start anew. I've spent so many decades intervening. Now when I become anxious about God's timing, I sit in this moment and thank Him for sheltering me from the drama of another's life and helping me unfold my soul to a deeper level of faith and understanding. Sometimes, I may be ready, but someone else is busy picking up their puzzle pieces because they are not ready. I will trust in God's timing more than mine!

Adaptation, Not Expectation

It is said that where I put my energy and what I focus on will come to fruition, that where I choose to put my energy will result in what I desire. Expectations have led me to disappointments, judgments, and resentment. It takes one more step to merely wish or hope for a certain outcome. Instead of expecting a specific result and becoming disappointed, I am learning to say what I desire and then wait. In not knowing, in this empty place, I am letting go of expectations and replacing them with anticipation. I am placing my energy in my faith and know that I will receive what I need when I need it. Thy will, not mine, be done.

FLEXIBLE IN CONCRETE

When I walk on concrete, I know it will not be flexible but will sustain my weight. When I set a boundary, being flexible does not mean I have to either bend and compromise my truth or be too stiff and close myself off. It does mean that I am willing and able to listen and hear another opinion. When I'm set in concrete, I cannot see, hear, or feel anything but me. How does this support a relationship?

GROWTH IN TURMOIL

It is said that there are no guarantees for a pain-free life and that it is in times of adversity when growth is promoted. Doing what needs to be done when I don't want to do it causes me to explore what is making me uncomfortable. Facing my fears of being judged or abandoned may cause me to revert into defensive mode, but when I know I am forthcoming in my truth, even if it may differ from another's story, I can rest easy knowing the outcome will be beneficial for my growth even if the result is different from my expectations. Having uncomfortable conversations and addressing uncomfortable issues that are caused by miscommunication may cause discomfort, but knowing there is a life lesson will bring peace. So when I can anticipate instead of expect, I know all is well. Let God take my pain and turn it into joy!

RENEWAL IN GOD'S PLAN

I spent decades living with the expectation that we all followed the golden rule. This led me to decades of disappointment, which melted into resentment. At times, I wanted to stay mad and get even, but I knew that a hater of haters was still a hater. So now I have faith in knowing that others' behavior is not about me and that I cannot make anyone show up to follow any rule, golden or other. I have faith in knowing that God is in control and that I am not His only child; we all are.

Joy in the Heaviness

Sometimes, there is a heaviness in my heart, and I don't know why. I sift through all my unanswered prayers, broken dreams, or unresolved issues and know that all is well and that I am where I am meant to be. Still, the heaviness of acting as if all is well harbors the seed of unfulfilled dreams. This is when I choose to let go of expectations and choose joy. I watch a bird ride the wind, watch ducklings imprint their parents' behavior, or listen to the laughter of a child. I look for many joyous moments in the heaviness of my heart, and then I am reminded that all is well and meant to be.

Expectation versus Anticipation

Expectations result in disappointments, resentments, and judgments. Anticipation is faith waiting and trusting God's will. When I expect something I want to go my way, I tend to become agitated if it doesn't, and this may harden my heart, and I become disappointed. I may judge a behavior because it does not align with mine. Yet when I let go of expectations, I anticipate God's will and enhance my faith. What is the easiest way toward my joy and happiness?

If I

If I were promised that all my hopes would come to fruition, how would I live? If I knew that I was being protected from the very situation I thought I needed to be happy, how would I react? If I were given a choice to have what I want, which might be filled with drama and pain, would I take it? If I knew that the way I fantasized someone

160

to be was really a facade, how might I then want to have that person in my life? When I can let go of what I think is best for me and accept what God thinks is best for me, I can have a life filled with joy, peace, love, and faith. My choice!

SPECIAL DELIVERY

When I asked God for something that I really thought I needed to be happy and got something quite different from what I expected, my first reaction was disappointment. My typical reaction was to ask why I didn't receive what I wanted and prayed for. Now I know that what I did receive was exactly what I was meant to have. Special deliveries are the best kind of gift that we can receive from anyone who loves us. This proves that God knows better for me than I know for myself!

WHERE MY JOY LIVES

When the pain I feel is attached to a memory, its origin is usually holding on to the indiscretion of others as well as my own. When I forgive these indiscretions and release the hope that all will change, I can then give these burdens to God. When I live with expectations, I forego the need to have faith, because I have set myself up for a specific outcome. When it doesn't turn out as I expect, I then react, which, in turn, causes resentment, disappointment, and judgment. When I live in faith, then this action turns expectations into anticipation, because I know the results will always be in my best interest. Trusting and knowing that all will work out as God plans will keep me in peace, which is where my joy is.

ONE MORE TIME

When I think a behavior is changing and I become a little bit more open and vulnerable for the exchange, my expectation is that it will be different this time. But my expectations only lead me down the road toward bitterness, because what I think is there isn't. I react

161

with resentment because it seems like nothing is changing. So one more time, I come home to me and reflect on giving up the old and being prepared to live empty. It calls for developing inner stability, not engaging in the old ways while waiting for the new to arrive. So one more time, I heal, grow, change, pray, hope, let go, move forward, and learn how to depend on God and myself.

JUST BECAUSE...DOESN'T MEAN...

How do I have a relationship with a loner? How do I have a companion or collaborate with a controller? How do I remain interested in wanting to be intimate with someone who doesn't think about intimacy or doesn't have the need? How do I trust someone who hides themselves behind lies? How do I continue to have hope and have faith that my relationship will be restored? Just because I expect a certain outcome doesn't mean I will get it. I am only disappointing myself with my expectations. So I will show up as my best, true, kind self and leave the rest to God.

GOD HEARS PRAYERS

It's odd that once disappointment from unanswered prayers has passed, there is a peace and calmness that all is as well as it was before the unanswered prayer was uttered. Putting my hope and faith into a prayer request can lead me to focus my energy into a result that I want. This will lead to disappointment and despair when I don't receive the results that I pray for. I am learning that a prayer request is asking God to fulfill what I want, and all the while, He is fulfilling my prayer request with what I need. So after my tears are dried, I look at the results and find meaning in what He has given me, once again blessed with knowing that He is looking out for my best interest.

LOOK AT TODAY

I always thought that if I had everything I wanted and became exactly who I wanted to be, then I would be happy. It was interesting that when I did get something I wanted, the thrill of receiving it was diminished by the desire to have it. When I thought I was content with who I was, I was given one more opportunity to peel away another layer to see my potential greatness. I always put my happiness in the hands of tomorrow instead of living with the contentment and grace of today. So when I say a prayer for something I want to come to fruition, I will find gratitude for the blessings of where I am today.

I See Me

When I told you I loved you and I didn't get the same in return, I used to think that I was unlovable and not worthy of hearing those words. Yet I know that no one can complete me but the love of God, and even if my words are not affirmed by you, I know I am loved.

Throughout the day, I make sure that I say hello to those I see on my walk and that I give someone a compliment or a kind word. I do this because I know how it feels to receive that kindness. Sometimes, I just want to hear it too, for someone to tell me that they love me or that I'm appreciated. Sometimes, I just want to receive a hug. I know that I am. It's just nice to hear it. Today, I will affirm myself! I am loved, cherished, and appreciated. I see me!

CHAPTER 7

Faith and Trust

GOD'S LOVE

When I wondered why you didn't show up, I asked myself, "Why didn't I?" Asking someone to complete me is a death that I will continue to live over and over again until I empty all that defines me in the name of love. Now I need to be open enough to receive love, so God says, "Let me love you!"

MY QUESTIONS

I am aware of my behavior choices. Am I reacting in fear with a closed heart, trying to punish, or am I acting from a place of love and faith knowing that it's not always my story? Give me the knowledge to know if I am withholding my openness to a past behavior that is still present or if forgiveness means one more chance.

PRAYER

The only place where no one can travel with us is within our soul. This is where only God and I can commune and visit. We all have the same ability, and when visited, it can bring peace, joy, and comfort so that from within, we can share this blessing with others. This is what prayer is.

Distinguishing the Voice

We all have an inner core of truth and goodness. When seeking advice from my truth, I sometimes get a very clear picture of what to do, and there is no confusion. Then there are times when I get stuck with what I want to do and what I know I need to do, and I choose not to follow my truth. As we all do in times of fear and turmoil, I can get carried away with behaviors that I know are not to my benefit. Learning to follow my truth and do what know I need to do is an ongoing testament of my faith, so when I am at that crossroad, I will distinguish the voice of truth from the voice of fear and follow the path of truth and love and leave the darkness behind.

When Grief and Joy Collide

It is amazing how one can feel grief in the joy of the birth of a new child. As others welcome new life into their families, I can't help but feel the loss of not having what I thought I will have. When I feel consumed with the grief of deprivation, I hear that quiet whisper that all is meant to be. If it weren't for my faith and trust in God, I don't think I would have embraced the blessings that have been bestowed upon me. I can be happy for others as they enjoy their new rite of passage, and I can find joy in knowing I am where I am meant to be, and I am grateful for my comforts and blessings. I can live with the pain when grief and joy collide, but I will not live in the pain. I am blessed where I am.

When the Dust Settles

It's interesting that in one minute, all can turn around. When in a crisis, the pain can feel as if it will drag on forever, never to see the sun shine again. In joy, the fleeting moments are so sporadic that it sometimes seems difficult to recall the happiness. Yet in this in-between is where the nurturing begins and the healing takes place, and all is calm, and all is safe. In this safe haven is where faith is restored, and the knowing of not knowing becomes comfortable. When the dust settles, all is as it should be, and what a comfort that is!

Grateful Opportunities

It's interesting how one major event in my life can define me if I give it more energy than I need to. I can get so easily stuck in my grief and not recall the joy or the life lesson I have gained from the opportunity of experiencing the moment. The more I have faith in God and myself and trust that all is meant to be, the more I am able to look at these moments with clarity, not pain. When I feel it and acknowledge the message, I can then thank it and move on. After I've said my goodbyes, I choose to turn the page to see what's next.

All That Is

I wonder. At the end of one's life, do we recall the negative or the positive experiences? Do we relive past hurts and allow them to continue to hold us hostage in the present? Looking back on my life's journey and recalling some of the fondest memories I have lived, I know that all that is happening now is because of the foundation that was laid to pave my road.

The pain of the what-ifs and should-haves is fading away into the recesses of my mind and melting into fondness for the experiences and opportunities that have aided me in accomplishing who I have become. I truly doubt that at the end of my life, I will try to recover that which has been lost. Instead, I will savor that which I have managed to hold dear to my heart. Although I have spent decades grieving and mourning over what I have lost, I have come to an acceptance that what's done is done and that all that is, is meant to be. I am humbly blessed.

Giving Up or Moving On

How much longer will my grief last? How much longer are my insecurities going to take center stage? How much longer will anxiety wreak havoc on my soul? How many more countless decades will I allow myself to be controlled by past hurts and disappointments? How many more regrets and feelings of resentment will I feel from broken dreams?

How much more of me will I release into the abyss before I am no longer seen or heard and I just disappear? How many more times will I allow the past to control me and live in the pain? How much time will it take to see the blessings I have and the amazing soul that has evolved? When will I stop dismissing my amazing capacity to survive and thrive? When will I have 100 percent faith that God is taking care of me and that all that I have and meant to have is in His hands and in His plan for me? No more. It's time to trust and have faith and move on!

I Am Okay

How many times did I give my energy to worry and the results were better and richer than I anticipated? Even if my prayer is not answered immediately or answered with the result that I anticipate, it all works out for my greater good. That's when I am able to say, "I am okay." In my faith that all is meant to be and that I am where I am meant to be with those whom I am meant to be with, it is a choice to let go and allow all to be as it is meant to be, and I am able to say, "I am okay." When I get caught up in my fear and when I worry, I can ask myself, "Where does my nourishment lie?" And then I am able to say, "I am okay."

I See Me in You

How easy it is to look at someone else's dilemma and give all the advice in the world, yet when I am put in a similar situation, I will react the same way they do. It's so easy to make a judgment call on how someone is reacting, but knowing this behavior very well, I see me in you. What a gift this can become if I see this experience as a vital life lesson. I can either see the crisis as an opportunity or a dilemma. Either way, I will eventually come to understand that the experience is not to break me but to break me open to the light that awaits me. In that light, I see me in you and you in me.

The Spark

Coming home from an extended vacation can rejuvenate the familiar. What is becoming mundane, ordinary, and predictable can develop a new spark when coming home again. Do not take the blessings of financial security, emotional stability, and good health for granted, because they can change in a heartbeat or in the whisper of the wind as it blows snow across a road less traveled. It is in the tiny moments of gratitude when getting reacquainted with the familiar that the heart sings and the soul smiles. The familiar is comfortable and a blessing.

Come Sit by Me, and Let's Talk

When I see my struggles in the eyes and behaviors of another, it humbles me into a feeling of compassion and empathy. I have judged others too many times, thinking I am more right than they are, yet in all reality, all I want to do is share the knowledge that I have in hopes of opening my heart to theirs. I have found that when my approach is an open heart and an open mind, it will pave the way for my love to flow to them and for their love to be received. No one is more right or wrong than anyone else. We all have gifts to share. Come sit by me, and let's talk.

Faith Is the Answer

To just believe is an act of faith in the not knowing. This can easily roll off my tongue, but to put it in motion is quite a different feeling. I can say I believe in God, I can say I have faith in His wisdom, I can say I accept His plan for me, and I can act as if I do; but put an obstacle in my path when I feel betrayed or challenged, then where is my faith, and how do I act according to my talk? To think before I speak, act, and react is an act of self-talk and self-discipline to hold my tongue and release my fear to know God and to have faith. Either I do or I don't, but either way, I know the truth.

I Am Where God Wants Me

When I look at a grandmother playing with her grandchildren at the park or see family photos and I'm not in them, I can't help but ache for that life. I am watching someone live the life that I hoped to live. I always believed that there was enough love to share and that no one ever had to be excluded and that there was just more to enhance what's already there. I can't help but wonder about the what-ifs. But then I look at what is now, and I know all is meant to be as it is, and that's enough.

I Know My Worth

Living my life without outside voices to influence my decisions is a freeing experience of faith and trust in myself. Having lived in the shadows of others and having been defined by what they require in order to be accepted has been a life struggle for me when it comes to seeing and hearing myself as the powerful soul that I am. When I was seen with another, there was only one shadow that appeared. I had the need to keep them close because I did not believe in myself, and this caused me to disappear into their shadow. Shedding my doubts and fear of abandonment and learning my value and my worth have brought inner peace to my soul. I no longer allow fear to control me knowing I am loved and cherished and needed and accepted and appreciated.

Sharing in Truth

When asking someone to have a relationship, it is essential that both parties are willing to present themselves as their true, authentic self. When one fears rejection, they may say what the other wants to hear or do what the other wants to do even if it is against their truth. Too many times, we second-guess our friend or ourselves because of this need to comply. It is not beneficial if I am asking you to share your story if I am only telling you a story of fiction. How will you know me if I don't show you who I am? How will I ever know the answers to my requests if I am afraid to ask for what I want?

In this fear, we miss opportunities to be in one another's lives because we are not willing to open our hearts and minds to the possibility that all is possible or to open our closed hearts to the softness of being able to be so close as to hear the other's heartbeat. At the risk of being mundane, what is there to lose? Sharing my truth will only melt all the doubts of being rejected and enhance the story of a lifetime. Share your truth.

WITHHOLD THE ACTION

There have been many times in my life when I thought I knew better for me than God did, so I offered a helping hand, only to delay the results. In these hasty decisions, I caused more problems than those I was attempting to resolve. I had to discipline myself into faith and withhold the very actions that were causing me to move into more harm than resolution. In this lack of trust and faith, I spent decades in a darkness that only hardened my heart. Now with a simple request in prayer, I am guided into decisions and actions that will bring peace and serenity. What is mine to have, I will have, and I will always be grateful for the abundant blessings that have been given to me. I will cherish them always.

GIVING ME WHAT I'M GIVING AWAY

I was so proficient in meeting the needs of others in order to keep the peace. I did this at the expense of my own happiness and security. I did this because I didn't want anyone to leave. I was more available for them than I was for myself. Now that the dust has settled and they have left, I am in the situation that I fear the most. In my humbleness to let go and let God, I am still giving them my energy, thinking that if I bless them, they will return and that if I pray hard enough for them, then all will be restored.

With these conditional prayers and blessings, I am expecting what I want to happen instead of accepting what is. In giving them all my energy, I am once again depleted and leaving my best interests out of my own life. I have misinterpreted faith as getting my way instead of trusting God to fulfill me with His plan, so once again, I am bringing it back to God. When I bless them, I bless myself and let go. When I pray for their hearts to heal and let in God's love and light, I give that prayer back to myself. I am learning to trust that I am loved, I do matter, and all is as meant to be. What I am giving away in blessings and prayers, I am giving it back to myself.

I Choose Joy

The following is inspired by Madisyn Taylor: "Sometimes we become victims of negative thinking because we believe that focusing on all that has gone wrong will provide us with the motivation we need to face the challenges of survival." Automatically, I can change from joy to sorrow. My thoughts can hold me hostage to past desires that are unmet. I can instantly become agitated when I feel betrayed or disappointed. Why I would actually want to be miserable is beyond my comprehension.

There is so much joy in life to celebrate, yet I can easily find something to obsess about that can steal my joy in a heartbeat. I may have to live with the disappointments of unmet expectations, but I can choose to stay in that sorrow or look for the life lessons in the experience and move forward. I have faith that all is meant to be, and I know what I know when I need to know it. Until then, I choose joy.

I Know When I Know

When I am making plans for a new adventure, doubt and uncertainty may seep its way into the joy that is on the horizon. Rethinking and reanalyzing the plan may take the joy out of the mere experience and blessing that await me. I may second-guess the expense I may incur or what I may need to assure my comfort when I leave home. These tiny annoyances may inflict harm on my pending hopes and bring a heaviness that is not necessary for me to feel. If I live for this moment and cast all my worries to God and let go of my insecurities about my decisions being in my best interest, I can access each bit of information as needed. It's when I allow too much thinking to occur that I lose sight of this moment. All is well and meant to be. I will always know what I need to know when I am supposed to know it. This is faith!

I'm Okay with That

When I find myself feeling so overwhelmed with decisions, I can allow doubt into my thoughts, trying to sabotage the very decision I am trying to make. Working out problems or looking for new solutions can be painstaking if I am only looking at the goal and forgetting the many opportunities and experiences that come with the journey. The voice that asks, "What if I fail?" takes center stage, and my impatience to get to the goal can prevent me from enjoying the blessings that are in front of me. Now when I become anxious or impatient, I can step away, address my fear, and move into the process with a clear head and an open heart and mind. Knowing all will work out in my best interest is faith. I know that I don't know, and I'm okay with that.

Watch the Snow Fall

I watch the snow fall, then the sun comes out. I watch a neighbor pack her house, and the moving van drives away, waiting for the new neighbor to arrive. I watch, and then life changes. Life is as fluid as my heartbeat. One beat and then it's gone to make room for the next and the next and the next. Life is ever changing, yet when in the midst of the storm, the prospect of the sun shining again is only left up to the faith that it will, and it will. Having learned to step away and to have faith in the results has left me feeling vulnerable when trusting something that I can only feel. This new behavior keeps me in check when I want to add an ingredient toward achieving perfection. So I watch God do His miracles, and then I allow myself to feel the trust that is seeping into my soul, and then I watch snow fall.

Hurry Up to Be Loved

I was always showing up to fulfill the needs of others, to fill their agenda. All the while, I was neglecting what I needed to do for myself. Their opinions became my own. When I began to question or investigate my own truth, I was ridiculed, scorned, and dismissed. Being exiled brought me out of the darkness of their knowing and into the enlightenment of my own knowing. Now I am looking for the answers to the questions I was never allowed to ask. I am forming my own opinions, no longer fearful if they align or not. I am living in my own truth, searching for my own relationship with God and myself, without the need to hurry up and make a decision, because I am already loved.

And the Story Continues

Living a life in abundance and receiving the many blessings available take the risk of letting go and of the need to lend God a helping hand and having faith that He knows what is best. This is not to say that I should not be a productive member of society; it merely means that the more I try to control something that is not in my best interest or someone who is not mine to control, the more it postpones what inevitably is meant to be.

When something is effortless and I receive it in my timely manner, I may shrug it off as coincidence or don't give it much thought at all. But if I pray long and hard for something to come to pass and it doesn't, this may lead me to manipulate its outcome to serve in my timeline instead of practicing patience, perseverance, faith, and trust in the timely manner of its arrival.

I have always had what I need, and yet the wanting may override my desire to be grateful and humble enough to look at what's in front of me instead of what my heart desires, thinking it will compete me. What I have is what I am meant to have today. Who I am is who I am meant to be today. Let's chat tomorrow, for God may have another blessing to bestow on me or another prayer to answer. Then I may have another story to tell you.

That Time Is Now

If I could change something from my past, what would that be? If I could hope for something to happen in the future, what would I wish for? Putting my energy into changing the past or defining the future only makes me miss opportunities to celebrate where I am now. I wanted this house, and I got it. I wanted this relationship, and I have it. I wanted this lifestyle, good health, and financial security; and I have been granted those blessings. But if I get everything I want, when is it time to stop and be grateful? When do I begin to feel gratitude for all my blessings instead of reflecting on my past, giving energy to my unanswered prayers, or projecting my wants into the future? When will I just be able to stand still, inhale, and say, "Thank you, for today, I have so many blessing and comforts beyond my dreams. I am truly blessed and grateful!" Maybe that time is now!

Living in Faith

Four years ago, my house sold after being on the market for two months. People say that two months is not long at all, but ask a mother in her final trimester, waiting for her baby to arrive, if she's ready. In those two months, I packed two boxes a day, acting as if my house had already sold. This was living in faith! I've come to understand the concept of letting go and letting God. It's not believing in God after my prayer has been answered; it's believing that God's plan is better than what I could ever imagine. And if I let Him, then He will bring me what I need to evolve.

Living in faith is not affiliated with a specific religion. It is simply trusting 100 percent in something that cannot be seen but you know is there. It's the feeling that something greater than myself has the positive energy to sustain my life when I can't and knowing He walks beside me when I am lonely and assures me when I am making the best choice for myself and others. As I told my kids, it's that little bubble in your heart that speaks to you, and you know what to do, and you know all is well. Living in faith takes faith in the living.

I Believe

I believe in the power of unconditional love: the love of a parent for a child. I believe that this is how God loves me. My children have not always made the right choices, and even though I may have been disappointed and may not have agreed with these choices, I still love them. This is how I believe God loves me. He gave me free will, and at times, I may have swayed from the right thing to do in order to gratify that which I desire. I may have made these choices in fear of not being accepted or loved.

Anything decided in fear will bring pain and sorrow. I know this is harmful, and I've been given free will and, ultimately, have to ask for forgiveness from God and those I've offended with my choices and then forgive myself. But saying, "I'm sorry. Please forgive me," does not give me permission to continue the same behavior. It ultimately means I have to look at this behavior, access why I chose that behavior, and be aware that this behavior is harmful and must be changed.

Although God will never leave me, I may encounter a detachment from those I've harmed in order for me to empty the burden of my poor choices. In my aloneness, I have to give my fear a voice and decide how I will deal with my transgressions. I can say and hear from others, "I will love you forever even though your choices have disappointed me and broken my trust in our relationship, so I will ask you to stop and change your behavior." I pray we can all restore ourselves to be our best, true self for others and for God.

See the Blessings in the Sorrow

I have been given amazing opportunities to receive love and give love. I have the amazing blessing of having the comforts of joy, peace, and serenity. Within all my many gifts, which I can give and receive,

I can feel empty, disappointed, and resentful if my requests are not honored. When I am in a conflict where I see no resolution, I give my burdens to my faith that all will be as meant to be. In my hopes that I can accept the blessings in my sorrow, I can begin to adjust my thinking to become more positive than to give into the darkness of despair. It's interesting how when given free will, I would actually choose to react to situations that are not my life lessons. Empathy and compassion are powerful, positive feelings to share and receive, yet when I get lost in the drama of another's story, I then lose sight of my blessings in their sorrow. I will hold fast to the grace of today and pray for my acceptance of God's will.

MOTIVE

When I am consumed by my fear of what-ifs, I can find that my motive to resolve a conflict or to receive something comes from a place of expectations. If I do this, then I am looking for a specific outcome. I am capable of potentially sacrificing myself in order to persuade an outcome to heal my pain. Yet when I do this, I cause more harm to others and myself. Learning to live with the pain in faith can be uncomfortable, yet retracing my steps in order to right a wrong takes more effort and postpones God's interventions to heal me. When I am honest about my desire for a specific outcome and I am aware of the motive that drives my actions, I can pull myself back into the light of God and have enough faith to know that His plan is better than mine.

THE PUPIL OF THE EYE

The word *pupil* also means "student," and the word *eye* also means the proper pronoun "I." If you look deep enough into your own eyes, you will see that the black spot, the pupil, is a hole that allows the light in. Being a lifelong learner, I have looked at my own life lessons as I have encounters with others. So as the pupil of my eye looks at a situation, my student needs to see what I have to learn from the experience.

Not every situation is about me, and yet when I am drawn into another's life lesson, I have to see what I am to learn from being in this experience with them. Sometimes, it's just about reaffirming my worth with a boundary or just to pass on solicited advice that has helped me heal. The black hole of my eye can be filled with the light of love when I remember that we are all souls on an evolutionary journey and are here to help one another grow into God's love and light. It's not always about me but always about me.

AFTER THE FALL

"The purpose of a crisis is not to break us as much as it is to break us open, for it is through the cracks that God enters and healing begins." Mourning for a life I think I should have had is a waste of energy. I am grateful for the life God has given me. How many times have I stumbled and fallen, only to get back up? As children, we are taught that if we fall off our bike, we should get right back on; that way, the fear of the pain won't control us to the point where we are paralyzed. Yet when all our power is given to that which is a part of our stumble, it then becomes difficult to think how we will ever survive without that which we have given our power to. It is in that moment of doubt that we rely on ourselves, trust in God, and have faith that once again, after the fall, we can always get up again.

THE VOICE

Even when I feel powerless, I can always give a voice to my pain and hope that this is part of being human. The healing comes not by being heard but from the fact that giving voice to what lies within will soften my pain. Even in my deepest pain, the holiest of healings can occur. I am learning to give up my need to be accepted and loved by those who no longer accept or love me. I am giving up the need to fit where I don't belong.

There is a sadness in wanting to be loved by those who don't love me. I have to remember that I am still worthy of love and that I define me even if I am asked to live up to another's definition of who

I am. I am authentic and no longer wear a mask. I no longer speak lies that make me a part of a lie. I no longer sit by and watch injustice occur toward others. I accept that I don't belong, and I am fine being alone. This makes room for new experiences and opportunities that are waiting for me. "Never look down on someone unless it's to offer a helping hand up."

Pray and Pray Again

I will pray to help my broken heart heal from being dismissed and abandoned. I will pray to help me continue to trust and have faith in your plan. I will pray to help me stay out of your way and take care of myself.

What Is Not Mine

It's a simple equation when I have four items and they need to be equally distributed, yet when I am confused about what is mine and what is not, letting go and holding on can stifle any growth. In my desperate need to hold on, to belong, to be loved, and to just be, the fine line between what is mine and what is not can become cloudy. This burden then becomes a desperate cry for control, manipulation, abandonment, and perhaps death. So when asking what is really mine to control, it is in that quiet, peaceful thought that enlightenment surfaces, and God simply whispers, "I've got this." I humbly thank God for showing up with compassion, grace, and love. They cannot control me, and I shall honor them in the same way knowing that God's got them and that He's got me.

Live beneath Your Heart

I've heard that the head must be brought beneath the heart, or the ego will swell. If I do not bend, life will bend me. "Humility is accepting that my head belongs beneath my heart; with my thinking subordinate to my feelings," I will be subordinate to God. I know I am not facing my worst fears; I am living through them. I have lived in my head, so now I have to move from my head to my heart. I am listening to my heart to hear what it is telling me.

LOVE

Love is the only thing in this world that cannot be lost, because it is the only thing that is real. A closed heart cannot be penetrated unless there are cracks. The heart can be nurtured like the sun can open a rose. I can present my heart to the world when I have opened it myself. Love will never keep a heart closed.

RELEASE TO RECEIVE

In Tao, it is written, "The sage sees no nourishment in desires and lets it go. In putting energy into desires is an expectation of a particular outcome, to equal control and manipulation. In the letting go of a desire, this puts the energy back into abundance; that which is already and meant to be." After identifying what my wants are, the next step is to stop wanting and to let them go. This is a painstaking behavior for someone who tries to control the outcomes of situations by manipulation.

I have to give it up on an emotional, physical, and spiritual level. I have to get to the point of saying, "I don't want this. I don't need this. I am complete without it. I do realize that it is important to me, but I cannot control obtaining that in my life. Now I don't care anymore if I have it or not. I am going to be absolutely happy and complete with it or without any hope of getting it, because hoping to get it makes me nuts. The more I try and hope to get it, the more frustrated I feel because I am not getting it." So I ask myself this question: If I know this is all I am meant to have, will I be fulfilled?

SETTLE

In my emptying of that which is not mine, I see that my burden is that I either choose light or dark or positive or negative. When someone comes back or reaches out to reconnect, it triggers my fear

179

of trust and abandonment. I now have faith in not knowing, and what I do know is that I am no longer the owner of my mask. I know who I am. I am welcoming them with limited access to my heart, for although it is open, their presence is only welcome with compassion and empathy. I am so blessed to know how blessed I am. I have lived a purposeful, productive life, and now I settle into peace.

LIVING WITH

Not all problems are meant to be resolved. Sometimes, living with or living through is an integral part of my path toward my soul's evolution. Living with and through teaches me, so I ask, "What am I supposed to learn now?" I will trust God and have faith that if it is meant to be, then I will receive it. And if not, then I am exactly where I am supposed to be and who I am supposed to be.

ATTACHED

From my earliest memory, I have always been attached to someone or something. The origin of my being, my lifeline to God through my mother, was severed so that I may journey with God's wisdom knowing I am a part of something. Yet that mere attachment was disguised as a need, which then turned into drama. It was in the turmoil of another's life lesson that the attachment became distorted, and I questioned what is truly mine. So in my emptiness and silence, I was reminded to keep what was truly mine, share what was truly theirs, and bask in the glory of what God truly was. I am blessed to know I can walk away or toward anything because I know where I am truly attached.

EVERYTHING IS FOR A REASON

I wish things could have been different, but then I know everything is for a reason. I wish for a life where those I want, want me, but then I know everything is for a reason. I wish I didn't feel so damaged, but then I know everything is for a reason. I wish there were more happiness, love, peace, joy, and contentment; but then I know everything is for a reason. I know my truth. I can have what I want. Everything has its place and time, and everything is for a reason. I know I have a purpose, and I have a reason to be alive. I know this because I have faith in God, and everything is His reason.

BELIEVING IN

When the sun rises, it is just accepted, yet ask the person who has lived in darkness how they feel when they encounter the rays of light from the sun. When a mother is handed his or her child, whom she has carried within her, ask her how she can fall in love with someone she just met. When we are asked to trust and have faith in something that we have never seen, we hesitate. We are cautious, uncertain, and suspicious. Yet we all take the wind for granted and the ants diligently working to survive as nothing.

When did we stop believing in the goodness, blessings, and miracles that surround us? When did my heart start to question my truth? When did I start believing in someone more than God and myself? My need to be seen was futile, as I presented myself wearing a mask. My fear and my need to fit in or control what was said and thought about me were my way of trying to prove them wrong. I just had to prove myself wrong for believing them and prove myself right for believing in myself. Believe inward. That is where peace, joy, love, contentment, and happiness live. That is where God lives.

GOD'S PRAYER

I am now depending on myself because I do believe that I do matter. I believe we're all souls on an evolutionary journey—some we meet for moments, and some we meet for a lifetime. Those momentary meetings are so valuable and teach deep core lessons. I am embracing all God has to offer even if it means I'm traveling alone, without those relationships I thought to be lasting. God's plan is greater than mine. I have faith and trust in His plan to let go, accept, be patient, and trust in the unpredictability and to see my life through the eyes of a child and as ever changing and ever growing.

God says to me, "Have no fear, child, and have no regrets, for all is as it should be and all was as it was meant to be. Relinquish your resentment, and let Me take your pain. All you have is this present moment to be still and to be here so I can love you, so trust Me. All you have is you and Me and this moment, and that is enough. So breathe through the pain and just be free. This will center you and bring you back to Me. Just breathe."

A Secure Heart

In being allowed to explore and come home to a safe, loving, secure heart, I am blessed. The trees dance their last dance of the season, and change is, once again, upon my heart and soul. More change and deeper evolution, I understand, and I accept. I have faith in knowing I am not the fixer. I am God's instrument to help others.

Wait in the Lull

Staying in the light is harder than living in the darkness. I'm learning that negative behavior can be a challenge. I need to be aware of my pain; recognize my troubles, denials, and setbacks; and know that they are my teachers, guides, and allies. I need to keep my faith in the fact that I am cleaning my house to replace the old behavior with new ones. I need to control my impulses, anger, and resentment and change them into forgiveness, love, empathy, and compassion. I need to see you all in the light of love rather than attaching you all to an action of darkness. My thoughts originate in me, so if I am angry, I will be negative. Is this negativity worth putting aside my own peace of mind and potential for joy?

Not knowing when can be unnerving, but looking at this lull as God's way of dotting the i's and crossing the t's strengthens my faith and helps me feel comfort in the knowledge that all will be as God intends it to be. I look back on how I dealt with my lull and how my impatience only prolonged the outcome from the detours that I traveled, so now I choose to stay close to myself and trust God, savoring the new normal of the lull with no drama and enjoying the quietness of my faith.

True Origin of the Pain

Having found inner peace, love, trust, and faith, I am accepting all that was and is because God has given me a life lesson in every tear and laughter. I have been brought from a place where even though the initial reaction may have been fear, which quickly changed into acceptance, I was able and willing and joyfully partook in delving into the true origin of the pain. Ultimately, it comes down to trusting all I can control and handing God what I can't. I am protecting myself from negative voices, walking away, and living in my peace.

I Have Faith

What is my goal? To strive for faith, trust, love, acceptance, and worth. In my stillness and my struggle to remain in God's light, my insecurities of abandonment pushed me toward sacrificing me again. How will I ever be filled enough until I look within to fill me? No amount of compromise will ever fulfill me. That is not my job. This is how I must fill my void: with God's love, guidance, and presence in my life. I have faith.

Would I Again?

The biggest question I have to ask myself is, will I again do it if I know the outcome? Wanting a guarantee for a pain-free life requires no faith and a prewritten script. There will be no need for chance, experience, or growth if I feel that the destination is more important than the journey. So I'll answer my own question: Yes, I would again make the choices I have made and have those in my life who still remain or who have gone. I will because this is my journey—pain, bumps, bruises, joy, love, and faith. So it is with total acceptance and faith that I've come to this point in my life where I say yes to me.

Broken Dreams

How much energy have I put into my hopes and dreams, only to become broken because the outcome is different from what I expected? In this darkness, the tears that I shed wash away all the sadness so that I am able to come into the light of trust and faith with God's plan. I may never understand everything that has happened, but all is purposeful to help me evolve on my journey. I bless all of us as we heal our brokenness into the wholeness of God's love and light.

Accepting the Undone

There are certain things in life that can get a do-over—makeup, a sewn seam, a potted plant, a made bed—so if not done right the first time, these things can be redone. There are, however, things that can never get a do-over. These are the moments when a life lesson begins and growth occurs. Some questions will never be answered; I will simply have faith and learn to trust God that all is meant to be. Will I ever gaze into the eyes of a lost love or hold the hand of that stranger who holds my ancestors in their heart? I've come to accept all that I cannot change and know that these undone experiences are bringing clarity to my life. I may never know, but I trust and have faith in God.

Faith and Trust

I am of victor. I am victorious, not a victim. I survived! I trust God's timing. He does not have anything to prove to me. He does not bargain. I have to strengthen my faith. I trust in God. Forgiveness is letting go. It is accepting that we are all on a journey and will trespass against one another and ourselves. I don't forgive to get what I want. I forgive because it strengthens my faith in God's timing and His plan. I may not always understand why things happen, but I trust and I have faith that God's got this.

This experience in forgiveness teaches me to release my sadness, expectations, disappointments, and resentments and to find gratitude for the lessons I've learned. And with praise, I say, "Father God, thank You for working your eternal glory in me. Thank You for your blessings and unconditional love. Thank You for allowing me to cast my burdens and cares on You today. I now know my trials and troubles are temporary. Thank You for carrying me and giving me your eternal love and blessings on my life today. Thank You for guiding and protecting me by saying yes and no. I am humbled and grateful all the days of my life. I am grateful to be your blessed child."

THE MEADOW

If we are to believe that we are souls on a human experience, then we'll understand that being alive in a body takes time. It takes time to change a negative outlook and see the positive light of God's landscape and its scenery. Instead of looking at a solid brick wall with no cracks so God's light cannot penetrate, a walk to the other side of the wall and into the open meadow will heal us. This is where God is.

THE MORE I STRUGGLE

The more I try to heal; let go of what was, could have been, and the waiting; accept what is; live in the now; and be grateful for the positive energy in God's universe, the more I struggle. I have so many comforts, blessings, life lessons, experiences, and opportunities to help me evolve; yet the more I try to be grateful and to let go, the more I struggle. I know my fears come from lack of faith—"What might happen? Will I get hurt again, abandoned again, or abused again?" Living in this fear, that the past might happen in the future, does not let me see what I am now, what I have now, and what is now. It may happen, or it may not. If it does, I have God, and I have faith, and I will always land on my feet.

So I pray, "Help me stay in this moment, God. Help me let You do your work and help strengthen my faith. I am grateful that when the dust settles and the pain is at bay, when I humble myself and apologize from my heart, I can feel your peace. I know that the closer I get to my soul's healing, peeling away my layers, the louder the negative voices will get. Help me stay in your light and remember to trust your plan. Then the struggle is over."

Speak Words of Truth and Faith

It's easy to speak words of faith and truth; putting these concepts in the heart of my soul is the essence of my spiritual evolution. Truly living in faith is 100 percent believing in not knowing and trusting that God's got this! Emptying the burdens from my soul into God's hands is faith that all is and meant to be. Feeling the pain of abandonment and believing all the borrowed experiences from others have filled me with that which is not mine. I now trust God and myself to lead me on the path of truth. Having faith means believing in God and letting Him instead of me do it alone.

No Need for the Drama

I used to think that if I held on to the drama, I would feel alive. Fear, resentment, and anger and being a victim made me a part of the drama. But that wasn't living; that was dying, the dying of my soul. Today, I forgive, and I let go of the resentment attached to what was or could have been. All is meant to be so that I could evolve. I don't have to be finished in order to be whole. So here's a gentle reminder: It's all in God's time. His planning is the only thing that matters in the great scheme of things. I will be patient and live my life. I bless the yesterdays and pray for the tomorrows, and I live today in God's positive, loving grace. I have faith.

What If I Knew?

What would my life feel like if I have total faith and trust? What would my heart feel like if it is opened to every experience without the fear of ever being closed? What would I do differently if the only voice I hear is God's positive, unconditional message through my mind, body, and soul? What, then, would I do? How, then, might I live? A life without fear of pain, judgment, abandonment, lies, manipulation, control, and abuse—how might I think, feel, and act? My mind and thoughts are all that I can change. Now I live with the pain, not in the pain. I forgive myself. I did what I knew, like they did. Now I know better, so I pray that they will. I trust God and my own thoughts, words, and deeds. The only expectation I have is that God's got this!

Gratitude in a Praise

Thank You for working Your eternal glory in me. Thank You for your blessings and unconditional love. Thank You for allowing me to cast my burdens and cares on You today knowing my trials and troubles are temporary. Thank You for carrying me and for Your eternal love and blessings in my life today and every day. Thank You for leading me toward Your light and love and for teaching me Your protection of my yeses and noes. I am humbled and grateful all the days of my life. I am blessed to be Your blessing. I am safe in not knowing and trust that You do! I know life has its contradictions— darkness to light, joy to sadness, and havoc to peace. I choose to live in Your peace!

How Do I Know?

After years of dancing to another's song, speaking another's truth, and being another's scapegoat, how do I know who I am? How do I know my own truth? How do I know anything and trust that? Fear, doubt, panic, and confusion can lead me down others' path and get me stuck. It all comes down to trust, the trust of my soul's intuition, my God-voice, and my truth. So I will stop, make an assessment, and ask myself, "Am I where I want to be, doing what I want to do, and am I comfortable with agreeing with another's decision?" If I am at all uncomfortable, I seek the answers. My actions must mirror my words so that I know I am singing my own song, dancing my own dance, speaking my own truth, and knowing I am.

Hope and Faith

It's good to remember the soft breath on a birthday candle and how much hope that one wish held. It's good to remember the swift toss of a penny in a well that held so much promise with its clang as it hit the bottom. I have learned to act as if all my prayers have been answered by God's will, and at times, my wish or hope will bring a life lesson with this sting, only to utter, "Be careful what you wish for." It is through hoping that what I want will match what God wants for me that faith comes—things wished and hoped for, the evidence, unseen. What is meant to be and what is in my best interest is what God hopes I will accept.

Let It

In my emptiness, that which is not mine to hold and care for is no longer mine. The resolutions are not in my control; all I have is me. I trust myself as I have trusted others. I show kindness and love to myself as I have shown to others. This is my time to live in my truth, to use my voice, and to sing my song without fear. All that I have hoped for, needed, and wanted are in God's hands. All is as they are meant to be, so let it be.

Where I Am Safe

Safety takes on many forms—wearing a seatbelt, birth control, sunscreen, eating right, exercising, and many more things—but spiritual safety is not a materialistic armor. It is the belief that we are all safer in the hands of God. Not knowing and not seeing can be confusing in my need for immediate gratification, yet this is what faith is. This is where trust lies. Deep in my soul, I know where I am bound. The conflict comes when I look outside of myself for the feeling of completeness and safety. It is only when I relinquish all my trust that I'll know my true origin and the completeness of who I am. I am God's blessing.

In the Silence

In the silence of my world, I hear the thoughts of my heart and soul. This is not meant to be confused with the negative but for savoring my own love and worth, my gift from God. Being vulnerable allows anything to seep in through my brokenness and cracks, which is why I must be aware, kind, caring, and loving as I travel along this journey and I must know that all is positive in God. I will be patient, forgive my stumbles, stay empty, and believe in not knowing that God's got me. In the silence, I can hear Him.

The Promise

A promise is a bond of word to deed. It is the sunrise of God's glory. It is the fragrance of a baby, the butterfly that emerges from sleep, or the first buds of spring. It is when promises or expectations turn into disappointment that the heart hardens and relies on resentment to keep it closed. With trusting myself and trusting God's promise, which has the face of faith, I step into not knowing. I choose to be secure on the pavements of life even though it has cracks, and I may stumble, but I will be caught. So I open my closed fist to all whom I have tried to control and grasp to be mine. I have an open hand, a cracked heart, and a free mind for all that I am meant to be today.

Faith, Trust, and Peace

Within the stillness and emptiness, I am. I live with not knowing by trusting that God knows; this is faith. In the letting go of that which is not mine and in the acceptance of the emptiness and the not knowing, there is calmness; this is faith. There is a joy in the acceptance of all that is and is meant to be; this is trust. There is a peace of mind in knowing that God's got this and that I am where I am meant to be; this is trust.

Although I have free will, my pride is my weakness. I cannot, nor will I, do this without God. He's got this. We are all the same, trying to learn through our life lessons to evolve. He is my guide and my road map. Yet sometimes, I detour, and I wander away, and I suffer in my pain. I now know He is my home. I am blessed enough to be joyful. I know I am loved and cherished by God. In my faith and His grace and mercy, I trust this, and I live in peace.

God Is

When fear knocks, God answers the door. When fear enters, God is right there to close the door. When I stumble, He is there to pick me up. When I sin, He is there to forgive me. When I lose sight of the positive, God restores my hope and strengthens my faith.

In my deprivation of rites of passage, God protected me from the drama that would have swallowed my soul. For in faith, everything feared is gone. For with faith and trust in God, all is, and I am. Coming home to me is knowing that this teachable journey has taught me to trust myself, God, and my intuition and to be true to myself at all cost. I know that I am a blessing, and I am purposeful, worthy, and loved. The detours were harmful and painful at times, but it's time to go home in peace. In these heartbreaking disappointments, God entered the cracks of my heart, illuminating His light in me again. In not knowing, I have found comfort, and I trust God. I live in faith knowing all I can do is be my best, true, positive, spiritual, authentic self and leave the rest to God.

Prayer Requests

I reflect on my previous lessons about giving away my power to be loved, and I am now even more convinced that I will give my energy to Him. I wondered why someone didn't do something to help. Then I realized I was that someone. In God's time, I am learning perseverance; and with tiny steps, God will get me there. I have faith and trust that God's got this and that He will guide me to fulfill my purpose. My prayer is for God to help me stay positive in a negative situation. I pray to stay with God as others struggle to find their way. Help me walk my talk even if I'm the only one listening and hearing God's message.

The Illusion of Fear

It's ironic that I think someone can fill something in me or complete me. If I didn't get the response I craved for or the item that I desired, then I felt depleted and slighted. If God thought it would complement my journey, then I would have had everything I ever wanted and needed. So even when I stumbled or carried a load that was too heavy, the load of another's drama, God allowed this knowing that in the end, I would return and follow my path. The fear will never be fulfilled as I envision it in my mind; the unspoken dialogue of the what-ifs will never be spoken. So I have decided that having acknowledged what a blessing I am, I will continue to fulfill the destiny God has defined for me. And when a fearful thought comes to mind, I am reminded that I am, and so is He.

How Many Times?

Automaticity can be dangerous unless it's the body functioning to keep us alive. How many times has a negative thought controlled my mind without my being aware? How many times does the sun need to shine for me to trust the sunrise? How many times does my heart have to automatically beat for me to trust my body? How many times does God have to show His unconditional love for me before I know that I am loved and worthy? We are born knowing all these answers and spend a lifetime retracing our misguided steps back to knowing that we are loved, worthy, and blessed. How many times? How many chances do I get to evolve? As many as He wants to give me.

A Choice

There is a warm comfort in the knowledge that the silence of not knowing does not matter because of my trust and faith in God. Accepting things as they are means needing to release the disappointment and resentments of how they are not. Having faith that all is meant to be means what I want or what I think is my progressive entitlement has a different face now. I may never understand the whys or have all my questions answered, but I trust God. What I do have is knowing I have been blessed with the way things are and knowing I am loved.

RESULTS

I am able to celebrate what I have become because of the choices I have made to heal. Although detours into more dark caves have been explored, I've come back into the light. I'm now experiencing my enlightenment—that the past cannot be changed or relived. I have faith and I have restored trust in myself enough to know that I am where I am meant to be. The not knowing and my anxiousness to fix things or manipulate an outcome to stop the pain, which has only caused more pain, have melted into the light of my truth and faith in God's will.

FLASHBACKS

In the quiet time for reflecting on the flashbacks of my life, more joy and pain is felt. The birth of my children, graduations and diplomas, marriages, friendships, and jobs—all have brought me joy and to where I am. As I reflect on my life's journey, I look at the life lessons I've been able to experience. I know that in those fleeting moments of my memories, all is well. How I view the experience, labeled painful or joyful, removes me from what I'm here to learn, so why struggle? I am okay with God handling all the burdens. I live in faith and trust that all is and will be as He intends for me. He loves me that much, as I do Him.

ALL I CAN DO IS BE ME

Choosing words and actions that are positive will always be the task at hand, because I know the negative triggers, so I seek positive energy to guide me toward His light. Disappointments come from thinking others will walk their talk. Resentment comes from broken promises or believing their words. Expectations are only about me—who I am and how I will present myself. The hardest lesson is patience, but God's moments are timed differently. So let me trust Him to live in His time zone, and let me focus on my evolution. All I can do is trust, have faith, and believe.

LETTING GO OF THAT WHICH NO LONGER FITS

Letting go of that which no longer fits is an act of trust and faith, so not knowing how, when, and if it will be replaced is the basis of emptying. The need to be filled with anything is the root of my fear. Even if it is not meant to be, the struggle is in trying to replace the emptiness when there is no room for the new. There is a transition time. What's empty to be filled may leave a void, so getting comfortable with not knowing will allow the old to be replaced with the new. Holding on to everything while trying to bring the new into a filled space results in clutter filled with fear, so I am strengthening my faith and savoring the void time. Not letting go of that which no longer fits just prolongs the happiness that does fit. God is with me every step of the way. I'm reminded that fasting doesn't mean I'll never eat again; in His time, I will be filled with His treasures.

WHAT WE NEED WHEN WE NEED IT

God has amazing grace, and he will give us what we need when we need it. In reflecting on all my experiences, I realize that I have never been forsaken. God has always walked with me, occasionally carrying me and helping me up when I was down. Everything is temporary, just a fleeting moment, one more breath to take in order to evolve. It doesn't matter that I can't see far ahead. If I relax, I can see as far as I need to see for the moment. The situation may not be ideal, but I can get through if I stay calm and work with what is available. I can get through dark situations. I can take care of myself and trust myself. I can go as far as I can see, and by the time I get there, I'll be able to see farther; it's called faith in one more day. As I see myself change, I can quickly identify my feelings, triggers, and reactions;

and in my takeaway, I can see God. Nothing really does matter, yet all matters!

Enough Said

I awoke with the most incredible thought. As I was coming into my consciousness, I recalled the movie about a throwaway child, *Martian Child*. God spoke to me as I was reflecting about how I felt about being that child. "Why didn't anyone want me? Why did I get thrown away?" So God answered, "No one threw you away. Their actions toward you weren't about you. I have always and will always be there for you. You were born to fulfill your purpose. You're my child, and I love you." Enough said!

Accept God's Offer

I was taught to abandon myself for the service of others, so I gave and expected the same in return. My worth was in question by being told I didn't deserve anything, so I began searching for others to fill that which I kept giving away until my void became so vast that ultimately, I was swallowed and lost in the darkness. I decided that I would endure no more darkness or waiting to be loved, cherished, filled, honored, or respected. I decided to accept the light that brought only love, trust, and faith; and I accepted the relationship God offered me.

Complete

An interesting concept is the concept of letting go. The tighter the hold, the greater the burden and pain; so when released, it leaves room for that that which is required so that wholeness occurs. Once filled with that which is required to be whole, there is no more room for anything that does not complement the journey. What is left complements that which already is. The puzzle is complete; the missing pieces have been found and in place. No one can complete another. One has to believe in their own worth and purpose. The only definition of oneself comes from within. That's where God is.

WHAT FITS

Why do I become a slave to my past? Why do I hold on to the old after I've learned something new? The old has served its purpose; it's helped me survive. For that, I am grateful. So when it no longer fits, I pray and ask for help to let it go with gratitude, love, and appreciation. I pray for help to move forward and help me turn the page to the new chapter of my life. More is to come, without pain, without sorrow. Help me let go of what no longer fits.

AN INSTANT FIX

When I began my recovery, the ideal would have been an instant fix—to ask, believe, receive, and achieve. Yet the main step in this process was faith and trust. I learned that asking equaled prayer, believing meant trust and faith, and walking the talk was receiving. I've learned to have a daily check-in with God. Trusting God to show up after my prayer is one of the great lessons I have learned. Nothing is immediate; I've learned to live in faith and to trust that all will be as God intends.

IN THE MIDST

In the midst of darkness, I see light. In the midst of my aloneness, I feel loved. In the midst of being stagnant, I move forward. When I am confronted with a new normal and I am asked to embrace it through change, this can be difficult for me as I try to hold on to the uncomfortable and predictable. But knowing it is in my own best interest, I must let go, and I must embrace the new as I release the old. In the midst of letting it go, I may find myself empty and in a void. This is where my faith kicks in. So I take one more breath and inhale to make room for the new as the exhale releases the old. In the midst, I am safe.

Faith and Trust in God

Having faith and trusting that God's got this require the need to let go of that which is not mine. No one will ever react as I do, solve a problem the way I do, and love and forgive as I do. We all have our own journey, our own reactions, our own problem-solving strategies, and our own way of showing love and forgiveness. I honor all of us. We are all souls on a human experience, all evolving, all becoming enlightened in our own time; no judgments are needed. When my impatience is driven by my need to control, I give it to God and focus on myself. God speaks to me in the beauty I see, the positive messages I hear, the quiet voice in my mind, and the love in my heart. My ears, my mind, and my heart are where God's voice is. He says, "I've got this. Can you hear me?" For years, I showed up for everyone but myself. Now it's time that I include myself. I am worthy.

God Says

What is important, and what matters? Is it important that I am happy or right or that I am heard or healed? Is it important that I am accepted by wearing a mask or by being authentic? Is it important that I'm believed or faithful and truthful? I cannot, nor will I, put energy into changing someone else's mind, perceptions, or beliefs about who I am. I am trustworthy, faithful, purposeful, and worthy. Whether I am accepted, heard, or believed will not change my worth, my truth, or my faith. I am not because they say I am but because of who God says I am.

And Someone Said

"Once everything I have relied on has fallen away, great change takes place and I remember all that has enclosed, nurtured and incubated me, so when new life enfolds, the old is within." We get through it, but we never get over it. Transformation always involves the falling away of the things I rely on, and I am left with a feeling that the world, as I know it, is coming to an end, because it is! It is time for new beginnings and new journeys. "Out of the slumber, removing the Vail, all will seem fuzzy, yet all is clear! It doesn't take any more effort to stay filled with faith than it takes to develop a negative attitude."

PUSHBACK

When I am invited into someone else's journey and asked to assist them to heal, I can experience pushback. I can be a trigger of their pain. Some may leave, retreat, or stay. Their reaction about how I am helping them drill down to their core is not about me. What is about me is how I react. When they do leave, retreat, or stay, I pray for help to love myself. Help me feel my own worth and not be filled with their responses. Help me continue to fulfill God's request to help others heal even if their pushback stings. Help me see what is about me and let go of the rest. Help me honor me even if I'm the only one.

OUR DECLARATION OF INDEPENDENCE

I am worthy of a good life. I do deserve happiness, contentment, blessings, and love. I am a treasure unto myself and to all those I meet. I will no longer accept things as not meant to be but rather as how they are. All will come to pass when God thinks I am ready to receive His gift. I am given one gift at a time for me to process, internalize, and apply until it becomes a given. I am worthy of all of God's blessings. I do deserve it all, I do want it all, and I shall have it all; but only when God knows I am ready. With patience, acceptance, approval, fulfillment, joy, passions, love, and forgiveness, I know I am worthy; we all are!

WHAT IS ESSENTIAL

There comes a time in life when change is not only necessary but also essential to our well-being and to the quality of our lives.

For one like myself who has lived with the essence of the negative energy from false words spoken, there will come a time when the belief systems change. The drama that comes with the reaction of self-defense not only fuels the fire of the drama but also keeps the embers burning. When the negative energy is removed, it can be summarized—that while living in pain, it executed a fight worth fighting.

Even if the energy has now changed, I don't have to live in the pain, but I can learn to live with it. When there is too much silence, quiet, and serenity that positive energy brings, being uncomfortable with my new sense of power may send me back to the familiar, the uncomfortable, and the predictable. Even if it is painful, at least I know what to expect. But as the quality of life unfolds, the need for drama is replaced with the need for peace. I trust that peace develops a deep faith. I know I can remain peaceful and serene, growing in comfort that is defining a new quality of life and knowing a certain amount of pain will always be present. The act of letting go requires that something better will replace it, and that takes faith and trust. This is an essential practice toward peace.

How to Bring Peace

While I am engaged in the power of drama, either self-inflicted or a reaction to others', this turmoil will only distract me from the positive and the takeaway from the spiritual journey and the power within. There is a blessing in the drama, where a life lesson may be learned. Change requires something different, something better, to get different and better results. The goal is happiness, love, joy, peace, and serenity. It requires faith and trusting that the next unknown, unpredictable steps will move away from the darkness and into the light. It will be unfamiliar and uncomfortable, but with faith and trust, the light will wait to fulfill, to enhance, and to bring peace and awareness toward the first steps. This lesson is only about me, but I know that it's not always about me.

God and Me

Letting go, having faith, and trusting God and myself are the beginning of becoming familiar with myself after all the years of wearing a mask to be accepted and loved. I tolerated manipulation, bullying, and abuse because I was always allowing myself to be hooked to get love and acceptance. Although it was negative, it was familiar. My new norm is to be positive and savor God's love. Even if God and myself are the only ones showing up for me, that is enough. That's a blessing, and this is love.

I am undergoing the peeling away of negative layers, and I am constantly aware of my changes. This may leave me by myself, but I am never really alone. I spent a lifetime surrounded by others who only stayed if I gave some of myself, but no more sacrificing me for them. That's God's gig. I am to be who I am meant to be for God and me; so I will sing my song, dance my dance, think my thoughts, feel my feelings of joy and pain, honor my journey, celebrate my existence, acknowledge my growth, and love my soul as God loves me.

Within the Lessons

Letting go and trusting that God's got this is a new behavior. All the relationships I wanted, all the people I loved, and all the heartaches that were attached to all of them were the origin of the pain. Everyone I wanted in my life was attached to some sort of pain—a memory that hurt me or I thought of them and felt pain. I wanted them, and I felt pain. Why did I want to hold on to them if all I had with them brought pain in my life?

Then I decided it was time to thank them for the life lesson and the growth I made with all the pain, because when I wanted them, it was painful, and this was what I was choosing. Then I decided that if I could not have a healthy, loving, painless relationship, until then, I could wish and hope that we all would heal. No, I can let go of trying to manipulate outcomes to heal and stop my pain, heartbreak, heartaches, and drama. Although it may be painful, within the lessons, I am healing.

What Would Happen If...?

What would happen if I got everything I wanted? What would happen if everyone I loved, loved me? How would I feel different from how I feel now? How would I live differently from how I live now? The lottery drives people's dreams, hopes, wishes, and future; yet I am where I want to be and with exactly who I want to be with. So what would happen? Nothing! I would still be exactly the same. I would still be blessed for all that I have and for all I am yet to receive and thankful for all the life lessons, experiences, and opportunities that have helped me evolve. When I realized that "What would happen if..." was in my control through my reactions, I was able to listen and hear God's messages.

My Illusion

I had the illusion that if I was what everyone wanted me to be, then I would be loved and wanted. I had the illusion that if I loved my children and siblings enough, then they would want me in their lives. I had the illusion that if we moved away from the drama of others' lives and made a new plan, then it would be pain free. I had the illusion that if I was forgiving enough, helpful and compassionate enough, and empathetic and patient enough, then we would all love one another and get along. I had the illusion that we all wanted to live in God's love and light, heal our pain, and forgive one another's trespasses; and then there would be peace.

These are not illusions for me. I want all of this, but I accept that others may not, so I will be kind and love everyone. I will love my children and siblings forever with all my heart even if we are not to be together. I will say yes or no, but only if it doesn't compromise my integrity. I will honor my promises; and I will be forgiving, helpful, compassionate, and empathetic. I will live in God's light and ask to be forgiven, as I have forgiven. I now see all of us as souls in a human experience. Even if no one will, "I will, to will, Thy will."

The Answer to My Why

I asked God, "Why didn't they want me and love me the way I wanted and loved them?" This was the answer: "You did the best you knew how at the time you did it. You did the best for your children." Then I asked, "Why did I have to let them go?" He answered, "You did what was best for your children, as I have done for mine. For even though it is difficult, I love my children that much to let them have free will and choice. This is what a mother's love is. This is what my love is." I got my answer.

Take a Pill and Call Me in the Morning

In the 1950s, a doctor's advice could be echoed: "Take an aspirin and call me in the morning." I thought that I could use this advice when I started my therapy—if I took an aspirin, the pain would be gone. I thought recovery would be like stretching out a sore muscle to rid myself of the pain and to heal the wound. Recovery is a lifelong journey, not a destination. It's exploring, detouring, falling, climbing, swimming, sinking, digging, flying, tunneling, scaling, skipping, tripping, and jumping from one layer to the next. I have chosen to deal with the obstacles, detours, inconveniences, disruptions, and deaths knowing I am just being rerouted toward new life lessons, opportunities, and experiences. I am glad I have good workout gear!

Struggle in the Darkness

I am here to live in God's truth and use my voice. I am here to live void of drama. I no longer need to continue on any other path or journey but this one. I am learning patience to heal myself and focus on my truth. I am seeing all of us in God's love and light. I am aware of contradictions, and I choose to move into the light as I struggle in the darkness. I choose the new but integrate the life lessons from the old. I am giving my pain a voice, and I am listening so that I can ask for what I need. I am being as kind to myself as I would be if I were trying to teach a child something new. I am showing grace and forgiveness to myself, as I have shown it to others. If I am too busy trying to make their lives purposeful and comfortable, who will be doing that for me? They need to honor themselves, as I am learning to honor myself. Even if those I love choose to remain in the darkness, I can encourage them while being in the light.

Step Into

How long do I protect myself—teaching before learning, leaving before staying, and anticipating rather than entering? How much longer do I wait until the magic pill does its magic and I can live in peace and find joy and happiness? Life is going on right now! Each sunrise gives one more opportunity, and with each sunset, I can say, "Well done!" Each moment is a chance to live, learn, teach, love, accept, and grow into my soul's journey and purpose. Show up and step into the next moments, whether they are my last. I can say, "I see me."

When Fear Knocks

In a world of unrest, uncertainty, sadness, and miscommunication, it is sometimes difficult to rise above the clouds and to know that the sun is still shining. I spent a lot of my life in my own darkness, which I created because I felt responsible for assuring others' happiness. Yes, there may be unrest in the world, but only seeing the unrest negates the pure, true blessings of all the goodness. Being a pessimist is hard-core. It requires me to dive into the layers of my own unrest, heal it by forgiving myself and others, learning from all the experiences and opportunities that all is well, and knowing what truly matters. I've learned to see the sun on cloudy days and to keep my faith in God and myself when unrest is at my door. When fear knocks, I let faith answer.

Panic versus Faith

We've all been in uncomfortable situations. Sometimes, immediate action can fix the problem. Other times, waiting for resolution is the only course of action. We may hurry into recovery thinking that moving into the issue will help resolve the uncomfortable. What I've learned is, during panic, I only fuel the fire. The recovery algorithm that has helped me is this: acknowledge, let go, have faith, empty, and move forward. This has always helped me find solid ground while I felt as if I was sinking. Having faith surrounds the conflict with positive energy and hope. It changes my attitude, reaction, and behavior from panic to peace. I'm not giving up. I just believe in giving into my peace. This is all I can control.

Take One More Step

When I stumble and fall, I take the time to gain my strength to stand again and to take one more step. When someone hurts me or I feel dismissed or betrayed by another's actions, I take one more step. When I realize that I have kept myself hidden under a mask until I don't even recognize my own reflection, I take one more step. When I understand that I have enabled and allowed unacceptable treatment, I take one more step. When I ask myself at what cost I will stop at to see myself loved, accepted, cherished, celebrated, and appreciated, I take one more step. When I realize I am giving away energy toward worry or uncertainty, I take one more step. One more step out of fear and into faith and love is one more step toward God.

When All Else Fails, Open Up and Let Go

In the struggles of my life, it all comes down to, "God, what should I do? I've tried everything, and I am in such pain. Help me!" The answer has always been, "Open up and let go." Holding on too tightly has caused my fists to be closed with no hope or room to receive anything. I know no enlightenment can enter a closed mind and no light can enter a closed heart. No one or no situation can change until we all open up and let go. I can hope, dream, and pray this for all of us. Having this knowledge and enlightenment can be shared only with an open mind and open heart, so I will live this way and pray for all of us, and when confronted with drama, I will bless them with an open heart as I walk away and let go.

My Own Report Card

Results are up to the interpretation of the receiver. If one gets what one desires, it is labeled a success. I may give 100 percent to a task, but all the while, my ratings may not exceed 50 percent from another with a different product in mind. This is where I find myself exploring contradictions. If I find that someone or something is detrimental to my well-being, I follow my truth and inner guidance. If I fail to listen to my inner voice, I will allow myself to live by the definition of another. Someone else's perception is not my report card. I welcome solicited and constructive input to help guide me on my journey. It is when I relinquish my control to their words that I lose my voice. I may not achieve 100 percent all the time, but my journey is not yet finished.

I'm with God

Too many times, out of my fear of rejection and abandonment, I moved forward, only to stumble over my own two feet. I hurry to silence the uncomfortable voices that ask, "Will I fail? Will I be abandoned? Will what I have all be taken away?" All my hopes and dreams are held in my emptying of others' burdens and in my faith that in this moment, God is with me. So instead of negotiating or giving bits and pieces of my heart away to the owner of the first smile I see, I stay with God. This is an empty-handed leap into my void but is a true test of my faith—that in this moment, I am with God. So I will celebrate the deer grazing outside my window and the tree dancing with the wind. In my silence and in the emptiness of all others' burdens and drama, I stay with God.

One More Layer

As a child, I can recall getting ready to go outside to play in the snow. I was always dressed in layers of clothing—boots, gloves, and hats—all to keep out the cold. Having lived a life of layers to keep things out, I also have not allowed to let things deep within. While keeping out the cold, the warmth of my heart was smothered. So as I peel away one more layer, I allow the warmth of my own soul to fill me with the joy, love, passion, and blessings that have been kept at bay with all the layers that I wore to protect me from the cold. As no cold can enter, neither can warmth. My heart's warmth keeps me trusting and having faith.

Restore the Cracks

We are all born pure of heart; our hearts are wide open, trusting and allowing ourselves to be vulnerable. Yet the first hurt hardens the softness within until we become stone from the inside out. It then takes decades to see that the hardness does not allow the light in to melt away the pain of trespasses. As I have begun to trust myself and to have faith in all that is, I know that all is meant to be for my soul's evolutionary journey. I allow the cracks to let in the light. I may never be able to restore the past, but I can learn from it. Given the opportunity to choose to live wide open again, I restore my cracks with love and light and once again live with the vulnerability of having faith in God and trusting myself again.

Life Is Fluid

Everything is temporary and fluid and needs to change. Nothing can or will remain as it is now. This is how growth occurs, this is how a soul evolves, and this is how progress moves us forward. Where I place my energy, it then becomes passion. This can be confused with obsession, control, and manipulation from past experiences; but now that I trust myself and have faith, I can sift through and know what is mine and what is someone else's. There will be no more gravitating toward drama to feel alive or a part of something. There will be no more focusing on that which I cannot control. My burden comes when I do not let go of that which is not mine or refuse to move forward. Knowing and accepting that all is temporary and subject to change free me to experience the abundance that is waiting for me. I can let go in faith knowing all is fluid and all is temporary.

Discontinue

It has been written that when I carry habits and attributes into my present situation, I have to look at what I am unconsciously repeating today that I wish to discontinue. The automaticity of my reactions was always for defending my word and deed. All the while, when I was raising my sword in anger, I was merely affirming the label that was branded on me by those who needed to control me out of their own fear. I became exactly who they were! Fighting my own shadow left me depleted, empty, and shamed. A straight or crooked line is just a line. I now live my life in peace, letting go of control and accepting not knowing. This is faith; the sword is a rose, and the need to be seen or heard has been replaced with just being. I have discontinued that which is no longer helpful on my journey to evolve.

Where My Trust Lies

Deep within us is our all-knowing intuition and consciousness. We're born trusting that our caretakers will guide us. My caretakers took me down the darkest of roads, which challenged me into my own thinking, because their lie became my truth. Through many years of praying and searching, they helped me discover my true self and my faith in God and in myself. My trust no longer belongs to their words. Like the trust of a child, I will continue to see the good in all people and situations. I hear my own voice, and I live in God's truth. I am learning to trust myself again and to listen to my own intuition. I am trusting that I am taking care of myself with a simple word: *no*. I can feel safe again, and I can trust. Even if they lie, the truth is known through God. I will live in that truth.

With One More Breath

When my heart got broken, I held my breath. When I got stitches or was put under general anesthesia, I took in a deep breath. When my breath was taken away in an instant by a lightning bolt, I thought that if I held it long enough, the pain would stop. And after they left, I used to hold my breath, waiting for them to come back to love me. But in depriving myself of a single breath, I once again found myself stumbling into their definition of me; so I walked into my light, spoke my truth with my voice, opened my heart to forgive them, and healed myself. I allowed my heart to beat again with one more breath. I can finally say I have learned how to breathe again on my own.

I Am Learning

I am learning that those who scurry around to buy supplies before a pending storm miss the beauty of the clouds rolling in. I am learning that all the wrong in the world can be alleviated by just believing that all will work out as they are meant to be. I am learning to enjoy life as it unfolds. I am learning that all my anxiousness to complete a project or restore a relationship makes me miss the journey of learning to love and accept all that is now. I am learning that all the unforgiving behavior that I've held on to doesn't matter to anyone else but me, so I am learning to let go of my past transgressions and forgive myself and celebrate the person I have become. I am learning to have faith and to trust myself and God.

An Open Heart

We are all born of love. Our navel scar is our attachment to this pure miracle. We are all born trusting and knowing our vulnerable state as we move into the light. Yet just one glance or one unkind act or word can begin to close the very essence of our being: our open heart. Our heart will very slowly begin hardening, and with each heartbeat, it begins to become suspicious and closes down. We do this to protect ourselves from harm, but the biggest consequence is that we close our hearts to ourselves. Learning to trust again is a risk, and learning to honor and to see our true goodness comes as we open our hearts again to God. With each heartbeat, we release our true kindness and pure love to others and ourselves. With each heartbeat, we see ourselves again, and we continue with our hearts wide open.

TRUTH ON THE TONGUE

When someone speaks, often, if it's a subject of interest, I will listen. When the truth of their words roll off their tongue, it is then that I decide to speak my truth. So what do I do when the truth of their tongue does not match mine? Do I become combative, do I try to speak louder so my truth will be heard, do I try to manipulate their truth, do I try to assimilate them, or do I give in and become submissive? I am learning that when a negative message is spoken and it does not align with me, it is not about me; so there and then, I learn to detach myself from their message and get back to the truth on my tongue. With respect, we can agree to disagree.

THE WORST THAT CAN HAPPEN

Living in fear of failure, abandonment, and judgment mobilizes feelings that can lead me to living in the status quo. Living with what-ifs or I-can'ts prevents me from reaching the purpose of my journey. But risk-taking is scary; they may continue to treat me this way if I succumb to their needs, or I may get hurt again. So what if they try the same behaviors again? When it happened the first time, it was on them. But allowing it to happen again and again is on me. What is the worst that could happen if I say no? At least I have me, and I am living in my truth, fulfilling my purpose. The worst that can happen is nothing!

The Fear of Risks

When taking a risk to try something new, my first thoughts are fear-based—"What if I fall again? What if I fail? What if they don't like me?" The what-ifs can paralyze me into an unspoken dialogue that I script in my head and that is never spoken. I still allow that one negative voice to have a voice, but thankfully, I am able to silence it after I evaluate its message to see if any of my fear-based thoughts have purpose, such as to protect or to defeat. I now take more risks. The "What if I fall again?" turns into "I stumble, but I always get up." Falling has now turned into an opportunity for a life lesson, and abandonment has morphed into knowing I am already filled with God. I have no more to lose with their opinions, because these risks have brought me into God's light, love, success, and faith.

So We Meet Again

After an amount of time passes when I meet someone again, we exchange a hug, smile, or kindness and share a bit of our stories. This social pleasantry is how we give and take from another, but we don't leave our hearts with them. This is different from an undesirable estrangement, where someone is dismissed, exiled, or abandoned, only to meet that person again. This is where a conflict may take root. In this moment of choice, I become silent, and I see this person as another soul on a journey to whom I give a piece of myself to be loved. I am reminded of how much of them I have let in before I no longer saw me. How much is the same, and what's different in them and in me? No longer willing to engage in the drama dance, I have new steps to take. So as we meet again, no longer needing to be acknowledged as the gift that I am, I extend my hand and say, "How are you?"

Living with the Pain, Not in the Pain

There are many things that have brought pain into my life—a scraped knee, a harsh word to close my soul, or a hug to keep the slap from a loved one from stinging. This has resulted in causing physical harm to others and to myself and not believing in myself enough to show up or to have faith. Living with the discomforts of pain has caused me to try to fix it so the pain would go away. Living with the discomfort of a swollen ankle is different from the discomfort of waiting for a loved one to come back to my life. I've taken this discomfort into my hands too many times, looking for an apology or vindication, only to drown deeper in the darkness, wearing the mask of shame. I am learning to live with the discomfort of the pain and move on with my life and not live in the pain. I now know all is temporary, and I have faith that all is meant to be in God's hands.

Teach Me How to Love

I've had love expressed as an emotional hostage taker with conditions. I have been expected to accept others' choices for me in the name of love. I have been dismissed from my needs in the name of love. I have been led to believe that only if I give someone what they want will they love me. I have sacrificed my own truth to receive what they call love, but it has only left me empty, and I have to give more to get more. Unconditional love is a giving and sharing of the heart to make someone happy without expecting anything in return. This exchange then brings love back to me. The love that a mother shows her newborn child or the first promise of spring by the blooming flower are signs of love, hope, and joy. Please, God, help me live in this definition of love and purge what I have been taught.

Impatience

Impatience is a sabotaging behavior where I think I know what's best. This has hurt me in so many ways, and what it truly amounts to is my lack of faith and trust in God, in others, and in myself. I do not need to list the countless of times I became impatient, uttering the words, "Are we there yet?" I can't begin to express the sadness I feel for missing so many opportunities to see your landscape on a road trip or to savor the situation that has brought me to cleansing tears or to just be in the moment and embrace all that is. It has taken decades for me to be able to enjoy and feel gratefully blessed for this life journey. If I could pass on any advice, I would simply say, enjoy, love, and be patient; for all that is meant to be already is!

LIVING IN THE PRESENT WITH RERUNS OF THE PAST

It can become a joyous or difficult situation when an anniversary is celebrated. Lighting a candle has multiple meanings, such as for a wish or for the memory of a loved one. Joyous occasions have memories of pleasure while the opposite is quite true for the pain of loss. Either one can rob me of living in my present. As I focus on one or the other, I can celebrate the journey I've taken to bring me to my present state, or I can remain in the loss of a loved one, harboring pain, resentment, and disappointment over what I wanted it to be. Either one, when visited too long, can prevent a celebratory journey that has helped me evolve. I have faith and trust that even if I never understand the whys, I know all is well in my present state of living.

FEAR OF NOT KNOWING

How many endless decades did I spend listening to the sabotaging voices within me and from others that I needed to do one more thing and then I would get the golden ring? My definition of my golden ring differed from others, yet it was because of the desire to attain it that the fear of not knowing caused me to act before it was time, wreaking havoc. Trying to change the nature of the past will always be an unsuccessful, fearful experience. But to live my life in the peace of having conquered the fear of not knowing has allowed me to come home to myself to experience joy, contentment, and satisfaction. This is what I can control. Now where do I want to focus and expel my energy, on what can never be changed or on what brings me home to be complete? I have to choose wisely.

God Has the Final Word

I am an adult, and I know the difference between right and wrong. I know what feels right in an encounter, when I am safe in a situation, and if I trust my own final word that I am blessed. The old, tired, screaming voices can try to sway my thinking; but that still, small, kind, loving voice speaks my truth. My conflict is not in defending my truth against another or to try to even convince myself what is really true. My conflict is in deciphering what role I have in the drama. Is it my own or theirs to hand back; or is it for both of us to be allowed to tell our story, to be heard, to agree to disagree, to honor each other's truths, and to strive for a resolution? This is difficult, and my conflict is if both parties are not willing to work for a resolution. My impatience speaks one opinion while my patience speaks another language. In the end, I know who has the final word.

The Lesson in the Waiting

I have learned over many decades that trying to fix a wrong before it's time can only prolong an outcome, so I am learning to wait, yet not always with patience. I'm also learning that in the waiting time, I am on an evolutionary journey. The lesson is not the price of my destination and of getting what I want. It's the price of what I am learning during the waiting on my journey toward what I am becoming. I have rushed so many years away from the pain, looking for that comfortable, safe place to land. But it has been in sifting through the pain that I found my true destination waiting for me. Though I am enjoying the journey, even when it gets a bit uncomfortable, I can wait and learn as it passes.

Hurry Up and Wait in Patience

We have all been in the situation where a car speeds past us, only to meet us at the same red light. I have been guilty of judging and saying, "What was the hurry, only to wait?" How much of my life have I squandered and ignored to reach my destination? How many times have I stuck my hand in the outcome, only to sabotage it and to go back a few steps to regroup? How many times have I lost my faith, not appreciating the gifts from God, the growth that could have taken place, and the lessons I could have learned if I had trusted enough to be patient and to wait? There is a simplicity in life: just be and be grateful. Within learning patience is listening, gathering, and understanding. It slows me down enough to experience each precious moment. I trust and have faith in my journey and see where I am and who is with me.

SEEING MIRACLES

In biblical times, resurrections, partings of water, death to life, hunger to plenty, and lepers to cleansed are the miracles that I have been taught; yet in my doubt, I waited to believe in the fireworks of life to show me they even existed. I have lost precious moments because I passed them over as ordinary or forgotten, that precious gift when a harsh word replaces a soft whisper. In the hurried living I call my life, I can recall so many times when a compliment that could have been celebrated as the fullest expression of life was overlooked. I can visit my miracles in recalling a memory, but the pure essence can only be felt when I humble myself. I feel grateful and truly blessed when I am present to see my own miracles—my bodily functions, the nature that surrounds me, or a prayer that is answered or unanswered. I am that miracle. We all are.

GOT YOU LAST

As a child, having the last word or the last touch became very empowering. It was as if I owned the situation, and it made me feel right and important. The "I got you last" syndrome maximized itself into a beast of its own, and an eye for an eye went to the extreme and morphed into bullying, manipulating, and even destroying the very essence of pure love. What once was a childhood game manifested into who was more justified to own the power of another. I am humbled in my heart to say that at times, I took this game too far. The golden rule has more love and light than "I got you last." Retribution against another or retaliation or conquering another does not enhance love. It feeds fear. I choose to act and react in love, truth, kindness, compassion, and empathy. Now I am humbled with grace and say, "I got you last," with a hug and a smile and the words, "I love you. You do matter."

React with No Reaction

When I am confronted by a behavior that is less desirable than what I am comfortable receiving, my best, first choice is to react with no reaction. Not giving away my energy or my power to that unfavorable behavior allows me to continue to be my best, true, positive, authentic self. For far too long, I have always reacted with a negative, defensive armor to defend my honor in hopes that I could prove the other person wrong or that I could change their mind. Yet with the negative bantering of aggressive dialogue, I simply validated them and bought into their manipulation by showing up to participate in their drama. I no longer choose this type of behavior. I will simply smile, center myself in the positive love and light of my soul, pray for them, and say, "Have a better day."

The Light Exposes What Is in the Darkness

There have always been opposites and contradictions—right/wrong, happy/sad, good/bad, or dark/light. The positives have always attached themselves to joy, whereas the negative has an attachment to sadness. Yet there is no way to know either without the other. The feelings of the positive are when we accomplish a task, learn something new, or greet one another with reciprocal feelings. How are we to ever know that which lies in the darkness if it is not expressed and exposed by the light? We can live in denial of our true self in the darkness and never know the joy of life, or we can take the chance and risk being seen and vulnerable to be exposed in the light. Shedding the darkness will be uncomfortable; change is difficult. Where shall you dwell?

All in God's Timing

As a young child, I used to play dress-up and acted as if I was an adult. Time flew by, and I became an adult so I could live my purposeful life. I came to grieve that I hurried through the journey, only to find that God's timing was better than mine. Having watched a child learn, they can no more do calculus at age six than I could do brain surgery without training. It is in these moments of clarity that we are given more to help us on our journey. By doing it on my time and ignoring God's timing, I had to relearn, reevaluate, and rethink my choices. Hungry to know my answers and to complete my product, I am no longer in a hurry to grow up, and I am slowing down to see what is next, all in God's timing. I am enjoying the journey because God knows my destination.

Faith in the Release

Having a hold on someone and not allowing their stumbles to help them learn is detrimental to their evolution. If I were to forever pick up a child every time they fall, there would be no celebration in their first steps. If I were to pay their way, they would never know that in debt, there is responsibility. If I were to always excuse behavior that is hurtful or meaningless to the benefit of the light and love in the world, they would never question their choices or apologize or own their own behavior or repent or ask to be forgiven and promise to change for the good of their soul. So let them fall, go into debt, and see themselves in the reflection of their pain. I have faith in my release; God's got this.

So Many Questions

As children, we are spoon-fed knowledge from strategies on how to feed ourselves to the very essence of our belief systems, even about our own being. When we love another, it's difficult to watch them fall. All the while, we lean in to catch them. But it is in the fall that we all learn. After being spoon-fed, it's time to question what

215

exactly I've chosen to ingest. With so many questions, it requires me to sift through all that I know and look for my deep-seated truth. Sifting through decades takes time, patience, love, understanding, compassion, and diligence. We all have questions, and we all have the ability to seek our own answers. Ask the questions, seek the answers, and live your truth.

The Will of Self with Self

The will of self with self is truly the complete disclosure, compassion, and acceptance. When I look into my eyes, I see me. When I let go of my own will and have faith, then all is as it is meant to be in the peace of my heart. I have learned to breathe; be grateful; find patience; be my best, true, authentic self; find my voice; live in my truth; become aware of my reactions; and heal the struggles of the self with my own will of self. My struggles become few and my burdens are lighter when I release my will on another and bring it back to God. In my anxiousness to complete my healing, I have unjustly robbed myself of some blessings from my journey. I now slow down, live in the moment, and give the will of myself to my truth and to God.

Conflict or Calm

In my life, there have been conflicts. Some of them I made myself. When there is a conflict with another, the blame-shifting does not resolve the issue. Accountability and truth will bring communication to the forefront, yet the inner conflict is much different. Even though there may be a problem and a solution, staying in the problem has been my past behavior. This behavior gave me a reason to be combative, and a victim and I would not need to change. Now that that behavior has been replaced with the truth of who I am, I know in my soul what is mine, and I can pick calm over conflict. Conflict within can be resolved with the truth of my knowing and my faith in God.

The Line in the Sand

The line in the sand is a boundary and is drawn to give notice that a behavior won't be tolerated. I've drawn many lines in the sand, only to allow it to be crossed and not taken seriously. I have reacted combatively and aggressively, only to become aware that I've allowed that line in the sand to be crossed. I would set a boundary yet not honor it out of fear of rejection or of hurting another's feelings or because I was not quite sure what triggered me to draw the line in the sand. Now I follow my intuition, and when I need to draw a line in the sand, I know it may cause potential conflict, and I will not engage. If it is not received in the light of love and honor, then that is not about me. I now show up for me.

Just for Today

We encounter so many situations and moments every minute of the day, every day in our year, and every year in our life. How we choose to show up, act, and react is based on our free will. We may not be able to control every situation, but we can control how we want to react, and if there is a life lesson, it is for us to grab hold. Just for today, I will live in my moments. Just for today, I will count my blessings. Just for today, I will savor my opportunities and experiences and celebrate who I've become. Just for today, I will walk purposefully in the light and stray from the darkness. Just for today, I will be happy and content, and I will feel the blessings of the just, just because I can and because I choose to do so.

You Need Proof?

We live in a society where truth needs to be proven. So much of what we read or hear is the result of an ego war between right and wrong and the need to control and have power. So what is the true truth? What proof is needed to truly trust and believe? You need proof? Look at a child at birth take his first breath. Look at a dying person take his last breath. Look at the seasons change from life, to

217

death, and to life. Look at the amazing machine working effortlessly to house a soul. Look at the comforts, blessings, and unanswered and answered prayers. Look at the energy that love holds, the evidence of things not seen. You need more proof? Look in the mirror and see that person's reflection; that is the miracle of you, God's masterpiece, miracle, and child. How's that for proof?

LETTING GO IN MY SOUL

That which is positive is of God. All that is in the past has served its purpose and has taught me what I need to learn. Letting go of what was or could have been is the letting go in my soul knowing that all is as it should be. I have learned not to confuse helping others with attaching any kind of self-gain. To find patience with myself, I need to go within when I'm frustrated with the negative. Geographically speaking, I've been removed from the toxicity, and now it's time to remove myself from the toxicity in my spirit. I am letting go of what will be, because I know God is in control and I have faith and trust in His plan for us to live in his positive love and light in peace. I'm just being asked to empty myself and be silent to get the answers.

IT IS DONE

These humbling words release most of the negative messages, manipulation, control, abuse, and pain into the total acceptance of what is meant to be. Trying to change the unchangeable can cause frustration and the feeling of worthlessness. Hopes, dreams, wishes, and a need for a pain-free life only come with the letting go of a need for a different outcome and the acceptance that all is as it is meant be. What is done is done. When I finally come to the end of my rope, instead of holding on longer with my blistered, bloody hand, I release it and move forward. Some things are never meant to be, and spending more time waiting for it to become so just prolongs the pain of putting my energy where it doesn't belong. It is done. I am moving on.

With One More

We live in a society so abundant that with just one more right word or behavior, our needs are met. We do have a responsibility to contribute, not just take. When shopping, we can order what we want with one more expectation to pay. With one more behavior choice, we can treat others the way we want to be treated, fulfilling our spirit by doing what's kind. With one more sunrise, we can bless our pending journey and be aware of our thoughts to remain in a positive light. With one more breath, an inhale of love, and an exhale of promise, we can continue to fulfill our purpose. How lucky are we?

To Live in Peace

Ask someone what he or she may want, and their answer may be good health, love, peace, joy, happiness, or money; the list may go on. Then ask someone how they may get what they want. This is where the excuses and blame-shifting begin. This is where the should-have and only-if become excuses to obstruct the outcome. But truthfully and bluntly, the only excuse and obstacle is us. We get in our own way by needing to control the situation or outcome or by judging what is right in front of us or by falling victim to another's behavior choice. The endless list that brings peace into our minds, hearts, souls, and bodies, it is enough to know it's already here. What is robbing you of your peace and joy? Maybe it's just you. Have faith and enjoy.

You're Right

We have been given a great gift, the gift of free will. As adults, we get to choose what we want and need; and with diligence, we get what we ask for. Yet when faced with adversity, we tend to give that difficulty more energy than needed. We can set ourselves up for success or failure based on where we choose to put our focus and energy. Either way, we are right. Handling the situation without reaction is the key to it being in our favor. Give it a negative reaction and expect a negative outcome and you will be right. Do what you can or must to resolve it and keep faith in knowing all is and look for the life lesson. Either way, you will be right. You get to choose how you want to be right.

SOLUTIONS

When confronted with a problem, the first course of action is to find a solution. But instead of looking at the goal, I sometimes tend to stay in the problem until the problem is me and I am the problem. Sometimes, it is about me; other times, it's not, but I make it about me. Solutions are merely resolutions toward the acceptance of an occurrence that either aligns with our growth or ascertains information to share. Either way, focusing on the problem will only rob me of my joy. I am learning that not everything can be fixed by me. I am learning to remain calm and to filter through the problem for any life lesson I may draw from it. At times, I just need to allow the other person to deal with it. Either way, there's always a solution, so I'll just have faith and listen.

WHY WORRY?

If I were to wake every morning with a light heart knowing that all would be well and that everything I had would be taken care of, would I worry? If I knew I would be healthy because I exercised and watched my diet, would I worry? If I knew I had enough money to buy what I needed, would I worry? If I knew that I loved unconditionally and all that I thought and felt was positive and productive, would I worry? If I knew that I could delegate my day to the passions and activities that bring me joy, would I worry? If I knew that I could give and receive all the positive energy in the universe from God, would I worry? So the big question is, why worry?

Be Gone

I have spent decades in and out of my moments of joy and clarity. I have been able to see the truth and have a voice. But in a moment, a sliver of doubt can enter and begin to suck the life out of my happiness with just one glance or word. In *The Wizard of Oz*, the Good Witch told the Wicked Witch to be gone since she was bringing nothing but negative energy into a beautiful, peaceful land. How many times have I allowed negative utterances to drum up fear and spoil a perfectly glorious day? Too often! So if I am in a peaceful moment and fear knocks at the door, let faith answer it with the words, "Be gone!" When I find myself being robbed of my happy thoughts, I can say, "Be gone!"

Hands Up

Go into a church and see the hands up toward God as one is lost in prayer. Go into a bank where a robbery is taking place. Hands up toward the ceiling is a show of submission. Hands up toward someone who is approaching us is a sign that we are setting a boundary. Hands up is a physical response that has taken on different meanings. Whether it is to welcome or deter, it can become a symbol of our body responding to a want or need. When I find myself reacting in a negative way, I choose to open my hands to welcome the healing of the positive energy from God's universe so that the light will travel from my open hands toward healing my cracked heart.

Step In

When surrounded by more noise than usual or when others push and pull on my energy, I have learned to engage in a respectful way and push away from the situation and step into my heart. People are lonely and want love; they need companionship and interaction. What happens if I am not on the same road? I have to be kind and view them as a soul on a journey, like me. I have to find compassion and treat them as I would like to be treated. Relationship is so vital to our existence; we need interaction to be seen, to be heard, and to be touched. I am learning that I can engage if I remember that I need to consistently step into my heart. I can release the judgment, disappointment, resentment, and expectations and just extend my hand and say, "Hello. How are you?"

HICCUPS

The old saying, "We make plans, and God laughs," is never truer than during a flight delay at the airport or a baby's arrival that is past due or a dinner that burns in the oven. These little hiccups in life can cause stress and anxiousness that cannot be controlled. These hiccups in life may cause temporary discomfort, but it will long be forgotten when one lands at their destination or a mom says hello to their newborn child or the pizza arrives at the door. It is in the in-between moments of the hiccups where patience, calmness, acceptance, and reflection on what truly matters lie. In the hiccups of life is where our character matures, and then an "Aha!" moment is realized. All is for very specific reasons, so take a deep breath and a long exhale and watch life go on.

UNCONDITIONAL

The definition of *unconditional* is without conditions—no rules, regulations, or guidelines. So when a mother meets her child for the first time, this feeling of being so overwhelmed with unconditional love is such a blessing. This blessing is carried through a lifetime. That's how a parent loves a child. Even if the child chooses inappropriate, hurtful behavior or forsakes his or her own parent, because of unconditional love, the parent shows up anyway. It's taken me a lifetime to know this; and now I'm on my own path to trusting, believing, and accepting God's unconditional love for me.

FAMILIAR

There is peace in the familiar. Participating in daily rituals can bring comfort and a burden. If the action that I participate in is to benefit me and is done daily, this will support my journey. If the action is one that keeps me from evolving, then it will only hinder me as I move forward. There is a benefit when I deviate from the familiar. It may be taking a vacation or just trying out something new that pushes me out of my comfort zone. At times, releasing the familiar may be uncomfortable and supported by fear. Challenges will always stretch me from the familiar to the unknown. This is when I become quiet enough to hear that still small voice tell me, "Have faith. I've got you."

RECONNECT

When I haven't done something in a while and I try to reconnect, it may feel awkward. Riding a bike for the first time in a while can leave me shaky and unsure, but then the memory of achievement sets in, and it becomes effortless. It may seem quite a different story when I attempt to reconnect with someone I have loved. *Awkward* is a mild word to attach to the feeling of once again feeling vulnerable. Guarding my heart is much different from catching myself when I stumble. But once the fear settles, so do my decision to forgive and to be humble enough to know we all have struggles. It is through the cracks that the light will penetrate and melt fear into love.

WHAT'S THE TRUTH?

With all the information floating out there, one may become confused and ask, "What's the truth?" Fake news has a history that stems back to biblical time, when all God wanted was to love us and for us to love one another. Yet in the need for power, glory, and greed, bullying and manipulation became the way for another's truth to be accepted by all in order to lead. Family, friendships, media, and propaganda all have the ability to give and receive the one great gift, which is love. So again, the question is asked: What is the truth? I have read a plethora of information from the 12 steps, the Bible, and the word of Tao; but the one great truth I can rely on is the power and energy of God's love and His want to have a relationship with all of us. What's your truth?

Dialogue in My Head

How many times have I allowed the what-ifs in my head to steal my precious present moments? While in a conflict, I always have a dialogue in my head to configure my defensive tactics and make my case so that I can have my voice and be seen. How many times have I held my own happiness hostage and waited for the outcome I've scripted to come to pass so that I could move on? Hurrying toward the end of a conflict, I play out the confrontation with the dialogue in my head because I want everything to be peaceful. This very act robs me of the very peace in the present, not having faith that God's plan is in motion. I now live in the present, leaving the conflict with God. Thy will be done.

Balance through Faith

Somewhere in the middle, we must achieve balance and know what is enough. This statement is true in a world of contradictions—what is right, what is wrong, what is strong, what is weak, who is rich, or who is poor. The list being endless speaks that somewhere in the middle of all this lies the balance. In the life that I've come to choose to live, now that I have 85 percent of it behind me, I look at the journey left to travel. I then ask myself, can I live with drama on one side and peace on the other? This is where my faith lies within my own balance of conflict or what I hope will be.

Not My Story

Often, when I read a novel and the main characters are in turmoil, I wonder why they are making the choices they are making if they are so miserable with the results. I'm not sure why we choose to be in situations that continue to cause us harm or sadness. In every opportunity, there is a life lesson and experience, so why remain in situations that continue to have the same outcome? And then it hits me. This is not my story to tell and not my journey to live, and even if I would not make the same choices that may result in pain, it's not for me to decide for or judge anyone else. It humbles me to know that I can support and love someone even if how they choose to behave and live differ from my journey. It's a nice blueprint for world peace.

In the Waiting

Dreaming about a certain outcome or praying to find peace can bring about an uncomfortable situation. It's called waiting. Once a request is made, I sometimes expect immediate gratification, like a behavior will change or the phone will ring or an apology will be awarded. Yet it is in my waiting that my turmoil festers. I can become impatient, judgmental, and disappointed that my expectation has not been met. Then it hits me. How much of me am I still giving away to you to complete me? How many more times will I continue to engage in the same behavior and expect a different outcome? It is said that once a prayer is spoken, the waiting begins, but you never have to pray for the same thing again. The prayer has been received. Now in the waiting is where I begin to live in faith, patience, grace, and abundance. I know and I am thankful that what I am meant to have now, I have. All is in God's timing.

The Bridge

On one side of the bridge are peace, quiet, and stillness toward all that is new and healed and accepted. On the other side of the bridge are the brokenness of dreams, the drama of another's life that has become toxic, and the souls longing for connection. My not having the ability to be on both sides of the bridge at the same time doesn't mean that I don't feel or want what's on both sides. I want what's on both sides, but I accept the fact that it can't happen. In this acceptance, I find trust and faith, even when the bridge stands in front of me, longing to have those connections and peace. Until the two sides can merge and be healed, I remain living with the pain, but not in the pain. I will find blessings when I feel deprived, I will find love when I feel alone, and I will live in the moment when my needs get too big.

PUNCTUATION

There are many punctuation marks, but the ones that hold true to me are the period, question mark, comma, and exclamation point. I have used the exclamation point and question mark more than any throughout my life. I am always questioning or screaming loud enough to be heard. I have come to learn that my answers are in the commas and periods. When I question why, God usually tells me through His use of a period that what's done is done, like my past is done period. When a comma is used, it usually means that there is more to come, even when I use an exclamation point. When I use a question mark over and over, it means I have come to accept and know that even though I may never understand, there is a bigger picture in the puzzle of my life, and I am only focused on one piece. In time, with the faith of knowing that all is as God intends, all my exclamation points and question marks will change into a period to show the flow of my life and for me to know that God knows better than I.

REACTION AWARENESS

At any given moment, silence can turn into a deafening sound that bursts a sunray through darkness. In the initial shock of what's happening, the immediate reaction is to ask, why is this occurring, and how do I protect myself from any residual backlash of the negative? Then I have to become aware that I may not understand the why, but I can begin to uncover how it makes me feel. Is it a trigger of a past indiscretion? Is it a trigger of a past trespass? Either way, I am aware of how it makes me feel. I assess its continuous hold of my heart and soul and then bless it for its reminder that all is well and all is as it's meant to be, and I can once again enjoy the dance of the trees in the wind. Awareness allows me to accept and know that all is fluid.

TRANSPARENCY

In my understanding, when something is transparent, it's almost as if a veil of denial is lifted, and the sun shines its brilliance to be seen for the first time. So much is still hidden in the depths of my healing. At times, I think I've truly healed or have a handle on an issue until something or someone ventures into my path, and then I am reminded of the layers. There are still so many layers that lie beneath my pain and that need to become transparent, but I do appreciate the subtle baby steps I am awarded; otherwise, it would shoot me back into the darkness of defensiveness and denial. Now when one more layer is peeled back from the darkness and into the transparency of the light, I can smile; and with a quiet affirmation, I whisper, "I am once again humbled and grateful that I am indeed healing, evolving, and able to continue on my path to fulfill my purpose."

A VIEW IN THE MIRROR

When I see a behavior that makes me uncomfortable, I humble myself so I could see what of that uncomfortable behavior I see in me. This mirror image concept has pushed me to the edge of self-righteous judgment of others and myself. This "I'm better than you" attitude has pushed me into my own humbleness to see others as complementary souls on a similar path to assist me to become my best, true, authentic self. Yet it is humbling to know that the lessons before me are to question if I've made the correct choices to be the best reflection of myself. So in that, I feel humbled to look into the mirror and not look away. I am humbled to look into what is in this reflection that gives me one more life lesson.

A New Page

Every day is a gift. The possibilities are endless with joy or sorrow waiting just around the corner. As I prepare myself for my day's lesson, I can decide how much of me I am going to give any situation that may cross my path. Each new day comes with a new page to script a new blessing. I am now so aware of the messages that come with each encounter. Although it may take shedding many tears to see it, once the pain or joy presents itself, I can look to see what it is I can draw from the experience. Even if the situation is not about me, being an observer can have its benefits. With a new page, I can review what I've asked God to restore but decide how long the visit will last. How much of me I am giving to waiting will draw from the joy that awaits me. I will send out blessings and enjoy the new page of the day.

Hands Open

There are so many opportunities for our hands to be open. This physical gesture may detect a letting go or a welcoming in. Either way, this action can catch and release and bring inner peace. I used to think that if I let go, I was giving up on a much desired need or dream. Now I've realized it is in the act of opening my hands that I release the burden of carrying another while allowing the flow of the new to enter. Waiting for restoration after forgiveness is the action of sitting Shiva. I can pray and grieve, yet it is in the gentle opening of my hands that I can give to God the burdens of my journey. Letting go is not giving up but is the mere act of faith and hope that all is well and that I can choose to accept or keep fighting. I can release all my burdens and forgive others and myself. I bless all of us on our journey, whether together or apart. I choose to live my life in the joy and gratitude of all my blessings.

Release, Breathe, Accept

There comes a time in everyone's life when we need to release that which has been held so tightly to allow room to breathe. I used to hold on because if I let go, then that meant giving up, and I didn't know how I was going to fill that void. So instead, I began to replace it; and consequently, I had to begin all over in the pain that I was avoiding. I have never died from pain, and letting go and releasing the dreams that I thought would bring me happiness has allowed me to accept all that I know I am meant to be. I can release, and I can breathe, and I now accept I would rather be where I am without that filled dream than where I thought I should be. I know now that my faith and trust in God and myself is where I am meant to be.

Melt Into

When I awake with a to-do list, I may forget to stop and melt into my blessings. I take time to say good morning to my home, thanking it for my protection and safety. I welcome the sunrise with the praise of another day of my journey. Yet I can so easily be distracted into a negative experience if the news is on or the dogs and kids are fighting or if I get a text or phone call. I can melt into a negative situation that can easily rob the joy and blessings in that moment, and I can be distracted into recalling an estranged relationship, wrongdoings, and feelings of abandonment or dismissal. But with a simple prayer and a rerouting of my thoughts, I can melt into knowing that in time, I can see me in you and you can see you in me. I then remember to own what is mine and bless you as I melt back into the blessings of my life.

Broken Tickle Spot

There are certain spots that when stimulated will cause us to flinch in pain or cause laughter. A tickle spot can move us from laughter to tears if pain occurs. It usually causes more laughter, pleasure, and love than pain. But when the tickle spot becomes broken, where does the laughter go? How can the laughter be found? How can laughter be restored? There are so many experiences in one's life that can bring so much joy but also in an instant turn to pain. It is in joy where love is, and even if there is a chance for the laughter to get lost, knowing it can be restored is how faith grows. As fluid as a river are the moments of our lives. We are ever changing, and when allowed, we see the joy and the possible pain in every situation. Look for the light and enjoy it with the laughter of a tickle.

My Story

If we were to sit down and share our experiences, we would see the similarities in our stories. We could share our first love or when we first felt that we were beginning to truly uncover our authentic selves by feeling the pain being burned away to allow the light in. Yet all too often, we are drawn to one another by our differences, all the while thinking, "I'm right, and you're wrong."

We spend countless amounts of energy trying to get one another to think, feel, and know what we think, feel, and know so we can be right. This doesn't complement us or allow our similarities to bring us together. Rather, it strengthens the rift that keeps us apart. This enhances the fear that we harbor so that we don't know who we are anymore. My story, your story, our stories—these are ones of joy, pain, love, fear, and ups and downs. Come to me, as I will come to you, so that we can share our stories—our similarities and differences—in the light of love.

The Rainbow in the Storm

At times, while I am reflecting on the decades of my life, I tend to focus on the painful times, when I felt abandoned and alone. In these desperate times, whether self-inflicted or due to another's choice, I would always look for the rainbow in the storm. I recall my first sighting of a rainbow. I did not know the scientific logistics of why there were rainbows. I merely gazed at its beauty, counting the colors, lost in its wonder. I think that if there can be a rainbow in a storm, then I can find happiness; and if there is beauty in the darkness, I can find the light. With the acceptance of contradictions and opposites, I know that life is as fluid as the river; it's ever changing and ever flowing, and the storms of my life have come and gone. The pain from my memories now fade into the life of abundance, joy, and peace; and in the midst of all the storms' turmoil, I am that rainbow.

God's Got a Plan

There are some things in life that are very predictable—fire burns, water is wet, the ocean and rivers flow, and the flowers bloom—but there are also many things in life that are very unpredictable. No energy is given to the predictable because no one can control it unless water is added to fire or a dam is built to prevent the river from flowing or a flower is dug up before its bloom. That control will postpone the beauty that is meant to be. Focusing on the unpredictable does not change its inevitable outcome; it only postpones the beauty that is meant to be shared. Yet fear leads to control, and control leads to inflexibility, and inflexibility leads to missing the opportunity to witness something better, something that can never be imagined. So what's next? Maybe it's a mystery, but having faith and knowing all is well is the greatest outcome of all. Just wait and see what's in store and what comes next.

Burn Off

Fire, although one of the most fantastic discoveries of our lives, also has a very dark side. It can make a meal or destroy a home. It can warm a soul or burn off skin. Just as fire burns, so do our negative thoughts. With the look of one person, it can cause us to harden or soften. With just one touch, it can embrace the heart or break it. The burn of anything can be as devastating as it is helpful. When the burning off of an emotional issue causes discomfort, sweat, and tears, what lies underneath is hope for a better tomorrow. As fire can burn down to the foundation, it can also uncover a new beginning. The burning off of something undesirable leaves us vulnerable enough to

231

reach out and say, "Help me." With those two words, which remain after all is burned off, come hope, prosperity, and peace for anyone who is heavy with burdens. Burn off, burn deep, and discover what lies beneath.

DELAYS

Anxiousness, impatience, lack of faith, and not trusting are all fear-based feelings that I have when I am waiting for something that I want and I am not receiving it on my time. I used to try to manipulate and control the outcome as if I knew better for myself than God did, but this only delayed the inevitable outcome. Whether I am meant to have what I want or not, I am gently reminded to look at what I already have. This postponement is only painful when I give all my energy into its arrival instead of trusting God, letting go in faith, and finding gratitude for all that is enhancing my joy now. So as I humble myself one more time, I thank God for my blessings and thank God for helping me live in my truth with my voice and knowing who I am.

WHAT'S THE GOAL?

There are so many things that go on in our busy lives that we can become easily distracted. A to-do list or a desired outcome can easily fall by the wayside with one distraction. So it is with our spiritual journey. Even if we have the goal to follow the golden rule or to live by God's laws, we can still be easily detoured with one distraction. Maintaining the high road when an encounter is not coming to fruition takes determination and discipline so we can bypass the distraction to reach the goal. What my goal is may differ from yours. Even when I am being a responsible, productive citizen who is doing what's ethically right and being my best, true, positive, authentic self, I can still become easily distracted with one unkind word from another or myself. So remaining aware of my distractions can help me maintain my soul's goal. What's your goal, and what are the distractions keeping you from achieving it?

RECEIVE, REFLECT, RELEASE

There have been countless times in my life when a simple life lesson turned into decades of grief, sadness, and pain. I am very capable of making a decision for myself, but I have a very annoying habit of second-guessing myself. I can ask for others' opinion and give my power away, thinking someone knows better for me than I know for myself. It's easy if someone agrees, but if they give even one ounce of pushback, I would then feel as though I need to defend or even persuade him or her that I am capable of what's best for me. I will receive many more opinions in my lifetime. I will also receive pushback from another who has a different opinion. Now instead of feeling unsure and doubtful of my decision, I can reflect on their information and then release it into God's hands. I know that I will never be placed in a situation without the assistance of God's guidance. I am safe and assured that I will receive what I need, and I will reflect on how to use it and release all criticism from others and myself knowing God's got me.

OFF-BALANCE

In times of unrest and being unsure, I can move in and out of a positive mood. At one moment, I have faith that all will work out, and I will give my energy to here and now. In another moment, I feel myself in doubt and drown myself in the uncertainty of not knowing. It is said that a person of faith travels through this experience and always arrives knowing all is well and meant to be.

When I reflected on my anxiousness and uncomfortableness with unfinished business, I ended up choosing behavior that prolonged the inevitable outcome as if I knew better for me than God did. I always land where I am meant to be, and then I reflect on God's goodness and on what He thinks is in my best interest. Traveling back and forth between total faith and anxiousness and insecure feelings of trying to maintain some patience in not knowing is when I am off-balance. But with one more prayer, one more inhale, and one more positive thought, I can live with not knowing, knowing that God knows.

Repent, Not Remove

There were many times in my life when I did not make the best choice for myself or for others. I spent years living in the past as if I could feel guilty enough to erase or remove it from my memory. More often than not, I am plagued by a poor choice and spend countless hours berating myself, thinking I should have known better. These are teachable moments. I know I am not perfect. I make mistakes, I say the wrong thing, I make poor choices, I can be insecure, I can be afraid, and I can be unsure. I am also a work in progress. I am healing. I am a good, kind, compassionate, forgiving, and loving soul. I am learning to look at my past errors and at the life lessons I have learned and humble myself to ask for forgiveness from others, from myself, and from God. I cannot remove what is done. I can only repent and move forward. With that said, I am sorry. Please forgive me. I'll keep trying.

Release and Move On

What I once relied on is coming to an end, because it no longer applies to my journey. The automaticity of my reactions is slowly turning from negative to positive and from fear to faith. Harboring anger from past transgressions will not change what has occurred. Life lessons and experiences are gifts from the residue left behind by pain. When I can feel a negative reaction coming on, I can step away, breathe, remove myself from the past, and morph back into the present knowing all is well, all is meant to be, and my not knowing is temporary. I used to think that if I stayed angry long enough, the situation would change. All I got from that behavior was sadness, and I remained stuck in my broken dreams. Now I release my need to control an outcome and rely on God's plan for me to move on with my joy.

A Closed Fist

A closed fist is one of my most detrimental acts; it depicts pain and anger and does not allow anything in, similar to a closed heart. Although it cannot be seen like a closed fist, a hardened heart cannot allow anything in while it harbors all the pain, not allowing it out to be healed. But when a heart can open, whether it is broken or just healed, love, light, truth, and compassion can replace the pain it houses. Such as with an open fist, it can hug or embrace, congratulate and praise. I have gone through life like a revolving door—swinging open in love at one moment and closing the next. Yet never at any moment in time have I ever benefited from being closed in with my anger and pain, so as I swing open to receive the grace of love and light, I extend an open hand to greet you.

Stop for a Picnic

I've had many encounters with not knowing. I've had many experiences when I was uncomfortable with not knowing. I've had many a prayer meeting with myself while waiting for answers. I went out and did the work myself, only to feel the results of my labor in the form of anger, resentment, disappointment, and failure, because I did not wait in faith. What I've learned is that once a prayer is sent into the universe, my faith falls in knowing that in not knowing, I will eventually know that all works out as God intends. So I've learned to send out my prayer request, have faith that it will be answered, listen for what I have to do to make it real, and then let God take over. So I've learned that in my in-between times, I have a life, and I can still breathe. Then I stop, and I have a picnic.

How Do I Live With...

I've learned to forgive a trespass when someone says they are sorry, but how do I live with their behavior if it's not changing? How do I trust again? When someone leaves me without including me in their decision, how do I live with this dismissal when I know how much I will miss them and love them and that they are following a dark path? How do I live with the ghosts that are keeping them in the past when all I want to do is see the light and live in its glory? How do I live with another's decision that hurts me, even when I know I cannot control their behavior or ease their mind? I show up every day and thank God for my blessings, and I look at the situations that others have chosen to follow and assess if it's good for me. I thank all those who have come and gone in my life for that little bit of light or darkness they have left and see if it will help me evolve. How do I live with darkness in life? I live in each moment that I'm given in faith and trust God that knows best and that if I am in the darkness, He is with me.

Hope and Faith

If I knew that I would never have a financial, physical, or emotional problem and that all my hopes, dreams, wishes, and goals would be answered and fulfilled, what would I do? Would I continue to worry? Would I continue to sit and wait for something to arrive? I've been given an amazing gift: to live the rest of my life healed. I am no longer involved in anyone else's drama unless I choose to be and unless it fulfills my purpose. How I choose to show up every day, in peace or in turmoil is a right I have. My days of being responsible for others is behind me. How do I want to live my life knowing all is meant to be?

In God's Way

Trying to manipulate or control an outcome may still not get me what I desire, so instead of putting all my energy into that, I'll get out of God's way and let Him do it for me. God isn't at work to produce the circumstance I want. He is at work to produce the version of me He wants me to be. I will never be placed in a situation that I can't handle without God by my side and in my heart. Life didn't happen to me; it happened for me.

Seeing What's Already There

It's so easy to desire something and to be diligent enough to strive to receive it. This works well with self-discipline, but not so well with striving to change another. I know all is well when I accept that I can control my own behavior and reactions, and seeing what's already there is an affirmation of answered prayers. Believing that receiving is coming is faith, and accepting what's about to take place and accepting its outcome is surrender.

Toolbox

As I continue on my journey of spiritual evolution to fulfill my destiny, I review what is in my toolbox. I am in a holding pattern of deciding what is in my toolbox that I still need to complete my journey and what I can relinquish that no longer serves me. During this stillness, I am allowing myself to let go of the fear that holds me in bondage and replace it with faith that allows me to accept that I don't know. By allowing this process to unfold, I am finding that my journey is becoming lighter, and I am replacing my toolbox with a bag of faith. I have what I need.

Stay Warm

Staying in a moment of peace can feel like a warm blanket on a cold winter night, but the minute the door flies open and fear blows in to smother the warm fire that glows within, it can be a momentary event that I tend to dwell on. Instead of asking fear to leave and just closing the door, I may continue to add fuel to its fire. Now I know that this is an immediate awareness, so I flip the cold into the warmth of my knowing that I am a blessing and that I am worthy of goodness and love. I can remain in the light when the darkness arrives knowing that the brighter the light, the bigger the shadow.

Roads

When I get agitated with all the obstacles in my path, I can decipher the why in what is keeping me from fulfilling my journey for the day. I know things are put in my path to affirm my journey and to help me question my deep-seated reason for choosing the road I am on. When I look at obstacles as experiences, then the judgment of good/bad melts into an opportunity. When I become fearful, I can tap into my support system to help me give it a voice. It can be as easy as a phone call or a visit that can affirm my decisions. I am not saying I should give my power of voice to someone else; however, another can help calm me when I feel I am alone on the road. Sometimes, traveling alone is necessary; but because I have faith, I am never alone.

Floating In Between

When I become anxious about an outcome, I can find myself floating in-between my faith and trust in the unknown and my self-doubt and fear. In these times, which do not benefit my own self-worth, I inhale positive energy and know that all is well, and I exhale my fear of my own negative dialogue. I am learning to feel my faith and live with my own contradictions and still feel love.

Looking Up When I'm Down

There will be guaranteed times when I am down in the dumps. This is usually a self-inflicted result of a negative reaction in the expectation of a different result. Wishing and hoping and praying for something other than what is can lead me down the path of self-pity and depression. Knowing that the past can only be accepted as is and knowing to look for the life lessons in the pain can sometimes be confused with the abundance of blessings that already are there. I need to stop chasing that which is not and be grateful for what is. When I'm down and I look up and look within, there is my faith and my hope for the acceptance of what is.

God Decides

In the past, when I was anxious about an unresolved issue, I would look for a loophole to try to encourage, persuade, or even guilt someone into a resolution that would ease my pain. When I offered my unsolicited advice to resolve an issue, it only made it worse. Now whether I am enlightened about the reason or not, I have learned to trust and have faith and know all is as it is meant to be for a specific reason. Whether the issue has been resolved or not, I have chosen to live my life with the pain, not in the pain, and this brings me peace knowing that the pain no longer defines me! I can learn to wait for God's resolutions and know all is well.

Open Fists

It's a wonder sometimes that with all the negativity in my own head, I can actually find my peace and joy. I was unaware of my thought process for decades. I never realized how much negativity was driving me until I became so overwhelmed with grief that I humbled myself and asked God to remove my burdens. How I did this may not be applicable to you, but this is how it unfolded for me. I was so overwhelmed with grief, and I was unable to find any joy. I exercised, walked, read, meditated, wrote in my journal, and gave to others; yet still, I was plagued with despair. One night, I was lying in bed in tears, and I became still enough to search for my answer and asked God why. He told me that I was carrying a load that was not mine to carry and that it was time to let it go. So I unclenched my fists and dried my tears, and with open hands, I asked God to remove my burdens.

He also told me that there was a life lesson in every experience and that He loved me so much that I would always be safe. Now when I am feeling overwhelmed with what is not mine or I fear an outcome or I doubt a decision, I ask God to guide me and remove my burden. In this simple act, I feel better, because I can trust God and I now trust myself.

Thy Will Be Done

If I had waited for things to change in my life, I would still be where I was. In order to continue my spiritual evolution, it was necessary to take the initiative to move forward. Learning to live with the pain and not in the pain has been one of the greatest growth points of my life. The pain of my disappointments and feelings of rejections has plagued me too long to give it any more of my energy since nothing will change but me. Learning to live with the uncomfortable is to understand and accept that I cannot change anything but how I choose to react. I know and have faith that all is. Thy will be done.

Down and Looking Up

At times, I find myself digging a hole of despair; and before I am even aware of my thoughts, I am, once again, down and looking up. We've all been given free will; and our thoughts, words, and actions are in our control. Sometimes, I don't need to react to anyone's drama, because I am drumming up my own through a trigger. The insecurities and the waves of self-doubt can encase me before I know it, and then I am, once again, down and looking up. These times call for my thoughts to remember my many comforts and blessings and to show how grateful I am with all that I have, who I am, and yet to be and receive. This is the time to remember with the blessing and faith of this one day.

Abundance of Blessings

In the culmination of my years, I have found my voice and have chosen to speak my truth. I have found my truth and have chosen to live in that truth. I have set boundaries and honored my own words and deeds; I walk my talk. I have released judgment toward others since I am not sinless and have made inappropriate choices that have taken my life into an abyss.

Having emptied all that is not mine that I've allowed to define me has left me void and ready to explore. I have filled myself with worth, love, respect, and honor; and I have forgiven my own trespasses against others, God, and myself. I have learned to continue to answer my deep-seated questions with my own research and to not live through the discoveries of another. I have an abundance of blessings, and I am grateful for the journey.

At times, the journey causes me to look deep into my soul, which causes me to purge what I think I need in order to receive what I am intended to have. I have learned that my ancestors have decided to leave out one very important point of information and a very important name: Jesus is God in the flesh, and He is the Messiah. I am blessed with abundance.

His Will, Not Mine

How often have I interceded into God's plan to think I know better for myself or for someone? How often have I doubted my own faith and worth to allow negative energy to steal my joy? How often have I allowed fear to dictate my actions, only to find myself in utter turmoil? Too often! So now I have a new year, a new attitude, restoration of faith, and 100 percent trust and faith that His will, will be done!

Not Only Read It but Also Live It

It's so easy to read the words of a self-help book or the Bible or the words of Tao but quite another to actually put those words into the dance of our lives. It's a humbling experience when we can look into the eyes of another, and as the words flow from our lips to their ears, we hope they can trust the blessing of our connection. It is our responsibility to walk our own talk and hope the same from others. Words can be read and comprehended, but when they become part of who we are, then that's our blessing to God, others, and ourselves.

What Does Not Bend Will Break

Many of us have never encountered anything but being cherished with unconditional love, being accepted, and feeling as if we are a true gift. But many of us have also been abused, manipulated, controlled, or bullied. Since I have not encountered the positive aspect of that experience, I think about my strength and how I have been able to survive from being the victim to being victorious. Knowing that feeling of defensiveness and waiting for the next punch, the heart may harden, and that which won't crack will not feel the warmth of a healing light.

Bending does not mean submission, permission, or compromise but finding compassion and understanding that we are all in fear of the pain of brokenness. Without the ability of light to penetrate, there is no room for peace or joy. That which will not bend will only snap under the weight of inflexibility, which will lead to restoration and forgiveness. Sway with the wind and dance in the light. Peace will come.

Clean Up the Mess

When I spill something, I clean up the mess, but this is not so easy to do when a relationship has suffered. All parties need to be available to clean up the mess. But when the fear of rejection and judgment sets in, it's difficult to clean up the mess alone. This is when disappointment and resentment may set in, and nothing gets cleaned. Being forthcoming and honest can be painful when both parties have to take a look at their own behavior and be accountable for their part in the mess. When I humble myself to show up with the intention of cleaning up the mess, then all fear of rejection disappears, and hopefulness toward resolution can take fear's place. I am safe when I keep my faith and when I know that thy will, not mine, will be done.

The Why Questions

Unresolved issues within a relationship or within myself can cause unrest unless I have faith that I am where I am meant to be. This faith can become compromised if I allow the negative voices of unresolved issues to trickle into my thoughts. It's as subtle as a tiger that is stalking its prey, and before I become aware, I have taken a turn into darkness. To become aware is a reward in itself. Giving fear a voice will help flip the negative back into faith. Knowing my thoughts are fluid, I can choose what to think, how to feel, and how to react. So the question is, why would I ever want to feel sadness when I can feel joy? Why would I ever want to live in bondage in the chains of fear when I can have an abundance of unconditional love and respect?

When the Pieces Come Together

When a puzzle is in progress, each piece that fits gives a feeling of accomplishment, because the picture will soon be complete. Only God sees the finished picture as we go about our life's journey with all our scattered pieces. We look for the just-right fit so we can understand the why even if we may not like the answer. This may bring clarity to a ruptured relationship—why were all the different pieces not meant to fit until they were meant to come together? This journey is not always without pain, yet during the hiatus from joy, self-exploration and healing do occur. So when the puzzle pieces are once again asked to be joined, the pieces come together.

Where Fear Is

Lack of communication and misunderstandings can engulf us in fear. There are so many components to this that it then becomes easier to ignore than to confront. Lies, judgment, expectations, disappointment, blame-shifting, retribution, and abandonment all hurt. As if a sugarcoated lie isn't still a lie even if ninety-nine of one hundred are telling it.

It is in the simple act of obedience that God's voice leads me out of bondage and into the light so that I can fulfill my destiny. I can't be a healer unless I am healed. I can't present myself as loving, compassionate, trustworthy, or kind if I do not show those attributes to myself. I cannot forgive unless God and myself forgive me. I cannot let go of judgment until I become accountable for my own behavior. I can't speak of God's grace until I feel worthy of receiving it. I cannot live in truth until I know the truth about God and that He loves me and that I am worthy. Marie Curie wrote, "Nothing in life is to be feared. It is only to be understood."

It Is I

The initial reaction to any discomfort is fear. Living with a conflict caused me to immediately react in a fix it mode so the pain would dissipate and I could be happy again. It was when I felt the need to go faster that I needed to slow down. It was when my grip got too tight that I needed to let go. When trying to resolve and restore, I used to think that if they changed, then all would be well. I waited with a closed heart until the apology came, or I ignored the pain until I talked myself into a false sense of security, trying to believe that all was well in my world. This only prolonged my pain and did not allow the positive flow of God to melt my hardness into brokenness so that His light could enter my darkness. It was then that I needed to change and trust and have faith. With an open heart, open mind, and open hands, I can welcome all that is meant to be.

Relationship Anchor

Relationships are a connection between two or more people. When we are born, our primary relationships are with our mother and with God. As we grow, we meet others who either compliment or contradict our interests and beliefs. God is the one person who will meet all our needs, yet we seek others to enhance our life. One person may like sports, and another may read the same literature or have the same political affiliation. All relationships are there to teach us something; they inspire us to be who we are meant to be or show us exactly who we don't want to be.

I sought out relationships to be my anchor and to complete me when I felt incomplete. I looked for affirmations to feel worthy of being loved. Consequently, I lost myself and morphed into them. I lost my own anchor, connection, and relationship with myself and God when I believed their definition of me rather than how I was truly defined by God. My mirror reflection became theirs, and when I walked with them, there was only one shadow, so I looked for my anchor, the only true connection with God.

I know there is no way to keep things from changing or to keep them where I want them to be. There is no way to keep anything where I want it all the time. The anchor is with God. Every moment promotes growth, so I am willing to let go of everything that I believe define me in order to live in God's truth as my anchor.

Even When I Want To, I Must Not

I kept praying for God to send someone to take this walk with me. I was told to empty that which no longer served me, and so I became empty. I waited, but I still remained empty. In my impatience, I went back to try to reconnect with those who left in order to fill the emptiness. I found myself in the same situation, settling for less than what was waiting for me. I became agitated that my requests were not being answered, and once again feeling ignored and not worthy of what I wanted, I started refilling that which was not meant to be mine. I found reason to complain when all the while, I was meant to be silent, patient, and empty in order for God to send me what I requested. I gave all my energy toward reconnecting with all those who didn't give me a second thought. In my impatient act of going back to reconnect with those who had served their purpose, I realized there was no room for the new that was waiting to journey with me. In this society that encourages immediate gratification, I have learned that when I want to run, I must walk; when I want to eat, I must fast; when I want to shout, I must remain quiet; and when I want to, I must not.

God's Got This

How easy it is for me to react in a negative, defensive tone when I am being challenged with information when I know I am right. For decades, I felt as if I needed to defend my honor, because I was trying to prove my trustworthiness. Feeling as if my voice had been silenced, I became an aggressive advocate to prove myself worthy of being believed but while also trying to regain the power that I had given away to be loved.

Although I no longer need to sacrifice my worth, I still get triggered every time I feel as though I need to keep my power and voice. I am learning that I can remain silent and step away, ask for information, honor my boundaries, and offer solicited advice. I can assess what is mine to own and remove myself from that which is not mine to hold. I will remember the golden rule and do the best I can by filling myself with positive energy instead of reacting in defense. I will let God fight my battles and trust that He is my vindicator.

Lifted Fog

When the fog rolls in, it can become a detriment to our view. When it lifts, an unexpected joy can welcome a new experience. Allowing myself to remain in the safety of a cocoon can block all the amazing experiences awaiting me. I find peace when I trust myself to have faith in what will benefit my growth, not depending on another to complete me but instead seeing my completeness in the reflection of my strength. When the fog lifts, I am still and always will be there.

Where the River Meets the Sea

There were so many times in my life where I just needed this one prayer request answered to find my peace, and when the prayer was answered, there was little celebration or affirmation that it indeed was the missing puzzle piece that would complete me. Then there was always one more prayer request and one more prayer request and one more prayer request. The thing is, I was here all along. My puzzle was completed, and I was fulfilled and with love and worth, yet I was always seeking fulfillment from one more prayer request. Metaphorically speaking, the sea of people in the world is as unique and yet as the same as me. I know the river within me will still be a river when it meets the sea.

Open Heart, Open Mind

When all is said and done and apologies have been extended and forgiveness is in motion, what needs to be addressed in staying in the moment of an open heart and open mind? This can be accomplished through compassion, understanding, and communication. We are all human and on an evolutionary journey, and no one is more superior than the other. Yet the gnawing feeling about trust and commitment come into play when the apologies have been extended before but the behavior has been continued. The decisions then become about me, and all I can do is keep an open heart and open mind.

Intentional Journey

At times, I can find myself so anxious that I think the only way to find peace is to resolve that which is troubling; so I plan, think, and maneuver through the discomfort. Then I realize how much my anxiety is robbing me of the joy of the moment, and I stop. I realize what is in my control and inhale/exhale knowing I've done all that I can do. I do not need to assimilate myself to make it work out as I desire, because being someone other than who I am is not my desire at all. I can be present, I can be authentic, and I can be my best, true self. If accepted, then I journey along with the new; and if declined, I travel along with the new. Either way, my journey is all that it is intended to be.

The Loving Voice

When I feel so overwhelmed with a to-do list, an information, or an issue with a relationship, I tend to address my feeling on a surface level rather than sit in the uncomfortable not knowing until I can be calm enough to listen and hear. I do not like being empty, uncomfortable, or not knowing an outcome; so consequently, I self-sabotage to look for a quick fix. This always seems to set me back because I take matters into my own hands or fight a battle that isn't mine instead of waiting, trusting, and addressing what is truly mine.

When I finally become still enough and silent enough to hear the root of my pain crying out from the depths of my soul, I embrace it, give it a voice, and release it into the light. Even if I am finding my answers and I acquire inner peace, that does not mean the storm that is still raging outside of my own control is safe. I may see things differently from when I find my inner peace and look from a compassionate eye, but I am learning to be cautious, because even if I am at peace, the storm is still raging. I can find my answers and the truth from within when I am at peace and trust the loving voice that is guiding me in the midst of the storm.

Inhale the Light

For so long, I harbored guilt, pain, shame, and resentment for what was done and what I allowed to be done to the point where I was suffocating in my own darkness until I could barely see a glimmer of hope or light. Now that I have voiced my silent pain and have prayed for peace, I am learning to forgive others and myself as I venture forward on my journey's path to fulfill my destiny. As I inhale the light and exhale the darkness, I am at peace.

Truth, Faith, and Hope (Inspired by Mark Nepo)

Truth, faith, and hope are all emotions that can only be seen through eyes that believe there is something greater than me. As I continue on my journey and purge that which is not mine into emptiness, I am reminded that "the call of the spirit that would have us participate most fully in our days" is the evidence of truth, faith, hope, and love. I know "faith is the substance of things hoped for, the evidence of things not seen," so help me on my journey not just toward knowing but also toward feeling. Open and soften my heart so that the darkness that has kept it hardened will seep out and be replaced by the light.

Illusions

The definition of *illusion* is "a delusion, fantasy, or false idea." I had so many illusions on how I thought my marriage would be. I had so many illusions on my definition of a partner and a collaborator. I had so many illusions about how I thought others perceived me. I thought that if I just heard the words, "I'm sorry," then all would be well. I cornered myself into this judgmental mindset, believing that if behaviors changed and walking the talk became the norm, then I would be happy. But the apologies came, yet the words didn't match the actions, and I, once again, was left broken because I put too much energy into their word and gave away my power. What's the worst thing that can happen if my illusions of happiness don't come to fruition? Nothing! But I will have to look at where I am depositing my energy and where my faith lies; my nourishment lies with God.

Sarah

Celebrating the life of a loved one is difficult knowing that the box sitting on the kitchen table houses the temple that once held that dear, sweet soul who is loved by many. But a life is not defined by the box sitting on the kitchen table or the many boxes of stuff that will be packed and donated to Goodwill. A life is celebrated based on the moments that are lived in the light of joy, not in the darkness of despair. If any life lesson can be learned as we say goodbye to the one we cherish, it is to celebrate the moments that are given to each of us in the heartbeats of our life. As our life's clock winds down and our presence here begins to fade, the one true, loving moment to be remembered is how blessed this universe has been with the smile and laughter that was that soul.

My Prayer for Today

God, please set my foot on your path. Help me prioritize and focus on those things that honor You and fulfill your plan for my life. There may be relationships, commitments, and activities that I have to let go of; so give me the courage to do so. I want to slow down, restore balance, and experience more joy in my life! God, thank You for loving me unconditionally without holding my sins against me. Thank You for forgiving me and giving me the power to stay on track and not repeat my past trespasses in order to fulfill my destiny for this day and every day. Satan wants me in bondage; he whispers my regrets and sins and reminds me of how I've felt unworthy and unloved. I hold myself in bondage by believing and listening to his lies. The only way to combat him is to pray him away. God, protect me from the lies and strengthen my faith in You. Let me walk with You on my journey.

Found

After all the fear has burned itself out and when there's nothing left but the ashes of worn-out masks, the untold truth is heard, and all the hurts and sadness that have been carried on the journey are gone. When others' opinions defined me more than my own truth, I was silenced, my voice only speaking their script, and I became their parrot. The spoken truth set me free, and now I can see my own shadow and reflection. Even if there is a risk that they will leave, I would rather stand alone in God's light and truth. After purging all the lies and beginning to fill myself with God's light and truth, this may leave me empty. In this emptiness is where I have nothing to lose because now I get to fill myself with God's light and truth. Now coming into my light, I can live authentically, not needing to compete to be accepted and loved. I am a blessing to all, as they are to me. When we live in that light, all that has been lost is found.

I Know

Sometimes, just being alone is the right place to be. It quiets all the noise that surrounds me. It alleviates any of the responsibilities I feel to have things any other way than what they are. When I find myself forcing an issue that I feel needs to be resolved, I miss all the blessings that are in front of me. I am accepting living in the moments of not knowing with faith that in God's time, I will know. For now, I know this is where I am meant to be.

God's Word

When I questioned why, You told me it was because You believed in me, and Your faith in my word was stronger than any words spoken against me. You also told me, "I love you enough to wait for you to come to Me and to let Me love you." Learning to trust has been one of my life's challenges. I was meant to be loved and cherished, but when I laid my trust, it was betrayed, so this left me suspicious. I then began to barter for love and relinquished my power to another to feel worthy and accepted, but this, too, was betrayed.

Now I am at the gates of a new behavior, where I am asked to trust that which I cannot see or physically feel. I am asked to relinquish my power to a father who wants to love me, but my lack of trust is preventing me from feeling it. So I am taking this slowly, at my own pace, not rushing into anyone else's story about Him. I am learning to accept a love that is unconditional and safe. Pray for my inner peace!

Wash the Floor

There are some days when my to-do list controls me instead of me controlling it. I have to wash floors, water the plants, clean the bathrooms, write, read, and walk. But when I look at my to-do list as a chore instead of a blessing, I may miss my joy! Washing the floor is not always a pleasant experience, but I can find joy in my accomplishments. At the end of my life, with my last breath, do I want to reflect on the moments that were given to me as blessings, or do I want them to be remembered as a burden? Not everything I do will be pleasant, but everything I do is purposeful. I need to remember to find the joy in all my experiences, even washing the floor.

Pray and Release It to God

When I want to fix it, I pray and release it to God. When I want it resolved on my time, I pray and release it to God. When I want that which is not mine to have, I have to wait for what is intended to be mine, so I pray and release it to God. It doesn't work if I try to control or manipulate an outcome or try to resolve an issue or heal a relationship that is not ready to heal. The only thing in my control is praying and releasing it to God.

Remember What Matters

What does it feel like at the end of a life? With one's last dying breath, what do they think about? How many of my broken dreams will really matter as opposed to how many lives I've touched with a gentle word or a kind smile or a warm hug? I pick up something at a flea market and wonder about the previous owner's story. Knowing another will house the materialistic decorations I've surrounded myself and that have brought me joy, will someone wonder about me? This humbles me to live each day as if it's my last in God's positive love and light and in faith and peace. It reminds me to remember what really matters.

Something Different

After decades of making the same choices, engaging in a new behavior can be a bit scary. What happens if my behavior isn't accepted? What happens if everyone leaves and I am left alone? These thoughts can leave me paralyzed in a familiar but painful situation where change must occur, but my faith will release the fear, and I will attempt something different. My what-ifs may come to fruition, but

I will never truly be alone. I will land in a better place in peace, not in pain.

THE BLESSINGS OF MY DAY

No longer living through the promises of another or looking for my identity in another's definition of me or needing validation of my truth, I can just be. No longer feeling the need to expect but rather have faith for what is and meant to be, I can enjoy my blessings, find my passions, and live in the joy of the day. If someone harbors ill will against me or if I am holding on to any resentment from a past trespass, then it is our responsibility to move toward resolution. I can just be and enjoy the blessings of my day.

CORNERSTONE

Before I ever had language, I knew that in faith, all my needs would be met. I knew that if I cried, then my parents would come to comfort my distress. I knew that if I had joy in my heart, then I would have my parents to join in my dance. Yet one word or one look of displeasure can rob anyone for an eternity of what their core truth is. So to live in faith is to come back to the very foundation of the truth and to know that we are all loved, cherished, wanted, and purposeful not only to bring joy but also to receive it. This is the true foundation of our being.

EVIDENCE OF THINGS NOT SEEN

It's okay to be where I am even if it means that those I love and want to join me have not yet arrived. I can continue my journey in anticipation of their arrival. Even if they never arrive, I can live with an open heart knowing I always hope for the best for them and will keep them in my prayers. "Faith is the substance of things hoped for, the evidence of things not seen."

FULL

I watch people who have more wealth than they will ever spend and whose physical beauty is beyond even Aphrodite's, but they still implode in their unhappiness. I have learned that no amount of money or beauty will ever replace love and faith. Without love and faith, all that is accumulated becomes stuff that will never be enough to fill an empty hole. But with love and faith, the poor feel rich and the unattractive become beautiful. It is in the light of faith and love that we all are full. With gratitude for my abundant blessings of unconditional love, financial security, emotional stability, good health, and spiritual enlightenment, I am full.

MOVE ON

When I can finally say that I have given it my all, then I am ready to move forward and, with acceptance, live my life in joy and peace. Things will not always work out the way I want them to, but all will work out for my benefit. That is where my faith lies.

I HAVE HOPE

When I have spoken my peace and have shared my requests with another, I then need to have faith that it will work out to my desire or that I will receive another outcome. I am no longer engaged in manipulation or badgering anyone to see it my way or do it to my specifications. The one thing that I do receive when I know that my request has been heard is hope.

DETOUR

"We often work harder in our dreams than in our life. We secretly hid our dissatisfaction with the life we've created and secretly hunt for an imagined cure for what it means to be who we are." How often did I wish I were living somewhere else or coveting someone else's life because I didn't have what I wanted or thought that if I had what they had, I would be content and happy? After knowing this scenario for many years, I have come into my faith knowing who I am and knowing I am purposeful, as are my experiences, opportunities, and life lessons. If it had been any other way, I would not be who I am, where I am, and with who I am with, fulfilling my destiny as it has been written for me. These detours have taken me on my life's journey, only to return home to me. Home is where the heart is.

BREAK THE CYCLE

Staying and living in faith means I need to let go of expectations that always lead to disappointments, judgments, and resentments. The cycle of my expectations is I forgive, I expect, I receive a behavior that has not changed, I get disappointed, I judge myself for being vulnerable again, and I melt back into resentment. When I expect, I give away my power to another or to a situation that only leads me toward negative feelings. To break this cycle, I need to show up for me, do my best, and allow the situation or other person to merely compliment or repel. Either way, I can stay whole rather than break into pieces of despair.

NEW ADVENTURE

When I am experiencing a new adventure that requires me to have no prior background knowledge, I am required to live in faith. This requirement means no control, no opinion, and no facts, just faith. This addresses my lack of trust in others who say one thing and show the opposite behavior, but I am not dealing with just one more person. I am dealing with the truth of my soul and the energy that lives in me that is all positive. This is what I bring along with me as I start my new adventure to live in faith and release the fear of the unknown.

ONE MORE LOOK

When I hear someone say they will do something and their words do not match their deeds, I can get so agitated and become so judgmental of them. Them not keeping their word is about them. What is about me is that I find myself building trust in them and that I look for their words and deeds to complete me. My faith then becomes about their actions, and I realize I have put my faith in the wrong hands. By remembering that we are all souls on a journey, that I am no better than they are, and that their decisions are about them, I am humbled once again. If their decisions are only going to affect them, I need to say a prayer, ask for God to bless them, and walk away. Then I take a good look in the mirror to find my reflection again.

Don't Give Up

When we are born, all our needs are met. When we cry, we receive the attention we desire. When children want things their way, they become combative when they don't get their needs met. This childish behavior can mask itself into adulthood—disappointment from unmet expectations results in resentment. I am learning that through unmet expectations, my faith can detour. When I think I know what's best, I tend to try to make it happen my way. Things may not happen on my timeline or the outcome may be different from what I hope for, but either way, I don't give up and live in faith that all is well and as it should be.

Discomfort in Growth

It is written that in the total acceptance and the letting go, the very thing that is the focus will come to fruition and be granted. This is a humbling example of how total faith and trust unfolds when wanting something so desperately that it becomes an obsession. Through all the vitally important lessons to be learned within the discomfort of growth, there is a good reason, and all will be revealed when it's time. With faith, trust, and hope that all is as it should be and that I am exactly where I should be and with who I should be, all is well.

A Life within the Waiting

While I wait for the answers to my prayers, I will let go of my need to control the outcome to my specifications, and I will let go of the resentment and heartache that I harbor in my heart. While I wait for the answers to my prayers, I will remain in my truth and use my voice and mind to keep forging forward into the knowledge that awaits me. While I wait for the answers to my prayers, I will continue to melt my bitterness and to live in joy and appreciate the blessings I have been given, enjoying this season of my life. While I wait for the answers to my prayers, I will live.

I Have a Praise to Share

Living in faith requires trusting that all I need will be supplied to me when I need it and that all I want is what I have right now. Living in peace is easy when everything I want and need is in the palm of my hand. It is in these quiet, remote times that I may overlook the blessing that has already been delivered. I may start planning my next adventure without even embracing what is already here for me. I will live in faith, trusting all is as meant to be. I will praise and thank God for what I have been given knowing I have what I need when I need it.

The Truth

For so long, I allowed my feelings to be dictated by someone else's mood or a situation where my voice was not being heard. I allowed that to steal my joy, and I allowed myself to fall prey to others and to situations that I could not control. This only agitated me, and my bitterness grew, and I became more judgmental and resentful while waiting for them. I know we are all on our own journey, which may intersect with one another, and that availability is where we are on this journey. So if I am waiting for a situation to work out in my favor or I am waiting for a person to show up, I am missing the joy of what's in front of me as I gaze into a hopeful future. Knowing this is the truth, when I live my life, all is well.

Sidesteps

When I get anxious and impatient about a destination, I may make mistakes that may cause a sidestep and delay my progress. I then find myself searching to right my wrong, and this delays my goal even longer. If I remain calm and trust in my process, I can achieve my desired outcome without having to clean up any messes I make along the way. Even though they are uncomfortable, these sidesteps are a blessing, because in the message lies my faith, trust, peace, and joy.

Little by Little

When I think I know better for myself than God does, I will detour and end up back where I started, so I am now making my request and asking for guidance. I will have what I need when it's time for me to have it. A five-year-old child will not be given the car keys just because he wants to drive, so in God's time, He will give me what He thinks I'm ready for. If I get everything I want that I think is good for me, then I will be overwhelmed with anxiety, because there is too much for me to process. Little by little, I will be given the tools I need for the task that is in front of me. I will be given what I need when I need it. Little by little, I will enjoy the journey, not worried about the destination. What's the hurry? I'll always arrive where I need to be when I need to be there and with who I'm meant to be with.

Pain Management

When I find myself feeling physically broken, I need to seek what deep-seated message is behind the pain. When I'm in physical pain, I know it is God wanting me to move forward in faith and to let go of what I can't change. When I resist this, then I'm in pain. I spend the next few days hobbling around while praying for the pain to subside as I release what is required. When I live my truth and live in faith, I have no pain unless I choose to visit it. When I make these temporary sidesteps, I can acknowledge how I used to live in it and how I now live with it. I am moving forward, managing the pain.

TRUST AGAIN

Some days are so gray that I feel the sun may not shine, although I still know it's behind the clouds, just waiting for me to join in its song. This is when I will huddle into my corner of despair and ask myself what it is that I need to feel loved, cherished, and wanted. Then God's voice tells me that I'm already there. I just need to come into the light and dance in the rays of the sun. I no longer have to live in fear of rejection, abandonment, and judgment. I am giving into peace and joy. I have been forgiven, and I want to believe we are all doing the best we can. If we want to know better, we will do better, but that is a choice. I can be cautious and learn to trust again, but that's my choice.

SOS

When I find myself feeling sad and everything that is said becomes a thorn in my side, I can send out an SOS and ask for help and ask to be surrounded in light so the darkness melts away. "Maybe I have some major obstacles in my path, but being discouraged is not going to make it any better. Don't waste another moment of my precious time being angry, unhappy, bitter, resentful or worried." Dance in the light.

I WILL SHOW UP

Despite knowing the love of my life may not want to participate in a life with me, I will still show up in prayer even if I am dismissed. I will show up with mercy to forgive even if it's not my fault and I am blamed. I will show up in love even if I am not accepted. I will show up even if I am a ghost to you.

GOD'S RESULTS

Sitting here with most of my days behind me, I can reflect without pain and feel grateful for my abundance and comfort. Learning to let go of that which I cannot control or those I love is a testament to my faith that what is not in my control is God's to control. I do not always like the idea that things won't work out my way, but I can still know that God's results are better than any I could ever imagine. I wait for His results and live my days in comfort, being joyful, and in peace.

THANK YOU VERY MUCH, BUT NO HELPING HANDS ARE NEEDED

When I think I know better for another and myself, I make decisions out of the need to control the outcome because I am uncomfortable with the present situation and think I've waited long enough for my desired results, so I give God a helping hand. But never has this ever worked out in my favor. The repercussions have only set me back to where I need to let go and to pray that I will accept what God has in store for me because it is better than what I could ever imagine. It is in my own best interest to move forward on my journey in love and peace, letting God's will be done. When He needs my help, He'll ask.

THE LIGHT THAT IGNITES

All is well when I let go of that which is not in my control and give it to God, where it belongs. I can then focus on fixing me. But doing this without faith can be heart-wrenching, as I will have to wait for someone else to be awakened. I have to believe that God's plan is far better than any intervention I could possibly offer. All I can do is continue to ignite the flame within my own soul and remain in the light. If I can offer hope and truth from my light, which shines within my own soul, that's the one true gift I can give in order to help God. God gives me this light through my faith and trust in His plan, and I pass that on to you.

No More

How can I have a relationship without compromising myself to be loved and while remaining true to myself? No more sellouts to be loved or accepted and remain true to God and myself. No more settling to enable someone else so they'll love me knowing it's not always about me. No more accepting inappropriate behavior or excuse to make me feel I'm not worthy. I am living in God's love and light and in faith and peace. It's as easy as asking and believing. When I am in need of something that is not in my reach, I can say a prayer; and if it is meant to be, I will receive it. I can control only this: believing that I am worthy of the request, having the wisdom to ask, and having the faith to know all will be as it is meant to be. We have a promise from this prayer: "This day my daily bread, forgive my trespasses, and deliver me from evil." This is something I can pray and believe, and all I have to do is ask.

Listening

When things start falling into place, I can feel a humble gratitude that I am receiving clarity now for what I didn't understand then. I don't always know why things happen, but in my faith, I know there will always be a reason. It may or may not be revealed to me, but either way, I trust that this is in my best interest. Whether or not I get the answers to my questions, I know that God is always listening.

Relationship

I can say I know about someone, but does that characterize a relationship with them? I can say I know about God and believe there's a god, but does that mean I know Him, trust Him, and have faith in Him? Does this mean I have a relationship with Him? He's made seven promises: "I am your strength," "I will never leave you," "I have plans for you to prosper," "I hear your prayers," "I fight for you," "I will give you peace," and "I always love you." Now why wouldn't anyone want to have a relationship with someone who offers these promises? Looks like it's time to trust again.

Red, White, and Blue

I'm not sure why things happen and may never understand, but I have learned to have faith and to trust in God. It's a comfort to know that He loves all of us. God does not have a political affiliation.

Evan Parker (February 16, 2013)

No one will truly understand the complete cycle of life until it's been experienced. Birth, life, and death are experiences we will all encounter, but how we live in the in-between holds our divine purpose. Even if our souls never encounter one another, our mere presence in a thought will have an impact on our lives. Heartbeats are a moment-to-moment occurrence, and until we heal by allowing our brokenness to bring us together, our hearts may harden, not allowing any light to penetrate, so that we may not see one another's pain. Heal by being open to the possibility that the broken pieces of our shattered dreams will reveal an abundance of possibilities to help one another fulfill our purpose.

Living in God's Love

After living most of my life in the shadows, I can now come into the light knowing I am safe and secure and that I am loved, cherished, wanted, and purposeful. In this humble self-proclamation, I know God's love for me far outweighs the bitterness and despair that have dwelled in my heart. Knowing where my true nourishment lies, I can move forward knowing that for the rest of my life, I live, and God loves me.

Faith Is in the Driver's Seat

I can watch an action-packed movie and desensitize myself enough so that I can be entertained without feeling it in my soul. This learned behavior of protection can be a blessing as well as a hindrance when danger is at the front door. Staying abreast of what lurks in the shadows can be counterproductive if I live in fear, but if I remain in faith with hope that all is well, I can remain detached as well as informed. I will let my faith drive my decisions!

What Matters?

Taking inventory of the necessities in times of trouble can cause anxiety that is not necessary and will rob me of my peace. I have to live in faith that for today, in my isolation, I am not alone. I have the comforts of food, water, shelter, and the love of God to sustain me. If this were my last day, what would matter? God will put more on our shoulders than we can endure because He knows our limits, so we will pray to Him to come and join us and guide us. He does show up when He's invited.

Love Is

I know love to be kind, gentle, compassionate, patient, and forgiving. I know how it feels to be disappointed when a promise is broken, yet this does not cancel out the love that has become the foundation of my heart. So I will remain hopeful that in time, we will all heal from the broken promises and begin to know love again as kind, gentle, compassionate, patient, and forgiving. I have faith in us all!

Faith

When I live in fear of the predictions of another's doom and gloom, I can miss my moments of joy, joining them in their destructive path away from faith. What will be will be, and as long as I am diligent in my responsibilities, all will be well. I have faith.

All I Can Do

Not keeping in touch with a loved one who has chosen to cut ties can be a debilitating feeling that aches in my heart. Not knowing how they are doing, all I can do is pray for their well-being and bless their journey. In my prayers, I trust that God's got them, because I know He's got me.

One More Promise Fulfilled

With one more promise fulfilled, the sun rose. With one more promise fulfilled, the birds sang. With one more promise fulfilled, the flower bloomed. With one more promise that God fulfilled, I awoke to a new dawn, took a deep breath, and thanked Him. When I live in faith and keep my hope alive, I know that those I love will be protected in God's light, and that brings me peace. How do I know this? Because He promised!

Tapestry

When I am hurt by another's behavior, I can feel like I am a victim. If I am a stakeholder in their choice and my opinion is not sought, I feel as if my voice is being silenced. This can bring back many memories of feeling invisible, unloved, and unworthy. My behavior is to rant and rage until I am noticed, but all that this does is mute their ears because they do not want to deal or engage in any resolution. This display of fear is a clear sign that I have detoured my faith from God and onto them, believing they have my best interest at heart. I settle back into the "Why me?" syndrome and implode into self-loathing and disappointment, turning my heart toward bitterness and despair.

Then in time, I gain my composure and, once again, look at the life lessons that are unfolding in the situation. Their behavior is about them, but my reaction is about me. I can see God's hand in my life once again bringing me to my knees to trust Him. I may not see the entire picture and the tapestry of my life as whole and complete, but He knows how this one incident, this one thread, will fit perfectly into the final tapestry of my life. I may not see the benefit of this experience, but in faith and hope that He does, I can find peace.

I may never know the why of what has transpired in my life, but either way, I know that God knows what is purposeful and essential for me to reach my destiny. God saved me from something for something, and I know that where He's taken me is where I belong. I have faith, hope, and peace in knowing all is well! He's here, and all I have to do is look for Him and look to Him. I'm not quite sure what it all means when a thought comes into my head that is so beyond my comprehension that I can feel unsettled, but I know I am not meant to understand everything or to understand all at once. Being spoon-fed what I need when I need it is a comfort. God knows better for me than I know for myself. I trust that!

The Truth

How do I know if it's the truth? How do I trust that it's the truth? Knowledge is a gift we share with one another; but sometimes, the truth of the knowledge can be misinterpreted by someone's opinion, interpretation, judgment, or bias. I am the only one responsible for me to seek the truth, to know the truth, and to speak the truth without my opinion, interpretation, judgment, or bias; and that's the truth!

Truth Is Truth

I lived my life in the truth and lies of others to be accepted, but now I have come to a place in the journey of my life where I can know the truth. Not to negate others' belief systems, I am now on my own quest to know what my own truth is. This is a slow process that needs my careful attention so as to replace the lies with the truth. I am in no hurry, as I was in my youth, because I now know I already am loved, cherished, and accepted. This is the beginning and foundation of my truth.

FHT

When a change occurs that is a welcome distraction, it can bring an illation of surprise and excitement. When a change occurs that is not welcome, it can bring fear that what once was may not be again. Faith, hope, and trust can bring peace in uncertain times—faith that God knows best, hope that all will be well, and trust that all will be as it is intended to be. I may not be able to control the distractions of the change that occurs in my life, but I can welcome it with my faith, hope, and trust.

Love Grows

Love grows inside the heart. It is a seed planted by God that will grow outward, toward humanity. Love is the universal emotion that is all positive. It brings joy, peace, hope, and faith. We all need to feel loved, cherished, accepted, appreciated, and validated. Yet when I put all my hopes, dreams, and emotions into seeking love from another, I was left hopeless and defeated, because I engaged in the dance of sacrifice and bartering. Now I know it is not necessary to receive love by bartering and sacrificing, because God has always loved me. It wasn't until I could accept His love that I could truly forgive and find empathy and compassion for another, feeling worthy of allowing God to love me.

Already

I read about salvation, forgiveness, and restoration; and then I asked when. Then I remembered that I was already saved, I was already forgiven, and I was already restored. I just have to be grateful that I am and pray that they will be too. I will not put my life on hold by waiting for that to happen to them, but I will pray for them and be grateful that I am already.

TRUTH SEEKER

How do I really know what the truth is? I lived my life in the shadow of another's interpretation of the truth. I always feared doubting their word, because when I sought an alternative to what they offered, I was threatened with banishment, Consequently, to my own detriment, I stayed in that shadow. I know that love is the opposite of fear, light the opposite of darkness, and truth the opposite of a lie. I know a lie is still a lie even if one hundred people say it is the truth. I just want to know the truth so I will continue to live in the light and in love and so I will have faith that when I ask for the truth, I will get it.

I CHOOSE PEACE

The peacefulness within the soul comes from faith and from trusting that all is well and as God intends it to be as the unrest keeps occurring in the world. Living with inner peace in a chaotic world, staying aligned with the positive while the negative rages on, takes discipline. Not engaging in the negative may require the click of the TV, a holding of the tongue, or polite excusing myself away from a conversation. I have a choice to stay or leave. I choose peace.

LOOK WITHIN

Frustration and impatience can cause me to act before it's appropriate in order to ease my pain or to receive my wanted outcome. Yet never in my life has frustration and impatience had a positive outcome, so I must reinforce my faith and trust in God's timing. I trust in God's timing and have faith that His outcome is in my best interest and my benefit. I must answer this question: What am I not giving to myself that I am looking to others to fill?

Small Steps

What is left after the heart has been broken and all the tears that have been shed are dried in the dust and the lessons of life still occur in spite of being paralyzed? What is left is the sunrise of a new beginning. Like a river, life is fluid and flowing. Although the heart may be broken, it can mend. Although the tears have been absorbed in the dust, more tears will come to cleanse the pain. Although life may seem like it's been put on hold, what has been paralyzed will lead way to new footsteps that will only move toward the light. Walk away from what has been done in the past and take the first small steps into the light. You will not stumble. God's holding your hand.

Redemption

De- means to undo and dispose while *re-* means to try again. In this world of easy access, immediate gratification, and throwaways, it's no wonder that getting rid of something that does not align with one way of thinking is easier and more prevalent today than ever than to look at what works or at what needs to be evaluated. There are people whose behavior will be deemed wrong or evil or unacceptable. There are bad parents, bad siblings, bad teachers, bad doctors, bad service people, and on and on. However, the good outweighs the bad, which leaves hope and faith on the horizon that good conquers evil. So the next time a judgment comes when you wonder how to label a person, think about all your behaviors and wonder if you should be de- or re-. I would like to think that I can be redeemed and forgiven; all it takes is a few more chances to redefine my behavior choices toward good. I have faith and hope that I can achieve redemption.

God's Plan

Most of my life was spent waiting for the outcome that I deemed worthy of my joy. I waited and waited, thinking and hoping and praying that if I just got what I thought I needed, then all would be well. But when the birthday wish blew away with my breath as

I blew out my candle, it didn't change anything. I placed my hopes and dreams on an apology or a kind word or a behavior change. I neglected to place my faith on God's promise that all things would work together for my good. Within my heart and in my soul, I know that the plan that has been laid out for me may be different from what I see, but I will continue to seek the truth as I purge the lies. I trust and have faith in God.

Forsaken No More

Sin separated us from God, but Jesus, or God in the flesh, loved us so much that He was willing to separate Himself from His spiritual God-self to take on our sin as a human sacrifice, washing away our sins. "My God, My God, why have You forsaken me?" were the words Jesus cried as He lay dying on the cross. This was His human self, separated from His God-self due to taking on our sin so that we would no longer be separated from God. He never left me. I left Him. I know what separates me from God; it's me. So I will ask for forgiveness, repent, and try to change my behavior.

Hope

If I don't have faith, then I allow fear to control me. I become anxious and careless as I try to fix the very thing that should be left alone, or I try to hurry through the very thing that needs time. If I don't have faith, then I look for something to fill me that will only lead to disappointment, resentment, and bitterness. If I don't have faith, then I will burden myself with carrying the very thing that is not mine to hold, and my hands will not have the room to receive that which is waiting for me. If I don't have faith, then I harbor that which only brings sadness, and I will not have room for the joy that awaits me. If I don't have faith in what is yet to come, then I cannot be still and feel what is already present. If I don't have faith, then I don't have hope. I have hope!

Sun

Allowing myself to feel sad is a new behavior I have learned to embrace. I used to think having a pity party and getting over something meant I was not allowed to feel what I needed to feel in order to heal. Perhaps this was the way I allowed others to control me and held myself prisoner for so long. Now I allow myself to feel what I need to feel. I nurture my wounds and wait until they shine in my darkened heart. There will always be light!

Inhale

Finding peace with the past is a rite of passage that requires hope, faith, and trust in God. I've heard it asked that if you can change anything, what would you change? I've thought about this, and if I were to change anything, would I still be who I am today, with who I'm with, and where I am? Learning to let go of that which cannot be changed or that will never happen is giving up the dream of what could be in order to make room for what is. I have faith in God that what will be, will be, and I have hope and trust that all will be restored. Living this way takes the burden off my shoulders, so with one more inhale, I gratefully see how blessed I am.

Everyday Blessings

As a child, when I learned something new, I got so excited that I proudly wore my accomplishment as a badge of honor. Learning to ride a bike without training wheels, driving a car, successfully landing on my feet after a cartwheel, or learning to read are just examples of the pride-driven accomplishments where I found my worth. Believing in myself when no one else does is one of the greatest accomplishments of my life. It is only through the grace of God that I am able to trust again. I know we all have a purpose, we are all worthy, and we all are lifelong learners. I am blessed with the ears to hear and the eyes to see the beauty of experiencing something new every day.

Live in Truth

I always wanted acceptance and to be seen for the gift that I was, so I sacrificed who I truly was in order to be a part of something that I was not. It was a difficult journey for me to let go of those I wanted in order to make room for those I needed. It would have been different if they had seen me and accepted our differences instead of still trying to pressure me with threats of abandonment. Although I do want to remain in contact with the others, I find more peace in being alone knowing I am living my truth instead of trying to conform into their lie. I will miss what I want in order to find peace in what I have.

In Need of Guidance

Help me flip all the negative messages in my head to positive messages. Help me silence the dialogue that will never be spoken. Help me let go of the pain of not being loved, understood, heard, or accepted. Help me give my energy to the amazing life I am leading today and not to what happened yesterday or what will happen tomorrow.

I Hear God's Voice

When I become anxious about seeking resolution for an unresolved issue or fear, I find that remaining calm and praying are my only hope. So many times in the past have I acted out in fear, only to cause more problems than I have ever imagined. If I truly have faith, then I know, in my silence, that finding patience will bring the results that I am meant to have. In the whisper, I will hear.

Guidance

When making a decision, I have to weigh the pros and cons of the results, and then I have to deal with the combative voice in my head that tells me I will fail or that it's the wrong thing to do. Once

I remove that voice from my negative list, I can clearly determine if I can live with the consequences of my decision. So I will stop and purge the negative and listen to hear what wisdom I carry to make the decision and the guidance I've been given to live with what I choose. With God's guidance, I can decide what's best for me.

THIS MOMENT

If I waited until everything I wanted came to fruition in order to find peace, joy, and happiness, I would never be alive with what I have now. Wanting more without feeling gratitude for what I have only leaves a void that will never be filled. Finding contentment does not mean I have to be complacent; I can still strive to be better and to do better while I am celebrating who I already have become. I will be grateful for my now as I anticipate what is yet to come, not in any way to be fooled that I will not indeed face adversities. But now I know I don't have to face them alone. I have happiness, joy, and peace in this moment.

MY DECISION

Making a decision that will affect the course of a life takes careful examination of what will happen once the decision is made. This is not a practice that many undertake in a society of immediate gratification. Pondering over a life-changing decision takes time, prayer, obedience, and patience, as it unfolds like a flower budding for the first time. I've made my decision, and I now can live with the results and die with peace and faith.

YOM KIPPUR PRAYER

I pray we see You in the eyes of a child. I pray we hear You in a child's laughter. I pray we feel You in the hug from a child. I pray we know You. I know that when I'm ready, then I will receive what I am meant to have. Until then, in faith and hope, I will enjoy today's sunrise and find joy in everything I see and feel and hear. Thank You.

If You Want to Know

If you want to know what faith feels like, listen to a mother's prayer for a sick child. If you want to know what unconditional love is, watch a mother redirect a child's inappropriate behavior and wipe away that child's tear as the child asks for forgiveness. If you want to know what peace is, stay in love, hope, and faith that all is well. This is God. I didn't give God my soul and believed in Him for His gift of eternal life. I understand that was why He came to earth and died for our sins: to reconnect us where Adam and Eve severed our connection. I gave my soul to Him because He asked. I trust Him, and I want a relationship with Him.

I Am Well

When the dust settles from the windstorm that has rattled the house of my soul, I am well. When I release all that is not mine to hold and give the heavy load that I carry to God, I am well. When I have faith and hope that all is as meant to be and all that I am intended to have will come to me in God's time, I am well. Living in contentment doesn't mean I've given up hope or don't have faith. It means I trust God more than I trust anyone else. He always makes sure I am well.

Endurance in the Promise

I don't know anyone who likes to be in pain, but ask a woman in labor and she will truthfully tell you that going through the pain of labor far outweighs the benefits and the wonderful results in birthing a child. Endurance and perseverance are aspects of our character that show up in times of sorrow and pain. During a difficult time, these tools will deepen my faith since I know that God will use all situations, whether they are painful or joyful, for my benefit and to deepen my relationship with Him. Why do I trust and depend on Him to ease my pain? Because He promised He would, and I trust Him.

We Are All His

Watching others, as others have watched me, or trying to find peace and contentment can be painstaking, but that journey is not as difficult as we make it out to be. We've spent our lives pushing away that which is pure and true in order to experiment with that which is tainted and a lie. Given free will, this is the journey for most of us: that we have to discount the truth to live in the lie, only to discount the lie to live in the truth. Within peace is contentment and the truth that will never ever change: God loves all His children. I am one of those children He loves, and so are you!

Today

Every day, I can struggle with losing sight of all my blessings by wanting what I don't have. I can get agitated at the littlest things, and yet I know that what I have I am meant to have and what is absent is not meant to be there. So I pray and find gratitude in the blessings that are right in front of me, and this helps melt away the sadness of my broken dreams. Knowing life is fluid, like the ever-flowing river of my days, I continue to move, and I can live with hope for tomorrow as I live in my faith of today.

Hear My Prayer

I'm not sure how to pray when I am at a crossroad in my life with a relationship or a decision that needs an answer. I'm not sure how to phrase my request. Do I ask a change for me or a change in the other person or clarity for my decision? Acceptance is the act of receiving and acknowledging. Although there have been times in my life when I had to force acceptance upon my heart, I did so with faith that all was meant to be. I acknowledge that God's will is greater and better than my own. I may not like it, but I will be humble enough to acknowledge it and accept God's will, will be done for good. So I remain silent enough in my thoughts to utter these words: "God, I pray that I will understand your will for me and your guidance for me. Give me the wisdom to succeed in your will for me. Help me!"

Living in Peace

After years of praying, waiting, and hoping, when the prayers were finally answered, I found that life moved on. When I learned to live without those I thought I needed and those I wanted to join me on my journey, I became quiet enough to hear the wind and faithful enough to accept God's will and hopeful enough that whatever prevented them from joy melted like a snowflake as it felt the sun. I will continue to pray for them and live in peace.

Humbled

There are days when I feel I will never get through the pain of my disappointments. I know the strategies that I have in order to remain in peace, yet there are still times when I feel so overwhelmed because there are so many unsettling things around me, so I detach until the windstorm of my life settles back into my humbleness. I remember that I am not in control; God is. I will settle back into my humbleness knowing we are all struggling and all have our own story that we are living and that I'm not the only one feeling this way. I will be humble and ask for guidance, wisdom, and peace; and then I will be still to listen, hear, and have trust in my faith. I am, once again, humbled.

God Knows

It used to hurt more. Every bone in my body ached, every thought I had brought me sadness, and every glimmer of hope faded into a mucky gray. But now my body feels healed, and my thoughts are those of joy, and my hope has been placed within my faith that all is as it is meant to be and all is well. I feel at peace. I know the concept of letting go in faith. I know this in my head, and I pray my heart will receive the message, "Let go, and let God!" I know in my heart that God's promise is true, and having faith in His promise eases the pain of waiting for the restoration of severed relationships that have broken my heart. But then I think that during the time of estrangement, knowing I have changed, how will the restoration of these severed relationships bring joy? So I let go and let God figure this out. How will my heart heal, and if or when these relationships ever rekindle, who will they be with me on my journey? God knows!

Availability

Being blessed with the knowledge of the truth, I can live in peace, even when I am confronted with pain. I can pray that the pain will find its way into the light, and I can hope that the pain will heal in the awakening of the truth, and I can have faith that what I believe will always sustain me in that light. While I wait for the reconciliation of severed relationships, I find peace in knowing that when I ask God and He tells me not now, it is because He's working on it. I trust that. I have found such peace in His promise! The hope and the faith of light and love that God offers are available to all of us.

Practice

Learning a new behavior may be difficult at first, but if discipline and diligence are practiced, it can become second nature. So how do you mend a broken heart? How does one keep practicing this procedure when all there is, is yearning toward restoration? This is when I ask God to heal me and strengthen my faith and help me believe that all is as it is meant to be. In there, I can live in hope as the pain subsides. I practice this daily!

CHAPTER 8

Forgiveness

I Asked God

I lived my life on the promises of another. I believed their truth, leaving my own behind. The expectation that their truth was right for me led me to disappointment, resentment, and judgment of them and of myself. Although another's truth may be their truth, it is not mine. They didn't believe me, but I believe me. They didn't pick me, but I pick me. They didn't apologize, but I forgive them and myself. I am a blessing, I have purpose, and God loves me. We all have our own intimate relationship with God. Their right is no more right for me than mine is right for them. We are all souls on a journey. We are given the opportunity to have a relationship, to learn, or to teach. I know my truth, and I believe in my truth. I asked God why I had to part ways, and he answered, "Because I love you so much that I was protecting you from their drama. You needed to fulfill your purpose. You needed to come home." So I did.

Listen to Receive

Each life lesson and emotional layer may result in pain. Pain is the cleansing of the old, the releasing of more negativity, and the learning of new ways of thinking and reacting. The push-pull can be painful; but ultimately, peace comes from prayer, forgiveness, grace, acceptance, patience, and love. With an open heart comes an open mind and an open soul; that's how God enters. How can God fulfill my prayers and dreams if I do not feel worthy of His precious gifts? It's time to listen so I can receive.

Look but Don't Touch

Looking with your eyes, not with your hands, is a way of teaching someone boundaries. That which is not mine requires permission. Yet in this world of self-gratification and entitlement, how many trespasses have occurred without a "Please," "Thank you," or "I'm sorry. Forgive me"? Too many, so let's get busy.

Forgive and Bless

Watching someone I love fall into darkness may lead me to be frantic and anxious, spewing out only-ifs. Yet my solution for keeping me out of the darkness and in the light is mine only to share if solicited. I have to let go of the burden and my arrogance that I know what's best for anyone. Focusing on me allows my experience to bloom, and if a request is uttered my way, I get to share my blessings. All we can do is pray they find their light as I stay with God in His.

Resentment

Melody Beattie wrote, "It is hardened chunks of anger that blocks the flow of my heart." Louise Hayes wrote, "The body will respond to the soul." I am blessed to know my past and what I have learned from it and who I have become because of it, yet when lessons are not learned from pain and our hearts won't heal, the pain remains. Forgiveness and letting go are the easiest words to roll off my tongue and the hardest to feel in my heart. Retribution, anger, or resentment are all parts of the dance that keeps anger fueling its fire. Yet the minute I rise above, find the compassion, and remember that we are all souls evolving, I can let go and forgive, and I can pray we all heal and love again.

JUDGMENTS

How easy it is to slap on a label just because I see things in a complementary or contradictory way. How easy do we all dismiss that which we do not favor? All is meant to be to draw knowledge from or enhance another's experience. It is sad that so many opportunities are missed because we see things differently. This does not apply to tolerating. It simply means to give love and peace a chance. I'm not implying I hold on to everyone or everything, yet a respectful kindness is warranted when a goodbye is spoken. Letting go, moving on, and releasing that which is not mine to hold is not a judgment. It simply means it isn't fit to assist my journey. It's neither good nor bad, just a, "No, thank you."

RESENTMENT FROM BROKEN PROMISES

Trespasses are interesting actions. Broken promises cause disappointments due to the expectation that actions will match the word. The only one who truly suffers by holding on to that dream to come to pass with an action is me. It takes energy to wait as if the apology would ever erase the pain, yet the pain gets deeper when holding on to that broken promise. Words and actions are our character, but the only one I can control is me by walking my talk and reacting when another doesn't.

UNKNOWN

Melody Beattie wrote, "The pain was necessary to know the truth but I don't have to keep the pain alive to keep the truth alive." I thought that if I didn't relive the pain and hold on to it, then those who hurt me wouldn't see what they did, and my suffering would have been for nothing. Now my clarity tells me to stop defining myself by what was done to me by those who hurt me and to love myself and validate my existence from my center out. I no longer resent them, and I pray that what's broken in each of us will reconnect our holy pieces. Forgiveness comes when I can give up hope that the past could have been different. I know that I can't change it, yet through the acceptance of what was, I know all is meant to be. I honor the experience that has made me the person I've become.

RELEASE

Forgiving someone doesn't mean condoning his or her behavior. It doesn't mean forgetting how they've hurt me or giving that person permission to continue their behavior. Forgiving someone means making peace with what happened. It means acknowledging my wound, giving myself permission to feel the pain, and recognizing that the pain no longer serves me. It means letting go of the hurt and resentment so that I can heal and move on. The challenge is to silence the mind. In the disconnecting and going within, compassion, grace, forgiveness, and love connect us. I do not have to lose myself anymore. Forgiveness does not invite the person to continue their behavior. It releases the other person's hold on me and sets them free to walk a separate path from mine. While releasing my anger and resentments, I will continue to walk my path.

MY TRUTH AND AFFIRMATION

What kept me from forgiving was the feeling that all I had been through would evaporate if I didn't relive it. I thought that if those who hurt me didn't see or own what they had done, then my suffering was for nothing. But the ripples from a stone thrown into the pond of my life vanished. I was left with opening my hardened heart to release the debris that settled there. This led me to stop being defined by those who had hurt me. I needed to love, value and validate my own worth, live in my own truth, and use my own voice. I didn't need to keep this wound open as perpetual evidence. I now have exchanged my resentment and being a victim for becoming victorious. I truly am a gift from God. I have a purpose for my existence, which is only defined by God and myself.

LET LOVE

There will come a time when all is said and done, when all the transgressions are addressed, and when all the apologies have been spoken that we'll see that all is left is love. If allowed, love can melt anger and despair into understanding and compassion. Love can melt fear into faith and judgment into acceptance. Love can melt the burden of control into a life where God is.

If I allow my past to dictate my present, then I will still be waiting to be validated by another, waiting for someone to tell me my worth, and waiting to be loved and accepted, still seeking another's approval. If I got all the apologies; spoke all my regrets; asked for forgiveness; received compassion, empathy, and acceptance; and felt worthy of living my life and if all my fears melted into love, then how would I feel, and how would I live? What is my greatest fear if I just let love in?

OVERLOOK

"I walked away because you were too busy finding faults with me, while I was too busy overlooking yours." How humbling is it for me to think that I have forgiven while others still receive my resentment in a passive-aggressive manner? How arrogant is it of me to think that I have overlooked another's hurts while I'm holding on to that hurt for revenge? If they change, will I be happy? Where does my true nourishment lie? How can I expect another to fulfill my needs if I don't accept what they are offering? What they offer is perhaps all they have to give, so shaming or blaming them into showing up the way I need and want them to will never bring peace. It's time to see what I'm missing.

I Matter Too

Having survived all my years of caretaking at the expense of myself, I can humbly say, this is not mine. It does not mean I don't have compassion. It simply means that I finally know that I matter too. I waited decades for apologies that never came and for my past to have a different ending, but this only prolonged my pain and kept me hostage in my self-made prison. I know I no longer need to wait until everything is perfect before I breathe. I have learned to live amid the turmoil and unrest in the world, but now I can find refuge in knowing I have a peaceful place to land.

No Need to Hurry

When I feel I am well on my way to forgiving myself and when I chose to react when I am hurt, I can feel the anxiousness to put it all behind me before I completely drill it down so that I don't need to keep coming back to it as a weapon. I may use the information that I've gathered from the lesson as a reference point, but if I don't fully feel the hurt from the pain I've sustained, my disappointment may morph into resentment. If I rush and hurry into it without exploring its fullness, I can find myself repeating the same lesson. I will no longer hurry through the journey, for the healing will be there when I'm ready.

Behavior Change

It's so easy to accuse someone of making me upset, angry, or sad. It's so easy to blame-shift my unhappiness onto the behavior choices of another. "You made me feel this way"—this is the expectation, that my way is the right way and that all should conform. But expectations come from a lack of faith, believing instead that what I think I need or know better for myself is worth fighting for. If I scream loud enough, then I will be seen, and I will get what I want. And if I don't get it, then instead of knowing it's not what's best for me, it's not my time, or there is a life lesson in the decision, I feel disappointed and become judgmental and resentful. I then spew all this onto another and make them at fault.

This is not a behavior I am proud of, but this is a testimonial. I, too, am who I accuse others to be. I harbor resentment, close my heart, stop communicating, and stop wanting to collaborate; and I walk away from being a partner, friend, or lover. I know it is not all about me, but in this humbling moment, it is! So I ask for forgiveness, and I begin again. I begin to have faith and release expectations. I keep an open heart, open mind, and open hand. I listen without judgment and communicate my needs without demanding. I love without expecting, and I am a friend without giving solicited advice. I collaborate with patience and an open mind to invite their vision into mine. I become the person I want in my life. I do unto others as I would have them do unto me, and even if they don't, I will!

Melt

I used to think that if I held on to my pain long enough, then the person who hurt me would apologize, and it would heal me. I gave so much power to another as if they held my happiness in their hands. Actually, that was exactly what I allowed them to do. Nelson Mandela said, "Resentment is like drinking poison and then hoping it will kill your enemies." I am now grateful to open my hardened heart to forgive trespasses that left me without faith when I dwelled on my expectations, resulting in disappointment, judgment, and resentment.

Steps toward Restoration

Asking for forgiveness is the behavior that leads toward repenting the trespass. When I remain connected to my faith, it dissolves resentment, judgmet, and disappointment from unmet expectations. I can then look at forgiveness and move toward restoration and healing. This can only occur if the behavior is discussed and if the person owns the behavior and changes it. And then healing can occur.

Forgiveness

Learning to forgive requires a deep conversation to explore what behavior needs to be forgiven. When asking for forgiveness, it requires the behavior to change. Learning to forgive myself has been the greatest challenge. I acted as if my transgressions were unforgivable, so I kept myself imprisoned thinking I was not worthy of forgiveness while I was being asked to forgive others and to get over it. I am aware of my word and deed and try to be my best self so I can forgive and keep my behavior in check. Others' behavior is not in my control, so I no longer get stuck waiting for them to change but rather accept things as they are. It's difficult for me to forgive if the behavior still continues, so now all I do is offer a prayer that the behavior will change so I can trust again. I can forgive, detach, and trust myself.

Forgive One More Time

Forgiveness is releasing the sadness and finding gratitude for the life experience and the lessons learned. Tears are the best words the heart can't speak. We all have a journey, and our path is our own and is unique to us. If I was once on someone's path on their journey and I am no longer there, I won't take it personally. Everyone is in one another's lives for a reason, such as a moment to help that person evolve. As others are in mine, so am I in theirs. I detach in love, thanking them for the life lesson so I can go out and practice what I have learned. This is where grace and forgiveness occur. There is always a gift waiting once the ache, fear, and greed settle.

Continue to Forgive

When behaviors are hurtful and ignored and the person acts as if the trespass never occurred, this can be troublesome. As I try to forgive with compassion in my heart, the behavior may continue because the person may think that with my forgiveness, I am enabling that behavior to continue. There is no healing without dealing with the conflict that may ensue. Trust will not develop if the behavior does not change. And so with this impasse, I let go, and I cautiously live my life. When in the midst of trying to heal my broken heart due to the failure of an action, I can let go of my need to have it my way and depend on God's way. All will turn out as He wants it to be for my own well-being.

Keep Forgiving

I've been struggling with forgiveness, thinking that it will exonerate the other person or myself of inappropriate choices. I found I could easily forgive another but realized I kept setting myself up for the same hurt if a behavior change was not presented. I only have the power to change my own behavior, and that is how I can forgive myself. I can look for restitution if need be as well as resolution and reconciliation with that person, but a behavior has to change. "Father forgive them for they know not what they do" are words of encouragement that prove that change can occur. I no longer expect anything, because this turns me away from my faith. I know God's will is the best for me. With unmet expectations, I feel resentment, disappointment, and judgment. I forgive to heal myself and take back all the energy I am wasting on thinking that their behavior change will enrich my life or make me happy. "It is finished" means I am willing to let go and forgive, but I can remain cautious as I regain my trust.

One More Time

One more time, I am approached by the lesson of looking to others to have my back and defend my honor or to look to others to agree with me knowing there will be conflict when I do not have these needs met. This is a behavior I have yet to master. I may feel betrayed or abandoned. In the end, not everyone will have my back, defend my honor, or agree with me; but I will. When my combative mind settles down and my bruised heart begins to heal, I can forgive since it is usually one-sided and they have not given me another thought. Holding on to this resentment will only hurt me and consume me with thoughts of bitterness, keeping me in a prison of pain. The only thing I can control is how I choose to feel, think, and act and pick my battles. I will "forgive them for they know not what they do," and if they do know, then that is about them, not me.

APOLOGY

I think it's ironic how a relationship can heal, but even after apologies have been exchanged and forgiveness is developing, the behavior may still not change. It's almost as if the definition of an apology gives way to the same behavior, and all is as it was before. Trust must be rebuilt, and the only way that will happen is if the words match the actions. I am very cautious when seeing how the words "I'm sorry" develop into a more loving relationship. I will look at the behavior that warrants an apology and change it to move us forward. I hope you'll do the same so that the words "I love you" matter.

THE JUDGE IN THE MIRROR

Releasing judgments toward healing requires that all masks be removed, all lies become a spoken truth, and all behaviors change toward the goal of restoration with full disclosure and 100 percent humbleness to ask for forgiveness. Having become a master victim and proficient in the game of blame-shifting, the hardest behavior I had to look at and justify was mine, because I was the judge in the mirror. It was so much easier to point a finger so as not to be accountable with my feelings of disappointment and anger and so I could stay with resentment and retribution. I was the only one who suffered, because I was choosing behaviors that did not compliment my truth. Now having begun the journey into forgiveness, I can comfortably say, "I am sorry, and I am learning, so please be patient as I am arriving." I say this to others and to the judge in the mirror.

SELF-INFLICTED

I have identified a place where I have been judgmental and hard on myself. I now look at myself with a compassionate eye. What I say to others in hard and difficult times, I now say to myself with the same compassion. I can trust that I will have everything I need. I am never intended to carry all the supplies I need at one time; the burden would be too heavy. I will have what I need when I need it. When I send messages, I make sure they are pure and don't contradict themselves. This will allow others and myself to keep our voice and know that our truth is moving toward a healthy relationship without manipulating outcomes.

So often through my compassion and forgiveness for others, I lose myself or cut others off to preserve myself. But compassion is a deeper feeling that waits beyond the tension of choosing sides. Compassion, in practice, does not require me to give up the truth of what I feel or the truth of my reality. Nor does it allow me to minimize the humanity of those to have hurt me. Rather I ask myself enough that I can stay open to the truth of others even when their truth or their inability to live up to their own truth has hurt me. I need to tap into me and remain God centered. I am not a pebble in anyone's shoes. I need to break things down in order to get them out. I need to let the cold thaw, let the warmth in and break and crack the hardness so the light may enter.

FAMILY

How fragile life is, yet watching the news or hearing a statistical number can harden the heart or desensitize and numb the spirit. Yet it's amazing how self-pity and anger can absorb compassion and empathy in a beat of the heart by receiving a text, phone call, or email from a loved who is sharing their pain and loss. I pray we can all feel the pain of another's loss without the need to find retribution or retaliation. I pray we all find peace and treat one another as if that life is a member of our own biological family. I pray we all heal.

A Child's Mind

When an adult's lie becomes a child's truth, trust shatters, yet there's always hope on the horizon for a new day. The pain of my yesterdays has paved the way for today, and the expectation that it will only get better gives hope for what's around the corner. With these rose-colored glasses, the new dawn becomes alive with ultimate possibilities. But the utterance of one unkind word can cause me to spiral into the abyss and can darken the light that awaits. In these moments of hurt, I wrap myself in the love that I know already exists inside of me and believe that what is transpiring outside of me will only infiltrate my peace if I allow it. With a smile and a gentle good-bye, I turn back into the love that is within and go about my day in peace, exploring the newness of the moment in my child's mind.

Notable Quotes about Forgiveness

- Forgiveness is the letting go of resentment, disappointments, and judgments. I value my serenity over my desire for revenge. I release my resentment knowing we are all on a spiritual journey and seek compassion and empathy.
- Communion = a co-union.
- Atonement = at-one-ment.
- Recreation = recreate.
- Authority = author it right.
- Listen to hear, and hear to listen; eyes to see, and see with eyes.
- Forgiveness doesn't build walls; it builds boundaries.
- My mind is consistently creating fears to hold on to not because I'm afraid to admit the extent of my hatred, but because I am afraid to admit the extent of my love.
- Prayer is my request to God. Meditation is hearing His answer.
- Outer world = mirror.
- Inner world = magnetic force that draws us and that we need to evolve.

- Forgiveness is when I stop giving my power to or identifying myself with the suffering that has been caused. It is when I no longer give the pain any energy to fester. Suffering comes from suffering.
- Who before I do = Who am I before what I do? Who am I in the midst of what I'm doing?
- Why before what = Why am I doing what I'm doing, and what is my motive?
- "We are asked to know ourselves enough that we can stay open to the truth of others, even when their truth or their inability to live up to their truth has hurt us. Tragedy stays alive by feeling what's been done to us, while peace comes alive by living with the results." We are all souls on a journey.
- The obstacles in my path can become gateways to new beginnings.

CHAPTER 9

I Am

I Will Learn

I used to think that if I were happy in a moment, then I could freeze it and remain in that bliss. But I know that life is as fluid as a river and flows with new experiences, some painful and others joyful. I am also learning that I don't need to be drowning in the river of life to learn. There are many life lessons and opportunities in all experiences. I can learn in the calm flow as easily as I can learn in the roaring tides. It's my choice. Either way, I will learn.

Not Mine to Rescue

So many times in my life, I took on someone else's responsibility to resolve an issue as if it was mine to fix. I became a warrior to rescue them, and I wore this suit like an armor, always making sure that no matter what, the person I was assisting would be so grateful that they would realize they couldn't live without me. I was so afraid to say no and that they would leave. I would do or say anything to be loved. In this insurance policy that I concocted, I lost my voice and my truth, assimilating myself into their story. Then I began to see my worth and began to say no, and in fact, they did leave. They left, which, in turn, helped me regain my voice and live in my truth. With or without them, I know who I am. I live in that truth now, and having rescued the only person I am responsible for, I now see me.

My Life with Me

I have been practicing letting go to see the very best in every situation, such as when I am triggered with a past transgression or a broken dream that did not come to fruition. When I encounter a person from my past and I see that they are still stuck in the same behavior that I've moved on from, I become disheartened that my hopes for reconciliation are once again dismissed. I pray for them, I bless them, and at times, I find myself immersed in them, once again leaving me out of the equation.

Attempting to get a life without them was one of my most difficult challenges since they defined my life. I am once again reminded that I have a life with or without their presence. I have worth with or without their validation. I am a blessing and I am purposeful with or without them knowing me for the woman and soul that I am now. I will continue to pray that they can face their fears and heal in God's love and light, but until they do, I am reminded that I, too, deserve the exact prayer that I am blessing them with. We may not be ready to have a relationship, if ever, but until then, I have a life with me.

Already There

What I need is already in me. I am my best teacher, and I have my best interest at heart. My intuition is tuned into my own soul. My mind penetrates the depths of me. No one can tell me who I am; my soul knows. God is my anchor. I am capable of knowing and learning what I need for happiness with my own faculties when I trust my teacher within.

I Know

I spent the major portion of my life either looking for another for validation or defending my truth. If I just fulfilled that one more request, then I would be loved. If I just screamed loud enough or stood my ground one more time, then I would be believed and deemed trustworthy. Now it just doesn't matter if I am believed or accepted. I know my truth even if another is lying about me. I know my worth even if another has abandoned me. I don't engage in that behavior anymore. What's the point? What's the goal if I do? People will believe what they choose to believe, and people will embrace or leave. Either way, I know who I am.

Allowing the Good In

I've spent many years opening and closing the door of my heart to loved ones or friendships. I've spent many years drowning in the toxicity of my warped belief system, giving my power to believing unworthiness. I've spent too much precious time giving away my energy to those who have moved on without me. I still struggle with the contradiction of good versus evil, but I now believe in the positive more than I do in the negative. Allowing the good in helps me see my worthiness and purpose to fulfill my destiny. We all have worth and deserve to be loved.

I Know My Name

I have watched my shift, and it is so subtle and simple. All of what I already know is peeling open; the layers of my flower petals are exposing all that I need to know in this point in time. Control, anger, and reaction to fear are all the behaviors I have in me that I am now healing from and that are becoming positive. I am able to feel it, and I see me. I am able, with free will and choice, to be the spirit I am meant to be—positive, loving, and forgiving. I am setting boundaries with my no, and even though I long for those whom I have set boundaries with and I want them to reach out and ask for forgiveness, I am still being my best, true self to God.

I miss them every day. I think of how I want our relationship to be, but I accept how it is. This is God's plan. I found myself by saying no to them. I found my voice and trusted my intuition because I stopped listening to them. I thought they knew better for me than I knew for myself. I love, honor, cherish, and believe in me more than their definition of who I should be. I know better for me than anyone does. I know I am worthy, and I am a blessing.

FROZEN IN TIME

Look at class pictures throughout your lifetime; that's where we are frozen in time. These memories that usually come with a smile are the one thing we cannot change. We are forever frozen in time with a smile on our face and with love and hope in our hearts. Change can be a welcome gift or a fearful foe, but in the end, the results are usually to benefit our growth. When I think back now, I am reminded of the joyful times that have brought purpose to my life. No longer feeling shame, I can view the photographs of my life with warmth, welcoming compassion, and empathy and with a slight chuckle for our hair and clothes. I have lived a wonderful life; just look at the pictures.

SCREAMS

I've finally looked over my ego's need to scream to have a voice. I've finally let go of my ego's need to control the materialism in my life. My materialistic items are an expression of my soul's happiness; it's a tapestry that defines my soul's celebration. I decorate and surround myself with the items that bring me joy. They do not define me. That's my ego, not me. I'm grateful to have let go of this, and now I come back to my soul's journey to love and be loved and to surround myself emotionally and physically with the positive.

WHAT MATTERS AT THE END

As I reflect on my life and look at my accomplishments and challenges, I see that each holds a time in my life when so much attention was given to get what I wanted. Now I can hardly remember what was so important that it held so much power to complete me. What

293

really matters is not what I got but how enhanced my journey is to evolve my soul. Money is nice to have for security, and I surround myself with things that bring me pleasure, but I can't take them with me. How I choose to enjoy my days will only depend on how I choose what completes me. What really matters as I take my last breath? Who I am and who I want to be is not about them, just back to me.

What Matters

With my last breath, as my heart beats its last heartbeat, what will I be grateful for? I am a blessing. I've lived a purposeful life of helping others and continuing to be hungry to understand. I have an amazing gift to forgive, I see life through rose-colored lens, and I want everyone to get along and to be kind to one another. I am grateful to have loved and to have felt the love of others. I've been blessed to carry another's life in my body and on my shoulders. I have lived with love, hope, faith, compassion, empathy, and understanding in my heart. I've been blessed with comforts, and I know I am loved.

The True Truth

We are all an accumulation of every life lesson we have ever encountered. Every person we have met has left their footprint on us, whether we have chosen to believe their message, incorporate their knowledge into our database, and become what they have presented to us. Ultimately, there is a truth to our being, the truth of our truth. This is our pure, authentic self as defined by God; and we know down to our core that no matter what words are spoken and no matter what action is taken, we know we have purpose, we know we are light, we know we are a blessing, and we know we are love.

First Connection

The umbilical cord is the first connection where the grace of God first touches us; our skin is transparent and soft, not yet worn from life. The hardening of my skin and of the shield that I've put on to protect my transparency is now shedding, and I'm reverting to the uncovered, original center, the umbilical center, so that once again my skin is becoming thin and transparent. God can see my cord, and now I am revisiting my cord, my connection to God.

NOTHING TO PROVE

When called a liar, the truth has to be articulated, and evidence has to support or negate the allegation. When one knows their truth, it just is. A butterfly does not have to prove its beauty, a baby does not have to prove his or her innocence, and a flower does not have to prove its fragrance. When one knows deep in their core, then it just is, and no proof is needed. It's taken me decades to truly know my truth, and now finally, I am letting go of my need to prove my truth. "The pain was necessary to know the truth but we don't have to keep the pain alive to keep the truth alive." The pain was the fire that burned away the lies for me to live in my truth.

FULL CIRCLE

I am grateful to be blessed and to be worthy of all the life lessons, experiences, and opportunities that have helped my soul evolved. I feel as if I am coming full circle, back to the self I knew I was and now am. I am gradually feeling the release knowing I can't do anything about my past and accepting that what was is done. I cannot change anyone but myself. Detaching from relationships and from those who are still sad, who are in the darkness, or who think they can treat me the same way has been painful yet healing. I am gradually letting go of those who needed me to be someone else when I was with them. I am grateful to have my voice, to know my truth, and to be my best, true, positive, spiritual, authentic self.

MY TRUTH

Caring, considerate, loving, compassionate, empathetic, patient, forgiving, attentive, accepting, appreciative, kind, trustworthy, respectful, responsible, generous, and humorous are the attributes that make me genuine and authentic in God's eyes. These attributes are my God-given gifts, which I have to share with others with unconditional kindness. I have shown up as a daughter of God, a wife, a sister, a mother, a teacher, a mentor, a writer, a painter, a walker, a dancer, a reader, a hiker, a camper, and a pet owner. These are how I choose to express my positive, authentic self.

Home in My Heart

"Home Is where the Heart Is" was a plaque that hung in my mother's kitchen, but the saying goes deeper for me. I am home in my soul because I know my truth and purpose. I am home in my body, and I nourish and cherish it because it houses my soul. I am home in my mind, and I know who I am. I know God. I am blessed to have taken this journey with the many addresses for my body and mind knowing the purity of my soul. I am humbled to have been able to experience and revisit where I started and to look at the contradictions, now knowing that where I belong and where I've landed are where I am in peace and where I am meant to be.

My Inner Voice

Today I will trust my own heart. The clear message that whispers within me has more to tell me than a thousand voices. I have God within me who knows what is best for me. There's a part of me that sees the whole picture and knows how it all fits together. My inner voice may come in the form of a strong sense, a pull from within, a gut feeling or a quiet knowing which equals my God-voice. However my inner voice speaks to me today, I will learn to pay attention. In my heart, I know what is going on. Though I was conditioned from childhood to listen to others, today, I recognize that it is deeply important for me to hear what God is saying from within. I will trust my inner voice. I'll control what I can control, that being how I react to a situation. I will find happiness within my story.

I Am Who God Intended Me to Be

I have learned to never waste my time trying to explain who I am to people who are committed to misunderstanding me. Some people won't love me no matter what I do, and some people won't stop loving me regardless of what I do. I choose to go to where the love is. When I was younger, I used to wish I would fit in; I'm glad I didn't get my wish. Nothing hurts a good soul and a kind heart more than to live among people who won't try to understand or who can't see the blessing. I know I am a blessing. I know I am worthy. I am meant to live a life filled with abundance. As the Talmud reads, "God will not judge me for not being Moses-like, God will be disappointed that I was not being who He intended me to be." I have only one obligation; to be completely who I am. I altered who I was to be accepted by others as if they knew who I should be better than I knew for myself. Even if no one loves me, I am lovable; even if no one hears me, I have a voice; and even if no one believes in me, I have a truth. Even if I am no one, I still am. Today, I know.

Cure Me

When I began my recovery, I thought that an acknowledgment and a few words would cure me and that I would be the person God intended me to be before the abuse. Now I know that the detours, tears, and fears are all a part of who I am meant to be today. This journey called my life can be described as joyful, peaceful, loving, forgiving, full of contentment, understanding, faithful, full of trust, and becoming who God intends me to be. I've learned to embrace my contradictions.

Magic and Miracles

When I was young, I realized I was a child of God, as we all are. I truly believed in magic and miracles. I saw nature from the eyes of a child. My laughter came from the depths of my soul as I danced into my life. When an adult's lie became my truth and when another's words became more real to me than my own intuition and my God-voice, I lost my way; this abyss became my home. And then the contradictions came into light. The words that harbored pain and hurt found their opposition, and the light began to shine again. I am thankful for the journey of my life dance and to be brought back to the eyes of my child, believing once again in miracles.

The Plaque

Growing up, a plaque always hung in the kitchen: "Home Is where the Heart Is." Not fully understanding this concept, year after year, I kept getting away from my heart, searching for its proper home. I forged ahead, yet it never did find the perfect fit until I came home to God. Since I knew my mother was my original home, I searched for that warmth, safety, security, and love; but I could not find where I belonged. From the origin of my soul, with my first heartbeat, I always belonged to God, for Him breathing life into me was where I first knew Him as home. I am home.

Rewind

As I rewind the story of my life in my mind's eye, I can see how the joy, the struggle, the growth, the denial, and the completeness called me. How strong and resilient I am to have endured and conquered; how blessed I am that even though an adult's lie was my truth, which consequently silenced my voice and confused my truth, I did prevail to become who God always intended me to be. So as I rewind and celebrate the movie of my life, I know we are all blessings. We are souls on an evolutionary journey, living our story to become and believe who we are meant to be.

I Still Am

In my silent, quiet reflection, I still am. After adversities, life lessons, experiences, and multiple opportunities, I still am who I've always been. There are no more masks and costumes that define what others think I should look like, and although alone and at times lonely, I would rather be who I am than who they think I should be.

THE DANCE

Interesting thing about birthdays is, it's the celebration of one's existence and one's life journeys in the space and time housed in the body, the temple of our soul. Being mind, body, and soul, sometimes, the dance is not always easy; we're coordinating a three-step movement, prioritizing who should lead—the mind, the body, or the soul? And then someone else invites us to join in their dance, and we forget to show up for our own dance. It becomes a life journey filled with backsteps, sidesteps, stumbles, and falls. Once on our feet again, we realize we need to show up and learn our own dance before we engage in another's. I am my own partner first with God.

UNDERSTANDING

To drill down until I completely understand has been one of my negative and positive interventions. I knew God since our visit when I was five years old, but I never understood why love had so many messages and faces. I never understood why pain had to rip at the very fiber of my soul, only to encourage me to wear a mask and hide my true self. What I have come to understand is that I may never understand everything, and this not knowing has deepened my faith and has brought deeper meaning to the message I got when I was five years old: that all is well and that God is with me and that He loves me.

THE FOOTPRINTS OF MY LIFE

As I reflect on my life and all the talking I did, how much did I really walk with honorable intentions to do the right thing? My initial, negative reactions usually got the best of me, and as I began to be aware of my initial thoughts, I started flipping from the negative to the positive. I became aware of the footprints of my life that I was leaving.

When one speaks of faith and trust, walking that talk should be an assumption that it will be internalized into deeds. Having released the burdens that are not mine, I now release my need to control my what-ifs and move into trusting that God's plan is playing out for me and all of us so that we may evolve. I continue to have faith that He knows best. I am blessed He's got me in His hands and in His heart.

WALKING MY TALK

As I reflect on this journey of recovering and uncovering all that has brought me down, I am healing and delving into the darkness to bring it all to light to heal. Walking my talk has been one of my goals on my soul's journey. Knowing myself before my mask hid my authentic self gave me the goal to live in that truth. My expectations that others would fulfill their words with actions became one of my greatest downfalls. My only-if led me into the darkness of being fulfilled by another, yet now in the light, I still hope and pray that walking the talk will be everyone's goal. Knowing I can trust myself to walk my talk for and with God is enough.

I USED TO THINK

I used to think that if I was just good enough to be loved, I would be loved. I used to think that if I prayed hard enough, then I would have my prayers answered. I used to think that if I was good, then everyone would be good. I now think I am love, I am enough, and we are all good despite our struggles. When someone's choice hurts another, a conversation from love can heal. How much time is given to waiting? Is this my struggle? Letting go of waiting and moving forward without brings a deeper comfort in knowing within. I know who I am, and I bless all those who have helped me arrive. In my aloneness, I am my and God's blessing.

A Do-Over

If I could get a redo, would I take it? If I could sidestep all the pain in the experiences that helped me arrive, would I? The fact is that this life journey is still resulting in growth, sometimes joyful, sometimes painful. Would I replace anything? No! I am because of all my experiences, the joyful and painful. I am because of the multiple opportunities from God that allowed me to stumble and sometimes fall, only to be helped up again so that I am able and willing to continue this life journey. I am blessed for all my experiences and for the other souls that have helped me by drifting through my journey to help me arrive. Thank you.

What Is Best for Me

I have looked at the problems I have encountered and given so much of my energy to. Now I've learned to focus on the solution. This way, I attract what I want. I'm grateful for all that I have been given in my life. At times, I let the problem rule my head. Someone would say something negative, and I would give it so much of my power as if they knew me or what was best for me. I may not always be in sync with others, but that does not make me wrong. I know what's best for me. I am aware of the situations I am in and choose the behavior I think will complement the best outcome for me; no one does that for me. I am true to myself. I have a voice.

Gratitude

Gratitude is being grateful and seeing all that I have accomplished, all that I've healed from, and all the experiences and opportunities that have helped my soul evolve. Having been reminded I am a soul on a human journey, I've had countless opportunities to move from judgment to compassion, darkness to light, resentment to forgiveness, control to faith, and depletion to trust. I am grateful.

Already Home

So I asked, "Why?" and God answered, "Because I was protecting you from the drama. You needed to fulfill your purpose. You needed to come home." I came home, and when they came back, I had already filled myself with God's love so that the void that they had left was already replaced. And then I said, "Why not me?"

Who Am I?

Without the labels and restraints that I allowed others to place on me and with the drama and stories I got caught up in like a tornado, I searched for me in other people's definitions of who I should be. I lived to serve them and to be loved. My purpose was to learn to love as much as I wanted to be loved. I was so busy making them feel loved that I forgot to include me, so I asked the question, "Who am I?" With that, I began a relationship with God.

Share Your Story

If I were to tell you my story minute by minute, day by day, year by year, and decade by decade, would I know who I am? I am a product of every choice I have ever made in my reaction to what I chose to do or how I chose to react to what was done to me. What is the source of my energy? Is it a hug or a slap, a smile or a frown, or a loving affirmation or a bullying insult? I found that I had given more energy into the negative energy that I was exposed to and chose to believe. Now I choose to believe we are all souls on an evolutionary journey, here to assist one another, to bring our stories to the table. With the masks off, we can truly see one another as we are. When you're ready, join me for a cup of tea, and let's share our stories.

Authentic versus Mask

When I meet someone for the first time, I have my guard up, not sharing too much information for fear of gossip or judgments.

This social mask is worn to assure my anonymity. When someone comes back into my life or if I begin to be vulnerable with the new friend, this social mask begins to reveal my authenticity. As I begin to share, I also begin to trust. Yet there is that still small, doubtful voice that tells me that I will get hurt again. I live my life on what-ifs and what others say about me. This has kept me hidden behind a mask of fear. I am willing to shed my masks, and I am willing to take the risk of presenting my authentic self. I am also learning how much to share and with whom to share and to remember to ask myself how much emphasis I should put into them before I lose me under a mask.

Who I Am and What Is about Me?

I used to think that I was wrong if I chose a behavior other than someone else's expectations, that if my choices did not align with theirs, I believed their judgment. Their lie became my truth. Ultimately, I lived my life this way, giving all my power to the approval of others. And when I trusted they were right, I shamed myself into thinking I was wrong. Now I am humbled to say I've asked God to forgive my sins and all the unrest I harbor. My shoulders, once tired of carrying the burdens of others, have been released. I am trustworthy; therefore, I trust. I am kind, loving, and caring; therefore, I show love, and I show that I care. I am accepting, compassionate, empathetic, and forgiving; therefore, I act this way. This is who I am. Tell me who you are.

Fleeting Moments

A candle in the wind burns with its vibrant flame one moment, and the next, the smoke carries away the memory of its being. Looking at old pictures of myself, I can recall that fleeting moment when the smile began and then life resumed. I have pleasant and sad memories where life was celebrated in pain that mumbled the happiness. I recall specifics that caused monumental changes in my life's journey, whether helpful or not. I've always seemed to get back on track toward my destiny. Fleeting moments are gifts of affirmations, growth, survival, and just being who I am and destined to be. What are your moments?

What Truly Serves Me?

When I make a mistake that hurts another, I ask them to forgive me. I look at my behavior choices that are made and question how this behavior serves me. When I ask another to forgive me, I then tend to prolong my punishment into self-loathing, feeling that it is one more failure. So again, I question myself. Does this mindset serve me? Hurting others for revenge or to regain my power no more serves me than them doing the same to me. Humbling myself means looking at my choices and changing my behavior that does not serve me. Moving into the evolution of my soul with choices that serve me are behaviors of love and light.

The Core

When a tree is stripped of its bark, soft, pliable wood remains. When the earth is drilled through layers of dirt, water is found. When I remove all the layers of hurt, pain, drama, and victim triggers, what is my core? I am humbled to know that what lies beneath is pure love, joy, and positive love and light. But having carried the pain of my own experiences that I had with others, I feel the conflict of letting it all go. But when I have all these questions answered, my core is all that remains. Will I still be seen without my coat of shame? Will my songs still be heard without parroting the voice of another? Do I need to hold all this drama to feel alive or to participate to belong? Will you feel my presence in the ashes of my broken dreams? Can I continue on this journey emptied of the past?

Irreplaceable

Having been replaced, ignored, and dismissed does not diminish the fact that I am irreplaceable. Rejection and opposition have thwarted me from making a life for myself without another's approval and has helped me get back my voice. Even though I am invisible to some, it does not diminish my being seen. Even though the lies of others have exiled me, it doesn't diminish my voice's ability to be heard as I speak the truth. I am done turning my life over to the expectations of others so I could be loved. Even if I have been dismissed, silenced, ignored, and replaced, I am irreplaceable. I have a purpose. I have the need to be loved, heard, cherished, admired, and celebrated. I have chosen to no longer wear a mask, no longer blend in, so I can be seen. No more being silenced. I can see me, and I can hear me. Do you?

A Cup of Tea

The old saying "Not my cup of tea" has a deep meaning for me. On the surface it is saying no thank you, I choose something else. But also it may mean my choice is right and your choice is wrong. This has sparked many conversations and conflicts. The deeper meaning for me is, we all have a choice. What I choose is right for me and works to enhance my spiritual journey, even if my choice does not align with yours, doesn't make it wrong or evil. Yet in the controlling and manipulative judgment of good and evil, this conflict pulls us on different paths, yet ultimately it doesn't matter. We either journey together or not, but my cup of tea may still be different. Would you like to make time for a cup of tea with me?

Buyer's Remorse

How many times have I made a purchase, a decision, or a move and then later questioned if I did the right thing? How many more times do I need to doubt who I am, what I've earned, how I've lived, or what I've done? Questioning myself can benefit me if I am not sure of a behavior reaction or if it leads me to make sure I've the funds for a purchase. This checking in with myself assures that I have given thought to an outcome. It is after the questioning and the action that I doubt if I've done the right thing. This self-doubt shows me that I don't trust my own power. It is then and there when I feel the weight of my own self-doubt that I need to let go, release the past, and move forward with my heart filled with love and gratitude. I need not sec-ond-guess that I am capable of trusting my own decisions and have faith in God that He is guiding my way. Who I am and where I am now is what is meant to be today.

Knowing My Worth

When a transgression occurred, I focused on feeling my feelings and waiting for the transgressor to own his behavior. Sometimes, I would receive the apology, which helped me move on because I did not feel invisible. Yet when I didn't hear those two words—"I'm sorry"—I would harbor my pain like a warrior, wearing my armor for battle. I then began to participate in the exact transgression that was shown to me. This behavior was how my clan identified rela-tionships. Now my intellectual knowledge on how to be seen and heard comes from within. I need not engage or give my power to a transgression to know my worth.

I Am What I Do

So much of my recovery has been focused on forgiveness of my own transgressions and the trespasses of others. I harbored anger, resentment, and disappointment as if it defined what I did and what was done to me. It was easier for me to believe I deserved that behav-ior rather than feeling the need to constantly sing my song of praise. Now I look back on my experiences and opportunities to evolve as a series of lessons to help me arrive to who I am and what I do now. When I stopped living in the pain and began to live with the pain, I was able to see all of us as souls on a journey. Anger turned into compassion, disappointment turned into gratitude, and resentment melted into forgiveness; and I can now sing my own song of praise and do what I am meant to do.

The Things I Do

The things I focus on and the things I do reflect who I am. I read, so I am learned. I pray, so I am hopeful. I talk to God, so I have faith. I write, so I care enough to pass along my wisdom and share my story. I walk, so I care about my health. I hike in the mountains, so I celebrate the beauty of nature. I watch chick flicks, so I believe in the power of love and happy endings. There have been times when I chose behavior that did not reflect who I was. Living with these contradictions caused pain to others and myself, for I was not presenting myself as authentic. As I lived under a mask, the true me was hidden. Now that I live without a mask, the things I do reflect my best, true self. What do you choose to do?

With One More Puzzle Piece, I'm Almost Complete

If I choose a metaphor, it would be that our lives are millions of heartbeats all placed in one puzzle. I could see the many opportunities and experiences it would take to complete me. I sometimes look past the puzzle piece, only longing for its completion. This is when I lose sight of the gifts and blessings within each piece of my puzzle. I've waited decades to be completed, complemented, and accepted by others, always longing for more. This is where they end, and I begin. I am learning and embracing this knowledge and beginning to flow in my own truth and faith. I know that not each puzzle piece I meet will fit, and if it does, it only enhances me; it does not complete me. I will continue to dance and celebrate each piece of my puzzle that fits or doesn't. Today, I have been given one more puzzle piece, and I am blessed.

Acceptance

When someone or something does not align with my greater good or I just don't see how they will complement me, I say, "Not for me." This declaration does not have to be harsh; it is a simple statement that it will or will not fit me. I can accept that the contradiction or opposite of who I encounter will either complement me or not. It's when the opinions and judgments cause a chain reaction of events that may trigger an old emotion. I may have felt the need to change their opinions so that I would not feel alone. I no longer need their validation or for their opinions to match mine. Misunderstandings do not have to hurt; they can heal. Clarifying conversations usually end a potential conflict, so let's chat.

ME INCLUDED

Sometimes, I can get so caught up in praying for someone or giving the just-right pep talk that I forget those words of wisdom and healing for myself when I am in need. I need to remember to include me.

TESTAMENT OF THE POWER OF CHOICE

Blaming other people for our state of being has led society to be filled with victims, angry souls, and those who refuse to communicate with one another to actually see, hear, and feel another person's soul. We are all a product of those we have met and the choices we have made. We have free will and can decide who we want to be, how we want to act and react, and how we want to show up every day. We do not have to be defined by another's words or acts. We can choose to make a statement of who we are by deciding how we are going to react to any contradiction that does not complement our soul. By owning my own choices and accepting yours, even if they don't align with mine, will allow me to live in peace. What is the testament of your true power?

WHAT PART IS MINE

In conflict, we tend to grab our sword, put on our armor, and prepare for battle. In a courtroom, the defendant always defends and the prosecutor will always prosecute, but to what end do we ask the question, "What part is mine?" I've been on both sides of the fence, victim and conqueror. Neither role has ever felt as if I belonged within that label. So it is in the humbleness of my soul that I lay down my armor and see myself wide open in front of my own eyes to look into my own heart and my own soul and say, "What part is mine?" I then explore who I have to forgive and who I have to ask to forgive me. This is my part.

PRACTICE BEING RESPONSIBLE

It is so very easy to have peace of mind when in my own little zip code. Yet with a few hours in a car or a plane, drama can arrive at the destination and want to pick up where it left off when I left. Having the need to make everyone happy becomes an all-too-familiar burden that triggers so much past hurt that I question my own intentions and wonder if traveling is really worth the conflict and the confrontations. Then I am blessed to have enough faith to come into the reality that this scenario is meant to help me practice what I claim to know. I am not responsible for anyone's happiness. I am not responsible to accommodate everyone's needs to assure their comfort and requests. I am responsible to honor my own truth. I am responsible to honor my own boundaries and to fulfill my purpose. I am responsible for me.

MY LIFE'S MIRROR

Looking for affirmations and acknowledgments, I asked myself this question over and over again: "How much of you do I need in order to see myself?" Having spent decades of giving myself away and being taught that self-love is an ego-driven behavior that is not acceptable, I've then looked to others to acknowledge my talents and to tell me I was worthy of being loved and worthy of being seen. So I continued to become the acrobat that others desired, jumping through hoops and wearing the masks of their choosing. I began to disappear in the words of others, and I began to fail to see my own reflection in my life's mirror because I wasn't living my life; I was living theirs. So I continue to learn, feel, and cry to see myself in the reflection of my own life's mirror. Now I see that I am worthy, whether they know it or not. I am purposeful, whether I am acknowledged or not. I am loved, whether they love me or not. I know I see myself in my life's mirror.

In Good Company

We are not meant to be alone but to be a part of a community. However, there are times when being alone is essential to remember where I am in my relationship with myself. I am then always in good company. I am learning to let go of controlling what is not mine to control. Manipulative controllers raised me, so now I'm trying to change my knowledge that their lie became my truth. I can no more control or manipulate anyone into healing than I want anyone to control me. I can control myself, explore who and how I love, let go of lies, speak my truth with my own voice, and choose how I act and react and what I focus on. I commit myself to my continued self-exploration and healing.

In My Time

"Hurry up and move on" are words that can cause stress if spoken before the time is right to actually move on. Having always needed to fit in and be accepted, I engaged in the "Hurry up and move on" before I was actually ready. I struggled to find my purpose and my worth and for someone to validate my reason to exist. From an early age, we've depended on our adults to love, cherish, protect, and honor us. From an early age, we've believed all the messages we received from the adults who were entrusted to take care of us; but when these adults did not receive love from their elders, they then treated a child the way they were treated. They were disregarded for the gift they were, and then they passed this on to the next generation. It is not until one soul stands up for her beliefs and chooses to believe the blessing she is that she can live in her truth and speak this truth. I am in no hurry. In my time, I will move on.

Follow the Directions

When I am at a crossroad, I may feel so overwhelmed that I begin to second-guess my decisions, not trust myself, and feel like I'm at a stalemate with what to do next or where to go. This is when I need to settle in and allow myself to give all my insecurities a voice. What do I believe about myself that isn't true? What are my obstacles, and what is my fear when facing these obstacles? I have learned that not giving myself processing time and acting on my anxiousness to fix something that may not even be broken can cause more harm than good. I need to relax and inhale my faith knowing that I will get all my answers when I can decipher what questions to ask. I will be led down the right road when I listen for the directions. I will know what to do and where to go when I can be calm and when I can listen and hear.

Live My Life

When I saw someone in pain, I wanted to fix it for them, and so I prayed for their salvation. I confused myself for decades by replacing my wants and needs with theirs and harbored their pain for them so that they would find peace. But in this act of confusion, thinking I was expressing compassion and empathy, I was told to fix it, but I got in God's way. I forgot me and neglected my wants and needs. I encased myself in their pain and neglected what I needed to free myself from this self-inflicted bondage of unrest, insecurity, and victimization that caused so much unrest that I could not escape it. So now when I am confronted with this scenario from others' life story, I can offer solicited wisdom that I have deemed helpful, and I can continue to pray for their pain to heal, but I will not replace my life with theirs. I am living my life and writing my own life story. I hand them back to God and pray they will heal.

Misinformed

When I was led to believe something other than the truth, my first instinct was to panic, and I reacted in a negative way out of fear.

I felt taken for granted and betrayed to the point where I blamed myself for trusting one more time! The huge trigger was that I was unable to trust my judgment of character. But now I see that I am a trusting person and that I walk my talk even if others do not. I am a person of my word; and even if they lie, cheat, bully, or try to manipulate and control, their behavior will not be met with the same from me! That is about them, and that is not who I am! I know my truth, and I know who I am.

Joy in the Ashes of My Sadness

In recovery, we are encouraged to face all our fears and trespasses in order to come to a place of acknowledgment and acceptance, which will eventually melt into peace, understanding, and forgiveness. Yet I have been known to focus on what went wrong rather than on what went right! I can only rewind my past so many times in order to peel back the layers into my soul's core to heal. I rarely visited my happiness because I allowed my sadness to cloud the growth and healing that I had accomplished. Misery is a moment of suffering allowed to become everything. There is so much joy and love to celebrate and that I can find if I look deep enough. I know there is joy in the ashes of my sadness, and I celebrate the me I've come to know, accept, and love.

We Are

After letting go of all that I could not control, I am. After becoming humble enough to ask for forgiveness and to accept forgiveness, I am. After emptying all that was not mine to hold and to become comfortable in living with not knowing what comes next because I burned my script, I am. There is a peace, contentment, and joyful feeling to knowing what is mine and what is yours. As I release you to live your life, I move forward with living mine. We can come together as two to embrace as one and know we are.

I Am

In this moment, God has painted His sunrise tapestry. In this moment, the babies of the world awaken with a stretch, a yawn, and a whimper to say, "I am here." In this moment, our breath enters, filling the body with life, and one exhale exits into the universe to assist in sustaining it. Each moment, as precious as the next, simply state, "I am." So when something disturbs the flow of peace, inhale one more time and say, "I am."

Who Am I without You?

Being surrounded by people who told me who I was, what worth I had, what to think, and how to feel left me filled with deception and lies. It got to the point where my reflection in the mirror was everyone else but me, and my shadow became invisible beneath the weight of someone else. I lived my life on empty promises of being loved and accepted, only to feel depleted and used. But when I became still and started sifting through the baggage in my life, I began to discard all that was not mine to keep. I began hearing the voices that defined me and listened to what was truly true about me. Now empty and void of everything that defined me, I am exploring who I am without you.

I Know Who I Am

Always ready for battle, I used to wear my armor, as I felt the need to defend my honor. I would relinquish all my energy to prove that I was not what they said I was. I would spend countless moments trying to change their minds about me so that I could believe it myself. It is human nature for people to talk, to judge, and to lie. What I can control is not what is said about me but how I choose to live my life in spite of what is said. If someone wants to take another's word without knowing the facts and if they do not want to engage but rather judge my merits on the gossip of others, then that is not about me; it's about them. All I can do is be my true, authentic self and live in the light of this truth. I can spend my energy proving who I am to others or living an honorable life for God and myself. I know who I am.

HOME WITH GOD

Keeping myself empty and open to possibilities has not been an easy task for me. If I weren't filled with someone else's perception or opinion, then what would I have to say, and who would I be? This journey has finally brought me home to myself. I can finally look in the mirror and see my soul. I can listen to my heartbeat and know its rhythm. I can think my own thoughts and know it's my own opinion, and I can look at my life and feel humbled enough to say it is good. I have finally emptied myself enough to welcome the new gifts of positive love and light into my heart and know I am worthy and I am home.

THE JOURNEY

I have gone through many rites of passage. I have completed my schooling. I have experienced being a mother, wife, sister, daughter, and friend. I have felt the joy of success and the pain of defeat, but I have always known I have a purpose. Whether I have been loved or dismissed, I have worth. Whether I have found a place to belong with others or am alone, I have purpose. As I continue to turn the pages of my life, getting close to the end of this journey, I know that I have lived because I have experienced joy and felt pain, I have loved and been loved, and I can look in the mirror and see my soul and know I am.

BEING ME

Fear no longer rules me, so now I can make decisions based on what is best for myself in the presence of God. I no longer wear a mask, which gives me permission to be my authentic self, no longer fearing judgments or listening to others' opinions of who I should be or how I should act. When I can look in the mirror and see my own reflection or walk with another in the sunshine and see my own shadow, I know I am no longer invisible. When I no longer wait for another's words to match their actions to make me happy, I find my own joy in being who I am meant to be by fulfilling my passions. Approval is never satisfying if I have to relinquish who I am to get it, and usually, I will never satisfy everyone, which means I will be on this continuous cycle of seeking others' approval and love. No longer engaging in this behavior, I think this is what it feels like to detach and let go.

The Battle Is Over

I no longer need to fight and scream to be heard because I hear my voice. I no longer need to fight to be seen because I see my reflection. I no longer have to fight to be right because I know my truth. I no longer have to fight anyone else because the only one left is me. I no longer have to battle with myself because I know who I am and who I am meant to be. The ugly reflection of fear and pain is now being replaced with the joyful soul that lives within my eyes. The battle is over.

New Year, New Decade, and New Beginning

I am letting go and allowing hurts, disappointments, and unmet expectations to live in the past, where I no longer need to call on them to defend my honor. I know who I am and who I want to be, and the sadness of broken dreams, which has caused resentment and bitterness, no longer has a place by my side. I am diligent in living my best moments now, and if a past hurt seems to seep its way into my now, I will kindly acknowledge it and send it back where it belongs. I choose to live in these precious, present moments and thank all the experiences and opportunities I have been given to help me be where I am and with who I am meant to be with. I bless all those who have left on their own journey and pray they all find their way home.

I feel so very blessed to know that this journey has been purposeful and rewarding. I have survived abandonment as a child, injustice in adolescence, and infidelity as an adult. I have served others by being a teacher, mother, wife, sister, daughter, and friend. I have been on a journey of healing, and I am no longer a victim. I have found compassion and empathy toward behaviors that I displayed when I was in pain. I no longer cast stones or planks toward others but rather send positive messages through my prayers and actions. I no longer identify myself by what was done to me but rather by who I became because of it. I am loved and blessed.

I Call Myself

I used to hold myself captive by the way someone treated me. I believed they knew what was in my best interest, and I called myself a victim. I used to beat against unopened doors and pleaded to be loved by those who were not available to love even themselves, and I called myself a victim. I used to loath myself and deemed myself unworthy because I made others my god and keeper while all along, they, too, were suffering, and I called myself a victim. No longer am I being defined by another, nor am I knocking on unopened doors or seeking relationships with those who are unavailable, and I am not accepting another's definition of me. I call myself loved and worthy, and I live in peace.

Compliment

When I find myself needing validation and looking toward others to fill me, I need to look within. So many times, I have looked to others to validate my worth, love me, compliment me, or fill my void. This has been a lifelong struggle. Yet I saunter forward to find my purpose and my worth and to be filled within. I know I am loved, worthy, and a blessing; it's just nice to hear it sometimes. So when I need to hear these words, I will look in the mirror and tell myself the truth about myself. I am lovable, I am worthy, I am purposeful, I am precious, I am a blessing, and I am God's child!

No Combat Required

I used to get so defensive when someone questioned my integrity or doubted my truth. I used to become so combative as if what they thought about me or how I was allowing their opinion to define me actually mattered. But in my past, it did matter. I did allow their reaction and judgments to make me doubt myself, my truth, and my integrity until I found myself actually becoming who they were telling me to be. Now I believe in me and know that I live in the truth and that I am a person of integrity. I walk my talk, and there is no need to be defensive, and no combat is required. What they think no longer matters. I know who I am, and if they take the time, they will see me too.

My Creed

I spent decades trying to give everyone what they wanted so as not to disappoint them. I spent decades living everyone else's truth and gave them exactly what they requested so that I would feel worthy and they would love me. But toward the end of my days, I came to realize that I had not been my best, true, authentic self, so I now understand and accept that not everyone will like me. Some may even be disappointed by the choices I make. Not everyone will trust me, but I will never give them a reason not to trust my word, for I will always choose the truth. Not everyone will understand my kindness as a simple gesture but will be suspicious of the giving. Some who claim to love me will leave when I choose to say no or when I disagree with their opinion. However, at the end of my days, I know I am someone you can depend on to speak my truth, walk my talk, respectfully disagree with your opinion, and love you until I die. This is my creed.

Living

After decades of trying to be who you want me to be and finally accepting who you are, I am living. We may not see eye to eye and may disagree, or we may not have much in common, but I am living. I can offer my respect, appreciation, compassion, forgiveness, and empathy; but I will be who I am as you continue to be who you are. We are living.

CHAPTER 10

Judgment

FAITH IN MY ALONENESS

When I am alone and I reflect on where I was and where I've arrived, I realize that being alone is sometimes necessary to hear the still small voice. When trying to understand a situation, it is sometimes necessary to get another's point of view, but only if it's a suggestion. Taking someone's opinion as only a suggestion is part of my life's journey. I do not make it my solution.

It is best to at times have a deep-seated conversation with God in order to figure out what to do next. When I depend too much on someone else, not on God, I'll do what's best for them even though it's not the best for me. When I am confronted with a future situation, I can find myself so absorbed in the future dialogue that I lose sight of my now. This is fear driven by the unknown. The simple prayer, "Thy will be done!" helps me regroup into faith. I will concentrate on my positive reactions and faith. It is all meant to be as God intends, and I trust that. I have faith that in my aloneness, I will get my answers.

TO BE SEEN

It can sometimes seem difficult to look at something that displeases me without judging. How often does a critical thought come to mind, only to be dismissed with an excuse? How often does that judgment block the vision of what is truly in front of me, wanting only to be seen? How often have I blinded myself with a mentality that snuffs out my inner light? By truly humbling myself, I can keep my gaze upon all and everything and still learn to be gentle, to forgive, and to live with the words, "I see you."

SHED THE SKIN

When we look at a newborn, it is so very easy to fall in love with his/her purity and innocence. We can hold this new life in our hands and breathe hope and joy into his/her soul without giving it a second thought. Yet when we greet another, we tend to judge the color of their skin or the clothes they wear. Why is it that we cannot extend the same nonjudgmental gift of love to them that we give to a new life? We become so tainted with society's judgments on race, color, and creed; and we harbor others' prejudices into our souls. The body that houses the soul is all that we see. We all become lost in the abyss of fear that we can't even love ourselves. When we can visually and emotionally shed the skin and the essence of our souls are revealed, then we can all be loved, cherished, and honored. If we can see one another in this light, then the purity of our love will illuminate through us and into God's universe.

WHO I AM

I continue to struggle with keeping my voice because of another's judgments. I keep struggling with the need to defend myself despite knowing I am a trustworthy person when I am called a liar. I continue to let go of others' opinions, judgments, and their definition of who I am supposed to be to continue to love myself and to know I am worthy.

In Front of the Truth

Facing facts can either debilitate or enhance living one's truth. It can be an interpretation or fact. Either way, when one's truth complements another's, there is peace. Yet when the reverse occurs, havoc and disharmony appear. Ultimately, the truth is real and within reach. Judging or giving our opinion on another's truth is not our job. Yet it defines the hierarchy in our life when we give our truth to another to manipulate or when we believe another's truth as our own truth. We have to wonder, who am I, and what is my truth?

Do What I Need to Do

When making a decision, I fear, at times, that I will be judged, and I'm afraid of others' reactions. What may be acceptable to one person may agitate another, so I have learned to do what I want and what I need to do. There will always be judgment, and I will never please everyone. I will live my positive, true, spiritual, purposeful life to my fullest potential to fulfill my destiny and to serve God. That is what I need to do.

Judgment

Who is right and wrong according to whose law? A million times each day, I pass judgment on what I deem right or wrong. How many times have I forsaken myself in a truth, forgetting we are all a story of life who have been blessed with opportunities to learn and teach. Yet if not done my way or another way, the label is applied, and judgment ensues. Who is to say there is only one path, one way, or one choice? In a split second, judgment befalls the act, which in turn is attached to that person, and that very soul on an evolutionary journey is just like me. So the appearance may differ, the behavior may not coincide with mine, and the choice of word and deed may not complement mine; but mine is mine and theirs is theirs, and God is the judge.

Let Go of Judgments

I am grateful that I can forgive trespasses knowing we are all souls on a journey. I am grateful that I can let go of my expectations that result in judgment, disappointment, and resentment. What others do in their life is up to them and God, yet when it hurts me, I feel the pain deeply. I, too, have hurt others, and the one hardest for me to forgive is myself. Yet now that I am striving to be my best, true self, I want others to strive as well, which is an expectation. I have judged, as I have been judged. I have resented, as I have caused resentment. I have been disappointed, as I have been another's disappointment. When another is drawing me into their pain, my reaction must be compassion and empathy as I search for truth and understanding.

My Validation

At times, issues may arise that lead to a disagreement, but the relationship doesn't have to suffer, and this doesn't even have to be an obstacle. I don't have to think like them or even accept the situation if it's not good for me. If I think it's wrong, I don't need the world to agree with me. I have the right to feel this way, and so do they. Relationships don't have to end when we don't see eye to eye. I don't have to compromise my beliefs to be loved. I know my special gifts, and I don't have to relinquish my control or my belief system to be loved. I have the right to voice my opinion, to disagree, to take a stand, and to say no. I am capable of taking this risk knowing not everyone will always agree with me or even like me. Knowing who I am is my validation.

Judge the Journey

It's interesting that when I was at that point in my life when life was starting to make sense, everything else was deemed wrong, negative, or toxic. Then I moved to the next phase of my life, shedding more of what I thought was not good for my evolution, only to uncover something better, something deeper and more profound, that would help me reach my destiny. Once again, I deemed that as inadequate. I judged the stages of my life as less because I was evolving, and now I see those experiences and opportunities as allies, not foes. I see everyone and everything as a blessing instead of something I have to step over or get over. I am grateful for all those experiences and souls that have helped me arrive to be able to face one more layer of who I am destined to be.

Pick My Battles

How many times a day do I find myself judging a person's word or action that does not align with mine? If they do not say or do what I would, does that make them wrong and me right or the opposite? How many times have I engaged in combative conversations to point out our discrepancy? How many times has this done more harm than good? It is when I can decide to speak or not speak or act or not act that I will find peace. I will pick my battles.

Relationship

Being in our mother's womb depicts an ultimate relationship with another being. When we are born, this is the start of who we are within this severed relationship. This is when we begin to learn how to be close to another without losing ourselves. How much of me is within you, and how much of me do I sacrifice to be there? Learning to be who we are within a relationship requires us to know who we are within ourselves. Help me stand when you are falling. Help me keep an open heart and open mind when yours are closed. Help me love when you are being judgmental and lost. Help me see my sins while I see yours. Help me love you, and help me let you love me.

Check In

When I think I know better for myself than God does, I don't. When I think my opinions matter about how someone should act, speak, or dress, they don't. These controlling behaviors and thoughts

323

have kept me in prison most of my life. This learned behavior does not make me happy, bring me joy, or promote peace and compassion. So when I think I know, I'll stop and check. When I think should, I'll stop and check. When I think, then I'll stop and check.

Making Sense

No one is more powerful than another. No one is more beautiful than another. No one is smarter than another. No one is more talented than another. No one is better or worse than another. We are all given special talents to achieve our life's purpose. No one's life journey will be same, although similarities may occur as we connect on our journey, but no one is identical. With that said, even though our choices may have an impact on our stakeholders, no one gets to be the judge. It may make us uncomfortable or bring us joy, but another's choices are theirs to make to fulfill their destiny. We are not to understand everything, yet we are all souls on a journey, and even if our choices hurt others or ourselves, we still are worthy.

Balcony View

Sometimes, I take the balcony view of what is happening before me. It may be a hostile situation that I refuse to partake in, so watching from above can bring me peace of mind as I choose not to engage. I find that when I am drawn into that which is not mine to encounter, I may become biased, and this may lead to unrest, because it is not mine to judge. So I will keep my distance as others work out the situation and say a prayer from the balcony so that they may be covered in love.

Feeling Loved

May you never know what it feels like to be dismissed as if your needs don't matter. We all have a purpose, and we all matter. Being made in the image of God, He sees our possible perfection; and if we allow Him to love us and guide us and if we engage in a relationship with Him, we will feel love. There is purpose in everything we experience and everyone we encounter. May you feel loved.

God's Judgments

Understanding right from wrong requires the truth, because it needs no evidence. It does not require interpretation, judgment, or opinion. The truth never changes; it just is. So when a person has wronged another and broken their body or spirit, the rules and laws of society determine how to deal with these crimes. It's not that I don't care anymore. It's that I now know I'm not responsible for your happiness, peace, and joy. I will continue to love and pray for your healing. I hope you find it and that we'll be able to continue our journey together with joy and in peace. Society takes care of judging the body, and God takes care of judging the soul. This is the truth.

CHAPTER 11

Masks

Why Me?

After decades of wandering to find answers to the question, "Why me?" I came home to the comfortable acknowledgment, "Why not me?" I struggled with self-worth, addictions, low esteem, and self-deprivation caused by listening to others' words that tried to define me. Yet in my silent struggle, despite knowing that the uncomfortable mask I was wearing was theirs, not mine, it took decades to know how blessed I was and to thank all who helped me see that. All is purposeful, always masterminded by God to get me to this point in time. Having shed the masks and the labels and their persona, I now know, as I knew in my silent struggle, who I am, and I'm comfortable with the words, "Why not me?"

Explore without a Mask

I am undoing years of negative survival behavior, where fear, being my initial reaction, warranted wearing a mask. Now no longer wearing a mask, I see, feel, and hear the fear of leaving myself in order to oblige. I am struggling with contradictions of the hooks, yet I am successful in seeing, feeling, and hearing, resulting in staying true to myself. In being alone, I am true to myself. Even as others filter back into my life, I am who I am meant to be.

I have removed the mask that I used wear to get what I needed to feel loved. Having chosen my truth alone rather than living their lies, I learned that no love completed me but God's. Having been so desperate to find my worth in their words, I knew that my worth was within. I thought I was alone, the only one ever to travel this road, but I know now that we are all travelers. I know we must be emptied of that which no longer fits the suitcase of our lives. This leads to not knowing. But how glorious to know He is packing my suitcase.

Live with Not Knowing

To compromise my truth and wear a mask to be accepted only leaves me more depleted than before the request is made. Expectations to have the voice filled always lead to disappointments, which melt into resentment. The "I deserve it" mentality comes with conditions and always has the same end result, which is depletion. Now being complete from the inside out will eliminate expectations. Not knowing outcomes, releasing what will be and my what-ifs brings me to trusting and having faith in myself, resulting in listening to the quiet, calm, loving voice within.

True to Self

How easy it is to fall prey to another's words, to an advertisement, or to a piece of literature. All these lead one to defining oneself and to partaking in the world. Yet one hurtful word or advertisement that does not align with who we are or one piece of literature that is opposite of what we believe in can place us in a whirlwind of doubts or affirmations. What we choose to believe about ourselves is truly up to us, yet we get caught up in others' perceptions of what is.

Being true to myself is coming home to security, love, peace, and contentment. Whether they believe it or not, I will find the positive message in everything. Old, familiar abuse and new, unknown peace are choices I have to make because of how often I have sacrificed myself for a want or a need. Despite knowing it was not in my best interest, I settled. How often have I settled on wearing a mask or staying with another who was so negative that their lie became my truth? So often, the very thing I needed to do was let go of the fear of aloneness, emptiness, and a lack of trust and faith. Trust that in the loneliness, the light within is the only fire I need to keep me warm. Selling out and settling for a negative will never bring joy and peace. Either it's God's, or it's not.

My Plans, His Laughter

How many times have I planned my days, weeks, or years according to the promise of another? How many times have my reaction and behavior been dependent on someone reacting negatively or positively? How many times have I chosen to stay in a harmful situation over my suffering? Today, I will walk my own walk and walk away from the negative behavior of another. I will detach myself from their inappropriate behavior. I will choose me over their choice. I will remain positive in God's love and light, and if I become a victim of another's choice, I will graciously move forward on my path knowing I can depend on the promise of my word.

How many times in my life have I wished I were someone else somewhere else or living the life of those in pictures in magazines? In being humble and in forgiving others and myself, I trust, I know, I believe, and I have faith that I am meant to be where I am meant to be. So love, self-acceptance, and forgiveness for myself can bring one to true, unconditional love. This is what we all strive for, to just be in God's love, light, and peace. We all have a specific purpose, designed especially for our own spiritual growth, so just be the blessing.

Rebuild

When the foundation is unstable, when the walls are discolored, and when the rotting walls no longer hold up the roof, it's time to rebuild. How many times have I ignored the rotting wood, only to slap on a new coat of paint (another mask) or throw a rug over the unstable foundation to present myself as a remodeled new me? I was unable to hold up the roof of my house, so before I crumbled and I lost me, I humbled myself to the most amazing contractor/carpenter to help me rebuild. I went into the foundation, got rid of the rotting wood, and rebuilt a stable, transparent, humbled, graciously forgiving, compassionate, trusting child of God. I now live in God's house, and He lives in mine.

Follow the Footsteps

My whole life has been about following in the footsteps of another, doing what was asked, and allowing them to fill me with their interpretation of life. I never trusted my own steps. With this burden of frustration, despite knowing that their choices did not fit me, I kept trying to fit in with them, so I finally let go of walking in their shadow. By trying to make me fit into them, my choices were not mine alone. Now I know we may either complement one another or not. If not, I will step into me and move forward knowing that all footsteps lead to God.

Waiting to Be Found

When we are born, our skin is almost transparent and thin; but as we grow older, our skin hardens, and our true self disappears under a mask that we are given. We try to show the world who we are at given moments of vulnerability, yet we continue to live in this masquerade, where assimilation is required. As we disappear into ourselves, we begin to truly know who we are and what fits, so we slowly and carefully remove our masks, willing to risk abandonment, judgment, and misunderstanding until we decide it's okay to be who we are. After all the fear has burned itself out and when there's nothing left but the ashes of worn-out masks, the untold truth is heard. All the hurts and sadness that have been carried on the journey are gone. In this emptiness is where I have nothing to lose.

When others' opinions define me more than my own truth does, I am silenced, and my voice only speaks their script. Yet now that I am coming into my light, I live authentically, not needing to compete to be accepted and loved. I am a blessing to all, as they are to me.

When we live in that light, all that has been lost is found. Displeasing others is no reason to disappear. If those I love can't recognize me with my soul out in the open, I will not pretend, and I will be who I am, not wearing a mask or retreating into the old, familiar behavior to get their approval. I don't have to do anything to be loved.

Why did I define myself by everyone else's promise? Shall I keep the secret or speak the truth? I define myself by my promise. I don't have to perform, wear a mask, earn a badge of approval, or be witnessed doing a good deed. The only thing that matters is how deeply I try to be my best, true self. Being who I am doesn't let others down, but not being who I am lets God down.

If You See Me

The first time a child sees their reflection or the first time we look upon that child's face, we see love. There is an overwhelming joy, and this unconditional love is deep into our core. Yet if we take part in a transgression, either against our self or not, then the fear of being seen becomes so great that we put on a mask so as not to be seen. We tell ourselves that if we are seen, then we will not be loved or accepted. We even neglect our own reflection. It is only when we take a risk by forgiving the self-inflicted shame, change our behavior, and remove our mask that we can then present ourselves as authentic and true, as we once did when we were that child who was loved so unconditionally, into our core, that all we did see was love. If we see one another in love, then no masks will ever be needed.

Approval

In my state of anxiousness and unrest, I need to step back in faith and release my fear. If I allow negative feelings to overwhelm me, I have a tendency to be combative and defensive. A confrontation may trigger my need to defend my actions, but when I can pause, then I can make a decision to either engage or withdraw. I no longer need to defend myself, because no matter what I may do or say, I can't change anyone's opinion, and they will believe what they want to believe. In letting go of this need for approval and validation, I can decide what is best for me. If the relationship is important, I will engage; but if it's just an acquaintance, I will smile, wish them well, and move on. I don't need everyone's approval to be me.

AUTHENTICITY

Living in fear of being seen can be so paralyzing that before we are aware, we have hidden our truth behind a mask of self-worthiness, shame, and abomination. All this is brought on because we choose to believe them before we believe God. After spending decades behind the mask of shame, brought on by believing an adult's lie, I have removed it, and now I am able to empty the darkness to live in the light. If you see me, you will love me.

Staying with who I am and risking feeling alone will ultimately be more help to me than trying to align myself with others for my security. Having worn masks for most of my life, when I took it off, I was not sure who exactly was there. So for now, after I spent so much time morphing myself to align with another, I now spend my days getting to know who I am. Patience to become real will give me time to see my hurt as a life lesson. What I have to do is search and learn, and then I will be able to live in my truth. I eventually remembered that we are all souls on this journey, and we are removing our masks so we can say, "I see you."

MY CONVICTIONS

In my youth, I was desperate to be included and loved, so I compromised myself to get that need met. Wanting to be included, I would leave one situation if a more desirable one came my way. This was an unkind act, which left others who were counting on me disappointed. This behavior had me doubt my own convictions, and I found I could not trust my own word. I no longer engage in that behavior. Now when I make plans with another person, I keep my word. I have learned that my convictions are my code of honor, and not only can others trust me, but I have also learned to forgive and trust myself.

Mask

I wondered if you would still love me if you saw me. Having worn masks for decades, I was always afraid that if you truly knew who I was, then I would never justify being worthy of your love. Then God told me, "The things you chose to do don't define you. I already know your heart, so it's okay to be who you are." Then I saw my reflection in the mirror and saw my worth.

My Takeaway

Contemplating where I've been, the conversations I've had, and the choices I've made with the people I know, I've realized that it all comes down to my takeaway from all these experiences. I believe what I hear without investigation, I become what I am told to be without exploring my truth, and I become who others want in order to find value and worth. Not to negate the importance of relationships, but what really, truly, humbly matters is how I am defined in my own truth by God. There will be disagreements and conflicts, but when I show up as my best, true, authentic self, the best takeaway from this journey is that I've made a difference.

CHAPTER 12

Outcomes

PEACEFUL OUTCOMES

When I am preparing for an upcoming visit or conversation with someone with whom I am in conflict, I may feel the need to put on my dialogue armor and prepare for rebuttals so that I will have a defensive comeback if blame is shifted my way. If I am focused more on defensive comebacks than listening or hearing, then in this mode, there is no resolution that will ever come to pass because I will be confronting this person with fear. It is when I enter a peaceful realm of empathy, compassion, patience, and forgiveness that resolution will be achieved. I would rather have peaceful outcomes than add more fuel to the fire of fear.

I am learning to find the source of the pain and recognize what has caused disappointment, judgment, and resentment; and I am learning to forgive. I am learning that forgiveness is not about exonerating another. It is about turning criticism and judgment into understanding, compassion, and love. This positive reaction can only heal a broken heart. This positive reaction can only open a closed heart. I have faith that all is, and I anticipate the outcomes knowing the answers will come from within.

Where I Dwell

Disappointment is inevitable, but misery is optional. It's difficult to admit that if I am miserable, then it is of my choosing. Not being attached to negative energy gives me the hopeful feeling that trusting God will give me what He knows I need to evolve. Not knowing the outcome or manipulating it to cause detours and pain is all in God's hands. No more blame-shifting allowed; I now know that "happiness is a choice and if I'm not happy, it's a consequence of my choosing and not the circumstances of my life."

The key to my happiness is my own contentment with my own choices. If I wait around for everything that I want to arrive and everyone's behavior to align with mine and the world to spin at my request, then I will inevitably be disappointed, miserable, and judgmental. The way I feel and what I think are in my control and how I choose to view the world can bring me joy and contentment or misery. If I am surrounded by negative energy, I can choose to find another place to dwell. I am responsible for my own happiness and how I choose to live in my day. I get to choose if I want to live with hope or continue to live with the pain of breaking.

What's the Worst That Can Happen If I Wait?

When I am at a crossroad or I feel the weight of a decision that is yet to come to completion, I can become anxious and fearful of the outcome. What's the worst that can happen if I wait? When I am confronted with a transgression or I feel uneasy about someone's behavior or response, I want to engage with kindness, yet I am fearful that I may not be heard or accepted. What's the worst that can happen if I wait? When I want something or someone in my life that is out of my reach yet I begin to put my spin on it to assist the outcome, I tend to sabotage what's already in the works for me. What's the worst that can happen if I wait? The answer is, I may get what I want if I wait.

Ready to Know

When I release my effort to change something that is not mine to change, I find myself a bit sad when letting go of an outcome that I may have seen is in my best interest. This acceptance can be challenging since I always think I know what is in my best interest. But now that I am receiving the answers to the questions in my life, I can see the larger picture rather than a small part of God's grand scheme. This has required me to live empty and in a state of not knowing and has strengthened my faith. When I become anxious for an issue to be resolved or when I strive to know the answer to my whys, I can sit in peace and know that all will be revealed and that I will have my answers and that I will know when I am ready to know.

God's Timing

When the silence becomes a friend and when voices speak the truth, this is when I am most comfortable to peel one more layer off me. It is said that all we need to know is already there, and layer by layer, it will be revealed to us when the time is right, so what I know in this moment is what I am meant to know. When the time is right, something new will be revealed to me that may either bring me comfort by validating what I know to be my truth or rock my world, bringing me to my knees, as I begin to unravel what I've identified to be part of my core. This may develop more questions or even doubt, and more purging may occur, but either way, I am now open to the possibilities that more questions will be asked and more answers will be revealed in God's timing.

What Now?

After the life lesson has been experienced, what now? After the heart has healed, what now? After the prayer has been answered, what now? If I were to look at my life on a movie screen and fast-forward it, I know I will arrive to this point in my life, where I'm no longer saying, "What now?" but, "Now." Having taken the past with me wherever I went, there was never room for new blessings. But now that I have viewed the whirlwind of my life, I have arrived living in the now.

WAITING

I listen to the clock ticking on the wall. The seconds that will never be relived or retrieved, years of waiting, and seconds of anticipation that are all lost are melting into becoming what I already am. Lost in the words of another's promise, emptying myself in the dreams of another's life, I am waiting, but this waiting is not wasted, because in all the disappointments, there are always glimmers of hope and faith that I will return. And now I am finding the road back, so no more waiting to arrive or to hope or to dream but now to trust that it's all here in me. It always has been. I just took a detour. The waiting is over.

OUR STORY

"Once upon a time" is the beginning of all of us. That one moment when prayer becomes a reality is when we are born, when we live, and when we die. What fills the in-between makes us real, and we become purposeful when we know the blessing that we are. And through this evolution of our soul in this body, we learn contradictions to help us achieve our goals. We've learned that in the darkness of our journey, we all come to the light. We can pray, barter, and bargain for specific outcome; but ultimately, we all arrive. What we choose to fill the pages of our story becomes who we are. That we are all blessed and are blessings are truths that cannot be untold.

PRESENT POWER

When a thought comes to mind that may trigger a memory, the only way to acknowledge the lesson learned from it is to look at where I am in the present. It is when what-ifs and should-haves rob the power that the past has given me to be who I am in the present.

Nothing except a time machine can change the outcomes of broken dreams and shattered relationships, yet when I acknowledge the gift that has been given from encounters, life lessons, and experiences, that is where the true power will be.

AND LIFE GOES ON

As I view my life in a rearview mirror, having traveled toward my new experiences, I sometimes feel lonely and afraid, wanting the predictable old drama that I call life to fill my void. Yet if I truly reflect on then and now, would I really want all that knowing what I am now, feeling what I feel, and having evolved into who I am? It's almost like having a keepsake from my childhood, like a favorite book or a doll I once called friend. Although these memories have brought me joy, they no longer fit. I can choose to be a person who has evolved simply from what has happened to me or from what I've chosen to be and what I've done about what has happened. Being who I am doesn't let others down, but not being who I am lets me down, so I humbly thank them for the lessons learned and place them back on the shelf of my memory. I am humbled to know my life has gone on.

THE GOAL

Although a sportsperson keeps their eyes on the goal, strategies and game plans are their lifelines to the goal. When I pray for guidance to lift the burdens I'm carrying or when I'm reacting to another, I am taking my eyes off the goal, which is for me to evolve into my purposeful self. When I fill my mind with past hurts or with present obstacles, I forego my faith as if I can solve the world's problems. I undertake that which is not mine to hold. How can I fulfill my purpose and be myself if I am plagued with thoughts of those who are struggling like I am? It's one thing to journey together, yet it's another to give my journey for or to them. I can join them without forgetting my own path.

Come Back

As I continue to empty myself of trying to fix the expectations of being completed by others, I find there is only love, joy, peace, and contentment where God completes me. We all have human imperfections that need to heal so we can evolve. The release of that which is not mine also means relinquishing my need for outcomes, and this leads me to hold on to my faith, trusting all is as it is meant to be. With no expectations or attachments, reactions are calm. Having emptied and let go, I am filling myself with me. Knowing my truth and having my voice with no need to defend, I now know it's time to learn how to continue to feel full in the presence of others. So in the anxiousness of trying to fix it, I come back to me, and I know all is meant to be. We are all on a journey; so with no judgment, no connection, and no definition, I will be attached to that which is not mine.

Out of the Darkness

After settling down into quiet times and trying to live a drama-free life, I am aware when negative energy crosses my path. This may be a detour, an inconvenience, a disruption, or an obstacle; but it may not necessarily be negative, just a rerouting opportunity to look for the positive growth agent in everything. I cannot live in the past or live in days that have not yet happened. I let go of what was or what might be to live now in God's love, light, and peace.

The need for the truth will lead me into the unexpected living of my life beyond all images of perfection. My need for truth to be my best, true, positive, spiritual, authentic self leads me to leave behind all that is comfortable and perhaps predictable. In my emptiness and alone time, I am reminded that all is meant to be and that all I can control is me. Unresolved situations or unanswered dreams are present; but I will live my life, evolve my soul, and move forward. This is surrendering, accepting, and letting go. Just let life unfold with no expectations and no disappointments and release resentment. Although it was painful, I was led out of the darkness to live my life by serving in God's truth and surrounded by His light.

MINE TO HAVE

When I get caught up in that which is not mine to have, I tend to try to maneuver it to fit what I think will fit with me. I may try to change it to fit, or I may assimilate myself to fit it. This may cause a lot of anguish if it is not mine to have. Instead of continuing this behavior, I'll walk away; and although frustrated and disappointed, I know it is not mine to have. I've learned that when it is effortless, then it is mine.

IT CAN HAPPEN IN A SECOND

With all the hopes, dreams, scheming, and manipulating, if it's meant to be, it will be. We are given the choice to believe, trust, and have faith that all is and will be. Never in the history of the universe has worry ever solved a problem; so every opportunity is given to us to evolve, to become responsible, to show up for life, and to be our best, true, positive self. We are given certain tasks to undertake to help us become stronger in our faith. The "Why me?" syndrome can only be answered with, "Why not me?" Every second has a purpose. In faith, knowing it will all work out in God's time is God's way of ending our sentences not with a question mark but with a period.

WAITING

Living with the contradiction of what I have and what I think I want to fulfill me has left me anxious and fearful, which will muddy the water of my soul's evolution. Waiting for a bus that never comes eventually makes me walk. Waiting for another's behavior to change to make me happy makes me miss the opportunity of celebrating what I already have. Thinking another completes another leaves no room for the emptiness to be filled with that which is meant to be. My waiting and my holding on before I trust enough to let go leaves

me waiting. My waiting to be empty and my living with not knowing will only strengthen what already is there: my faith and trust in
myself that I am already full with God's love.

In My Head

Conversations that have never taken place—no exchange of
audible words and no utterances or noise from my mouth—are the
thoughts in my head that sometimes keep me in the darkness. When
what-ifs don't happen, I find that I have put energy into a defense
that is not needed but that has resulted in fear. I am always ready
for battle, wearing the heavy armor of justification, and it takes so
much energy and power but results in nothing but sadness. When
that dialogue that will never be spoken or heard is silenced, the not
knowing and the trust turn fear into faith. The silencing of those useless thoughts brings light to darkness, and joy turns from sorrow, and
faith replaces fear. In that one second, the change of that one thought
brings peace. Living in my head with peace is a nice thought.

Change Is Inevitable

Being fluid is a reminder of how a river flows, the gentle tide
moving in and out of the shoreline. But add stress, fear, or change
to the equation and what is once calm and soothing can become a
raging flood. Such as God's liquid on earth is fluid, we are also fluid
with our soul's evolution. Knowing all will change cannot halt the
change. It is when we resist and live in fear or stress that our waves
come crashing to the shore of our lives, eroding growth and prolonging pain. Letting the waters of our life flow as they are meant to flow
can bring peace to even the ugliest storms. All is temporary; all must
be fluid for the joy of life to flow onto our shores.

Remembering

How often does a scent or a behavior or an incident trigger a
memory? I have happiness in my life, yet when triggered by a nega-

tive memory, I plunge into that hurt that has lasted too long while not remaining positive long enough. The habit of remaining negative overpowers me with its loudest voice while the sweet, quiet, gentle, positive whisper waits for me to live in joy, happiness, and peace. Remembering the positive and negative can enhance an evolution, yet staying in either one too long can halt the journey. So as I remember what has helped me evolve, I bless all my positive and negative experiences and opportunities.

ONE MORE DAY

How many days and years have I spent hoping and praying for peace, joy, happiness, contentment, acceptance, patience, approval, and love? How many years have I spent reflecting on past hurts and achievements, only to say, "That wasn't so bad." I have survived, and look what I've accomplished, and look at how I've healed and grown! Each day has been and still is a blessing. When submerged in the pain of a burden that is not mine to control, the pain is in my reaction. I can feel hardened and broken. But then when I release it, letting go with tears that wash away the hurt, I am able to thank the lesson in the pain. It's just one more day to enjoy life, learn, and continue to live in joy with one more day of blessings.

IT MATTERS

As I evolve, I encounter people and things that will assist me. Whether I favor them or not, I try to appreciate what's being offered. What truly matters is love and what it brings—kindness, compassion, caring, understanding, patience, empathy, appreciation, collaboration, communication, cooperation, and validation. The conflicts and contradictions I meet along the way come down to treating others with love even if I encounter resistance. The only approval that truly matters is God's. Did I evolve as He would have liked me to, to serve others? It matters!

Intentions

What do I do, and what do I feel? Speaking, acting, and reacting with positive intentions means I am not so interested in the outcome of what will make me happy and that I've got my way. So my intention is only to walk my talk, control my actions, and decide to be my best, true, authentic self. Help me accept my journey as well as the journey of another even if we are on different paths. Bless us all with the gift of knowing that the core of our differences is truly the same: to love and be loved.

Reflection of a Memory

I wonder if at the end of this human experience, materialistic items will matter. Will the money in the bank matter? My guess is no. I will probably reflect on my joys and the memories of how I've showed and received love. Since the past has no power unless I give it away, it melts into a lovely watercolor of memories that hold joy, laughter, and love. Reflecting on the journey of how I have arrived is a portrait of the woman my soul has evolved into, a woman of great passion for everyone to have kindness and to give and receive. What a lovely reflection to see in the mirror of my journey.

Complete

Finished, done, and *complete*—these are words to describe moving on. These words hold the hope for the future by accepting the past and living in the present. "What if" comes to mind; these two words have power to halt any kind of evolution unless there is positive energy with each breath when these two words are spoken. For today, what if I were to receive everything I want and everything I've prayed for, including the past to be rewritten? Is this really what I truly want? My guess is no, because my faith is in not knowing and because I trust that God will lead me toward being complete.

ENOUGH

I don't need to convince anyone of who I am. I don't need to rant and rage to be heard. I do not need to be flamboyant to be seen. I know who I am, and so does God. I can hear my own voice, and so can God. I see me, and so does God. Enough said!

JUST ONE WORD

With just one word, a life can be saved, a heart can either be mended or broken, a soul can evolve, and a life can begin or end. With just one word, a moment can be turned into joy or tragedy. With just one breath, I can focus on my intentions and feelings. How many opportunities to stop and count to ten have I missed? How many words spoken in the name of fear cannot be taken back? When the sun rises and the day is new, I get to try again. When the day ends and the world goes to sleep, I get to be renewed. With just one word, with just one breath, I get to evolve and become the blessing I am meant to be. We are all given this opportunity and gift.

JUST LETTING IT BE

In my letting go of outcomes that I think are best for me are my faith and trust in God. In my trust in not knowing, I am no longer putting energy into a thought or action that may sabotage the outcome. It will, as it always has, work out the way God intends. I have been brought home to heal. I have come to know and embrace my contradictions. No more coercing, manipulating, or trying to control that which I think is best for me. I now know that God's plan is best for me.

TEETER BACK AND FORTH

As I encounter all my blessings, even if I'm so grateful for the amazing life I have lived, I do teeter back and forth from negative energy. Whether it's my pain or my reaction to another's, I find myself retreating into my own truth, yet I still struggle with the energy being in my presence. I then begin to be flooded with all that is not yet complete, and my focus becomes fixated on the whens and whys, so I discipline myself to remain focused on what is in front on me in this present moment.

AFTER ALL OF IT, IT STILL IS

With all the fear attached to outcomes, trying to manipulate it into what I want it to be, it still is as God intends. I've spent most of my life trying to fit in, be loved, and be accepted, depending on others to tell me my worth, yet I still am as God intends. I've been so blessed, and I'm so humbled by my gratitude for what I have in abundance. Having lived in fear and now seeing how I am attempting to live in love, it humbles me that I still and always will be as God intends.

TRUE NOURISHMENT

What lessons am I supposed to learn? In dealing with the shadow and carrying burdens, I have the opportunity to recognize where my true nourishment lies. I chose a behavior that obstructed the flow of God, thinking I knew better when I didn't and thinking I could control when I couldn't. Now I am moving toward the emptiness and making as much space in my life as I can for the experience of God to fill me. Heart and love, mind and wisdom, and spirit and faith all equate to God. "Misery is a moment of suffering allowed to become everything. Look wider than the hurt."

OPPORTUNITIES, NOT OBSTACLES

If I didn't get my way, I looked at everything as obstacles rather than opportunities. I thought obstacles kept me from what I wanted instead of seeing them as opportunities to achieve my goal. But now I see it as an opportunity to trust and have faith, to set boundaries, and to honor my own word. Maybe it's not about fixing something that's broken but rather an opportunity to create something better.

Enlightenment

With awareness comes an enlightenment of the pain's origin and the patterns that must be changed. I can't change the past or what happened; but I can forgive, accept, go on, and let go. I can't control the situation or anyone, but I can make healthy, powerful choices to take care of myself. This will start a new cycle of love, self-care, trust, honesty, faith, communication, respect, consideration, and self-worth.

Temporary

I sometimes put my life on hold to wait for something to heal so I can be happy. Impatience and anxiousness give way to frustration for putting my happiness into the hands of an outcome that I desire. These are momentary feelings that can steal my joy. Knowing that everything is fluid and temporary helps me regain my momentous faith. I can react and flow through the discomfort as I anticipate what's in store for me. Looking for a life without sadness or pain will not allow me to embrace all the events that this journey bestows on me. I can find joy even if there is pain and sadness, because with a fluid life, all is temporary. I have faith.

No Longer

Memories and triggers are reminders of how I've evolved and what has helped. "Keeping old wounds alive is a curse that drowns out the past happiness and growth. What do I focus on? Do I focus on the pain and to what end since it can't be changed? Tragedy stays alive by feeling what's been done, while peace comes alive by living with the results."

I never have to settle for less again. I never have to give what I don't want to give or relinquish my control. I am worthy of the best.

If I want something now and I don't get it, then it's not my time. I never have to manipulate or try to control, for when it's time, I'll have what I need. I no longer need to settle for the predictable even if it's uncomfortable. I no longer need to engage in unhealthy behavior that is not appropriate for my best interest. I have the choice to place myself in abundant situations. I may make a mistake, but I am not defined by that mistake. If I commit an error, I can apologize and change my behavior.

ENERGY

"What resists persists." How many years did I have an inner dialogue, preparing myself for whatever was to come my way but always dwelling in the negative outcome? But it never came to fruition, and I wasted a lot of my energy in fear of a scenario that never played out. Although I did not get the answers I wanted or produce the outcome I thought I needed to make me feel happy and complete, I did get the love I wanted by finding my voice, knowing my truth, having my faith, and believing to disagree with all of them because I was worthy. So now how do I want to spend my days, and where do I want to focus my energy? I will let go of outcomes and of what was, what could have been, and what will be.

SURRENDER

If I wait long enough, when I've exhausted myself by feeling the pain, I can then see I am a soul on a human experience, as we all are. We are all trying to find our way to learn and grow, so I can honor all of us. I can walk away from fear and inappropriate, controlling behaviors. I can stay angry and try to force my opinions on them, but how would I be any different from them, and how will it change the outcome? That wasted energy will only make me feel as if I've sacrificed my goodness to engage in that behavior. I can set boundaries, and I can honor my no.

I am now at a place of surrender, so I can move forward as I empty their burdens that I've chosen to carry. Surrender is not weakness, because there is strength in knowing how much is mine to hold and what to relinquish. Even though we become an extension of those experiences and people we encounter in life, not every attribute will complement me or be an appropriate fit for me. When it comes down to it, I decide who I should be by my own definition.

OPPORTUNITY

If I continue to give an obstacle my attention, my question is, how do I feel when I focus on it? If it doesn't make me feel good and it does not serve me, why give it my energy? I have found myself giving a lot of energy to someone else's word or promise. I need to remember that we all have the capability to do what we can. The people I choose to have in my life have well-meaning intentions. I need to begin to trust my own intentions so that I can trust theirs. The days of putting all my energy into them have turned toward me, matching my words with actions. I am a product of many life lessons and opportunities, and all these experiences have helped me become the person I am. I am open to finding a resolution so the opportunity to grow can serve me.

WHAT I TRULY NEED

I've realized that the anger and resentment that I once harbored do not serve me but keep me imprisoned in my own grief. They sucked the energy out of me for decades. I thought that if I held on to them long enough and played victim, then I would get the apology I thought I deserved to help me let go and heal so I could be happy. I can say out loud that I have tried to resolve it, and I've struggled but have not found my way. After receiving the apology I thought I desperately needed to feel complete, I didn't feel any better, so I realized that I didn't need their apology to let go, to move forward, to be happy, and to find joy. It was never about changing their attitude toward me but rather about changing how I saw myself. I am already here.

Decisions for a Positive Outcome

In making a productive decision for myself, I incorporate the following steps. My choices should be responsible and loving.

* Stop and get in touch with my feelings.
* Give a voice to the part of me that is afraid.
* Ask myself if I want the fear to control me.
* Ask myself to make a decision as if I were a person showing myself love and compassion.

Outcomes

My entire life, I have been known to say, "I'm not trying to be difficult, but I don't understand." At times, I was closed down, and I felt shame for needing clarity. I began questioning my own questioning and doubting my own requests as if my words were whispers in the wind. Consequently, I began to utter sounds of fear as if by speaking louder, I would be heard. Now when I find myself in this whirlwind of questioning and requesting, I will not doubt my needs. I have the power and self-worth to get my answers and to get my needs met.

The Right Thing for Me

When I am confronted with a decision and I am at a crossroads—should I, or should I not?—I have to weigh the options and answer the question, "What is right for me?" I have now come to this point in my life where my opinion matters and is the final word. I may ask for guidance and information, but ultimately, the decision is mine to make. I am the only one who knows what's right for me, because I know I have a voice and because I live in my truth.

WITHIN THE FIRE

Fire does not always get a positive reaction unless it is used to warm someone or cook something, but give it a devastating label and it can be construed as destruction. We all have fires that burn in our hearts. Call it passion or rage. It is there for burning off that which is no longer needed to hide the beauty within. When one has been covered with layers of life, it can take decades to peel and chisel away toward the purity of the soul's core. With the fire that burns within, if it is used with love, passion, joy, and good, positive intentions, it can burn off all that is no longer needed to reveal who we already are.

TRUSTING

In all my experiences, I had always been able and ready to accept the pain of my abandonment issues, which led me to fear and anger, yet I found it so difficult to trust in the joy and love and faith of goodness. It came down to allowing myself to believe in the goodness and to let go of deprivation. I started trusting myself, and now I see I am worthy of goodness, love, and joy.

SAFE IN DANGER

When I am confronted with negative situations or someone's drama, I may rely on my old instincts to become a character in their play or react by giving them my energy, which leaves me depleted. But now I choose to see them in their fear and pray they find their enlightenment as I return to mine. I am never again straying away from my light and into their darkness. It is now the reverse. I will invite them out of their darkness and into the light. If needed, I will walk away to sustain my positive energy. I will always pray they find their way out of the darkness.

Why? Why Not?

I can sit and wallow in self-pity and live my life as a victim, feeling nothing but disappointment and resentment to harden my heart. I can continue to ask why—"Why was my innocence stolen, my right of passage silenced, and my opened heart closed countless times?" I can learn that nothing happens by accident and that everything has a purpose. I am a soul on a spiritual journey to evolve, so the answer then becomes, "Why not?" That which does not kill us makes us stronger, so I will say goodbye to broken dreams and disappointment from unanswered prayers and replace it all with faith and with the answer, "Why not?"

Get Through

It is said that letting go frees the soul of resentment, disappointment, and judgment. Although the pain may be deep into the core, the soul is never harmed. It is through experiences and opportunities that letting go releases the burdens that I carry and my want for things my way. My soul's purposeful journey is to fulfill love of others and God and pass that forward. In letting go of wanting and moving to the fulfillment of what is, I release my power to God. I'll allow myself the memories of lost hopes and dreams as I get through the pain and into peace.

Reflect into a Memory

For a very long time, I reflected into a past memory and drew all the negative experiences into my present. This made it extremely difficult to see the joys and blessings of the present. I gave power to my past and moved it into my present moments and robbed myself of the reflection of a memory that brought me peace and growth. I now think of my past and smile as I reflect on a memory knowing all has purpose and all houses contradictions, but I choose to dwell on what brings me peace.

Back to Me

Ultimately, every decision I make is one that I have to own. The years of the blame-shifting victim are finished. I used to barter to get love and sacrificed my own worth to feel worthy, yet when I took a step away from the give-and-take that was always conditional, I saw that I brought on my own pain by accepting the conditions of my decisions. This enabling that has caused blame-shifting has come to an end, and I am responsible for my own choices. I no longer need to barter or sacrifice myself to know my worth.

Forced to Push and Pull

I can recall so much energy that I put into people and situations by forcing the outcome I wanted. Some called this a sidestep or a detour, but I usually knew it as a burden I put on me because I thought that if I pushed and pulled hard enough, I would get what I wanted. Yet my history showed me that in my gentle surrender, my letting go, and my giving up control or manipulation, I always received what I needed. I spent decades pushing when I should have pulled. Now leaving my frustration behind, I listen and am equipped with that which I need, and I trust the faith that empowers me to do anything I am required to do.

Freeway

Have you ever noticed how drivers drive on a freeway? They are locked in their own world, not really paying attention to their surroundings, yet put a storm or an accident in their path and all of a sudden, the freeway becomes still and becomes their present destination. In the stopping of their travels, they may glance at another or sit idle in their car, immersed in their world. The freeway means no distractions, no obstacles, and no drama. This is how we can choose to live our lives, but it does not guarantee a pain-free life. We can engage with another in a freeway of positive communication, so when the storm subsides or the accident is cleared, we can count on our journey, free of drama, just finding a way on our freeway to say, "Hello. How are you?"

WHAT'S MY GOAL?

It is our daily practice to be responsible citizens and to be productive members of society by working, paying taxes, and being our best, true, ethical self. All the while, as we show up in society, our souls evolve; so when a plan is made, I have to keep asking myself, "What is my goal?" If I engage in an activity where I choose to share a part of myself with others, how does this help my evolution? If done with love, then all is positive; but if engaging in a battle, I have to question what my fear is. Why am I defensive, and why am I agreeing to something that makes me uncomfortable? What are my battles within that still need attention? What is my fear? If I hold on to my fear, then what is my goal?

NOT HELPFUL

When I see an image, hear a sound, smell a pleasant fragrance, or remember a memory that brings me comfort, then I am at peace. When confronted with a situation or when I have a to-do list or a future meeting with someone I have had issues with, my mind may begin to script my responses so I am prepared for my inevitable doom. This is not helpful, and it is in this moment that I must stop and flip my negative into positive. Giving energy to my future will never benefit my spiritual growth. Responsible planning is necessary; however, pending doom, it will never bring me peace or joy. My thoughts matter, and there is no need to prepare for what-ifs. All will be as God intends.

ACCEPT RATHER THAN EXPECT

When a plan is made, the expectation of a certain outcome may turn out differently. It is then when I come to a very familiar crossroad of how I may react. If I get what I expect, then I am content and happy; but when the outcome differs, my familiar reaction will be disappointment, judgment, and resentment. I no longer need or want drama, so accepting instead of expecting will bring me peace. What is the goal of my expected outcome? What comes my way is now examined as I ask what life lessons lie in this new experience.

I Already Am

When I was young, I played ball with my brother and went to the movies with my sister and cousin, and my world was perfect. I woke every day to the possibility of joy. But when sadness took the front seat of my life, I slipped away into darkness. I strove for decades to get back my joy. Occasionally, I laughed until I cried; and when I cried, the laughter rarely came. I kept thinking that if only I could recover, then I would find joy. It was in the gentle whisper of God's love and truth that I heard that a pain-free life was not available, yet He was where I could find my joy and peace knowing my life was a journey, not a destination.

I Can Find a Friend

I sometimes get stuck in a painful memory. I have learned that if I give it a voice and talk it through, I can flip the sadness into joy. I have been known to look for support from others who have no support to give. This may trigger the feeling of unworthiness for asking for help from them, but I still have the right to ask. Just because they are not available doesn't mean I can't continue my search for another to share my journey. In this universe, I can find a friend.

Shiny Diamond

There comes a time in one's life when materialistic collections and social status are no longer important to define who we are. Growing up in a society where money makes the person and an outward appearance brings judgment, I have found myself so caught up in the validations that I've sacrificed my purpose in order to please them. It's so easy to react to a look or a word than to stay in the moment of peace, where my true nourishment lies. There are mementos in my life that either help me toward my destiny or hold me back. I get to choose that which I want to hold on to—the boulders that get in my way, the tiny pebbles that get in my shoes, or the precious diamond in the rough I've now become and that now shines.

Expose

In the midst of despair, when the outcome is different from my desire, I have to take a step back and tell myself that regardless of what is uncovered, at least the truth will be revealed. Even if it's not the truth of my truth, it will illuminate what is meant to be. It's always darkest before the dawn!

When Enough Is Enough

When I have had a disconnection with another, it is difficult for me to stay away from justifying or defending my truth. After the conversations, I have to humbly forgive and, if need be, walk away from their toxicity knowing their choices are not about me. I do not need to allow the triggers of fear to consume me. I do not need to wait for another battle to begin. I need to just breathe and know that I've done my best and know my truth, and that is enough.

Reflect on the Answers

What do I truly believe about myself today as I reflect on who I am? How have I lived my life, serving others and healing myself? How am I presenting myself in the light of love rather than from the darkness of despair? How do I walk my talk as I move about my day? Where does my true nourishment lie? What are the distractions or misconceptions that I still have that are holding me back in the past? How do I think, speak, feel, and relate to others and myself? These are questions that I will seek to answer.

God Knows

What if I knew that everything I wanted would be delivered? What if I believed that I no longer needed to manipulate outcomes because God would give me everything He knew was in my best interest? What if every time I felt fear of not knowing, I would feel a warm hug and receive a soft whisper that all was well? How would I have lived then? Live in the peace of knowing that God is!

I Lived

Sometimes, I look at things as they are and where I am in life and review the journey in my mind. When I was going through the difficult times, I thought I would never smile again. And when I was going through the happiest of times, I prayed the moments would freeze in time so I could remain there. And now as I am in the twilight of my life's journey, I look at the serenity that awaits me as I celebrate all the joy and sadness that encompass my life. All is well, and I have lived a good life.

Not Mine to Fix

When I am confronted with a situation where I know I have no control and where my influence may not be accepted, I can acknowledge that I am not a part of the scenario and send out a prayer. When I see a loved one suffering, I need to know that I cannot ease their pain other than by offering a smile or a hug or a prayer. The outcome may not be as desired, but a prayer of acceptance will ease the pain. I may not be able to fix it, but I can pray that God will.

Make Room for Something New

What's the point in talking or feeling about what's in the past? The point is that unless a hurt has a voice, it cannot heal; and if it is not given light, it will suffocate in the darkness and eventually rupture into an all-consuming resentment, disappointment, and judgment. Living in the pain can be detrimental and can keep me stuck with a hardened heart, going nowhere.

There comes a time in my life when I have to access what I have in my soul that is serving me. If there are words that have yet to be spoken, speak them. If there are feelings that have to be uncovered, uncover them. If there are hurts that need to be healed, give them a voice and begin to heal. All these years, I carried the pain but never really felt joy, for there was no room in my guarded heart. Now owning what is mine and releasing what is not, there is room for joy as my heart opens to faith and trusts that I am in the light. I can learn to live with the pain, not in the pain.

All That Remains

After the apologies are spoken, after my heart has been opened, and after my soul has been humbled into forgiving others and myself, all that's left for me to do is live my life. If my behavior has changed, then there is no need to apologize again for my past. If I have humbled myself to another to own what is mine, all I can do is hand back what is theirs with a prayer. All that remains after all the pain is revealed is to continue to heal and move into the light of life. Whether I am alone on this journey or not, I can honor God and myself by striving to fill all that remains with light and love.

Balcony

Having spent decades in fear, when I became afraid, I fabricated an outcome to my favor by making sure I had the upper hand. While I was planning this in my mind, life was happening, and the outcome was usually different from what I feared. Now that I am beyond that reaction, I can see myself through a different view, as if I am in a balcony, viewing my past from a bird's-eye view. Not judging or resenting unmet expectations or broken dreams, I can find compassion, love, and peace in the past experiences of my life and say, "Well done. I did survive, and although I may have detoured off my path, I have come home to me." I am learning that when the ghosts of past experiences try to make room in my present, I can acknowledge them for the lessons I have learned and send them on their way. They do not have to stay long for me to know I am no longer in need of that behavior to know joy, peace, and love.

Purposeful Choices

It is said that we are all born with a purpose. Finding one's purpose can be difficult if that person has lived their life through the eyes of another. When making a decision, I have learned to stop and ask myself what the intention and outcome I am searching for are and if it will serve to fulfill my purpose or to gain strength in the eyes of another. Staying in the light can be a challenge when the shadows of my past follow me. I am cautious when remembering to check to whom I am listening and what behavior is appropriate to fulfill my purpose.

Start Anew

If a relationship is going to be restored, then the problem must be discussed and a solution must be agreed upon so that the parties will know what is anticipated to begin to heal. I'm not angry. I've just gotten to a point in my life where I am no longer waiting or expecting your words to match your actions. I will be cordial, polite, and respectful; but that does not mean I trust you. If you want a relationship, then journey toward it with new behaviors.

No Regrets

"When I can look back into my past, doing so without regret and instead seeing only lessons that brought me to my current strength and wisdom, I can embrace the fullness of my experience. I can help those around me to build upon the past as I do. And when I choose to create my desires, I place my power in the present and move forward with life into the future, knowing God's plan is my best plan." I live with no regrets because I know where I am today, what I know today, the truth about God, and who I am with.

FUNK

When I desire something, I can usually acquire it and then move on. When it comes to wanting from another, this requires patience as I await my desired outcome. After spending decades waiting, manipulating, and sacrificing to get what I thought was in my best interest, I now find myself practicing a new behavior called patience. Waiting for another can cause me to slip into a funk that drains my resources, and I become lethargic, and I mope around knowing that this fear-based behavior is counterproductive. After allowing myself to pout, I brush off my funk and put my prayer and blessings into the universe and give them to God and begin to live my life again.

BE A LIGHT

I heard a whisper, and it spoke to me in these words: "Be the change you want to see in the world. Be the person you want to stand in front of you. Be an inspiration as you wait for others to inspire." And so I asked myself, "How is my behavior and faith inspiring others?" I can complain about another's injustice or lack of compassion or inability to be kind or forgive, yet when it comes down to the bareness of my soul, how do I deal with injustice, compassion, kindness, or forgiveness? Be the person who teaches others by being an inspiration of hope and light.

ENCOUNTERS

I'm not sure that I can pinpoint exactly what has been my greatest influencer. Perhaps it's Anne Frank's ability to forgive and see goodness regardless of the circumstance. Perhaps it's the bullies I've encountered whom I allowed to take the power to control me, all the while knowing my deep-seated worth. Perhaps it's the kindness in the simple words that are spoken to tell me to seek my truth and heal my soul and define and believe in myself. Regardless of the origin, I thank and bless all those I've encountered for helping me become who I am—those who saw my worth and those who feared my truth.

It Is Finished

I feel humbled to speak these words, for they are a special gift that remind me that what is done is done. What is in the past cannot be relived, only in my mind's eye if I choose. This phrase, these three special words, means that a goal has been met. Whether the results are of triumph or failure, the life lessons within the experiences are priceless. At the end of my days, the physical life of the things that have brought me joy will be housed in boxes and will end up in a garage sale. Another box will be filled with my heartfelt experiences, written on the pages of my life, while my ashes will be spread in the wind of eternity. At the end of my days, I will say, "It is finished."

Embrace the New

I have felt unworthy of my feelings for decades, and it now takes me awhile to give myself the opportunity to remove my mask and purge the anger, resentment, and disappointment that I've harbored in my soul and that have become my armor. When I present myself in a respectful light, there is always a warrior ready for battle if someone questions my motives. Now seeing that letting go has allowed me to explore my feelings and actually feel them before I am ready to make room for something new, I know that this effort is timely and purposeful. I understand the concept of caution, but it comes with the price of retribution if not dealt with on the soul level. I have the right to feel the way I feel, but I also have the right to release that which no longer serves a purpose. I no longer need anyone's approval, validation, or permission to exist.

I used to feel like I was sometimes the only one showing up to sustain the relationship. Now I have pulled back and have detached. I can see that this enabling tactic has only caused me to live in their truth and to become a part of their shadow. If it is meant to be, then it will be. No amount of effort, money, or sacrifice will ever put us on the same path unless we are willing to explore the possibilities of letting go to embrace what may be.

GLIDE

Moving along without feeling rushed can bring inner peace knowing that all is well and all will happen when it is meant to happen. I can let go of anxiously waiting for the destination to be seen. Now I know this journey is filled with so many blessings along the way, toward that destination. And even though I don't know the outcomes, I am willing to have faith and glide through my day.

MY BEST INTEREST

When I am asked to engage in a situation that may not be in my best interest, I need to review the desired outcome and decide if my presence will be a help or a hindrance. When I am unable to assist another in a request due to its toxic environment, I need to honor myself and step away. If I engage and I am not going to bring anything positive to the situation, I need to detach and say no. I am not someone who fixes anything for anyone else. It is not my responsibility to save anyone. I can be a friend and offer solicited advice or a shoulder to lean on, but I cannot fix anyone but myself. I can only wish them well and pray for their journey.

LOOK FOR IT

There's peace that comes when one finally understands that any kind of unrest can result in a positive outcome toward growth and peace. I know that worry and disappointment will only harden my heart, and resenting an outcome that is different from what I want will only hurt me. But the acceptance that what is meant to be is and that all is fluid will bring a calming peace that will help me look inside the outcome for the hidden message that will help me move forward one step at a time. There's joy in every opportunity and experience if I choose to see it. Look for it. It's there.

No Reservations Needed

I used to think that if I was not rolling out a product every day as if my life was an assembly line, then I was useless and unproductive. I used to think that if I didn't manipulate an outcome to my specific request as if I was ordering a fine, expensive meal, then I was being taken for granted and being abused. Now I can express my wants and desires and accept the outcomes as meant to be without reservation and without trying hard enough or doing enough to make it come to fruition. I have learned that any time traveling on my journey has not been wasted, because I have arrived exactly where I am meant to be with the knowledge I am meant to have. Every experience and opportunity, whether it brought pain or joy, has been a testament that I have lived.

Peace

When disappointment sets in from an unmet expectation, it can cause my heart to harden, and I can become bitter as I fester in my resentment of the "How dare you!" syndrome. But when I send out a prayer and my hopes for resolution are in the faith that they may or may not be answered in my time, I can still hope for the acceptance of the outcome that I receive. I have more faith in God's timing than I have in my own wants and needs. I bless them on their journey and pray for their peace and joy.

What Can I Do?

If someone is acting unkind, there must be a story behind it, so I will only assume there is a struggle within them and that it's not about me. I can take a risk and inquire if there's anything I can do to help, which may result in some backlash. I will convince myself not to take it personally and decide how I will continue to show up for those who are struggling. I will not allow any of their pain to hurt me, so the only thing I may be able to do is pray for their enlightenment and healing. That I can do!

Anxious and Impatient

Making a decision too soon can cause more harm than good. When I become anxious about a situation and impatiently waiting for the outcome, I can make a decision to resolve it to ease my discomfort. Knowing this is a temporary fix and not the real decision, I will now have to deal with making a decision before it is to be resolved and the backlash of its potential postponement. All will work out in God's time when He thinks I'm ready. I'm learning to live with hope and faith.

Hopeful

Waking with a heavy heart can cause me to feel hopeless. When I'm dealing with unrest with a loved one or a friend, I can become so anxious and impatient for there to be a resolution that my thoughts get tied into a knot of despair instead of hope. In these times, I will shed my tears, bless them, and give it all to God. If I allow Him to heal my brokenness, then I can find joy while things move toward resolution. Whatever the outcome, I have faith that all will be as God intends it to be!

Go-Round

After the dust has settled from the storm in my heart and in my mind, I can understand and reaffirm the life lesson and experience. I may not fully understand everything that I have encountered in my life, but I do believe there is a purpose for me to learn. The best part about life is, I will be given another opportunity to revisit the lesson if I don't get it the first go-round.

Seek the Truth

Elders are responsible for molding children into productive, ethical, moral participants in society. Children are hopefully taught through positive role models about responsibility, respect, trustworthiness, fairness, and kindness. We are to believe what our elders model and teach, and therefore, we can have a life journey that fulfills our purpose. Yet there are so many truths that it takes a lifetime to empty all the opinions, judgments, and prejudices and to truly know the truth. The cost for truth seekers may be great, but what matters most is that the truth is revealed and that we all have a choice.

Done for Me

Harboring ill will is a poison in the soul that can steal the glimmer of hope if not resolved. I used to think things were done to me because I was not worthy. I looked at all my pain as a consequence of just being who I was. Now I am looking at the resentment and bitterness that are festering and ask myself if holding on to any of this can serve me and bring me peace. Then I receive the clarity of the positive outcome. Rather than resenting, I am appreciating; and instead of bitterness, I am seeking joy. The vital life lessons and experiences have brought me many opportunities to seek the truth and live in the light rather than to disappear into the darkness. I've come to learn that it wasn't done to me; it was done for me.

Doing Better

When I think of all the choices I have made in my life, I have clarity about what was driven by fear and what resulted when I lived in faith. Trying to live by the golden rule and the Ten Commandments resulted in feeling that I always fell short of what was expected. Now after looking at my behavior and changing, I can be humbled to feel forgiven and learn to do better.

Motives

When I offer advice, money, or a piece of my heart, what is my motive? Is it coming from a place of control or coming from a place of love? Am I placing my wants before the needs of others? Does my giving come with conditions, or am I giving freely? Do I have expectations that may lead me to feel disappointed or taken for granted? Will my heart harden, and will I become resentful and bitter if I don't receive the results I am seeking? What is my motive? It is to do unto others as I would have them do unto me. It is to show kindness, compassion, empathy, and love. If it's not driven by these actions, I will not engage! I need to be very clear about my motives. I'm not sure if my faith is the foundation of my hope or my hope is the foundation of my faith. Either way, I'm blessed to have both!

One More Sunrise

I wonder how I've managed to finally accept my past as finished and done. Having lived in the pain, I became a victim at every sunrise. So it is with the state of the world. What exactly can I control in this time of unrest? What events can I change to bring me to a different outcome? I know I have to abide by certain restrictions. I know the sun will rise every morning. I know I have joy and love in my life. I know I have to seek God more and fear less. I know I have to accept what I can't change and be grateful for where I am. I know all will be as it is intended to be, so today, I will live one more day of my life in peace and joy and with love in my heart and thank God for one more sunrise.

Lie

A lie is a false statement made with deliberate intent to deceive. It is an intentional untruth, a falsehood, and a behavior that is chosen to not do the right thing. So when a lie is discovered and when trust is broken, all that can be salvaged is the hope for restoration, as forgiveness will melt away the resentment, disappointment, and bitterness that are left behind. So how do I move forward if I choose to continue to be a part of a broken relationship? Where is the foundation of this relationship if lying becomes a part of it? How do I maintain a healthy distance while trying to mend that which is shattered? I can learn to trust again and be cautious and aware of how much of myself I am giving away as I heal my own heart while I am trying to live in the moment. How much of this lie is part of me? Who is this person that I once held in my heart?

AND THEN WHAT?

Sometimes, it seems like forever when I am just sitting and waiting for something I want. I think if I only get what I want, then I will be complete and happy. But then what? Will I feel any more fulfilled, loved, cherished, or purposeful? How much energy, time, and power am I putting into my wants? I am missing the beauty and the blessings that are right in front of me. I know that I will have what I want if I am meant to have it. So much time has been wasted on the question, "And then what?" It's time to live again!

TRUTH NEEDS NO EVIDENCE, NOR DOES IT NEED A DEFENSE

I spent most of my life defending my truth as if it even mattered if they believed me or not. This very action took my power and faith away from God and placed my destiny in their hands. This very action held my soul in a prison of despair and sacrifice. I feared that if I spoke louder with the same story, someone would believe me. We all make our own decisions with our words and actions. When I look in the mirror, who do I want staring back at me, a person of integrity or a person who is willing to barter with her truth to receive an affirmation from someone who is living a lie?

THE WAY I SEE ME

I may have an acquaintance reach out when they are depressed to ask for support. I may have a friend pray over me and speak amazingly kind, gentle words about me. I may have someone affirm a kindness they see in me or tell me I am supportive and encouraging. I may hear that my words of truth are a comfort in a corrupt world. These kind words sometimes astound me, that I am seen in that light because of the struggles I wrestle with within me. It's not as if I feel I am presenting myself with a false narrative or that I am not worthy of the affirmation. Rather, this is the person I aspire to be; so I will continue to show kindness, speak words of truth, be supportive, and encourage others. This is who I want to see in the reflection of my mirror. This is how God shines through me.

Living with the Promise

Living with the promise that all will be as meant to be can be interrupted by my anxiousness of one word: *when*. It is because of this word that I am tempted to offer unsolicited assistance, and this will only prolong the arrival of the promise. So when I become anxious and put all my focus on the outcome I desire, I will read a book, watch a movie, write, take a walk, hug my puppies, smell a flower, or look at the flowing river. In these peaceful experiences, I will be surrounded with the now, and the when won't matter. I can live with the promise and enjoy what I have now.

What Will Matter at the End of Our Days?

At the end of my days, what will really matter, the amount of money in my bank account or the fact that I shared it? Will it matter that I held on to my resentment because of someone's behavior against me or that I offered forgiveness? Will it matter that I was more proficient at a task than another or that I only wanted to be a better me than I used to be? Will it matter that I chose fear to drive my anxious decisions or that I had faith that God always knew what was best for me? What will matter at the end our days?

The Garden

How do relationships begin, and how do you get to know someone's story? Communication is the foundation of a relationship, and only by being present can a relationship bloom. Being attentive to the words that are shared will help develop intimacy, where I see you and you see me. No light can penetrate walls that are built around the mind and the heart, so it is with kindness, compassion, empathy, patience, attention, and appreciation that a relationship can blossom into the flowers of the beautiful garden of humanity. We can heal hate with love and sadness with joy and fear with faith when we come together to start anew. The past cannot be changed, but the weeds can be pulled and replaced with a new seed that will flourish into a beautiful flower called hope.

Where Joy Lives

There comes a time in life when all the tears have been shed into the pool of healing, and this is where joy lives. There comes a time in life when resentment melts into the light of dawn, and this is where joy lives. There comes a time in life when a hardened heart melts into softness, and this is where joy lives. When all the battles have been fought and the conquest no longer takes on a life of its own, this is where joy lives. Enter into joy, and enjoy your life.

God's Outcome

While I reflect on the memories of my life, I sometimes give more attention to the pain than to the joy. These hard knocks that we all encounter—junior high school, cliques, prom disappointments, unmet affections, or people leaving—are all parts of the journey that does not kill us but makes us stronger. Even though the events may be painful, the outcome always seems to work out for our good. Not seeing the entire picture as God does, I can get caught up in these little snapshots of disappointment; but now that I am living in faith, hope, and truth, I depend more on God's outcome to do good for me than anyone could ever promise. So I will live in His promise that all that was done to me was done for me.

All Is Well

Sometimes, I just am. Sometimes, it just is. All the time, it is well.

> Truth is never dependent on the consensus of others. Truth needs no evidence. If you worry about what other people think of you, then you will have more confidence in their opinion than you have in your own. Poor is the man whose future depends on the opinions and permissions of others. If you are afraid of criticism, you will die doing nothing.

Where I Dwell

Life lessons that brought important experiences that promoted growth were what helped me change and move forward. Pain from my past can only be relived in my mind if I choose to dwell there, but I can't undo the past, so why focus on an experience that can't be changed and will only give me grief? Tolerating unacceptable behavior has taught me that I do not have to be a part of that circle even if it means I am lonely. I can celebrate the lessons I have learned by not reliving or undoing them but moving forward in peace knowing I am loved, cherished, and worthy. I get to choose where I dwell and where my true nourishment lies.

Release

Having lived my life with a few disappointments, I've come to realize that the outcomes usually benefitted my life. Although I may not have always gotten what I thought I wanted, I always got what I needed. I've learned that letting go of what I want is far less painful than holding on to the disappointment of not receiving it. Why would I want to hold on to something that causes me pain? What would be the purpose for doing that?

*****

Watching a child take their first steps, wanting to prevent their inevitable fall, or sending them off to kindergarten are some of the hardest things a parent has to do. It's a natural instinct to feel heart-ache. As they are pushing away, we want to draw them closer. When a loved one is taking a different path from mine, I want to encourage them onto my path, or I may even detour onto theirs, stirring the feeling of letting go and remembering how I felt when my children wandered off onto their own paths. Yet I know that no one will join me unless they make that choice and that no one will see the world through my eyes, and I cannot welcome love into my heart unless I release the pain that lives there. So as I have learned to release my child into the world and encourage a loved one to follow their own path, I am learning to release the pain in my heart to welcome the love that is waiting to fill it.

PAIN FREE

In the beginning of my recovery from brokenness, I thought that if I followed a certain recovery plan, I would be healed and pain free. I thought that if I chanted affirmations, read the right recovery books, went to therapy, joined a group, believed in God to save my soul, and repented for my sins, then my life would be pain free. I thought that if I had all my issues resolved, all my relationships restored, and all my trespassers punished, then I would be happy. But now I've realized that all that was done to me, either by my choice or the choice of others, was used for my good. I am where I am meant to be, and even though my life is not pain free, I know I am not alone, and I have faith and hope. I can be happy and find joy right where I am.

The Only One

It's interesting that when I have a conflict with someone and hold on to the pain, I am the only one doing that. The other person has moved on and doesn't give it a second thought. All the while, I am immersed in the pain and anguish of what has been said and done. How in the world does this serve me? Will it make a difference if I worry more or cry another tear or become angry and resentful since I am the only one behaving this way? I will let it go, and I will forgive. I will look for the life lesson in the experience, and I will learn to live with the pain but not in the pain, because I am the only one who can control this and make myself happy. God opens doors to happiness, but it's my choice to walk through.

Truth

When I think or do things that I know are not in my best interest, I not only try to change them but also seek the origin of that thought or behavior. I may not always get an answer, but I do know I am capable of seeking the truth, as I am continuing my journey to know the truth and live in the truth. I have the amazing gift of awareness—if it feels wrong, don't do it! I also have hope and faith that I know the truth, and if I'm not sure, I will seek the truth, and it will be revealed. I choose truth.

Journey's End

Making decisions have not always been easy for me. I'm usually the one with buyer's remorse after an expensive purchase or doubt myself by the way others react when I share what I have chosen. Never in the history of my life has regret ever made me happy or brought the outcome I was looking for. After being told who I should be and what I should want, I started thinking if the decisions they were making for me were in my best interest. When I made the decision to search for the truth, I was going to make it about purging the lies so I could replace them with the truth. In my journey, I found the truth. My prayer is that everyone will.

A Friend

I can't say I trust you and not believe in you. I can't say I love you and then do things that harm you and myself. I can't say nasty things to you or about you and be able to look you in the eye. I can't call myself honorable, trustworthy, kind, or respectful if my behavior doesn't match these attributes. I pray to be my best self for you and for myself. I believe and trust that you will help me accomplish this prayer. Thank you for being in my life to help me succeed.

Ponder

There are times when I have to make a decision and it is effortless. Then there are times when I think I've made my decision and I doubt myself. In the past, this practice brought on much anxiety, as if this decision was the most important in my life. This self-inflicted drama kept me on edge and took my focus away from the desired outcome of my decision, as it kept me in doubt and desperation. I would seek advice and relinquish my power, only to blame the others' advice if I was unhappy with the outcome. This took all the responsibility and power off me as I reacted to what they told me to do. Of course, all this was within my own power, yet it was so much easier to displace it onto someone else. That way, if it was the wrong decision, I could blame them. Now knowing and believing in my own free will and God's will for me, I ponder over my desired outcome and make my own decisions.

Contentment

Being content does not mean I have settled for the status quo; it means I have peace with all that I have been blessed with by God. Finding compassion for another as they struggle through decisions that are all too familiar is an act of kindness and support, not an act

371

of enabling and complacency. Speaking my opinion is not an act of judgment, claiming that I am right; it is a platform for my convictions of who I am. I live with a contented mind and have a compassionate heart and know my truth. I respect the same in you.

Joy

I used to live in anxiousness, awaiting what I wanted to have. I would put my happiness on hold depending on what I thought I needed to bring me joy. Now I live in joy in each moment, and I appreciate what I have been given to fulfill my needs for the day. I know that in God's timing, He will provide me with what He wants me to have to enrich my life. For now, I am enriched by the joy I feel for each moment I have been given.

REQUIREMENTS

I spent many decades watching myself go in and out of pain and joy. Never did I find the secret on how to remain at peace until I found my truth. That process became the most painful experience, yet the outcomes were joy and peace. It required me to examine all that I truly held in my mind and soul as being the truth. It required me to take an inventory of who laid the foundation of my truth, and then it required a sifting through what was true. The pain came from becoming empty and having faith to live in the void, which soon filled. It required my finding patience and forgiveness for myself and others. It required my asking to be forgiven, which now required living in the truth. The truth needs no evidence, opinion, judgment, or interpretation. The requirement to live in the truth is to have faith in knowing that He is the truth.

CHAPTER 13

Reactions

Better Than

During a healing period, I may surround myself with the pain that I am trying to heal. Reviewing the hurt will help me see things more clearly if I am willing to dig deep into what part of the pain is yours and what part of the pain is mine. This is not to blame-shift or to remain a victim. It is merely opening the closed doors to welcome you back into my life so that we can apologize and humbly ask for forgiveness. Although we do not get a do-over to change our past hurts, we can look at what led us to our decisions and come to an understanding that what transpired may not have been the result of us being our best self, and we can learn from our experiences and change our behavior.

While I dread voicing my fears and hurts, not wanting to be judged or abandoned and dreading to be seen as vulnerable, it's the only way to resolve this. Asking for or receiving forgiveness does not give me a free pass to continue my hurtful behavior. There are no excuses to be hurtful, and it does not give me permission to stay a victim or to not be accountable for my part in the scenario. I can learn to live through the pain knowing it is a part of me and may revisit me as a trigger, but I know it does not define me. I can be better than my trespasses and my abuse.

Just ask

I am sometimes confronted with too much that I react in a dark way, allowing the negative to engulf me. I react in a short, abrupt manner or begin to be judge and jury. When I finally shake myself out of it, I can then ask someone if they will help me. Humbling myself to ask for forgiveness and assistance will only benefit my journey. This can also be challenging if I get attached to an outcome. I can appreciate the journey and leave the destination for another day. Having a traveling buddy sure does help.

The One Constant

Sometimes, when my anxiousness to resolve issues sets in, I will start plotting my own destiny. I will begin to recall events that will rush me to resolve the issue without finding patience and keeping my faith that all is in God's time. I can begin to justify why I need to remind others that I deserve to feel the way I feel and defend my actions. In this danger zone of self-sabotage and doubt, this fear can drive me back into the darkness of lies whence I came. This is when I need to stop and find compassion in my heart and remind myself that I am no more perfect than another.

In my waiting time, I can gently forgive and remind myself of my own journey and how it's taken decades for me to heal from my own choices that hurt me. This is not to negate the abuse but to look at my part in my own life. Consequently, the choices that I make in fear keep me in the darkness. It isn't until I have shed myself of others' belief systems that I take a leap into the unknown and aloneness to find my own truth. Some may leave, and others may stay, but ultimately, the one who will always be a constant in my life, besides God, is always me. I can be me!

In the Mind's Eye

What I see, what I think, or what I hear is all about my perception. What may be my interpretation of a situation will make me either right or wrong. I look at the experience and try to draw the life lesson from the encounter. This may differ from another's interpretation, so when we share, we can embrace our perceptions and thank the other person for their point of view.

We Meet Again

When encountering another after years of discourse or separation, I may feel the need to recall what is mine and what is not. I can go into the visit with a new reaction: embrace and forgiveness. I become aware of my triggers, and if need be, I set a boundary as I present who I am today. I choose not to engage in the old bantering, I choose to step away from accusing voices, and I choose to only engage in positive encounters. I have defined myself in my own truth and have my own voice.

Making a Choice

When I get caught up in the negative behavior of another, I feel as if it is my responsibility to make peace. Since no one likes discourse, I take it upon myself to take on his or her burden even if it's not my business. This gets in the way of God and sets me back when I don't get the results I crave: to be loved and appreciated. What they choose to do to me is about them. What I choose when I allow them to treat me this way is about me. I am not out to punish anyone, but I am aware that I am the only one who can allow or reject any behavior choices from another. I choose to take care of myself, as they are in the process of dealing with their own behavior choices.

Not a Target

In my reactions to someone's language or tone of voice, I can become very agitated and close down. I can fabricate the meaning of their words or actions to mean that I am not worthy or good enough to be loved based on the language and behavior they have chosen, and then it dawns on me that their behavior and language are not in my control unless they are directed at me. My emotions have been driven by my reactions to others' behaviors rather than to reflect my true self. I have allowed myself to be defined by others' opinions. It's time to take back my life. That is when I can set a boundary and walk away from trying to change their behavior to suit me. No one will pick their behavior to meet my needs, but I can walk away if their behavior infringes on my soul. I am no one's target!

React in Love

Most of the things I fear I conjure up in my head, and it's not worth the energy I give it. I script a dialogue in my head that is never needed and will never be spoken. I imagine the worst-case scenario when in fact, it never turns out that way. This is fear, not love. I am blessed to know the difference, and I am becoming more aware of its pull on me. I will react in love.

Refuel

How easy it is for me to feel depleted in my isolation that I can immediately blame-shift my unhappiness onto another as if they are responsible for making me feel loved and appreciated. When I find myself isolated, that is when I need to reach out. When I'm hungry, I eat; when I'm tired, I rest; and so when I'm feeling depleted, I ask for help. Giving to others without being refueled can leave me feeling depleted, and then I will find myself looking to get filled from another. These are dangerous times for me, as I can look to be filled and not take any responsibility to fill myself. I will continue to be aware of my needs and fulfill myself as needed.

Boomerang

The next time I pray for a situation to change, I will extend that prayer back to me. If I pray for someone's broken heart to heal, I will pray my heart will be healed. If I pray for someone to forgive me, I shall forgive him or her and myself as well. If I pray for a situation to change, I will look at how I can make that situation better for me as I assess what is my part to change. My joy or misery is my own choosing, not contingent on someone's behavior or the circumstances of life. Just as a boomerang returns, so will the extensions of my prayers for others.

SIGNALS

When I see a behavior that doesn't align with mine, I have a choice to either let it steal my joy or pray for that person that they heal and pray for myself that I stay in peace. Being reactionary to unsavory behavior is becoming part of that behavior when I engage with word and action, so I need to remain mindful of how I allow others' behavior to affect my peace and how much energy I am giving to them. Will my displeasure change their behavior, or will my displeasure be a signal that I am not in control of them? I look for the signals that tell me how I am choosing to behave. This choice is about myself and what I can control.

LET IT RAIN

In the stillness of just breathing, I can hear the rumble of the storm in the distance. If I allow it, it can come in and disturb my serenity; but if I acknowledge it instead of ignore it, I can decide how much of the storm I want to infiltrate my peace. Sometimes, a gentle rain can wash away the film that is impeding my judgment; and other times, I just need to allow it to trickle over me. Whatever the situation is, I can decide how I want to react. Let it rain.

PEACE OR UNREST

When I am confronted with an opinion that differs from mine, I have a choice whether to be combative or to welcome the opinions with an open mind and open heart. It is when I am dismissed or my opinion is drowned out by another's attempt to bully me into submission that my choice can either be to put on my armor and engage

377

or walk away. What truly matters? What will bring me peace? How will I choose to engage to be heard? How will I be perceived? What is my goal?

New Reactions

Knowing when an issue is my life lesson has helped me learn about my own fear-based reactions. When I am confronted by a situation that makes me uncomfortable, instead of my old reactionary method of yelling or crying, I can now take a deep breath and silence the fear with a few clarifying questions: Why am I reacting in fear? What is this reaction telling me? What has it triggered? Is this life lesson for me, or am I a mere participant in another's lesson? When I can settle myself into faith, I can then give the fear a voice and answer my questions. Then I'll know what to do.

Agree to Disagree

When I am confronted with a behavior that may make me uncomfortable or make me feel as though I need to defend my choices, I can become agitated, and I may engage in a combative response. This is when I need to pull myself in and know I do not have to defend who I am or my truth. If another's truth contradicts mine, then I can let that be and know that my truth is what matters. If there is some truth that contradicts mine, then I can listen with an open heart and open mind; and if there is a resolution to be had, then we can agree to disagree. We may not see things the same way or remember the same facts, but we can respect one another enough to apologize and try to do better.

Stay in the Light

In my continuing recovery and journey toward my best self in God's light, I am reminded of how I am so reactionary to others' opinions. It reminds me how easily I am able to question my self-worth. No one but God and me can determine my worth or what is best for me. The core of my darkness lies in my ability to believe that someone knows what's better for me than I know for myself, and this only dims my light. I can get lost in the negative, but then knowing I am worthy of the light, my reaction flips to the positive.

Having lived my life in the shadow of reactions, I no longer want or need a detour away from my heart and soul, so I step into a drama-free void and into the emptiness of situations left behind and move into my own heart and my own soul and into who I truly am. This comes with no label and no definition, only who I am in the quiet and stillness. With a heart open, renewal time, clarity, joy of unconditional love, forgiveness, and staying in the light are new behaviors. I chant, "Heal yourself and keep it simple so that I may see God's image in the souls of my fellow human beings. Things in God's time according to His plan have always worked. Trust and live in faith, peace, joy, and love."

TAKE IT BACK

My emotions have been driven by my reactions to others' behaviors rather than reflecting my true self. I have allowed myself to be defined by others' opinions. It's time to take back my life. In my aloneness, I am reminded how I need to give myself all that I am sharing with others—love, acceptance, compassion, generosity, and blessings. Being my authentic self is how I choose to live my life. Alone or with others, I am living as God intends—as the blessing I already am.

WHAT IS TRULY MINE

From the time I am born until the day that I die, what is truly mine? My thoughts, my choices, my body, my feelings, my breath, my heartbeat, and my soul—everything that I choose to attach myself to can either teach me something or is something that I can enhance in someone else. Either way, none of it is mine to own, so I can decide if I will carry someone else's burden or engage in their drama and check to see if it's worth disturbing and losing my inner peace and serenity for. They are only thoughts and feelings, and I can change them if I so desire. How I choose to think, feel, act, and react is in my control. How should I use my choices to benefit my soul's evolution?

POSITIVE INTENTIONS

Reactions to that which I cannot control are battles that wage in my heart. It becomes a burden to think I know what is best, only to cause arguments that can be avoided if only I react with compassion and kindness. I will observe in silence and offer only solicited advice that is free from judgment so that even if I do something a different way, it doesn't make them wrong or me right. I will decide for me and let them be.

Reactions to outcomes that I expect may cause a negative trigger. The outcomes may not be what I want but are surely what I need to help me evolve. The initial reaction is disappointment, and this may soon deepen into resentment if my faith and trust are not called upon to help me see the grander picture. Once again, I may not understand or even get an answer, but my comfort lies in knowing that not knowing is in God's control. Change is inevitable, but misery is optional, so why not enjoy the journey and watch the blessing unfold? I call on my inner strength when reacting with positive intentions.

MY CONTROL

How many times did I live the days, years, and moments of my life in disappointment? How many endless hours did I spend scripting my resentment? How many years did I do this dance of continuing to hurt myself as others had hurt me? This life journey has taken a turn, and now I am choosing to get back on my road toward the light. As I disown that which is not mine to hold knowing it isn't an asset to my light, it will wreak havoc. The loud message will try to dim my light, yet it will know I am not leaving me again. I trust myself and have faith in God and know I am His blessing.

In my alone time, I reflect on what is mine, what I can control, how I react, and what I judge and why. My reactions that morphed into resentment were ultimately my fear of not being worthy of love and acceptance or not being validated. Fear brought on my anxiousness to fix it so the uncomfortable abandonment would be filled so I could feel loved. But as I experienced through many unanswered prayers, my reaction to manipulate an outcome only prolonged my connection to myself. My biggest fear became my own reality when I left myself to fill another, hoping that in return, they would fill me too. Now I know that God is my truth and that His voice guides me toward the light.

I Define Me

I decide what my attributes are and what are mine to enhance. If I am a stakeholder in someone else's decisions, then I take care of me, voicing my needs and opinions. Boundaries and detachment with empathy, compassion, patience, and forgiveness for others and myself are my ways of engaging without control or manipulation. I don't need any more pain or drama to feel alive and blessed. I can live with the pain but no longer need to live in it. I've loved and cared for others my entire life and have put others' needs before my own, but now all I have to do is be who I am and offer assistance without becoming their shadow. I can include them on my journey without losing me.

Anticipation, Not Expectation

I used to think that others would treat me the way I treated them—showing kindness, compassion, empathy, understanding, and love. I would wait for their acknowledgment and validation of my worth, disregarding the fact that I was already worthy. I gave to them to seek their approval and to define me. I gave them my voice and power and lived in the truth of who they defined me to be. The energy that I poured into them left me depleted, and eventually, I became resentful in my disappointment.

Help me remember that we are all souls on a journey and that no one else's journey defines me. The detours may have been inconvenient or disruptive, but the rerouting to my desired path has given me opportunities that will help me on my journey. There is always joy, love, and peace once the drama has subsided and the pain has healed. There is always the gift waiting once the ache, fear, and grief have settled.

Now I know I was worthy all along. They did not define me. My expectations have not turned into anticipation, and instead of waiting for them, I now have faith that God's got me, and them too. In my alone time, I reflect on what is mine, what I can control, how I react, and what I judge and why. How I perceive something is different from others. How I react, feel, and live is all about me.

Quiet Reflection

When I feel blessed to have faith and trust in God, I must speak the words, write the words, or read the words; and I must believe them. I will keep saying, writing, reading, and praying that my thoughts and actions depict this. I say I am letting go of what was or could have been to have faith in what will be, yet I still long for that phone to ring, that knock on the door, and those three words. I pray to keep on letting go and showing up for my life.

If the phone does ring or the knock on the door happens or I do hear those words, what would change? I am meant to be where I am and who I am with and meant to be with. I would not have found me or be living this drama-free life with them in it, so for now, I find peace and contentment in my quiet, reflective healing time without the drama those relationships bring to the table. All is a work in progress, not yet done. As my river keeps flowing, so does my life. Sometimes, it's calm; and sometimes, it's roaring with high waves and rocks; but either way, God has taught me how to swim.

Relationship

Relationships aren't about competition or outdoing each other's strengths; it's a cooperation that needs our differences. Relationships aren't about two people dashing across the bridge. It's discovering that after a lifetime, they've built the bridge together with their own hands. We do not have the power to make one another happy or unhappy. That is our individual power. We can make ourselves happy and share that happiness. The guidance we share with others is our own example of the highest, most advanced human beings we know how to be. We all have our special gifts. Try to remember that there is a reason I have chosen what's happening around me; I live my life the best way I know how. My inner teachers and guides are here to help me remember things I've already learned and known.

Having lived my life in the shadow of reactions, I no longer want or need a detour away from my heart and soul. I step into a drama-free void, the emptiness of situations left behind, and into my own heart and my own soul and into who I truly am with no label and no definition, only who I am in the quietness and stillness of God's light. Heart open, renewal time, clarity, joy of unconditional love, forgiveness, and staying in the light are new behaviors. Heal yourself and keep it simple so that I may see God's image in the souls of my fellow human beings. Things in God's time according to His plans have always worked. Trust, faith, peace, joy, and love are my goals.

TRUST

I will act in my own best interest. Occasionally, my choices will not please others. This action will help me take true responsibility for my life and my choices. I will own my own behavior and speak my own truth above others. I realized that all those people who helped form me and those who tried to assimilate me into who they wanted me to be were all mistaken, as was I. They thought I was supposed to be who they wanted me to be, and I agreed with them and allowed the assimilation. Only God can create me, and I am led by my own truth, and I create my own life. I don't have to be perfect. I just need to accept that I'm not. "I don't need to remember the pain of every experience that taught me the lesson, only the lessons themselves. Forgiveness is giving up and letting go of the hope that the past could have been different. The outcome will never change, only how I react to it."

SEEK THE SOURCE

When I begin to look at what's mine versus what's theirs, I feel my push-pull because I am so easily swayed and manipulated, yet this does not bring cause to do unto others as they have done unto me. When I am quiet within, usually, my initial reaction is a mask, so I am delving into the source. Sometimes, the behavior choice is not really the issue. It's the vessel to travel deeper into the source and usually come into the light.

COMPASSION, NOT CONDEMNATION

When I encounter a behavior that does not align with mine, I may be quick to condemn rather than stop and access the situation. Even after the assessment, I may still need to rise above the need to judge and condemn knowing we are all souls on an evolutionary journey. So as I am learning to find compassion, rather than settle in my judgments of condemnation, I am also offering the same kindness to myself.

WITHHOLDING

When I sit in front of another without knowing their story, I wonder about our similarities and differences. Do they have a story like mine? Behind the smiles and clothing and social status, I wonder who they are. I can see a grandmother with her grandchildren and wonder about her relationship to her child or see a couple walking hand in hand and wonder how they manage to remain intimate. The outer will always mask the inner, so when I ask the why questions, it's because I am on a different path and because my story, although similar and different from theirs, is mine to live. If I spend my time longing for that which I don't have, I am likely to miss the treasures I carry. I can embrace what I've been given as much as I can embrace that which has been withheld. God is holding me with love. I am blessed with the life I have.

KEEP TRYING

When I fall down, I get back up. When I'm faced with an obstacle, I find a way around it. When I have a mountain to climb, I equip myself with the necessary equipment and climb it. When I feel pain, I find a way to ease it. When I need to find a way, I find my way. All is possible if I keep on trying; just keep trying.

RESCUE

When I watch someone I love in pain, I want to put on my armor and rescue him or her. In the past, I would sacrifice me in order to assure their peace and safety, leaving me out of the equation. I saw their struggles as my own, not advocating for myself or honoring my own boundaries. There is little I can do for another but offer encouraging words of love and prayers. I can honor myself in the same way I offer support to another, but the only one I can rescue is me.

CONDEMNATION VERSUS COMPASSION

Am I examining my motives toward self-conquest, or am I trying to dominate another? Am I finding compassion for another's differences, or am I condemning them that they do not align with me? These deep soul questions help me find my humble core so I can know that I am not better or worse than another. We are all loved and cherished. What goal am I seeking when I treat another in this manner? Does this behavior enhance or impede my growth? Is this the way I want to be treated? Is this the person I want to be?

MY WHOLENESS

Who I am in the midst of having relationships is a matter of keeping my voice as I welcome yours. It used to be so easy to for me to be swayed into your thinking as I melted away. I thought that if I said or did just the right thing, then not only would you love me but I would also receive the same in return. Knowing that my completeness is totally dependent on me, I can welcome you without disappearing into your shadow. I can welcome you into my life to become a part of it, not to be my whole.

Not Often Enough

When I was a young girl, I hoped for physical beauty, money, and love. I would receive something, and instead of savoring the answered prayer, I would be on the next wish. I rarely celebrated my accomplishments or acknowledged that I was already beautiful and had all that I would ever need and was already loved unconditionally. How often has my unhappiness from an unanswered prayer outplayed a true blessing? How often have I gone through my life not noticing the little things that truly hold my joy? How often have I not been grateful for the amazing life that I live and yet to live with all my abundant blessings? Too often. It's time to change that!

How Will I Know?

Perfection is excellence, exactness, precision, and flawlessness. If I strive for this every time I want to undertake a task, I will lose myself in the destination rather than in the joyfulness of what I can experience on the journey. Getting lost in the finished product can make me feel as if every move I make must be a certain way, or I will be a failure. Against whose standards do I hold myself? If I am to meet someone's needs, then in turn, another will be disappointed, because their needs may differ. But if I always present my best self, approving and accepting my own behavior choices knowing my efforts are my best, then if another is disappointed, that's not about me. How will I know if it's the right path or the right thing to do? I will always know if I communicate with God.

WHISPER

The more I listen to the voice in my head that delivers messages that make me feel insecure, unsure, or afraid, the more I know it's not God. It may be the voice I believed to be true and that defined me, and it's the voice of the lies of my adult's truth. Sometimes, the voice has to scream to be heard; and usually, this is a sign that I am disconnected from God. The other voice reassures me that everything is okay and is usually heard in a whisper. Once I hear God, I know that is the voice of truth. Once I hear what He has to say, I revert to calmness, and the other voice is replaced with peace and reassurance that all is well. Within the whisper lies peace.

CHANGE MY THOUGHT

How often do I allow one negative thought or comment to steal my joy? Why is it that the negative is easier to believe? What's the worst that can happen if I soften my hardened heart and forgive others' indiscretions as well as my own? How would I then live without waiting for the other shoe to drop? If I allow the opposite to occur, would I then live in peace and be joyful?

SUBTLE ENTRY

When a lobster is prepared for cooking, it is placed in a pot of water that slowly comes to a boil. The future meal is unaware of its subtle and imminent death. Just like toxic thoughts that subtly enter my mind, I may be oblivious to them before I allow myself to react in a negative way that may cause harm. My voice of condemnation enters my heart before I can process the words spoken and access how it's making me feel. Being cognizant of my thoughts and reactions is a moment-by-moment practice, and I am beginning to become mindful of its power. Once noticed, I can turn condemnation into compassion and send out a blessing through my prayers. I may not always be cognizant of the subtle entry of a thought, but my goal is to alter it as soon as I am.

I Choose

When I am confronted with a decision, I have free will to choose either to accept or deny the outcome. If I want someone to help me and they are not willing or are unavailable, I get to choose how I will react. If I don't get my way, then I may become disappointed, because I expect a certain behavior to meet mine. But this has not always been the case. I have experienced remaining in my disappointment to the point where my expectations may melt into resentment if I harbor my desire too long. This is when I get to choose how long I will remain with these feelings and what exactly I can control if my needs are unmet. Not always being about me, I can decide what the life lesson in this experience is and how I will choose to learn from it. I get to choose how long I remain wherever I am led.

Helping Heart

When I'm comforting a friend who has shared their pain, I am very cognizant of how much of me I will allow to become part of their healing. Immersing myself into their story can result in giving too much of me. There is a fine line between honoring someone enough to assist them and trying to learn what it is to be in a healthy relationship with them. No one can complete another; all I can do is offer a kind word or a helping hand to assist them on their way from pain to joy. With a helping heart, I can remember what is mine and what is theirs and the wisdom to know the difference.

Listen in the Quiet

In my aloneness, I am reminded of how I need to give to myself all that I am sharing with others—love, acceptance, compassion, generosity, and blessings. Being my authentic self is how I choose to live my life. Alone or with others, I am living as God intends—as the blessing I already am. In my continuing recovery and journey toward my best self in God's light, I am reminded of how I am so reactionary to others' opinions. It reminds me how easily I am able to question my worth. No one but God and me can determine my worth or what is best for me. As the core of my darkness lies in my ability to believe that someone knows what's better for me than I know for myself, this only dims my light. I can get lost in the negative, but then knowing I am worthy of the light, my reaction flips to the positive.

Drama Free

I don't need any more pain or drama to feel alive and blessed. I can live with the pain, but I no longer need to live in it. I've loved and cared for others my entire life and have put others' needs before my own, but now all I have to do is be who I am and offer assistance without becoming their shadow. I can include them on my journey without losing me. Help me remember that we are all souls on a journey and that no one else's journey defines me. The detours may have been inconvenient or disruptive, but the rerouting to my desired path has given me opportunities that will help me on my journey. There is always joy, love, and peace once the drama has subsided and once we know the pain has healed. There is always a gift waiting once the ache, fear, and grief have settled.

My Own Best Interest

I've chosen to remember that there is a reason why I have chosen what's happening around me. I'm learning to live my life the best I know how, and I may find out all my answers. My inner teachers and guides are here to help me remember things I have already learned and known. I will act in my own best interest even though occasionally, my choices will not please others. This action will help me be responsible for my life and my choices. I will own my own behavior and speak my own truth above others, and I will be true to the me I am meant to be.

I realized that all those people who helped form me and those who tried to assimilate me into who they wanted me to be were all mistaken, as was I. They thought I was supposed to be who they wanted me to be, and I agreed with them and allowed the assimilation to take place. Only God can create me, and I am led by my own truth, and I create my own life. I don't have to be perfect. I just need to accept that I'm not. I'm no better than anyone else. I just want to be better than I used to be.

I now look at myself with a compassionate eye. I can trust that I will have everything I need. I was never intended to carry all the supplies I needed at once; the burden was too heavy. I will have what I need when I need it. When sending messages, I make sure they are pure and don't contradict themselves. This will allow others and myself to keep our voice and know that our truth is moving toward a healthy relationship without manipulating outcomes.

WASTED!

I no longer offer unsolicited advice. I walk away from any exchange of negativity, no longer having to justify my integrity. I refuse to believe anything other than the truth about me from others or myself. I refuse to see anything but positivity about myself. I am not the cause of others' pain, only my own. I refuse any blame-shifting from others. I refuse to give anything about me to anyone to be loved or accepted. After or before a confrontation, I allowed fear to drive me into scripting a dialogue in my head so I am ready for battle. I spent a lot of energy into this behavior, and usually, it never happened as I fabricated it in my mind. I have wasted a lot of time and energy preparing for a confrontation that has never happened. Wasted!

HEAL THE WOUND

I know who I am by defining what I am not. It is through these life lessons and relationships that I am able to remember myself with God. As painful as some of these lessons have been, I know who I am. In spite of everyone's definitions and efforts to control me into who they want me to be, I know who I am. I can let go of expectations because I live in the faith that all is meant to be, and I cannot change what has already happened, but I can learn from it. The way I embrace these lessons and react will bring me peace.

It is only through the crack that the wonder of life can enter. My authentic truth guides the way to enlightenment. One moment, one look, one word, or one negative encounter allows suffering to become everything. That one splinter does not have to define me. Take out the splinter, and let the break heal. Give the power back to the whole, not to the tear. I look back to when I made a conscious decision that someone else knew better for me than I knew for myself. That power I gave away to a person who was supposed to love me. My fear was abandonment, so I did what they wanted, but they left anyway. But now there's no need to assimilate myself. I'm already loved just the way I am.

SERVANT

I was told that in order to help others, I had to help and believe in myself. I couldn't teach a child to read unless I knew how to read and learned how that child learned. I couldn't help another heal unless I knew their pain through feeling it myself and knowing empathy. I can help them if I know the pain firsthand and can find strategies and interventions to heal it, and I can only teach through modeling by walking my talk. The people who have dismissed me and labeled me their trigger are not ready to learn and heal. What I can do for me is to keep going without being responsible for them but to pray for their healing, showing compassion.

LIFE IS

Even if no one hears me, I have a voice. Even if no one sees me, I still have a shadow. Even if no one believes in me, I still know who I am and still live in my truth. Life is exploration and having fun figuring out what fits. Life is an experience with contradictions. Life is embracing all that I have been offered. I can discover who I am by detaching from who I clearly am not. I will never forget that once upon a time, in an unguarded moment, I recognized myself as a friend.

TRY AGAIN

The only mistake I can make is to think I've made a mistake, because everything I have done has purpose to help make me become the person I am. When I am judging myself or label a circumstance as bad, I am asked to change the judgment to adjust my thinking and behavior. I can look at all circumstances as opportunities to continue my journey to grow. There are no failures, only more opportunities to try again.

ANSWERS TO MY QUESTIONS

I wonder why I keep having these useless, endless, worthless dialogues in my head, planning a confrontation that never takes place? Why do I need to plan a defense when there's nothing to defend? The fear I've let build up in my mind is worse than the situation that actually exists. Why do I need to justify my choices when there is no justification needed? Why do I need to state my definition of myself when it doesn't matter because others will believe, think, feel, and judge the way they want to anyway. Why put so much energy into nothing that matters? I won't let another's issues define me or get me down. All that matters is, I have so many blessings and opportunities to evolve.

CHANGE THE NOW

I always thought I could manipulate or control an outcome to feel I was doing something to change the past, but all I was doing was prolonging the pain and sabotaging myself. Repeating the same behavior was just getting me the same results. Enlightenment has brought me to the fact that I am powerless over anyone or over what happened in my past. My past was who I was and what I did to help mold me into who I am today. Those behaviors were just what I did, not who I was. When I change what I believe, then I can change what I need to do. When I move beyond my fear, I free myself to evolve. So what would I accomplish if I weren't afraid?

I Know What to Do

When I began recovery, I became aware of my first reactions; they were fear based due to my issues with abandonment, judgment, abuse, and neglect. I became agitated, defensive, aggressive, and mean. I became the bully I feared. Now that I know better, I do better. A hater of haters is still a hater. I am no longer a hater but a forgiver and a person of compassion and empathy. When an adult's lie becomes a child's truth, the cycle will continue. The moment I decide that what I know is more important than what I am led to believe, I will understand. I already know what the problem is, so I will put my energy into solving the problem instead of complaining about it. I know what to do!

Matter

I am reminded that when I give to others, I should not expect anything in return, because the giving will be conditional. I am aware that when I spread myself too thin and forget to take care of my own needs, I will not be there for them if I am not there for myself first. I know that no matter how others treat me, I do matter. No matter what others may say, I know that I matter. I am just as worthy of all the goodness I feel I put out into the universe. I will continue to strive to be my best self even if others do not.

Accomplishments

My denial used to keep me safe since there was only me to protect myself. I wished things could have been different, but they weren't. I lived a misguided attempt at positive thinking, and it cost me my truth. Now knowing better, I have learned to let go of expectations and outcomes. I no longer feel my detours as unnecessary but as opportunities. I see my struggles in the reactions of others, yet I see how we all try to hide. I will live my life in the light of truth, not under a mask of denial. Every day is a new day filled with so many opportunities, experiences, and blessings. Some days are easier than others. The closer I come to the person I am meant to be, the more frequent the lessons will be to help my conviction. There are days of ease, and there are others that test me to my limits. I try not to dwell on the side steps and heartaches that come with being disappointed because of unmet goals. I will try to react in a positive light and remember the accomplishments, not the struggles, that have gotten me there.

In the Deep

I look at this journey as the depths of an ocean. At times, the waves may be crashing on the surface; and sometimes, I will experience tiny waves of unrest while a tsunami may be ensuing. But at the depths, the deepest part of the ocean is my soul. It is always calm and remain a constant, endless stream of peace. This is a reaction to a storm and a reminder to go within the depths to always find peace in God. When the waves get too big, I become a diver. I know that when I ask, I will receive, not always with what I want but with what I need. I choose to act in faith, love, compassion, and truth; and rest assured, I always receive all that God intends me to have.

Knock on My Door

At times, I have to deal with a conflict as I continue to use my voice to live in truth at the risk of a confrontation. At the risk of losing myself, I have had to be willing to sacrifice that which does not align with my truth. Before, I would find myself knocking on the doors of another, thinking that this was my entry to happiness, but it was just one more door labeled Assimilate. Now I know that the correct door to knock on is the door of love, faith, and truth. I will grieve for those who have left because I will not conform. I will miss them every day, but I will miss me even more.

Freethinking

I have been blessed with awareness of my thoughts, the ones driven by fear and love. I have learned to become aware of fear but to not let it take me hostage. I am done chasing after others who don't want me. I'm done asking someone to fill me with love and to accept who I am. My new reaction is not to react in a negative, defensive manner but to ask God for guidance and have Him show me the way out of the darkness by using His light as my guide. This frees my thinking toward faith and anticipation. I pray to continue to flip my negative dialogues toward positive blessings.

Humble

Out of all the possibilities to choose from to overcome obstacles, mine are to heal from abandonment, to regain trust in myself, and to deepen my faith and walk with God. I have been reminded to remember with my soul. I have learned to ask for forgiveness when I trespass against others and myself. I have learned to humble myself to listen to God and watch my reactions when dealing with a painful trigger. All I need are love and faith. I know I can no longer give the past any energy for a different outcome. It is what it is, and I am who I am because of it. I know that I will no longer take part in my own abuse by continuing to allow others to abuse me.

Nothing hurts more than living among others who don't see me. When I stop letting what other people think of me define me, then I can truly see who I am. I know that the distance between two people is a misunderstanding, so if they will not take the time to see me, then I am walking away from them and toward the light of God and myself. I will forever miss the thought of what I wish it could be, but now I let go of that so I could be opened to a new adventure. Forgiveness is not earned; it's given. The pain will end when I forgive those who have trespassed against me and when I forgive myself for my trespasses. This is done out of grace and generosity when I learn that I need forgiveness more than I need to be right.

Goodness, mercy, compassion, and understanding are all forms of light. Forgiveness and patience and strength and courage are forms of kindness. I will be a helper in times of need, a comforter in times of sorrow, a healer in times of injury, a teacher in times of confusion, and a student in search of knowledge. I can let go of trying to manipulate outcomes when the situation is difficult.

What Matters

At times, I will find myself reacting to things that, in the end, really don't matter. I can allow a situation to dictate how I will use my power to resolve my inner conflict, which is the only thing that I can truly control. I don't need to change the situation, only how I deal with it when I'm immersed in it. What do I really want? What are the barriers that prevent me from getting what I want? What must I do to get it? The more I try to fix things, the more they fall apart. If it's not about me or if it's not mine to fix, maybe I should just let them fall apart.

If I feel I'm going to act in a negative way, I detach from the situation and take a deep breath. Compulsive reactions will only harm the situation and outcome. I will have to keep things in perspective. There are no immediate solutions that will benefit the situation, so I will slow down and deal with one crisis at a time. Insecurities make me hurry to resolve the problem to stop the pain, so I will ask myself why I am feeling this way. Security comes with patience, acceptance, faith, and time. I shouldn't allow situations to control my moods. I can accept the present situation, accept who I am at this present moment, affirm the journey I have left behind, and welcome with gratitude the journey I've yet to explore.

To Be Seen

If I want to be seen, then I need to show up to be seen. If I want to be heard, then I will use a tone that will be received. Others' image of me does not define me. I define who I am and how I want to be seen. I need no reassurances, for I have all my answers within.

Why take time to see my truth? Or do I accept everything I hear, see, and read at face value? When I know something from within, then nothing or no one from without can shake it. It is something so real to me that it will not matter if the whole world is against me and telling me I am wrong. I have the strength of inner knowing, so whenever I am in doubt, I go within and seek God's truth. Darkness always turns to light.

Who Do I Want to See?

There comes a time in our lives when we have to take responsibility for our actions. I may have gotten away with blame-shifting for years, which, in turn, fed my victim and kept it strong. No more time will be spent asking someone to show up for me when I have the capability to be present for myself. If I don't fill my space with my authentic self, then the ways of others will fill my space for me. I will no longer expound energy and give my past any more power toward something that can never change. When the dust finally settles, what's left is my mirror and me; and as I look into my own reflection, who do I want to see?

More Me

When things don't work out as I hope, I find myself asking this simple question: Why? I call it a simple question because I already know the answer: God is in control, and He knows what's best for me. So I continue my quest to fill my own need from inside out, and I am reminded of how enhanced my life truly is as I become less of them and become more of myself. Now I can say, "Why not me?"

Joy and Contentment

I am responsible for my own reactions. I am responsible for my own joy and contentment. I was taught that love came with conditions and that my needs would be met if I met theirs, and I learned the hard way that this was not true. Giving is an unselfish act of free will that is without expectations of reciprocation in kind. Joy is a self-seeking feeling housed in faith and trust in God. Learning appropriate give-and-take is the basis for a healthy relationship. When I can give and receive without expectations, then I can anticipate joy and contentment. A life without pain will bring no joy, because it is through the survival of that suffering where joy lives.

I See Me

Always wanting to be loved and to belong at times caused me my voice when I chose to assimilate into them as I disappeared. Now no longer willing to sacrifice, I can negotiate for what is comfortable without trying to squeeze myself into a shell. The struggle is not how to keep my voice and live in my truth but how to continue to honor and respect myself when no one else is willing to see me as who I am. They would rather see me as the way I was. Remaining loyal to my core may cause loneliness, but I am never truly alone when I know who owns the reflection in the mirror.

Where the Pain Is

I have experienced both physical and emotional pain, and I have learned to look for its root cause. Usually, my pain is the result of what has happened to me and how I've chosen to react. Physical pain is usually associated with an emotional issue, so as I stretch my stiff muscles and give a voice to its core, I can calm my fear by giving it attention. When I am in a tumultuous conflict, I give rise to my fear of abandonment and become defensive in my judgment calls. As long as I relinquish my power to the other person's indiscretion, my victim grows larger and will have the capacity to keep me prisoner in my own reactions.

When I own what is mine and learn to let go and forgive what is theirs, then the burden of carrying all the pain for the both of us melts into acceptance. I know I am only responsible for my own behavior by examining what has caused these feeling within, searching my heart for what is my true fear and righting my own wrongs. No longer neglecting myself while I focus on them, I now can concentrate on what is within me that needs to heal and evolve. When I know where the pain is, I can begin to heal.

PROMISES

When I continue to expect others to walk their talk, I can find myself being impatient as I await their arrival. I have been known to shut down my life in anticipation of their promise. Life is fleeting, and I know life is busy, but I also know that if someone is important, then I make time to include him or her in my life. If someone says something and does not match it with their actions, then that is not about me. I can only trust their word if it is followed through with action. When I get agitated because this doesn't happen, then that's about me. I will go on with my life without the need for them to be a part of it. I will be aware of how I am giving away my power to another's promise.

MERRY-GO-ROUND

In times of uncertainty, when everything around me is spinning, I need to remind myself that I need not stay on the merry-go-round of life. I can remove myself from unpleasant experiences and react with a positive attitude knowing that I am not in control. What I can control is how I choose to engage and react. If I become tired of being dizzy on the merry-go-round, I can get off and move on.

CALM

Anxiousness over the unknown can be detrimental if I hold my breath every time I react in fear, yet with just one inhale, all is calm. I notice that when I am scared, I hold my breath. Yet with just one inhale and exhale, I am calm. Just breathe!

LIVE WITH THE PAIN

"How to feel the pain of living without denying it and without letting the pain define us, so the choice being to become the wound or to heal it?" Healing a wound is a journey into love and faith after living in pain that houses fear. My initial reaction can cause the pain to remain alive or to choose to heal it by remembering that I am now safe and loved and cherished. If I see someone in pain, I may expect them to react as I would, but this is not about me, so all I can do is offer a compassionate heart. This then takes things back to me to examine how I actually do deal with the pain of living without letting it rule my day.

Words

When I carefully listen to others before I speak, my words have more integrity, and when I take time to center myself before speaking, I truly begin to harness the power of speech. Then my words can be intelligent messengers of healing and light, transmitting deep and positive feelings to those who receive them.

I need to show myself the same kindness that I offer to others!

Refocus

Uncertainty, doubt, confusion, and lack of faith are all little gnats that fly around to annoy us and to allow the floodgates of negative energy to open. When I allow all the voices of my fear cloud my head, I'll lose sight of what really matters in my life. Giving energy to the unknown robs me of my pleasant blessings, and when I engage in this all-consuming fear, then I have no life at all. Knowing all this helps me refocus on what I need to do to take care of myself. In faith, I can let go and trust that all will be done on my behalf.

Out of the Shadow

Staying aligned within an unaligned situation can sometimes draw out the darkness instead of the positive light. I sometimes see myself crawling out of my own shadow as I seek something encouraging to say about myself or a situation I may be experiencing. In these moments, I am reminded to keep asking for guidance and keep moving forward toward what's beneficial in this moment to help me heal. I may not be able to control the situation, but I can control how I react.

Pray for Peace

When I see someone in pain and I know their history, I can begin to feel guilty as I recall my part in their pain. The act of forgiveness is vital not only toward another but also for myself. I can ask them to forgive me for my part in their pain, but then I will need to forgive myself. Having the knowledge that I have done the best I can and now knowing that I have learned a better way do not exonerate my part in their pain. But keeping my part in their pain alive is not in anyone's best interest, because what's done is done. So now that I know better and am doing better, all I can do is ask for forgiveness, forgive my own behavior, and pray we all find peace.

Yo-yo

I am asked to leave and then to stay and then asked to leave again until the time when I evaluate how I am allowing myself to be used as a yo-yo. It is said that we will be treated the way we allow, and if we don't like being a doormat, then we should get off the floor. When a loved one displays this behavior, the hardest thing I have learned I have to do is, when asked to leave, I have to say goodbye! I then have to ask myself why I need this person in my life. I can wish them well, bless them, and live my life without the ups and downs of their yo-yo.

The Tree

How I react in a moment of uncertainty can bring great joy or harm to me as I process the event. A tree falls on my house, and I panic. My first thoughts are to access the damage to anyone or anything that may be in jeopardy. Then my anxiousness kicks in, and I want it removed so that I can get back to my peace. The damage may be minimal to the house, but the emotional damage can be catastrophic if I allow it to consume me. But in the midst of my emotional turmoil, the tree remains where it is. There is nothing to be done until it can be removed. I will have to temporarily live with the tree on my house as I find gratitude that no damage has been caused. Many trees have fallen and will continue to fall. I know I cannot stop this event, but I can control how to live my life in peace with a tree on my house.

Resolve

When the voices of condemnation settle into my conversation, I must immediately address the reason why I am thinking these thoughts and then address the fear. Self-loathing is just a continuation of a past relationship that no longer controls me, so it is my responsibility to remove any doubt that may flow into my soul and affirm my worth. When confronted with a problem, I refuse to continue to give it any more energy than what information I need to draw from it in order to find my solution. Turning condemnation into resolution will always reinforce my faith and give me joy and peace.

Keeper of Pain

I am a very sensitive person, and if not careful, I can take on other people's issues and become the keeper of their pain. Detachment is the successful reaction that keeps me from being engulfed by them. It doesn't have to hurt me or threaten my peace or make me insecure. I can remember that it's not about me, and it doesn't have to spill into my world. These are choices I can make as I react to their issues.

SEEING ME IN YOU

It's difficult for me to watch someone in pain without taking on the responsibility to fix it for them. If their pain mirrors mine, it is a reminder of the work I'm doing for myself. As uncomfortable as it can be for them and for me to become witness to their pain, that's how validating it can become to constantly reinforce their self-worth and self-esteem. I can offer support and an open hand and heart, but I make sure that my reactions are not to fix them but to offer support and express empathy. By engaging in this behavior, my reaction can be internalized by hearing and feeling what I am saying to them; and in turn, I can say them to myself.

BETTER NOW

Triggers are just memories, and it's my choice how to react to them. I can relive the situation, which will cause pain, or look for the message in the trigger. I don't have to submerge myself in the memory, only draw from that which is meant to help and teach me. Where I am is better than where I was. Sometimes, what I think I want is not really what I need. If I don't want to slip, I must avoid slippery places. Leaning against someone does not mean they'll hold me up.

DIFFERENT CHOICES

When I make a decision, it may or may not align with another's. I may get flack. I am learning that others have their opinions and that we don't always have to agree. If they are uncomfortable with what I choose, we can discuss it, but I don't have to change their mind any more than I want my mind changed. I don't need their approval and don't have to change my decision even if it means I won't be accepted. I will strive to accept others' choices, as I hope mine will be honored.

Life Is a Risk

If I don't try, then I'll never know where I can go. It's okay to be wrong, but there is a life lesson in every fall. There's a lesson to be learned in all opportunities and experiences, but if I don't try or take a risk, I'll never know. If I'm not accepted, that does not mean I'm a failure. Maybe my potential is not yet ready to be seen. At least I'll keep trying, and I'll keep evolving. I can handle situations, and I need to remember that. The choice of how I react is important, because I don't want to cause harm to anyone by not agreeing with them. Even if they have hurt me, I can take responsibility for my reactions, but not at the expense of hurting another.

To Heal

Guilt is not a friend. It has kept me prisoner in my own jail. So in order to heal, I need to make amends and solve the problem. If I make an inappropriate choice, guilt will not rid me of these feelings; so then I need to admit my behavior, acknowledge my inappropriate choice, change my behavior by not allowing myself to engage again, quit prolonging my guilt by letting go, forgive, and do better next time.

Analyze, Then Wait

When I have a situation that needs resolution, I may find myself making hasty, careless decisions in order to stop the pain. Yet it is this very reaction that causes more setbacks because I don't allow it to play out. I can be aware of my feelings, accept where I am, and deal with them and decide if I will act or not on these feelings by analyzing if acting on them would be beneficial to the situation. If I don't know how to react, then I am best to wait until I have clarity instead of having to clean up a mess because I acted too soon. I will view my lessons as learning experiences with the goal of growth and healing. I will not rush, but I will look for opportunities. I know that impatience will only bring more pain, so it's best to wait. What's the hurry?

The Soul

When my journey and life lessons cross with another, we call that a relationship. When these two lives journey forward and cross paths and touch each other's souls to enhance the spirit, that is called love. What does one do when the soul suffers from the choices of the other's journey? What does that soul do, and where does that soul go? The soul heals with God's love, but where does that leave the relationship? God knows. I sit and ponder my hurt feelings and wonder if this will be the last time I feel pain from this relationship. Probably not, but to have guarantees would be nice!

I want love in my life. I want a pain-free love with someone who will love me as I love them, but that is only a love with God. All the other loves have been placed in my life not to fill voids but to help me with my life lessons and my journey. We are all on a journey, and if I find someone to travel with, then I have been blessed to not be alone during my journey. This is God's gift.

Release in Joy

Although the injuries of my past do surface, I am willing to acknowledge the issues and know it's my choice to continue to react to the issues just as it's a choice to react to others' issues. When all is not in harmony with someone close to me, I still take on their pain; and at times, I take it personally. I need to be able to feel my feelings without being dragged down by others' issues, which is a pattern I have fallen into all too often. I need to remember to nurture myself and, if need be, to continue to help others but not be dragged into their drama. I want to be able to love and help others without feeling their pain and allowing it to dictate my moods.

As I continue to practice letting go, I am moving through this more gently by not losing myself in another. I am aware of how I have been able to get caught up in another's issues and allowed my moods to be dictated by their. I am being released, and I am allowing myself to live my life with all my feelings, and I am giving myself permission to trust and feel joy. I will celebrate each day of my life and deal with the challenges and obstacles in my path.

ONE MOMENT

I want to love and allow myself to feel the joys in life, as I have felt the pain and sorrows in my fear. Help me work as hard at accepting what's good as I have worked in the past at accepting what was painful and difficult. The pain and tragedy were predictable, so I knew what to expect and how to react. Now I am learning to handle the good the same way I handled the difficult and painful experiences—one moment at a time. I am my own person, free of the expectations and insults of others. I am a better person than what others have led me to believe about myself.

LETTING GO IN FAITH

When I refuse to feel my deepest fears, I give them life, because the energy it takes to refuse them gives all my energy to that task. What resists persists. I remember that there is nothing ugly or worthless about me; and if I hold myself in the light of compassion, love, and forgiveness, then my deepest fears will heal. I don't have to be perfect. I just have to accept that I am not. I need to ask God to meet my needs by believing that I deserve to have needs and desires and that I deserve to have them fulfilled. I'm not better than anyone else. I just need to be better than I used to be.

PRESENTATION

I no longer need drama to feel alive, nor do I need to react the same way I did as a child. I realized that all of us were mistaken. It was wrong of them to think I was supposed to be who they thought I should be, and it was wrong for me to agree with them. The pain was necessary to know the truth, but I did not have to keep the pain alive to keep the truth alive. I do not define myself by those who have hurt me. I define myself by knowing my truth, speaking my voice, and defining myself. God comes first. Offering myself to another means I present myself to them; it does not mean they come before God as authentic and true.

No Issue Required

Have I always found comfort in always having an issue? If I am worried about something, I can allow myself to feel the feelings and focus on my happiness instead of the obstacle. I can live with my past. I just won't live in my past. I can live with contradictions by flipping a negative into a positive. One moment of pain does not define or control me. In the pain, I see what the truth is: atonement (at-one-ment) with God.

God's Catcher's Mitt

God has to let everything happen so that I can evolve. I have to accept all that God wants for me so that I can accept His love. When everything that's false is destroyed, only the truth remains. Once I empty all the lies that I have once called my truth, what will I be filled with? Who will catch me once I let go of their hold on me? God will. He's just waiting for my fall.

Free Will

God's will, will not change another person's since He has given all of us free will. No one can control another. It is up to that person to decide what he or she wants to do, how to behave, and how to live. This can be a perplexing feeling as I wait for the behavior choices of another to restore our relationship. As I have waited for the healing of others so that we can move forward with our relationship, so God has given me free will and has waited for me to come to Him for a relationship. But in this waiting, life must go on and be lived. I can only change my behavior and the acceptance of another's choice.

God will help me if I ask. Although my pain and sorrow come from the fear of never experiencing that restoration, I live in my faith that I am where I am meant to be, doing what I am meant to do, and who I am meant to be with.

Flip and Pick an Alternative

When I have a negative reaction, what is my fear? Is it a lack of control, a fear of repercussions, of speaking up for myself, or fear of abandonment? I can flip my negative into positive and learn to do better next time, because there's always a next time. I have forgiven unkind acts against me. When I look at my loved ones' behavior and how they choose to treat me and continue to think they can, I am no longer angry, resentful, or combative. I no longer have to have a dialogue in my head, scripting what I will say when they defend themselves. What I feel now is loss and sadness over how I want it to be and how I would like to share new experiences with them.

I am able to let go of what happened knowing we all do, and this can't be changed. I let go of what could have been because we are all trying to heal and stop the pain. Until we all heal, change our behavior, and let go of our hurt and anger, I will move ahead in my journey without them. I grieve for their absence, but I will no longer abandon myself for them to be in my life. I am happy and content now, and it is only thinking of the past that brings sadness, so I've decided to stay in the present and trust God's plan for today according to his positive love and light in faith and peace. I will gather what I need to make me happy. I will prepare how I will take care of myself. I will put down that which I no longer need to be happy and enter joy and happiness.

Meet Needs

I do not need drama in my life to have a life. I am worthy, whether anyone agrees or not. I used to fear disappointing others if I didn't show up wearing their correct mask. I was always disappointing myself and suffocating under that mask. It was not, nor will it ever be, good enough for anyone, because I could never meet anyone's needs but my own. The only way to ever coexist is to commit to unconditional love. I am so very grateful for the life God has led me to live and grateful I have chosen Him to show me the way. Serenity lies with God, and I can live with my past. I just won't live in my past. I will look at myself before I judge another. I will seek help from God before I include another. I will look for life within myself, in my own eyes, before seeking a life with another. It may not always be about me, but it is always about me with God.

I WILL

In the silence of my life and my mind, all that matters is love. I speak the truth, keep my word, honor myself, and walk my talk. But that's me, and not everyone is me, nor is everything about me. But I will still show up and trust God's plan, and I will continue to honor other people's boundaries and live my own life. If their life intersects with mine, then I will continue not to judge knowing that everyone is on their own journey. I will show up for myself, love myself, and complete myself with acceptance, approval, appreciation, and validation. I will do unto others as I would like them to do unto me. I will show them empathy, compassion, patience, forgiveness, and love. I will stop making drama where there is none knowing that reactions in the negative feed the negative. I will identify my feelings, react in a positive, kind manner, and know I do matter.

What else is there at the end of my days on this earth? In the end, what really matters? What do I really have? This life is a gift from God so I can experience opportunities with all the negative and positive life lessons to help my soul evolve. What else do I want? It's time to live my life in my truth, sing my song, and dance my dance. What really matters? My journey with God does.

Knowing we are all on our spiritual journey to evolve and are present to help one another, I can forgive. We are doing the best we can at this moment, and when we know better, we can choose to do better. So I pray we are open to being our best, true, positive, spiritual, authentic children of God and to knowing our soul's emotional layers to our core and to evolving.

My Own Life Lessons

In every life lesson for me or someone else, there are always opportunities to grow, whether I am the student or the teacher. The teacher is always the learner, and the learner is always a teacher. Only in our aloneness do we meditate and pray on the lessons. Helping one another completes the circle of growth. Their issues are not mine, and I do not need to react to their issues with nothing but grace, understanding, empathy, compassion, and love. Letting the winds of heaven dance between us, I can teach and learn. In my solitude, I can either hide or pray my way through pain. Either way, I am not the cause of anyone else's sadness. I am only responsible for my own.

Growth

Every moment, opportunity, or experience in my life, whether it is painful or joyful, is a moment of growth in faith. It is neither good nor bad. It is meant to teach me something, or it means for me to help another learn. My memories or triggers are not to remind me to live in the pain, but it is to remind me how I have learned to live with the pain and survived. It is an affirmation of how I once was in denial but now aware that I am worthy. No more anger, regrets, resentment, or disappointments. All was purposeful, and how I choose to react and embrace it is a deeper level into my soul to evolve in God's love and light.

On Our Own Road

What helps us to remember is that we are all going through experiences, and although they may be different, we are all in the light of love. We may not be on the same road, so there should be no judgment. We are here to help one another even if we travel on the same road or we say goodbye at the crossroads of our life. Either road we choose is the right one for us. We all have a purpose, and I need to focus on my own. Trying to change that for another is taking away my evolution by focusing on them. I seek understanding rather than revenge, compassion rather than resentment, and love rather than fear to justify picking love of God to fill my heart.

Self-Conquest

"Is it self-conquest which you are concerned, or are you trying to dominate another?" The more I accept that we all have been given free will and God does not intervene unless invited into a relationship, then the more I know that all I can control is self-conquest. Knowing that all can be resolved when discussed and behaviors can be examined and changed, it puzzles me that denial is still a course that we all seem to follow. Perhaps it's because of the discomfort of having to speak the raw truth or because a comfortable, desirable behavior has to be replaced with a healthier choice, requiring change. Giving up what's comfortable can lead to a void where only faith can blossom. I now know that when I own my own behavior and engage in my own conquest of giving up the need to have it my way, I accept that we are all here to help one another evolve.

Focus

When my focus moves to the future, I may lose the opportunities of my today. When I wallow in the pain of my past, I may get caught up in my own blindness and not see the blessings of today. What happened in my past has led me to my today. What will happen in my future will enhance my footsteps on these present moments. So I will thank my past for lessons learned and opportunities that were given to help me become who I am, and I will give my future to my faith that all is well and that whatever happens will result in my best interest.

Patience and Self-Conquest

Patience is an attribute that requires me to have faith that all is well as it is in this moment and that all will be as it is meant to be in God's time. Self-conquest is my ability to put this in motion, yet there is an alternative side to me where all I want is things my way, and I want them now. Thinking that this childish behavior will bring me peace and joy may postpone my need to be fulfilled when I desire something that I am not meant to have in this moment. So by this humble acknowledgment, I will wait for God's timing and be grateful for what I have in here and now. There is peace and joy in every moment. I just have to be still and ask for guidance, and it will be revealed.

Metacognition

When I think of the times I am my most anxious, I live in fear. When I think of the times I am most calm, I live in faith. Knowing this simple statement can prevent or enhance my journey, so I need to constantly ask the question, "Why am I choosing what I am choosing through my thoughts and actions despite knowing the consequences of either living in peace or living in pain?"

Let's Chat, Shall We?

To heal an issue with another, the problem of common ground must be discussed, and a solution must be agreed upon so that both parties know that the road they are traveling is compatible. If a person is having an issue with a memory that only brings pain, then assistance, if sought, is available. Yet it is pride that prevents healing, and it is the lack of compassion that stands in the way of restoration. So I will drop my sword, and I will speak the truth of love, and I will learn to forgive and live with an open, compassionate, empathic heart.

Resolution

I'm not sure why a confrontation gets such a bad rap. It is merely a conflict between ideas or people. Confronting a situation can only allow solutions to be voiced, but if the fear (judgment) overrides the need for resolution, then all is lost. If a relationship is to sustain itself, then the joy and sorrows need to be shared. What makes us happy is usually the common thread that draws us together. But if different opinions come into play, unless they are discussed, discourse will build a gap where joy was once present. It will fade into sorrow, which can only be healed if discussed. Resolution usually occurs when a behavior is changed and a need to remain in contact is consistent. All we have to do is talk about it!

Getting Results

What thoughts cause me to become distracted and to spiral into fear? When there is discourse between me and a person I love or a situation that does not have the results I desire, I can become distracted from my faith and give my energy to fear. I then tend to think that my way is best, and I begin to make a plan to have it come out my way. This only leads to more anxiety and pain. I am learning to trust in God's plan and to be grateful. This does not mean I will put my life on hold for my outcome, but it means that I am learning to appreciate the gifts I am given as I release what I want and what I think is best for me. I am learning to appreciate how God is taking care of me and answering my prayer requests.

In the Light

All is revealed in the light. When something is not visible, it's given light so it can be seen. My fear lies and dwells in the darkness and is given power when I allow it to engulf my thoughts. But when I enter the light, all is revealed. How much energy is given to the boogeyman of my soul? But it all melts away when I enter the light. When I am in the darkness, I can call on my inner light, which is from God, to illuminate my soul so that all the fear in the darkness melts away.

Slap

I remember how the first time I said no resulted in me having a welt on my face. That sent the clear message that I didn't matter. But having purged all the welts that only exist on my soul's heart, I now can say no and deal with the repercussions of another slap on my heart but knowing it beats so strongly that only love can penetrate it.

Surrounded

When I make a conscious effort to hear my own heartbeat, then I can give thanks. When I hear my own thoughts, I can listen to the messages and decide what to believe and what needs to change. When I encounter another soul, I can decide if I need to stay or bless them and move on my way. Having spent decades surrounded by others who were also victimized and who became victims, I decided that what was done to me did not define who I was. So I will bless them and pray for their healing and move on to be surrounded by the light that awaits me as I move from my darkness. Vernon Howard said, "The one thing that evil cannot stand is for you to quietly observe it in yourself, without self-condemnation, without panic and without fight."

More Faith Than Fear

Taking a risk after I have been hurt is a process where I experience denial, then anger, then sadness, then acceptance. This process can take moments or, in my case, decades, but either way, the outcome is the same. I can detach, let go of what is not mine, release my burdens to change the situation, and have faith that within the experience, there is a life lesson. These words have echoed in my soul for decades, but now that I'm putting the words into action, I can live in my today as I release my yesterdays and tomorrows. I now live more in faith than fear.

Defending My Truth

For many decades, I lived in silence so that others' truth could define me and so I could feel loved. Initially, I always knew my truth; but early on, I muted it for acceptance. Defending my truth then became my life's mission. I tried to right the wrongs that were spoken about me and tried to change perceptions that were made by others who defined me. Now that I know my truth, I no longer need anyone else to trust it, believe it, or live it, except me. I do find myself triggered when I'm questioned what is real. Knowing what I know is all I need to trust, and God can take care of everyone else.

The Voice of My Reaction

Something will always happen, and we all have the opportunity to have a voice. My voice tells me how I am reacting and asks about my inner connection to fear and love. It is the inner calmness to help me off the ledge of how I may either sabotage my outcome or move forward. Either way, I am given the amazing opportunity to evolve or to live in the fear of manipulating the outcome into something I think it should be, which ultimately gets me stuck. So when my voice speaks in reaction to whatever happens, I get to choose how I want to respond.

When Ready, Move Forward

When a feeling surfaces, there may be judgment from others. They may advise me to let it go and to get over it. I believe that those who witness my growth may only be comfortable when I am doing our happy dance, but the minute I am confronted with a life lesson, I may or may not react from fear or peace. When I do react in fear, it is there where my life lesson is. I trust and have faith, but I need to process this for me, not for anyone else or under anyone else's time. I am learning to pick faith and love over fear and aggression. I am still practicing being respectful and assertive in my reactions and not to close another's soul. I am learning to trust and have faith that all is meant to be. How long I stay there before I move forward is about me. I am safe with my own reactions even if I'm judged by another.

To Save Another

A lifeline can take many forms, such as a life buoy thrown to someone struggling in the water or a kind word to help heal someone's pain. Yet it is in the moment of help and safety that I may overstep my responsibility. Some call this caretaking into codependency where my way is the only way. This is where disappointment, resentment, and judgment arrive when what I offer is not accepted. It is no more my responsibility to save another than it is theirs to save me. That's God's responsibility. I am here to help, not save.

Origin of My Pain

To claim I make myself frustrated and miserable would be very humbling. It would require the blame-shifting to end and for the victim to move into greater healing and for me to my own behavior. The reactionary excuses—that it was done to me—would end. In essence, I am the origin of my pain when I become responsible for saving another. All that this does is remove me from my own story and replace me with another. I live from the outside of me to be in another's story, responsible to save them. I am nowhere to be found but in someone else's shadow. When I learn that I am not responsible for anyone but me, I am then able to offer assistance without disappearing. The origin of me is in God's hands, not because someone else is validating me.

The Eye of the Storm

It is said that in the eye of the storm, there is peace. In an eye is where the dark-centered pupil can expand or retract and allow all light to enter to be processed. Judgments and expectations are burdens in my journey, the storm in my life. Yet when I enter the dark center, I become the pupil—empty yet full. There are no accidents, only life lessons and experiences to evolve. Where I am is where I am meant to be. Even if life's storms and drama may challenge my peace, the only choices I have are to react in either love or fear. With each decision, I will either be a participant of the storm, or I'll be taken to the center of the eye, where there is peace. My burden is composed of judgments and expectations, and they can disappear when I am in the storm, but not when I am of it. If I live in fear, I tend to do nothing except rob myself of the possibilities of being joyful. I am learning to be confidant with who I am so I don't miss out on God's purpose for my life. I am His pupil, surviving the storms of my life.

Drama versus Peace

In the middle of drama, there is a sense of aliveness, of always thinking and recalculating with no downtime. Yet in the middle of peace, there just is. I used to spend too much time acting and reacting to drama. Just to feel alive, I made my own when everyone else was calm. This was how I felt alive, and I got my worth by rescuing someone from drama. My drama was, I expected them to rescue me; and when they didn't, it caused more drama. Now I live in peace, and I know I am alive when I hear the birds' song or see the trees' dance with the wind. I know I get to choose to live in peace or to participate in drama. What is my burden, and what can I control?

It's a Thought

It's only a thought, and a thought can be changed. These are some of my most difficult struggles: (1) being aware if the thought is positive or negative, (2) the origin of that thought, (3) flipping negative into positive, and (4) staying positive. This four-step algorithm plays out like a song all day long. At times, being stuck in the groove of a long-playing album of the combat of my life can bring pain, anguish, triggers, shame, and frustration, which all equal to fear. With the automaticity of a thought, it requires constant recalculating and awareness. This is a thought I can live with.

We Are All Souls on a Journey

I can continue my journey with those who are still with me and carry memories of those who are not. I can see how we each struggle to stay in our truth while dealing with life experiences. Each opportunity helps me grow, although I am not always aware of how this situation will help me progress. It is when I am aware of my thinking and reactions that I am truly humble about how God is so present in my life. Practicing my reactions, I choose to remain silent and listen to the stories we all share without judging. Reactions do not have to be defensive. Reactions can hold compassion and empathy.

Change

Change is inevitable; all I have to do to affirm that statement is to glance in the mirror. Physical change requires a responsibility to honor the body to house the soul. Spiritual growth requires that the emotional instabilities heal through exposure to the light. Coming out of the darkness, which is predictable and comfortable, can stretch me to a point of anxiousness. It makes me ask the questions, "Will I fail, or will I be loved and accepted?" No one can do this for another, and all I can do is offer a kind and gentle heart, leaving judgment in the darkness. Help me trust the light so I can change and move out of the darkness.

Achilles's Heel to Heal

In mythology, Achilles was slain because of that one small spot on his heel that allowed evil to penetrate, control, and destroy. Whether I am tired, under the weather, or I have been insulted or mistreated, I can become Achilles's heel. I can allow every negative thought, memory, and feeling to envelop me until I become that negative energy. My immediate negative reactions are then followed by remorse, defensive excuses, guilt, and repentance. I am forgiven way earlier than I forgive myself.

In this repetitive self-loathing, I begin the cycle of healing one more time. This pattern is slowly but finally coming to an end. My mere awareness can complete this toxic cycle in moments, where before it took decades. I know the truth of my being, and I know the goodness of myself. Forgiveness and compassion can set me free. The loving way of my being matches the truth of my being.

Open yet Cautious

"With a closed heart, life is not possible. How to feel the pain of living without denying it and without letting the pain of living define me?" The heart is the most vital organ. It can be broken and mended in a beat with a word, a touch, or a glance. Keeping open to all of life's blessings, opportunities, and experiences is a risk; for not all outcomes bring joy. We live in contradictions, and there's always a possibility that not all outcomes will be positive, but each one will be vital to learn. So it is a risk to accept one more apology, it is a risk to begin to trust again, and it is a risk to say yes. Being open means living in and with all that is. Proceed with caution.

Refrain or Remain

At my first thought in the morning, while listening to the birds' first song, which is sung in praise and joy, is then where all possibilities are born. In an instant, change can alter any situation, yet the outcome is already determined. All I can do is offer a positive reaction and stay positive when confronted with a behavior that is less desirable than comfortable. I can choose to remain or refrain. When I allow myself to become entangled with that which is not mine to solve, I become negative, agitated, and judgmental, looking for a positive outcome while feeding it with my negative reaction. I can choose to remain in the light or refrain from the darkness.

If-Then

Things happen for a reason. People will come and go in my life. All is meant to bring a life lesson to the table to be learned through experience and opportunity, and then I move forward on the journey of my soul's evolution, but put an if-then into the scenario and it is halted. All the growth takes a detour off the path, and all becomes contingent on the outcome. When the destination becomes more important than the experience of the journey, then nothing gets done. I've spent a lot of time waiting for my if-then to move fully into my purpose. Stuff happens, whether I engage or not. Help me focus on my purpose and leave the rest to God.

If Only…, Then

This statement cripples me and puts my life on hold, waiting for another's life to enfold so that I can know how to limit myself by those I encounter. My life has been contingent on the reactions of others—"If they are, then I am." I continue to empty that which I have accumulated, and this process has been painful yet has taught me how to be whole again. I continue on this path of who I am and fill myself with the wonders of how positive life is.

Comfort Zone

When I am in my comfort zone, I feel secure, at ease, and comfortable. But put a hotel room in the mix, a visitor in my home, or any other situation that is not of my daily routine and it can cause a new awareness. Whether that awareness is confusion or excitement, the feelings are different from my daily comfort zone. Stretching myself to try new experiences can cause me to be excited and anxious at the same time. Yet with these new experiences, it tells me that I trust and believe in myself enough to engage in something new to learn, to feel, and to have fun. My comfort zone is expanding.

Vacay Every Day

When I decide to deviate from my daily activities, I call this a vacation. I get to sleep late, I eat food that I won't ordinarily indulge in, I see sights out of my normal backyard, and I just let myself be. Letting go of the daily grind allows me to just be, and it is in that inhale and exhale and release that the vacation begins. So any day, I can look at the sunrise or sunset and take a walk by a river or hike in the mountain and just be.

What Comes Next?

Suppose I had all the financial security I could ever want or need. Suppose I had good health with no worries that my loved ones or I would suffer. Suppose I had emotional stability and unconditional love. Suppose I had no worries, no negative images, and no negative self-talk. Supposed that all that I loved, loved me back. What then? What would I possibly be worried about then? What could the negative voices sway me to think, act, and react to? The "What comes next?" in any given moment is a gift, like a present on my birthday, something I always wish for. Yet with all the worry or negativism that I allow to penetrate my soul, I do not cherish or celebrate the amazing gifts of my next moment. This is what comes next for me if I don't celebrate who I am.

Enjoy the Journey

When I have a to-do list, I tend to focus all my energy into a final product. I tend to become anxious about the perfect outcome. This anxiousness and product perfection rob me of my purposeful journey. They steal moments of creativity or a life lesson to let go in faith, and they ultimately bring me unrest. So with one more blessed, deep breath, I relax, I create, I embrace, I enjoy, and I bring myself back to this one moment; and the what-ifs melt away like snow on a sunny day. My fear of the burden of control is carried off in a cool breeze. I am once again peaceful, joyful, and content in my happiness.

When the Dust Settles, Then What?

At times, I live life within a storm, whether it is self-made or someone else's drama. I enter into situations that may or may not enhance my growth. Some storms are a gentle rain that just need a hug while other storms feel like a sacrifice from my soul. This is where the aliveness of my life dwells. Although I have exited these storms, I am still engaged in others' weather forecasts, so I ask myself, "When the dust settles from my tornado or the hurricane of another's life, then what?" I now know the storms are unresolved and unhealed traumas. I have found that I haven't looked at my own trauma but wanted to forgive others and myself, so then what? Now I have begun to live each day by just breathing in gratitude. The dust will settle, I will heal, and the next part of my journey will unfold. Then whatever comes my way will be a blessing.

Listen to the Story

As children, we love when we are told stories of good versus evil, where good always triumphs. We listen attentively as the dragon is slain or the wicked witch melts. Yet do we ever ask what makes the dragon so angry or the witch so wicked? It is by asking questions and listening to the story that we bring empathy and compassion into the heart, which can melt away judgments, resentments, and bitterness and soften a hardened heart. So when my initial reaction is one of defensiveness, which is brought on by the origin of my story, let us all listen to one another's story in love, not fear. When you're ready, tell me your story.

My First Thought

Becoming aware of how I present myself to the universe has been life-changing. I've always received what I ask for in one form or another. Either way, I have been fulfilled and blessed. My first thought can be harmful toward my growth, or it can be helpful. How I choose to react and what I choose to think at any given moment are callouts to the universe and to God, saying, "This is what I want." Awareness is the key. If it's positive, it's God. This is so simple. So when I am at a crossroad, I will choose the positive; and even when I am aware of the millions of reactions I have to choose from, I will choose the positive. I will let go of everything within that has been keeping me from my happiness and well-being.

What's in Front of Me

At times, my mind spins with everything I have to do. This is a self-inflicted list, and some of it are responsibilities and accountabilities. Most of it comes from unresolved feelings and loss of relationships that I deem important. When I find myself in this tornado of unrest, I take a deep breath and look at what's in front of me. I ask for peace, and I will receive peace when I do not allow drama into my frame of being. Even though there is unrest within my family and the world's family, I do not have to be sucked into that tornado. I say a prayer of enlightenment and healing, bless them all, and keep showing up as my best, true self.

Lives Passing Through

As I reflect on all the lives and souls that have passed through and touched mine, whether it is for a minute or a lifetime, I am humbled to be reminded that we are all souls on a journey. How the encounter begins or ends is not as important as the footprint they leave on my journey. When I can remain in my spiritual realm, I lose sight of any judgment, disappointment, or resentment for their visit. It is now replaced with gratitude and blessings for having brought wisdom to me or for sharing a little piece of what I have to offer. I now use the word *borrow* because what is mine to give is a choice; I get to pass on knowledge while keeping my life lessons pure in my soul's journey. I am now moving forward.

In the Midst of the Storm

There is usually a warning when bad weather is on the horizon so one can be prepared, but storms in life are never really apparent until they're right upon us. It is like this when change is occurring in life. Being pulled into another storm can trigger my old behavior of caretaking, and my life stops to assimilate into theirs. It is not my responsibility to fix anyone other than myself, but as I watch myself being drawn into the deep abyss of another's drama, I am reminded of what is truly mine to hold and control. So in the midst of a storm, I will take care of myself and hand the burden of others back to God.

Permission

When we are young, we ask permission from our elders to do things. When we become adults, we give the same courtesy to others so that we do not cross a boundary. We also give a part of ourselves, and at times, we do give permission to be treated in ways that may not be to our benefit. Agreeing to others' treatment is our power and right to do, yet we also have the right to say no and stop the behavior. For many years, a behavior may continue without a word of permission but in the act of submission. If we don't like being treated like a doormat, we have to get off the floor. Only I have the power to say yes or no when it comes to how I am treated.

Eye of the Storm

During a major storm that wreaks havoc, spreading negative destruction on whatever is in its path, there is always the eye of the storm. Within this eye lie peace, calmness, serenity, pure light, and love; but the biggest obstacle is how I can remain in the peace, calmness, serenity, pure light, and love while I am surrounded by the negative destruction of the storm. I am learning to feel my feelings, question my reactions, and be mindful of how I am allowing this to have an impact on my peace. Usually, I try to battle the raging storm around me, realizing I have sacrificed my peace to become a part of the storm. I choose to remain in the eye while dealing with the storms.

COMPASSION

Compassion is the feeling of oneness with another, showing them support to further their journey. This is a way of being kind and caring, by giving prayers for one's difficult journey. Say, "I'm sorry you're in pain, but it does not make your pain mine." There is a very thin line in past which I may allow myself to get sucked into the drama of their pain if they sling some my way. That's when I need to keep my reactions in check and to be mindful of them knowing it's not about me even if they try to convince me that it is. I will continue to show compassion even if I have to dodge negative energy.

REGARDLESS

When a situation occurs, there are choices to be made. If this does not hinder my journey, then my reaction is positive and welcoming. If this occurrence is not in my repertoire of what I expect or find helpful or useful, I become aware of how I might benefit and react in a way that aligns with my highest well-being. Everything and everyone I encounter is put in my path for my growth or to assist another, so regardless of who I need or what I expect to happen, all is meant to be. When I accept, I can find peace in the moment and let go of expectations.

INTERRUPTIONS

In the midst of the day's busyness, there will be many detours off my beaten path. These interruptions come with many opportunities that I may interpret as a nuisance. When I am about to react, I begin to experience an immediate peace that there are blessings in all experiences. We are all souls on a journey, so instead of looking at these interruptions as getting in my way to my destination, I embrace the journey. I look at how these interruptions are enhancing my journey. Spending my days in anger because someone has done or said something will only prolong my pain. This detour wreaks havoc on the potential joy of my just being. An interruption, like a fly, will eventually find the wind and be on its way.

Move On

When I sit in the presence of those I've known for as long as my lifetime, I can't help but wonder why some of us choose to be combative and judgmental when there is so much joy and peace to be had. Having had the opportunity to see myself in them, I can choose to continue to live as if I am still in the past, feeling like I am treated unjustly, and this gives me cause to stay as a victim or choose to forgive and know we are all on a journey at our own pace. I don't want to be judged by another about my pace toward joy and peace, so I will release that behavior. I don't want to engage in a combat, trying to rewrite the past, so I release that behavior. I can bless them and move on at my own pace toward joy and peace.

How to Change What's Done

Trying to change what is done is like trying to go back in time to redo that which has caused pain, yet it is in the pain that healing begins. It is in the sorrow that joy is born. It is the tears that are shed that nourish new growth. My pain is my reaction to others' drama and to the choices others have made that have affected me, yet I can no more change their choices any more than I can change the outcome that has caused pain. I get through it and live with the pain but not in the pain, and I know how blessed I am to be where I am and who I am.

Packing for the Journey

As I face the final years of this life, I am packing what I need to make this final journey—the memories and those who helped me learn my most vital lessons, helping me become who I am meant to be and helping me shed that which no longer fits. I have been blessed by knowing love, holding life in my hand, and learning what truly matters. It's not the delivery of the pain, but it's how the pain is received and utilized to help learn the life lesson. So again, I thank those who said yes to me as well as those who said no. All have been a blessing in my life. I now pack light.

My Choice

When I am faced with the repercussions of another's actions, I can become agitated for the choices they make that affect me. I can also look at the situation as a life lesson and know that it's not always about me. If the action is made in error, then I can accept the apology and move forward. If their action is deliberate or intentional, I can call them on their choices that affect me. If they are remorseful, I will look for a change in their behavior so that we can move forward. If it keeps repeating, then I need to access how I want this person in my life. I can make a choice, then the choice can make me.

In My Control

When I find my thoughts being absorbed in another's discomfort, I may guilt myself into a frenzy, and I may try to figure out what I've done wrong to make them feel the way they do. But in my long history of this journey, I have come to embrace that sometimes, it's not about me. No matter how many blessings are bestowed on that person, they may never see the joy or gratitude in their blessings, and they may find comfort in being a victim. So I will change what I can about myself, and I will pray they find their happiness and joy no matter who crosses their path. I know that as long as I am my best, true self, that's all I can control.

One More Time

How do I live again after the death of a loved one or a relationship? How do I trust again after giving countless opportunities to

427

see the truth? How do I feel again after my hardened heart has been glued together? How do I see the light again after the darkness is my shroud? How do I breathe again? I will love again, one experience at a time. I will trust again, one word and action at a time. I will feel again, one melting heartbeat at a time. I will see the light again, one step at a time out of the darkness. I will breathe again, one inhale at a time. With one more time, I am.

The Right Thing

It's difficult when someone is not doing the right thing, and I have no control over that. The difficulty lies in my frustration with the person's unethical or unkind choices. Although I am not judge or jury, there are some fundamental, universal statements of right and wrong. When I encounter another whose choices may only benefit them at the expense of another, although I may not be able to change that person's behavior, I can be thankful that I know that is not a behavior I would choose, for it will conflict with being my best self. I will continue to pray that we all show kindness, compassion, empathy, and respect.

Not My Remedy

As I watch others struggle with the same behavior that I am learning to purge, it's heartbreaking to not tell them what to do to move forward, but I've learned that what is meant for me may not be meant for them. Even though we all have similar struggles, our remedies may differ. Too many times, I offered advice that was not taken, and this left me frustrated. My job is to heal myself and show compassion to others as they try to heal. I will offer an open heart, an open mind, and a closed mouth so that we may continue to journey together toward restoration.

Continuous Kindness

When I decide to show a kindness and I get ridiculed for my offer, I can be reminded that their refusal to accept it is not because they are suspicious of my motives but because they do not feel themselves worthy of accepting. I will continue to show kindness even if another does not accept my offer. The roots of my continuous kindness are my gratitude and blessings, which help me pay it forward.

COMA

We've all been asleep and have been awakened by an epiphany, an enlightenment. Living in a coma for many years, my life was a virtual reality, and I was a player in someone else's life. Now that I am waking from my coma, I am allowing light to be shed on my darkness, and I am thanking my teachers. Not needing all this information that I have learned, I can purge that which is not needed and expound on the knowledge that will help me reach my destiny. When it's time, all of us will have that moment of clarity; where once we were confused, we now understand. I am choosing to awake from my coma to see what awaits my understanding.

TRY

When I find myself in the darkness of indecision or regret or burdened with what I can't control, I can make a conscious choice to remain in the darkness or come into the light of hope, truth, faith, and blessings. If I remain in that fear, it will suck the life out of the joy that awaits me. I continue to try to stay in hope and faith rather than in fear and despair. Thy will be done!

I STILL AM

Amid my fear of retribution, sarcasm, and abandonment, I will still live in the truth and light of what I know is God's will. Although my viewpoint or belief system may differ, I will not discount or try to assimilate another into my way of thinking. We all have the ability to seek the truth. Our paths may differ, but that will not discount the journey. I will share with an open heart and open mind and hope I will receive the same, but if not, I still will be who I am meant to be, with or without you to share my journey.

I Can Say No to Me

When I continue to struggle with a decision, I have to get to the root of my need for resolution. The battle within my mind can lead me to an inappropriate decision just to satisfy and quiet the voice. The anxiousness I may feel may cause me to sabotage my own safety or integrity. Yet when I can uncover the cause of my conflict, I can comfort myself knowing all is well and I am safe. I can learn to say no to myself when my decision may risk my peace and joy.

Useful

Hanging on to a person, a thought, or something that may never come to fruition is like holding on to a piece of memorabilia that has no useful memory anymore. How long I choose to keep myself stuck is something I need to explore. This old, useless behavior only keeps me in bondage in my own prison. If it's no longer useful, I can always remain hopeful that maybe someday, but not today. Take off the slave ring! Today, I will live with my joy and satisfaction that I can only do what I can do. When I get anxious waiting for the results I want, I will miss all the opportunities and experiences of this present moment. Just be!

Risk

When I am confronted with a decision, I am aware of my first reaction, which is usually fear. What if I fail? What if I'm abandoned? What if I am judged again? If I allow these fears to lay the path toward my decision, I will never move forward and only live with regret, bitterness, and disappointment. I have reviewed the decisions of my life, and the path I usually choose is risky. I may have been hurt, I may have been abandoned, or I may have been disappointed; but at least I tried and took the risk, learned something new, purged something old, and lived! No guarantees can be a cumbersome feeling; but when I can take the risk, live in faith, and trust, I will always land where I am supposed to be. I can live.

DIVE

I know what I know. I am a child of God. I am a blessing. We all are. I know that we are all souls on a journey and that no one is better than another, because we all have a purpose and a destiny to fulfill. I have a defense mode and a short fuse that I use when I am threatened with abandonment, bullying, or manipulation. I have a loving, kind heart that can be closed when injured, but it can reopen for forgiveness and grace. What is standing in my way that I need to continue to say, "I don't know"? What is preventing me from knowing the answer? It's time to delve deeper.

THE SAME

We all have the capacity to condemn or find out the story to show compassion. We all have what we think right and wrong should be. When another's right and wrong conflict with ours, we become their judge and jury and try to force our opinions and belief system on them by shaming, manipulating, or bullying them. Never in the course of history has this ever turned out well for anyone involved in this situation. We are all made the same, but our experiences may differ. It is only when we ask someone to share their story that a means of communication may open that will show our similarities, not our differences. The next time I become the judge and jury of someone else's choices, I might want to think how I would like to be treated.

PARTS MAKE THE WHOLE

When I allow myself to relax and rejuvenate my energy, I am more willing to continue without being combative. Feeling depleted after giving my energy into another person or project can cause more harm if I do not acknowledge my needs. Taking a break can help me celebrate my accomplishments as I replenish for the next part of the journey. I can also revisit other passions that may have been put on hold while I was busy doing what I was doing. All parts of my journey are important.

CONDITIONS

Having allowed my identity to be contingent on others' definitions of who I should be, how I should act, and how I should meet their needs has led me to engage in a 180-degree turn away from that behavior and close my heart. I pray to keep an open heart and change my hardened heart to be able to find out who I am without their definition and beliefs while still maintaining a relationship. Help me learn how to love and receive love without conditions or expectations.

EXAMINE THYSELF

Trying to do better than what has been done to me requires me to be humble and without judgment. Knowing we are all souls on an evolutionary journey and have specific, handpicked lessons to learn, I cannot judge someone who is struggling with a life lesson that I have already experienced. The "I don't get mad; I get even" mentality only keeps toxicity alive. There is a saying that when we know better, we do better, so I will strive to do better.

WHAT I WILL DO?

Even when I know that fear is negative and love is positive, it is very easy to get caught up in either if that behavior is presented. Defensive, suspicious reactions come from being continually hurt, having a lack of faith, not believing in my own word, not trusting myself, and causing my heart to close. Knowing it's not always all about me, I can confront situations with a more positive reaction than the behavior I receive. What is about me is what I can control and hurtful behaviors that I can forgive, not looking for revenge or retribution but rather saying a prayer for those who are living in fear. I will show integrity in an unjust world. I will show kindness to the unkind. I will show respect to those who are disrespectful. I will be honest to the untrustworthy. I will show compassion and empathy to those who are filled with fear. I hope we all heal in the light of love and peace.

Open

Remaining open in the midst of a disagreement may make me vulnerable. Once my heart closes, it begins to harden with the bitterness of past hurts, and resentment will rise again. Knowing I have nothing to lose by keeping an open heart and an open mind, I may be able to seek resolution before the walls close in on me again. I can speak my mind from my heart and begin to heal. If I don't, then I risk revisiting the hardness that no light will penetrate. I can choose to have an open heart and mind and live in the light or close it and live in darkness.

The Key

In the midst of confusion, miscommunication, or disagreement, I must be able to keep my heart and mind open to my options and to the opinions of another and not engage in the assimilating battle, insisting that my opinions or my options are the ones to follow. We can all be our true self as we try to help one another along the way with kindness, compassion, and patience; they hold the key toward resolution.

Turn the Page

Being a lifelong learner can be as easy as turning the page in a book, but it is the study and comprehension of the new knowledge that will take time, especially to evaluate what is pertinent and what must be discarded. Sometimes, the comfortable status quo may lead to complacency. When I feel that I have enough to think about, I stop. This recess is helpful if I'm trying to understand what I am learning but can be detrimental if I choose to walk away from new information because I am comfortable and don't want to change. It is with discipline that I make myself turn the page.

SEND OUT A PRAYER

After the dust settles from the effort of trying, I can honestly and humbly say, I am only in control of my own choices, behavior, thoughts, actions, and words. Even if I have vital information and knowledge that can help another person, unless it's solicited, all I can do is send out a prayer. I cannot drag anyone into the light, but I can send out a prayer. I cannot save anyone from anything if they do not want to be saved. All I can do is send out a prayer. I may think I know what's better for them than they do, but I don't. That's God's job. Despite my arrogance, I will humble myself enough to send out a prayer.

RESPOND

I used to feel so uncomfortable if I expressed my feelings and it became a conflict. The practice was usually either me pleading my case after a misunderstanding or me standing my ground after I laid a boundary. This led me down a path toward frustration and into fear. I'm learning I can share how I feel in an appropriate way, and instead of reacting with aggression, I can kindly respond. I don't need to change someone's mind or expect the results I want, but I do honor myself enough to try and accept that I am protected and loved. When I am feeling lonely, I tend to focus on what I want rather than celebrate what I already have. I am blessed to be aware of this so I can turn my loneliness into abundance. When I feel immersed in toxic regret, I can either remain in shame, or I can accept what has been done and seek the life lesson and do better. I will listen to what messages I am receiving in order to check my behavior. I will keep an eye on myself and listen to the thoughts in my mind to determine how to respond kindly rather than react aggressively.

Aware

I lash out at the first sign of feeling as though I need to defend myself. I judge something that does not align with my thinking. I see the goal, and every other opportunity or path becomes a blur as I forge forward. I feel slighted when I am not treated with the respect I offer. Although I am not proud of these behaviors, I can humbly say, I am aware. Now the next step is to change.

Doubt

Too many years of my life have been spent doubting my beliefs and believing in my doubts. If I know that what I truly believe in is the truth, would I keep doubting myself? So what if I believe that with God's unconditional love, grace, forgiveness, and guidance and my faith, He will save me and protect me? Would I allow my past lessons and prior knowledge to get in the way of continuing to search for the truth, or would I doubt this too? I am learning to doubt less, and I am learning to trust again.

Sometimes, It Just Is

When I am experiencing a calmness, I review the situation and ask, why is this different? Is it because things are going my way, or is it because I am accepting things as they are? Learning to give up control will keep me calm. Accepting where I am and who in my life is meant to be with me will bring me peace.

I Understand

I understand that I have a deep-seated need to have faith and trust. I understand that all of us are souls on a journey. If I choose, I can live in the light instead of the darkness. I understand fear, for it has brought me to my breaking point: disappointment and heartache from broken dreams. I understand that I have opportunities and can learn to have joy from my experiences. I understand. Now what?

While I am waiting for my broken dreams to mend, I can take a walk and talk to God or connect with a loved one, read a book, or watch a movie, merely engaging in one of my passions. My brokenness, which is waiting to be healed, need not steal my peace or remove a passion that brings me joy. I will continue to pray, have hope, and live in faith, accepting that all is meant to be as I enjoy what already is.

Lay Down the Sword

When I anticipate a conversation that may go toward a confrontation, I may step in with my opinion instead of waiting for the other person to complete their thought. This does not work toward positive communication; so I am learning to think before I speak, act, and react toward a positive response. I don't need a sword for a battle that may not occur. I just need an open heart, an open mind, and a closed mouth.

Special Delivery

When I see the fruits of my labor working, I get a calmness that makes me smile. It's not a smile of arrogance, and I'm not being condescending. I am merely experiencing the joy I feel within my heart and soul, because when I do have hope and when I do live in faith, I may not be delivered what I want, but I will be delivered what I need—my daily needs, forgiveness, and protection.

What's Next?

After the dust has settled and the storm has moved on, what's next? Looking at the rubble left behind can be a devastating experience, but what's next can be determined by how long I choose to remain in what's in front of me. I can either look for hope or remain fixed on something that cannot be changed. What's next is up to me. Hope sounds good!

Cautious

As words change and behaviors start to align with promises, I remain cautious and know where my nourishment lies. Having lived on the promises of someone's words that have left me brokenhearted, I now wait to see how much of me will engage. Drawing back into my own heart, I continue to allow the depths of my truth to unfold as I become an observer before I participate. I will explore new possibilities as I continue my journey.

Help

When I am faced with a dilemma or a negative thought, my simple prayer is, "Help!" I then take a deep breathe, inhale the positive energy that is available, and exhale the combative thought. Then I shift my thinking into my possibilities instead of the hindrances that block my way. It's a good start for me to move forward.

Today

In isolation, I can become closer to God by depending on His promise for each day. He states that He will provide food (daily bread), forgiveness (trespasses), and protection (deliver from evil). When I remain in His promise, I can protect myself from the fear that illuminates the world. If I am finding myself reactive rather than proactive to the world's troubles, I can turn it off! My faith, joy, and happiness are a click away.

Watch

When I watch the sunrise, a blue jay eating a seed from a tree, or geese in a perfect V formation flying across the sky, I know all is well in the world. When confronted with something that interrupts my normal way of living, I may become anxious and fearful that it will hurt me. But if I trust that all is meant to be, then I can continue, in a responsible fashion, to live my life and watch the blessings that unfold in front of me.

STAY WITH GOD

When I ask for help, God asks me to stay with Him so He can solve my dilemma. How often have I looked to others' experiences, knowledge, and opinions to solve my dilemma? How many times have I not remained silent and still to hear the answer? Patience is not my strong suit, and being uncomfortable with my unsettled dilemma can cause more heartache if I don't remain with God. So instead of handing it over to someone else's knowledge and opinions, I stay with God so He can show me the answers in His time, when He thinks I'm ready. There is still work to be done, so stay with God.

THE STRUGGLE CONTINUES

I still find myself triggered by someone's negative reaction. I play right along, and the bantering leads me down a dark path. I find myself in such pain as I continue to display this behavior over and over. I pray and hope that I will pause and take a deep breath and not become a part of unhealthy conversations that do not have any positive purpose for me. I will also pray for their peace as I struggle to remain in mine.

PRIORITIES

When I awaken with thoughts that fill my head, I start to categorize them by importance. My mind may take me on a detour that is not purposeful toward my goal; so I will write them down, review what I can control and what's important, and go about my day. When I get stuck in negative thoughts that do not serve me well, I can say, "Not helpful," and move on. When I am confronted with the negativity that lives outside of me, I ask myself if what I am thinking is purposeful or harmful. I am aware that the only place where I will find peace is to go within my own heart and focus on what's right in the world and in my life. I know where my true nourishment lies. My priorities help me feel purposeful and successful.

CONSTRUCTIVE VERSUS DESTRUCTIVE

There is a history we all share called childhood. In there lies the very foundation of who we believe we are. This may or may not be nurtured, but either way, destiny is tenacious enough to find a way out of the darkness of despair and into the light of hope. This is what faith is, that in time, all that is not yet seen will be revealed. But in my anxiousness to get to a feel-good place, I may become destructive as I tear down the walls in my way. These walls are built by believing in someone else's interpretation of who I am. Rather, I will be constructive, not destructive. Others have what they believe is their truth, and I have what I believe is mine. It is when our truths conflict that pain ensues, so I will set a goal to listen and to agree to disagree. I choose to be constructive rather than destructive.

THINK WISELY

I am very diligent about what I ingest into my body for my physical health, but how so with my mind? I eat healthy for a dozen reasons, but what of my mind? What thoughts do I inject that are beneficial toward my mental health? What do I still carry from the past that is beneficial for my journey today? What belief systems still ring true about who I am and who I am meant to be? As important as my diet is to my body, so are the thoughts for my mind. I make the choice, then the choice makes me. What do I choose to ingest? Think wisely.

WELL

Trying to make something happen before its time is a futile attempt and a waste of precious energy. Thinking I know better for me than God knows for myself is a sign that I am living in fear. Waiting has never been a strong characteristic of mine, but seeing the results of my impatience has driven me to my knees, releasing fear and renewing my faith that all is as it is meant to be and all will be revealed in God's time. I can wait; and in the meantime, I can read a book, plant my garden, take a walk, or watch the snow fall while knowing all is well.

CHANCES

I've spent decades doubting my decisions and fearing my doubts. I've spent decades worrying about others' opinions and what they thought of me more than what I thought about my self-confidence and truth. Never has anyone ever been totally accepted by anyone else if their views differ. If I fear what they think or what they will do, I will be paralyzed in self-inflicted chains. I choose not to live this way and take my chances. I'm happier being me than trying to become who they think I should be.

THE FINAL WORD

Change is inevitable. The only events that are predictable are that the seasons will change, a baby will grow into an adult, the sun will rise and set, sadness will turn into happiness, pain will turn into joy, and I will live and die. These changes are not only predictable but also necessary for growth to take place. During these inevitable changes, I can choose to stay positive in joy or negative in disappointment. Either way, God will have the final word. I just get to speak with my voice and live in my truth until He does.

NO-BRAINER

During time of waiting, I can make it a pleasant experience by having hope and faith that my prayers have been heard and will be answered in accordance to God's will; or I can live with impatience, anxiety, and fear. Although my heart understands this choice, my head may not be so cooperative as to try and assist God with helping me get through my uncomfortable waiting time. Never has this ever worked out for me, and it only causes more anxiety and fear. So in the time of waiting, I will wait with hope and faith and try to live in peace. It seems like this choice is a no-brainer.

Prepared

I used to be defined by how someone showed up in my life. If they came with the armor of battle, I was prepared. If they came with a sarcastic tongue, I was prepared. But waiting for an apology that might never come was like holding my breath. I could barely move. This was my life. First, they chose for me, and then I chose for myself.

Little by little, I found that being prepared for doom and gloom led me to that negative life. I had no faith that anything good might transpire; so I prepared myself for nothing but sadness, despair, resentment, and bitterness. Now when those familiar old thoughts prepare me for darkness, I choose to live in the truth that in faith, there is hope that something better and more joyful is yet to come. I will live today in faith, and that promise that I can depend on will come to fruition. For that, I am prepared!

Mine to Hold

When I finally settle into my soul after I have been hurt, I can replace confusion with compassion and anger with empathy. I can seek understanding for the behavior choices of another that have offended me, yet I need to honor my journey the same way I honor theirs. I can forgive and still set a boundary, I can be kind and still be cautious, and I can stop enabling without the fear of retribution. What's mine is mine, and what's theirs is theirs. I do not need to carry their load. I only need to maneuver what is mine to hold.

Whisper

When faced with an unpleasant situation, what is my first reaction? Is it one of despair, anger, disappointment, and fear; or do I react in faith? Always feeling a hint of defensiveness, I will take a deep breath, usually shake my head, and smile to myself as I process my feelings in my head. After I assess the situation, I pray for patience and wisdom; and I figure out what is mine, what is theirs, and what is God's. Then I whisper to myself, "I know God's got this."

We All Matter

Does it matter if the sun is shining for us to find joy? Does it matter that we are accepted, loved, and appreciated by everyone? Does it matter that what others think or say about us is true or just their opinion? What matters is truth, joy, how we act, how we choose to treat others, and what we think and say about how we feel. This matters; we all matter!

Clash or Compliment

Failure is not the result of not making an attempt; it's the result of not persistently trying. If my future depends on the opinions and permission of others, then I will accomplish nothing. Nothing will be accomplished if I am afraid of criticism. If I worry about what they think, then I will base my confidence on them. All these affirmations are reminders that we are all on a journey and that we may, at times, clash or compliment.

I used to fear conflict if my opinion was different from another's, so I hid, fearing that I would be seen as different, not knowing that my difference was my strength. If we come to an impasse, I will no longer compromise my truth to seek approval. I will not give up my truth to be accepted by anyone even if that means I will travel alone. Either way, I will respect your point of view, and I hope to receive the same, and I will respect you from my own truth.

Heartache

When I am watching someone misuse their power to do good for self-gratification, my heart aches. When a loved one is making poor choices and I cannot do anything for them but pray, my heart aches. When I want to help but it's not my place, my heart aches. Having compassion and empathy for another requires patience and prayer while the heart aches.

BEHAVIOR

When civility gives way to war, what then? Protesting against something that does not align with my belief system is my constitutional right; however, I am not given the right to cause harm to anyone else in my angry state. If I have been bullied, then why would I choose to bully someone else. Would that not make me a bully? Unjustified behavior does not bring cause for more unjustified behavior; otherwise, aren't we also a perpetrator? He's taught us to love one another. How would I feel if I see my child engaging in harmful behavior? We are all God's children. I wonder what He's feeling about us right now.

UNREST

Unrest is defined as a state of dissatisfaction, disturbance, and agitation in a group of people, typically involving public demonstrations or disorder. There comes a time when unrest occurs. It can cause an imbalance in the peace within the soul and in the world. So how does one escape the turmoil of fear and hate? My answer: turn off the negative, do a lot of praying, and turn the fear into faith!

FOUNDATION

God's timing is impeccable as I wish, hope, and dream for a prayer to be answered. If I were to receive everything I pray for in the moment I pray for it, then would I be ready to accept it as the blessing it is and see its true meaning in my life, or would it just be piled on top of everything else I have come to know? While I wait for my prayers to be answered, I must be prepared to receive them by having a firm foundation, or the cycle of fear will infiltrate, and all that I strive for will be shaken and perhaps crumble. A house cannot be built on sand and be expected to weather the storm. Where have I built my foundation?

ENOUGH!

When I hear about injustice against a race or poverty within a people, I can't help but wonder why the emphasis is on blaming rather than on assistance. It gets to a point where complaining becomes so much easier than finding a solution. It's almost as if staying in bondage gives us the excuse to be reactive rather than proactive, as the blaming only causes more discourse rather than healing. It would actually require a change and an accountability in order for peace and love to take the place of fear. Why do we want to live like this, and when will be our time to change? Enough finger pointing. It's time to look in the mirror.

MOVE ON

When I recall monumental events in my life, I like to only remember the happiness it has brought me; but at times, the consequences of my choices will seep into that memory and taint it toward sadness. As I continue to stay in joy, I combat those few poor choices from my past. What's done is done. I am who I am because of the choices I've made. I can't go back, but I can move forward and do better. I can remember the good times and the happiness and joy because they do outweigh the sadness.

SHARE

After a man conquers others and has all the power, all the land, all the money, and all the riches he wants around him, then what? After he has conquered, where's his joy, and who will want to share it with him if he has all the power? Being king of the hill is lonely when you're the only one up there. I would rather have love, compassion, forgiveness, patience, kindness, empathy, joy, hope, truth, and faith within me, which I am able and willing to share with anyone. Join me?

Available

When faced with a dilemma, a decision has to be explored. Many choices may arise when trying to resolve the issue. It is there that the lines must be drawn and boundaries set in place. This does not require violence or abuse; all it requires is a conversation that must state what is acceptable and what must change. Misunderstandings occur when there is a lack of communication, so when you're ready and willing, let's pour a cup of coffee and sit down so we can move forward by resolving this dilemma. Let me know when you're available.

Guidance

Resentment is still an emotion I struggle with. I know it is futile, because all it causes is pain as I relive the hurts that still exist in my mind. Even if the behavior is continuing, I do not need to attach myself to that pain. A hardened heart gets very heavy as I teeter back and forth between holding on and letting it go. As I continue to ask for guidance, I am reminded that the only thing that is about me is my reaction. So once again, as my anger melts, as I detach myself from the outcomes I hope for, and as I learn to live in my now, I can find compassion. "You have to pass the test of being faithful where you are. Keep stretching, praying, and believing."

Now

There comes a time in our lives when our worry for our loved ones must end and the pain of past hurts must mend and all the disappointments from unmet expectations must melt into the joy of today. This time is now!

Move Forward

Once an apology has been spoken, it's time to move forward. Healing can only be prevented by two things: if the behavior does not change and if the apology is not accepted. This requires trust, faith, and hope. Moving forward is inevitable; however, moving forward requires change and acceptance. An "I'm sorry" requires a change in behavior, and "I accept your apology" requires acceptance. It's time to move forward, so let's walk our talk.

Hopeful

When I sit and think about my life, I can see moments of joy and moments of sorrow. During the times I experienced joy, I want to freeze those moment and live there forever. Conversely, when a moment of sorrow slips into my journey, I want to fast-forward as quickly as possible so as to forget the pain. Life is fluid and temporary, and I can find peace in my faith knowing that all is well. I am learning to live in the moment, still hopeful that the joy will somehow outweigh the pain.

Attention

Where I place my attention is as important as what I eat to nourish my body and what truth I choose to follow to nourish my soul. I can be swayed into darkness by a reaction from a behavior that is displayed, but where I focus my attention can make all the difference whether I remain in my joy or follow my feelings into resentment. I must be very aware of how and where I place my attentions so that I can live in peace with the hope that things will work out for good.

God's Guidance

Being a very reactionary person, I have come to the point in my life where I will wait to respond so that I can think before I speak. Yet when becoming aware of my own thoughts and of how I self-sabotage through shaming myself with my past transgression, I can react without giving it a second thought. I may have made some poor life choices, but God has used everything for my good. I can make a decision to allow the behavior of my past to define who I am today or quickly ask God to guide me and give me wisdom to live in the moment. I can allow what does or what may not happen rob me of the joy that awaits me today or believe in God's goodness and promises.

CHOOSE JOY

How easy it can be for me to allow my joy to be stolen in the blink of an eye. Whether it's someone's reaction or something I read or hear, I can allow myself to feel distressed. I may feel an overwhelming sadness when someone I love does not reciprocate my feelings; my abandonment may turn into bitterness and resentment. In these moments, my joy is being stolen, but I choose to make a conscious effort to walk away or say a prayer. I can find compassion for them knowing I can't make someone else do the same, but as for me, I choose joy.

MY BEST

Pleasing others should never be my goal, but I will always strive to do my best. Despite knowing that I will never please everyone, I will do my best. Whether my best is good enough for others, I will always strive to be my best, true, positive, authentic self for God. If others benefit from my behavior, then they will see Him in me. When I do what's right for God, then all can see how He works through me. I will remain humble and do my best not to feel that I am better than another but to strive to be better than I used to be.

PRAISE

When I feel depleted and deprivation is my only thought, I have to stop and say a prayer of gratitude for the unconditional love

God has given me. He's given me an abundance of blessings—good health, an open heart, and an open mind to continue to find peace. Even if I don't have what I want, I will always have what I need.

Every Day Is a New Beginning

How heavy my load is when I begin my day if I drag something from yesterday into my today. Unfinished business from yesterday may cloud my decision for today, so I will examine what is needed for my journey and discard the rest. I find that when I pray for others, I forget my own needs and worries. When I give my burdens to God, the heaviness from carrying the load ceases to exist. I can recognize poor choices, for I have made some of my own. So instead of judging another's behavior, I will show kindness and compassion, and then I will release my heavy load from yesterday and show up as my best, true self for God today.

U-Turn

When I come to the edge of my joy, all I can do is decide if I am going to plunge into the abyss or take a U-turn back toward my joy. I am now aware of my resources, my greatest being my hope and faith that all is being worked out for my good. I have no control over anything else, but I can choose to remain joyful even if the sadness shows up.

Humbled

It's so interesting that I can be so quick to point out someone's behavior and judge it kindly or meanly. I can also smell or taste something and judge it pleasant or nasty, or I can look at something and judge it good or bad. It's also interesting that if someone's views don't align with mine, I can quickly judge them to be right or wrong. It's humbling that I am judging the exact things I am being judged for, and I call it unfair. Humbled!

No More Worry

I never have to worry again about anything. I never have to worry about abandonment, assimilation, or abuse. I never have to worry about believing who I am supposed to be through someone else's definition or what I am supposed to trust or how I am supposed to live. I no longer have to worry if I am loved and cherished. I can choose to live in the truth or die in the lie. I never have to worry because I choose the truth and I believe in God.

My Cup

When I woke up this morning, I felt alone, and You told me to check my cup. I began feeling deprived of relationships I wanted and connections I desired, and You told me to check my cup. I was focusing on the negative situations in the world and was feeling sorry for myself for what I didn't have, and you told me to check my cup. When I did, I found that it was filled with unconditional love, financial security, good health, and emotional stability. I found myself apologizing for not seeing that my cup was running over, and for that, I am humbled by your blessings. When my darkness sets in, I will turn to the light and check my cup.

Goodbye

After all the countless hours waiting for that one voice to be heard, it's time to say goodbye. After one more attempt to make peace and being rejected, it's time to say goodbye. After all the tears have been shed and the prayers have been spoken, only to accept it as it is, it's time to say goodbye. Sometimes, it's just easier to say goodbye.

Challenged

When I'm confronted with something that I don't remember saying or doing, my defensiveness may come twofold. The first is that I am not comfortable with the behavior that I am being accused of, and the second is, I don't remember saying what I am being accused of saying. Instead of lashing out, I begin to recede into my memory as if it is a file cabinet of my past, and I look through all the folders to find the truth. Even if I don't recall saying what I am accused of saying and even if I don't remember engaging in the behavior that I am told I've done, I can respectfully acknowledge it and become aware not to do that again. I can't change what I've done or remember what I no longer hold in my thoughts, but I can be aware of how I react when my behavior is challenged.

DETACH

I never totally understood the concept of detachment. To detach meant to separate from; therefore, if I were to practice this concept, it meant that I would have to stop engaging emotionally. Having always been a person of deep passion, this was a difficult scenario to put into practice, yet what I did learn was that I could show up and still be kind and still engage. I just didn't have to do their work too. I did not have to ignore. I just had to be responsible for what was mine and find the compassion and patience for others to do the same. I learned to find my own life and to live in the joy of rediscovering who I was meant to be.

DEALING

I know that I will not always get what I want, but I know I will always have what I need. It's an inevitable fact that problems will always show up in my life, yet if I remain in faith, I will always receive the tools I need to deal with them. And if I choose, I will see the life lesson they're trying to teach me. There is no such life as living pain free, but with God, it won't hurt as much.

GOD'S WILL BE DONE

When I ignore God's will and try to journey through the day with my will, it never seems to work out the way it would if I allow

God's will instead of mine. So I will allow God's will to guide me instead of thinking my will, will get me the results I desire. God's will, will always bring me what I need. My will, will always lead me into frustration. God's will is better than mine. I will my will to allow God's will to guide me.

Turn the Other Cheek

"Do unto others" is not a difficult standard to follow if, in fact, it's what I want to do. But when it should be the right thing to do and I don't want to do it, then I do have to follow the rest of the standard by acting as I would want them to do unto me. Having been the recipient of another's cruelty, I don't want to inflict pain onto another, so I will do unto others as I would have them do unto me even if they don't show me kindness or respect. I will be kind and respectful because it's the person I want to be. Even if another hurts me, I will not hurt them. I will turn the other cheek.

Gratitude

How easy it is to find joy when everything is going my way. How easy it is to feel downhearted and dismayed when things go awry. I know that all is meant to be, and in good times, I may become complacent and not always find gratitude. I also know that all is meant to be, and during tough times is when I am brought to my knees. Time and time again, I am drawn out of being complacent and drawn back into gratitude. In tough times, I pray; and I also remember that in good times, I need to pray and be thankful as well.

Kindness

When I'm confronted with a behavior that differs from mine, I have a choice: I can react in kind, or I can rebel. Usually, rebellion comes with the agenda of assimilation, whereas a reaction in kindness comes with compassion and empathy. I would rather be given the platform of kindness than to have to engage in an endless war of detours. I choose kindness.

I Know What to Do

There comes a time in my life when I encounter a conflict where what to do or not to do becomes more important than what I should do. I know what to do, and having a combative dialogue in my head only prolongs that. Fear of not being accepted may set in, and I may imagine all the ways I will be hurt again, but I still know what I must do. My choices are not contingent on whether the outcome will be in my favor or accepted. I will do what needs to be done, because it is what I am meant to do. I'll do it and move on.

Listen

When I engage in a conversation that takes a lot of my energy, I have to remind myself that I am not connecting with that person to change their opinion. Rather, I want to share our beliefs in an honorable, respectful way. Without listening to the other person and just focusing on being heard, the engagement can become combative rather than keeping the lines of communication open for further discussion. How often am I more focused on what I am thinking or saying rather than stopping to listen? I will honor you with the two ears I have by hearing you and the one mouth that I have will remain closed until it's my turn to speak. Let's talk.

Done

When asked to do something, there are many reasons I don't want to engage; but if there is an innate reason not to engage, I won't. Otherwise, I will just do it. If I am supposed to do it and I become combative knowing I will eventually succumb to the request, I may as well save myself a lot of wasted energy and just do it. Then I can move forward to the next request knowing what I've accomplished; it's done!

Blueprint

When I am asked to do something that does not have a blueprint to follow or a road in which to travel, I may look for the easy way out by making excuses why I shouldn't engage. But I've come to learn that in the most difficult times, God has a designed plan for me and that I will be equipped with every tool I need to succeed. It is only when I think I can do it myself or totally ignore it altogether that I deem myself a failure. So in the most difficult times and in the most unfamiliar circumstances, without a clue of where to go or what to do, I will pray for guidance and wisdom and feel safe in knowing that God's got my blueprint.

Aware

Negative thoughts are like subtle little cuts that infiltrate my mind, and before I realize it, I have wondered off into a painful memory, and it has stolen my moment. I've never truly understood how much a negative thought can rob me of so many precious moments. I am grateful to be now aware of when I detour from joy into sadness, and with that awareness, I am awakened by a gentle push to come home to joy. I'm aware.

Vision

It's interesting how my thinking can change when I learn all the facts or step back far enough to see the entire picture. It's interesting that tunnel vision or blinders or a veil can distort my perception and lead me to believe something other than what's in front of me. I'm sorry if at times, I don't see the entire picture. I've learned to seek the truth and investigate all the facts before I make my decision. Forgive me. I will aim to do better.

Thanks, but No, Thanks

Having to deal with a confrontation can leave me scrambling for words that defend my position. Some will come at me to tear me down and drag me back to the place where they can control me. If this is why they are engaging with me, I can kindly decline to go with them. Yet if I am speaking the truth and live in the truth, I need no evidence to defend who I am presenting myself to be. I'll just show up as myself. I can pray and wish them well and be on my way.

No Defense Needed

When I prepared myself for a confrontation with someone who had different views from mine, I can recall loading my tool belt with specific rebuttals to their accusations. I had to be prepared to defend myself against anything they deemed untrue about me. This was an exhausting task, because my integrity was in question and because I felt the need to defend my honor. Yet now no defense is needed, because I know my truth. If I present myself in any other way than who I am, I am responsible for questioning how I present myself that may lead another to have these misconceptions about me. Knowing it's not always about me, I need not be defensive to show others who I am.

I Choose

How often has fear played a dominant role in my life? I can become anxious if I am waiting for something to come to fruition, or I can become apprehensive as I enter a new experience, or I can become agitated if I am asked to prolong my gratification. In any event, I can choose that, or I can choose better. I choose hope, faith, truth, and God.

Wise Words

Contradictions are difficult for me to comprehend, especially if there are hurtful words and actions attached to someone's conversation. I am learning to choose my words wisely, as if they are spoken to me. I am choosing my time wisely, accessing when I need to have a confrontation or when I need to walk away. When there comes a time when I feel the need to speak up, I will. I hope that what I offer into the conversation will be an awakening of how hurtful things are. I pray I will choose my words and actions wisely so as not to fuel the fire but extinguish it into healing.

Smile

There are some days when I wake up in a mood that I can't describe other than feeling unsettled or melancholy. There is really no reason why I feel this way, but I just do. I then embrace my heart and become very aware of my reactions. Knowing this is temporary, I will encourage myself to step into the sunlight, and maybe I will find relief from my sadness in the joy of the birds' song. A smile is a frown upside down.

What I Can Do

When I feel at peace, I know I have flipped my fear to faith. There are certain things I can control, and yet when I am confronted with another's inappropriate choices, all I want to do is give them the "You should do this" lecture. I can set healthy boundaries and walk away so that their behavior does not hurt me. I can pray for them to seek the knowledge they need to come to the truth. I can be the role model for this, and yet all the while, I know it is up to them to seek the truth. We may not agree with how to arrive, but I pray we can all live in peace with the one truth: I know you are, I know I am, and I know God is.

Circle

Coming full circle becomes a celebration, because what is strove for has been attained. This comes with joy and a little bit of sadness, because something has to be released in order to make room for the new. Giving in does not mean giving up, and letting go does not mean losing. It means I've made room for something new. There is no conceding or losing when what has been waiting for me far outweighs what I am holding out for or holding on to. When there's room for the new by letting go of what no longer fits, then I will have what I am meant to have. I will have peace, joy, and contentment.

Prideful

Sometimes, I just feel so much conviction that I set my feet in concrete and refuse to move. In these times, the wind blows, the rain falls, and the sun burns; yet being in concrete, I am unable to escape my self-inflicted cage. I can make things difficult for myself when I know what I want to do doesn't align with what I need to do.

These are the times when I need to let go of my pride and release the negative thoughts that hold me captive in my self-inflicted cage. I may find what I am asked to do uncomfortable, but I would rather live with a few moments of discomfort than decades in a cage of despair. This conflict usually results in a therapy session with my prideful self, weighing the pros and cons of the consequences I may suffer if I don't do what I need to do but rather choose to do what I want to do. When I submit that what I know I am asked to do is the right thing, I can shed one more prideful layer and move on with my day in peace, because I know I'm about to do what is right.

I Will Pray

When I become aware of all the unrest in others' lives, I can become depressed for them and actually assimilate myself into their drama so as to live in the pain with them. When I watch the news and witness all the unrest, sadness, confusion, and hate that we are sharing, I can become so unhappy in the darkness of all the despair. This very behavior steals my joy, because there is nothing I can do for them to resolve their issue except pray for their healing.

We have all been designed with different and special gifts that may or may not align with one another, but it still saddens me when people who claim to love one another continue to hurt one another because of our differences. I will still love you despite our differences. I will still show respect even if you're disrespectful. I will still pray for you as you continue to curse me. I will still be my best self as you struggle to find your truth. When I don't know what to do, I pray. When I don't know what to say, I pray. When I feel a defensive, combative reaction, I stop and pray. I have found that if I detach and seek guidance within my feelings, I can bring it all back to me and give it to God. When I'm in doubt, I will pray.

Uncomfortable

Acceptance can be uncomfortable even if it means learning to live with that which makes me uncomfortable. Knowing I can't always have it my way doesn't deter me from wanting it my way, but I know that if it doesn't work out my way, then God has a better plan for me. When I can accept God's way, then I can learn to live with His decisions as I watch life unfold. He sees the entire picture, and His purpose and vision are greater than mine. I can live with uncomfortable.

Focused

When I'm confused, I can become agitated as I await the answers to my questions. Being a truth seeker, I dig to uncover layers of deceit until I arrive where the truth is. During this quest, my agitation melts into determination and elation so that when I arrive, I know I have purged fear to accept love. I pray to stay focused in the light of the truth as the darkness of lies fade.

Guarantee

When I reach out, there are no guarantees that my salutation will be reciprocated. I can say "Good morning" to someone I pass on the street and be ignored. I can send a birthday card, but my birthday can be overlooked. I can approach a relationship with an open heart, but I may be met with resistance. I may be ignored or overlooked or resisted, but I am not defined by someone else's responses or reactions. I can continue to show up in the light or become submersed in the dark; I choose light. My behavior comes with the guarantee that I will live in the light, so good morning, happy birthday, and I love you.

Step Back

When in pain, I know how to take care of myself—eat right, exercise, rest, and pray to hear God's wisdom and guidance. I can offer the same advice when I see another in pain, but I sometimes get stuck in feeling their heartbreak, so I've been known to enable their discomfort so they don't suffer the anguish of defeat. When I am confronted with a negative story or attitude, it is not mine to fix, but it is for me to remain hopeful and pray for an outcome that will be accepted. That is what is in my control. The rest is up to God! Solving another's problems does not work; I need to know when to step back and offer prayers, compassion, and empathy as I watch God go to work.

Forward

Remaining in the status quo will not enhance my journey; it only keeps me captive to the same situations that hold me hostage to the past. I may be moving forward even if those I love remain in the past. This does not mean I remain with them, nor does it suggest that they are right or they are wrong; it's just where they are. There may be a time when we aren't able to coexist without tension, so I can pray they find peace as I continue on my journey. I pray I remain in peace as I move forward on my journey.

DECISION

When I have to make a decision about something that will change my way of living, I have to think about the choices that will have an impact on me on a positive or negative scale. I usually know that if I am at peace in my thinking, then it is the right thing for me to follow. If there is any doubt or anxiety, then I need to seek the origin of the fear and pray for clarity and peace. Rash decisions made during a painful time may cause more damage, so I'll seek guidance in meditation and prayer and get centered. I'll make changes when I'm ready to accept my journey, not because I want to stop the pain while I'm experiencing the journey. Stop, look, and listen for guidance and wisdom. I know what to do.

NO DETOUR

There are so many blessings to be grateful for, yet an inappropriate word or one frown can detour the blessing into a whirlwind of victimization from past transgressions, so I will be cognizant of my thoughts so as not to detour faith into fear. Hurrying up to elevate the anxiety and pain may cause more of a disruption than the pain itself. Making decisions while struggling can detour away from faith, hope, wisdom, and guidance. When in pain and doubt, say a prayer; my favorite is, "Help!"

HEALING

Finding gratitude can be a more difficult task for some who are used to living in the status quo or victim mentality. I will never negate someone's pain, yet I will always offer a ray of light and hope. Everyone wants to be needed. Waiting for an invitation to help a friend can be difficult. Not making it about me can ease the anxiousness, and I can turn that into a prayer and send a blessing for their healing. I can learn to wait in prayer. Life is fluid, so the pain will eventually flow into love, and the life lessons and opportunities will be revealed. Life is!

Mindset

I know that when I try to tackle something that has changed or to learn something that is new, I can become agitated as I confront it with the same mindset or my prior skill set. I have to purge that which no longer is applicable to make room for new instructions. Such as it is with a new life—a job or retirement, a new home in a new state, or a relationship that is starting or ending—these new experiences require a new mindset. It's always exciting and a little bit scary to confront something different from my norm. I am setting my mind toward something new.

Pride

Offering support, wisdom, and guidance is quite different from enabling. This fine line can turn a sage into a god if not careful and if not keeping a watchful eye on pride. I am a child of God, and I allow Him to speak through me when others need a prayer. I will keep my pride in check, so when I am agitated with a behavior choice, I can revisit its origin and then take action. I can apologize to the person and ask to be forgiven; instead of it holding me in my prison of shame and embarrassment, I can make amends, then I can move forward, aware of not repeating the behavior. I can heal.

May the Lord bless you and keep you; may the Lord make His face to shine upon you and be gracious to you; may the Lord lift up His countenance upon you and give you peace.
—Numbers 6:22

Behind the Clouds

It's interesting that when cleanup on isle 6 happens, the results are the same; isle 6 will get cleaned. The initial reaction when the spill occurs can make the task to clean up isle 6 either effortless or a joy stealer. It's always a choice. Gloomy, snowy, or rainy days that block the sun behind the clouds can make me feel closed in and small.

Despite knowing that the sun is still shining behind the clouds, I can still give in to the gloominess of the day. Yet I can thank God for the beauty of the season and take advantage of this downtime from outdoor activities while nesting and keeping warm by a fire. The sun is always shining behind the clouds.

Do Better

Feeling disrespected by another's words or actions can set me off into self-doubt and anger. I start judging them, thinking, *How dare they treat me like this!* or *Why was I treated like this?* or *How am I supposed to turn the other cheek?* I allow their behavior to dictate my mood and self-worth while I know that their words and behavior are not about me but about them. My reaction is about me. So I forgive my self-doubt and judgments and forgive them for being misguided. I pray for the both of us and hope to do better and be better.

Be Better

The game of blame-shifting and retribution can become tiresome and exhausting. The mentality of getting even does not bring out the best in people. It only holds them captive in fear. So I will send you blessings even if I am a ghost in your life. I will speak kindness even if I am cursed. I will speak the truth to you even if you lie to me. I will forgive even if you're cruel and abusive. I will show you compassion and empathy, because I, too, have been in pain. I'm no better than you. I only strive to be better than I used to be.

Encounter

When I encounter someone in pain, my immediate reaction is to ease it. Although I cannot control their behavior, I tend to offer advice that has worked for me or sway them away from behavior that has caused me harm. It is not my responsibility to fix things for them; all I can do is be a support system and ease their pain. When encountering angry people, I feel the need to be kind. This, however, can be interpreted as an acceptance of their behavior. I am learning to say no and to set boundaries, even with the underlying fear that they will leave me. I can still be loving when encountering fear. I can still be kind when encountering anger. I do not need to engage because I am protected. I am safe.

GRATEFUL

When I come to the end of a relationship that has been toxic, I can experience regret and grief as I say goodbye. I will allow myself to feel this way until it is done. I can reflect on the life lessons I've learned from having known this person and thank them for the gift I have been given by knowing them. Even if it was toxic, I learned something. Perhaps what I learned was that I deserved better than what they were offering or that their definition of who they thought I should be was inaccurate. Whatever the case, I am grateful for all who have crossed my path and have faith that if they are gone forever, all is as it is meant to be. It is done.

OPPORTUNITIES

A reflection of the past may sometimes focus on negative experiences, yet with this focus comes enlightenment on how those negative experiences have brought me growth and prosperity. Although restrictions from life may halt a journey, the purpose will always remain steadfast when restrictions are softened and opportunities begin to arise. In the midst of restrictions and halts, I have found peace spiritually, emotionally, financially, and physically. I am grateful and blessed.

CHAPTER 14

Silence—Stillness

THE GIFT OFFERING

I am so confused with the way people treat one another. If we have a different political affiliation or a different religious belief, then we have to bully, badger, and abuse one another so that we will all think alike so that you are no more right than me. In this insecurity, we alienate ourselves from the very people who hold so many blessings and life lessons to offer us; yet in our fear, we push them away. We fear that we may have to look at our truth and change it a bit so that we can truly align with our own ultimate truth.

In my confusion, I have come to a point in my life where if I am not welcomed, I will leave; and if I am not given the same respect and voice that I am giving you, I will bless you and not engage. How sad it makes me that we are not willing to put down our sword or open our clenched fist to welcome someone amazing into our lives. An opened, softened heart can have the capacity to love and be loved. This is the gift that is being offered, so why not take it?

WHEN I ALLOW

When I allow myself to think I know what's best for me, then I can become anxious and engage in behaviors that will only delay and prolong what's inevitable. When I allow negative thoughts to seep into my peace, then I am able to become aware and change my thinking into a positive reaction, believing that all is meant to be. When I allow myself to see my unrest in another's fear, then I am able to acknowledge me in them and withdraw my judgment knowing we are all evolving souls. When I allow myself to enjoy my passions and the flow of life, uninterrupted by my anxiousness or need to control an outcome to make myself comfortable, then all is well.

THE VOICE WITHIN

When I am looking to resolve an uncomfortable feeling or trying to bring peace to an uncomfortable situation, I may get messages that are not to my benefit. I may hear my inner voice giving me advice, but I may become confused if the message is making me feel the pain instead of resolving it. I know that my true voice within comes to encourage the resolution, gives me hope, and pushes me into believing I am worthy of love and peace. It helps me understand and speak with love to reassure my worth and helps me find compassion for others and myself.

If my voice is only adding to my anxiousness and keeping me in turmoil, then I know that it is my saboteur and that the message is not in the best interest of my healing. The more I listen to and believe in what my truth is telling me about my value, my potential, and how much God loves me, the stronger that voice will become. The more I silence the voices that can interfere with my peace, the quieter those voices will become. Saying no to voices that are judgmental and that make me feel ashamed will help me stop believing them as I replace them with God's truth. I will be able to ignore the conflict those voices harbor and pick out the one that speak the truth: God.

RELATIONSHIP

Being a wife, mother, teacher, sibling, daughter, cousin, and friend gave me an excuse to become involved so deeply with the lives of others that it defined the life I led. I was always someone else's go-to person to solve a problem. I gave so much of myself that I had too little left for me, so I became invisible. I participated in their story, and this, in turn, was my life. Now that I no longer engage, except with a pleasantry or a blessing and a prayer, I am learning to sit still and enjoy the moments. Who am I in this silence? Who am I now that I have shed the definition of who I am in the lives of the others?

My thoughts occasionally drag me back into the drama of who they are without me. In the silence, I will occasionally look for some noise to get me involved so that it will distract me into being who I was instead of who I am now. I am learning that I don't need to participate in order to care. I don't need to assimilate in order to send a prayer. I don't need to worry because they are on their own journey, and they will figure it out without me, as I have figured it out without them. I am now learning what it's like to be in a relationship.

Before You Know It

Before you know it, you're an adult with responsibilities, a job, a family, and a mortgage. Before you know it, you're celebrating your kids' graduations and twenty-five years of marriage, and now you are collecting social security because you've retired. The "before you know its" creep up like a snake hunting for food in a garden. It can show up so suddenly that in the blink of an eye, what was new is old.

I have encountered my thoughts in this manner. I can awaken with gratitude and joy in my heart, feeling blessed for my comforts and joy. Yet before I know it, a negative, worrisome, troubling thought can creep into my mind, and I feel negative, scared, unsure, and uncertain. This is when I smile, realize what I'm doing, say a prayer, ask for the thought to reveal its message, and move on. Before I know it, I'm on to something new and exciting. Enjoy each moment because before you know, it will be gone.

Stop By for a Visit

When a friend comes by for a visit, we can chat for a while, share pleasantries, and then say goodbye. Not so much for a negative thought that stops by for a visit. I can extend a welcome, question its purpose for the visit, and then allow it to pass through me but not become a part of me. I do not have to engage for too long to decide what the negative thought is trying to persuade me to do. The one thing evil detests is me observing myself without self-loathing, without panic, and without a fight. How amazing to hear God's truth in the quiet stillness of my own mind and to decide what stays and what goes. Thanks for stopping by for a visit, but it's time to say goodbye.

RECOVERY

When I started on my quest to find myself in the depths of my own despair, I found books to read, people to talk with, and words to chant. All the while, I was thinking that if I was diligent and disciplined enough, I would heal, the pain would stop, and we would all love one another again and be a family. But that is not how it works. There are no magic pills to take, enough books to read, words to chant, or people to talk with to heal the pain.

It was in the quietness of the soul that I found me. It was in letting go and emptying all the words that were spoken to define me or to define God. It was in seeking my own truth with the deepest connection that only I could have found within myself. It was in believing or not believing where one found the truth. Dismiss all that is said, take time to go into the silence, and find out that in that peace and stillness is where patience and faith live; and that is where all will be revealed. This is where God is waiting for us.

REVISIT THE PAST

While I was fully immersed in others' lives, I neglected my own. When I became still and silent enough to hear my own cries in the darkness, pleading to come into the light, I was able to empty that which was not mine, and I began to immerse myself in my own life. Even after accepting my journey as God's will and healing most of my painful memories by forgiving in order to move forward, I still wonder, how many times do I need to keep revisiting my past?

Fleeting flickers of light that hold a memory may pass through my thoughts, yet how long I choose to dwell there will determine how much more time I need to devote to a past hurt that still needs my attention. How long do I need to revisit? I can revisit for a while, but then I need to leave, because I have a standing appointment with my present.

Stop, Look, and Listen

When we are taught how to cross a street or a railroad crossing, we are taught to stop, look, and listen. We're taught this to avoid potential danger. How often have I not used this helpful childhood lesson in my communication with others? In the past, I did not feel worthy of having an opinion, so perhaps needing to be heard made me talk louder to make my position known. Perhaps thinking I was an expert on a specific topic made me think that I knew better for me or for another than they knew for themselves.

I want to be heard and honored, but choosing this type of communication will not resolve my issues and is only keeping me from letting go of control. I will stop and address my trigger, I will look at the other person as a soul on a journey, and I will listen to their point of view. I will then continue to think before I speak, act, and react.

Take a Moment

When I was young, everything I encountered had purpose. I would spend hours exploring and learning, making an attempt to try and understand everything and everyone. Through the eyes of my innocence, I loved. Then life happened; challenges confronted me with choices. The luxury of spending time, taking that moment, was replaced with a deadline and a demand, and my just being became assimilated.

Now years have passed. I sit and watch the snow fall, much like I did as a child. I see a flower bud, and I stop to smell its sweetness. I watch a bird build its nest, awaiting its child. I become amazed by the acrobatic skills of a squirrel as it scurries across a wire. I watch, and

I see, and I am once again that child. This is my prayer and blessing for anyone who reads this: Like the innocence of a child, may your life be filled with snowflakes, flower buds, bird nests, and scurrying squirrels and the essence of taking a moment to know that you are a blessing.

Silent Enough to Hear

Pain has a message, so be still and silent to be able to hear it. Have faith and trust that God's plan is pure and filled with love. We are all particles, like dust in a sunbeam. Trust that we will land where we are meant to land. Trying to control all those particles will make us miss the vital lesson of the journey and the moments that hold so much to help us evolve. There are past worries and future concerns, yet all the good will outweigh the hurtful and painful memories. I thought that if I screamed loud enough, it would drown out the need for the pain to be heard and felt, but there's no need for drama or noise to feel alive.

Contradictions have a message. I have been given a voice, and now it's time to take time to listen. Be still and listen for the sweetness. What do I hear? In my stillness, I am filling myself with all that God has spoken to me, not from the words of another. His pure words are filled with love, hope, and peace. I choose to listen to my own inner voice, my intuition, and God's silent whisper to fill me with all that I am meant to know, hear, and become.

In My Stillness

I am still evolving; each experience helps me learn patience, consistency, and perseverance. I am remaining in His light to find contentment, peace, and happiness. In my stillness, it is drama free, quiet, and empty of the burdens I used to harbor as my own. I am allowing processing time to refill my cup with me after I have emptied myself of them. I am resting and allowing myself to just be to discover who I am meant to be. I am coming out of their shadow and resurfacing into the light. I am removing the mask and the veil that I hide behind in order to feel loved and worthy.

CONTRADICTIONS OF MY STILLNESS

In this time of stillness and emptiness, I am learning to appreciate and validate the lessons in each moment. Although this new behavior is uncomfortable, I am willing to have faith enough to know it won't last too long. Through the pain and discomfort, there is joy; through the tears, there is laughter. In my emptiness, I find me; in the quiet, I hear me; in the void, I am not alone. God is with me. He sees me and hears me. I am accepting the contradictions of my stillness.

NO NEED

In my stillness, I am emptied. When I am anxious, I try to fill the emptiness with drama to feel like I belong, but there is no need to do that anymore. I am at peace where I am and who I am with. I am able to relinquish control or the need to fix things or be the peacekeeper. In the quiet and stillness of my mind, I am becoming more aware of how I am letting go of the burden of hanging on to that which is not mine. The more I empty out that which is not mine, the more there is room for God's positive energy to fill me. I know God knows better for me than I know for others and myself. In the stillness of my mind, I hear God, I feel God, and I know God; there's no need for anything more.

WHAT FITS

In the emptying of that which is not mine or that no longer fits, there is peace and a drama-free contentment. I am embracing the silence and accepting just being. I trust and have faith in not knowing. I look for life lessons from every experience and for opportunity for the lesson's purpose to apply to my growth. In the stillness of my emptiness, I am aware of the what-ifs, and I am aware of the compromises that are attached to the contradictions. I am aware of the positive energy that waits for me to heal. As long as I stay true to God and myself, I never have to fear where I am being led. In letting go of being a peacemaker and trying to fit in that mold, I am at peace knowing what I know. This is what fits.

Begin Again

When the silence got too loud, I needed noise to know I was alive. When the void got too big, I needed the emptiness to be filled with whatever I could get my hands on just to fill it. It didn't matter if it was positive for my growth or not. When not knowing became uncomfortable, I needed to manipulate and control the outcome. When my trust was compromised, I began to live another's lie as my truth. An adult's lie became this child's truth. Then I fell, and the only hands that reached to help me up were His!

I began to trust myself again. I began to have faith in God again knowing He never left me. I began to accept the silence and listen for the small, quiet voice. I began to accept the void and the emptiness and the not knowing, and I began to restore my faith in God. I began again.

We Are All Evolving

According to our own timeline and through our experiences and opportunities, we are all evolving. This is where enlightenment occurs. Being able to pray for others and myself is grace given by God. There is no room for competition or conquest. I am only responsible for my own enlightenment, being allowed to share in my humbleness. The "Fix it, or hurry up and arrive" attitude only brings unrest and turmoil to a peaceful soul. It dims the light and causes havoc and drama. I am at peace, and I am enlightened. I pray others will find their way into this light and will see what a blessing we all are as we continue to evolve.

Those I Have Loved

In my quiet stillness, I see all those I have loved who have walked away from me. When one leaves, the pain of not having closure drills into my soul. All the whys keep pounding in my head and heart, and then when the quiet silence emerges to still my soul and purify my thoughts, I see the blessing in all those who have passed through my life. Even if I was not ready to let go, it was God's will that they left. So as I heal my sadness, my brokenhearted dreams never to come, I say goodbye.

Silence in Prayer

In my aloneness, I still struggle with the silence. So when the silence gets too loud, I reach for the old, predictable behavior that will cause some noise, and then I whisper my prayer: "Help me stay in the silence of love rather than settle for the noise of fear. Help me embrace my contradictions and listen to the message so that I will stay in the light." I know God's plan is greater than any of my wants or needs, so I pray, "Dear Lord, help me remain in your love and light when the darkness hovers over me. Help me remain with positive thoughts and deeds." My faith and God's truth are more important than masks and veils.

In the Moment

Being at one with myself is easy when I am alone and all distractions are silenced. Then I am truly comfortable with who I am and what I've become. Becoming who I am meant to be has taken the huge risk of no longer relying on the approval of others or the acceptance of others' truth or becoming a part of their drama, so I am walking toward my inner self and letting go of what is not within my soul.

In the past, I struggled to stay in that silence when it got too quiet and the drama had subsided. But now that I'm here, I reflect on where I was then and compare it to how peaceful I am now. Now there is a lack of drama, and I am getting comfortable with just being and just breathing. I now can show the reflection of my light, so I choose this moment, and I feel blessed.

THE WHISPER BUBBLE

How many years have I lived in the shadow of someone else's lie? How many times have I ignored my truth? In the stillness and silence in my soul beats the heart of my origin. In the whisper of knowledge, I know what to do. In the bubble of indecision, the whisper leads me to the light. Knowing God's truth, hearing His whisper, and feeling the bubble of reality in my gut is true living. When in doubt, the stillness, the silence, and the emptiness make room for all that is needed to know and all that is needed to guide me. So in prayer, I ask my question, and I become still and silent enough to hear the answer in the whisper of God's breath and feel the bubble in my soul be filled with blessing and truth.

IN A MOMENT

What have I chosen to do in my moments? How have I chosen to feel, to act, or to just be in that moment? In the past, when the silence got too loud, I needed noise. When the stillness got too quiet, I needed drama to fill the emptiness. I searched to hold that which was not mine to hold. I looked to make decisions for that which was not mine to decide. I stirred up noise and the stillness to feel that I was a part of something that was not mine. What is mine to live is mine to share, as I live in my moments. In a moment, I stop, take a deep breath, look at my reflection in the mirror, and look within my soul. In a moment, a smile or a tear can appear. In a moment, my life can begin or end.

WAIT A MINUTE

In this world of immediate gratification, how many times have I had to redo or try to fix that which I broke in my hast and impatience? Pacing, unrest, and manipulation will not ever get the desired results. All the impatience, all the effort to be patient, and all the letting go yet still holding on tightly will never bring me joy and peace. So ask the questions and take a minute to listen for the answer: "Will you show me and guide me and help me?" By silencing the voices, it will bring patience and peace and allow the answers to be heard. In this precious minute, what I need to hear will be heard. What I need to see will be seen. What needs clarity will become clear. Within a minute, it can bring faith and trust and hear God's answer.

FOLLOW THE VOICE WITHIN

Some say that the voice within is our God-voice and our intuition that what we know, we know. Yet after following some soft voices and some assertive voices, I know it is difficult to decipher what voice I should be following. In my self-loathing, self-gratification was the voice. In my self-doubt, I followed everyone else's voice. But now in forgiveness and in my coming home, I listen for that small whisper in my soul. The positive, joyful message I receive is, "I am, and you are. We are all one." Now in my haste to follow a voice, I stop, I breathe, I listen, I hear, and I finally know what voice to follow.

WILL YOU HELP ME?

Often, when I was faced with an adversity or a challenge, my initial reaction was to rely on my old reactions. In order to feel as if I was surviving, I would become defensive, then justify my behavior, advocate for my voice, and then surrender to the request. Within the battle, where I screamed at the top of my lungs to show I had a voice, I once again got lost in the sorrow and darkness of a broken dream. As I regrouped and gathered my disappointment and resentments as my next coat of armor, I was reminded of the simple request I made that was left unanswered: "Will you help me?" Yet within all the noise, I never heard the answer. How could I hear anything while the pain was drowning me? Not until I became silent, willing and unattached to expectations and judgments, did I indeed hear the answer, "Yes, I will!"

He Answers

We know only too well that sorrow often breaks the crust of a superficial life. It uncovers its deepest realities. Not always at our highest but sometimes from our depths do we best see God. The Lord's Prayer has always been my greatest contradiction and affirmation that there has never been a guarantee for a pain-free life. Yet in the depths of despair, when on my knees, feeling the implosion of the last tear I shed, I ask, "Will you help me and show me what to do?" Having been broken open again to the light that does shine, the green valley filled with sunshine can turn into the shadow at any moment. Either way, when silent and my last tears have fallen, I hear my answer: "Yes, and always!"

When Will I Know When to Do What I'm Asked to Do

Because I did not trust my own inner voice, ignored my intuition, and justified being unethical to my own conscience, I struggled with what was enough. While teetering in and out of life, I searched for clarity of what yes and no meant. I lived with a blurred vision. Then faith came back into view, and it required that I listen, hear, seek the truth, and see what can only be seen with clear vision—the vision that I am and God is and that you are and we are. I know, as I have always known, when to do what I'm asked to do. I know what my inner voice softly whispers as what *enough* means. I know, as I have always known, when.

Melting into Peace

In my experience, the more I hurry toward my destination, the more I stumble and fall. I lose sight of the beauty along the journey. I feel that if I hurry to the next thing, then I will not have to act as if

474

I'm trying not to feel the pain. This "Get over it" mentality can lead me toward carrying unfinished pain with me. Inevitably, not dealing with the pain brings it along on the journey and taints the beauty along the way. I can ask for clarity and move into forgiveness as my resentments and disappointments melt so that I can move forward on my journey, pain healed, and can see the beauty and blessings of my life.

Drumroll

When going to a circus or a concert, the roll of the drum usually signifies a presentation of great proportion. Yet after the drama stops, life still is. In the very silence after the sound echoes is where peace is. Peace is in the sigh of the heart when it knows all is well or the exhale from the body when all just is. So why is it that expectations of the drum roll are given so much energy? Is that because that's where the drama lives? No drum roll has ever given the peace, joy, contentment, and the knowing to just be. As I am learning to live with the cool breeze instead of the tornado and as I am learning to just be with each blessing of peace, the echo of the drum roll is now the hum of the favorite tune that brings joy.

A Pain-Free Life

In the movie *The Shack*, Wisdom says, "If you're looking for the guarantee for a pain-free life, there isn't one." This quote depicts the very essence of an unattainable goal, for with joy comes pain. It is learning to live, breathe, grow, and love through pain while in pain. This is when I am at my best for giving my burdens to God, when I need to do my own inventory of that which is truly mine to choose and control. My joy lies in the sunrises and the sunsets, a child's laughter, and a rain that washes away the old to bring the new. My passions are bringing laughter and happiness through my mere being. I am so very blessed to have learned to live through the pain, not remaining in it.

Not My Stage

During a time of unrest, the waiting time can be so paralyzing, so much so that an inappropriate decision can be made. This not only puts the situation into a tailspin, making it spiral more out of control, but also pushes me back into my darkness. It is in this darkness that I question my faith and I doubt myself in trusting my choices. Some opportunities may just be to strengthen my faith and trust and to see if the life lesson is not mine. Sometimes, I am just an observer, not invited to advice. So I will bless them, offer solicited advice, and live to my fullest potential. If it's not my stage, I'll just be in the audience to watch a miracle.

Next Chapter

As one scenario ends, another begins. This is the fluidity of life, ever changing, ever flowing. And at times, the rivers of our lives may rear off to another flowing stream or become dammed up with drama. Yet what is and has always been is inevitable: that life does go on. So with and without those I love, I go on. Resolved, forgiven, and healed, we all move from one phase of life to the next with so many rites of passage awarded to bring us to the next chapter. We are always flowing and always moving, yet it is in the stillness, silence, and passage that I know that I am.

Taking Time

We live in a society where immediate gratification is expected and desired, yet it is in slowing down and in the quiet stillness of the wind dancing through the trees that I find my gratitude. The "Hurry up, get over it, and move on" mentality can be as harmful as quicksand. In time, usually, it's with the acceptance of God's timing that I heal. I take my time to feel. I take my time to heal. I take my time to move through knowing what I am learning from the experiences are life lessons. I am learning that the deeper the pain, the more profound the lesson. In my stillness, I once again empty that which is not mine and thank the experience and move on.

A Bruise

When I bump into something, I usually bruise. This pain is a reminder of where I am walking and that perhaps I need to watch my footing or take an alternative route. When my soul gets bruised from another's transgressions or my own, I am also reminded of the solution. Yet how many times do I ignore this warning and continue to allow myself to bruise? My self-connection has been bruised due to not listening to my inner guide. Once again, I'm healing from a self-inflicted injury even when I know I always have the power to set a boundary and trust myself enough to honor myself. I am worthy.

My Truest Voice

There are so many thoughts throughout the day. At any given moment, I can go from happiness to sadness or confusion to clarity. These feelings are usually attached to a certain outcome I am seeking. Whether it is a solution to a problem or a question to be answered, my truth lies within my heart. My truest voice is that of simplicity, a voice that is positive, clear, joyful, and happy. It brings clarity and peace as if I already know the answer and what to do. But when it is in the drama of another or my own that I seek to feel alive, I've learned to become silent and still enough to hear my truth. By just being accepting, celebrating, grateful, and living as a child, I am at peace.

Balance

Having lived in the noise of a big city and having been associated with the drama of a clan, it is sometimes difficult for me to stay and just be in the quiet and stillness of my life. I used to look for something to bring the noise of life back, but now I know that in this quiet silence, I can hear the birds, I can hear the river, and I can hear the wind. At times, I will need some noise to get me to challenge myself to continue to grow, but for now, I have balance.

Sharing the Road

When I venture out for a nice, quiet, peaceful drive or stroll, it is one thing to be alone and take in the beautiful landscape while listening to my favorite music. But putting myself in a crowded mall or a congested freeway makes the journey quite different. It is only when I can sit and let go of the noise and the drama that surround me and that isn't mine that I can find my positive core and live in it but not become a part of it. I see this in the unrest in the world, how divided we all are, even in my family unit. But it is also in the quiet, peaceful stroll that I can learn to share the road and avoid potholes.

Light Switch

A simple message is to just be free, enjoy, find passion and live it, and just be happy. The art of the light fills the holes. How many times have I defined myself, my worth, my truth, and my belief system to match the definition of another's word? How many times have I refused to believe the light switch could be flipped on within the second of my owning my truth? My clarity of being depends on my own clarity of doing. If I truly believe in myself and that my soul is on a journey to evolve and so is everyone else, then my existence and my actions will embrace the switch of my being and will be flipped on to take risks, be curious, be passionate, and love. The purpose of life is to live it.

Fluidity

As a river flows, so does my life. Stagnant water can be infested with slime and other unsavory things due to its lack of flow, so life has to keep moving. Photographs of happiness, frozen in time, are reminders that life changes with the click of a camera. Nothing can remain, because it is in the fluidity of experience and opportunity that I evolve. When caught up in the memory of happiness, I can bless that moment and continue to remain enjoying peace. When a negative trigger infiltrates my peace, I can flip it to become positive and bless the changes that have occurred to make me who I am.

From Chaos to Silence

When I awaken the morning, all is quiet, the air is clean, and the birds have begun the day with their morning song to welcome another day. There is silence, yet when I put on the TV or watch the dog chase the cat, in a moment's time, chaos ensues, breaking the quiet. In these transitional moments, I watch myself go from tranquil to agitate, only to allow my inner peace to melt into turmoil. This wreaks havoc on my soul, and what was once a simple exhale becomes hyperactive breathing. This is when I need to detach, set a boundary, and remove myself from any situation that may cause distress. In this retreat, I am not showing weakness but a strength that allows me to say yes or no. This chaos can turn into silence when I go within and let go of the control of what is happening around me.

Live in Peace

After living a life of reacting to everyone, whether it is a positive or negative outcome, I no longer want to be associated with drama. Old soap operas were immersed in drama; how else would anyone be hooked unless there was some sort of an issue? Yet no one is ever really comfortable in the quiet, the stillness, or the emptiness of just being. After coming home from a tranquil trip filled with positive peace, I have a choice to live a life that mirrors that experience. I will find compassion and empathy for those who still struggle, but for me, I am choosing to live in a quiet, peaceful existence, just being, living in peace.

Peace

Having the ability to breathe without effort and to depend on my heart to beat life's liquid and for my organs to dutifully work their magic for this body to house my soul are such blessings. Yet put one piece of drama into the mix—some news story, a family crisis, or a friendship quarrel—and those blessings become unnoticed. It is in the silence where all that I once filled myself with is emptied, and a mere snowflake can bring peace to my world as it blankets my life. In the thaw, I am once again looking to the sun's light, to that one breath, that one heartbeat, looking to my soul and to God for peace.

Longing

"If you spend your time longing for things you don't have, you're likely to miss the treasures your carry," so just be, stand still, be silent, and listen. For most of my life, I believed that the formula of desire and expectations equaled to disappointments. How many years did I dump energy into another's promise and another's drama, only to lose the most important ingredient: me? So I will thank the life lessons and experiences, missed or learned, for all the opportunities to evolve. For one more day, I will just be, stand still, and put the energy of my longing into that which I have acquired—God's love and all my comforts and blessings—and focus on fulfilling my destiny and journey.

The Right Time for Me

I have made many wishes, had many dreams and hopes, and had many disappointments in my life; yet with every wish, dream, hope, and disappointment in my life, there had been a life lesson attached. In my judgment and disappointment, I may have lost sight of the meaning I intended to learn. It is now that I am living and appreciating my abundant life. I know what is right for me, and I trust in God's timing. I pray, in my emptying and silence, that I can evolve from all of God's messages.

The Quiet Whisper

When we meet a deaf person or a monolingual immigrant, we tend to speak louder and slower as if that behavior might help us be heard or understood. The loudest voice is not always the voice to be listened to or heard. It is in the quiet whisper that God is. It is the cool spring breeze that breaks the still trees into a dance. It is the soft ripple of a clear stream and the first flower of spring that bring a fragrant hope of tomorrow, like the soft touch of another. The quiet whisper is how God's message leads me toward the light of my soul.

To Be Heard in a Whisper

"The squeaky wheel gets the oil" is a saying that may translate into this: Who has the loudest drama? For it is in our nature to pay attention to it and perhaps heed it and sometimes get involved in it. Yet if I were to present myself as a whisper, would I be heard? If I were to present myself as a soft breeze, would I be felt? If I were to present myself as a snowflake among thousands, would I be seen? It is in that whisper, that soft breath of life, that we are. How we choose to exist is quite another story.

Be Still, Be Eempty, and Listen

I have been making prayer, meditation, and journaling practices in my life for many years. They have helped me purge the wrongs I have felt; helped me find my inner children to help them heal; helped me strengthen my faith; and helped me get through my heartaches, fears, and sadness. Disciplining myself to stop controlling, manipulating, and emptying and to just be is a life practice. When I ask for guidance and help, I need to be still and to empty myself to make room for that which is intended and then listen. I will hear the message when it's my time.

Passion

Passion comes in many forms—a hobby, a career, or a loved one. With passion comes a draw unlike any other. Although it may be difficult to articulate the interest to any given idea or person, the soul knows. Intimacy also takes on many forms with a variety of people, from a lover to a friend, yet when the origin is unknown, it is when I can become confused. When I can let go and feel what I am intended to feel, I will know what I need to know. My draw toward another or toward a thing becomes purposeful for my life journey. Short-lived or for an eternity, we are all given experiences to love passionately. It is our choice to decide when.

Good Health

When we wish for good health, that mere blessing holds so much positive energy, for it is not until our good health is in jeopardy that life stops. Having had a few medical issues in my life, the worry about finances takes the back burner. How I feel productive that day doesn't matter, and neither does a miscommunication alter my life's path if my health is suffering. A health crisis really takes us into a specific moment in our own mortality. As we will all get ill, we can truly live each moment in good health, enjoying all our blessings. When we come to the end of the journey and can be thankful that we did not squander any opportunity to see the beauty of life, warts and all, we are at peace.

Silence to Listen

When it got too quiet, I sometimes inhaled with such power that I could hear myself breathe. I used to be uncomfortable in the silence and with no drama, so I would sometimes drum up some drama to feel alive. When I got an urge to feel as though I needed to be a part of something that was not in my best interest, I took a deep breath, closed my eyes, and asked myself, "Why is it that I need to feel alive? Why do I need to be seen, heard, and acknowledged for my worth?" I can receive this gift and message and not have any toxicity to clean up. I am in peace, and I am grateful without drama.

TRYING SOMETHING NEW

I have always strove to be my best, truest self, even when I knew I was still clinging to a mask to be loved and accepted. I have always engaged in a fight with myself, dealing with shame and pain, or I engaged in a conflict with someone else by defending my honor and truth. Some of my behavior was from the belief that if I screamed louder, they would hear me or that if I dressed in bright colors, they would see me, and then they would notice me, and I would be loved and accepted. I gave a lot of energy into severed relationships, thinking that if all was well and we said sorry, I would be whole again. But by receiving an apology, no longer choosing inappropriate behaviors, and having faith, I know I have always been worthy with or without them. In my silence, I am home in me.

WITH ONE MORE GOODBYE, I LIVE

I defined myself based on the interests and needs of another, silencing and saying goodbye to myself more times than not. Yet there were small, silent, stirring affirmations that I, like them, was worthy and that I mattered. I have striven to let go of the contradictory voices that say I am not, and I am standing my ground that I am. With one more goodbye to a negative thought or a manipulative behavior or one more putdown, I live. When the fear subsides, the truth comes to the surface. I am worthy, I am a blessing and purposeful, and I do matter. Having been treated like a ghost, I now see me, I now know me, and I now love me. I am learning how to live.

THE GREAT SILENCE

At the break of dawn, before birds break into song and break the great silence, there is just my heartbeat with my thoughts and me. It is there that I begin my humble prayer of gratitude for my health, finances, and blessings. Now that the children have gone on their own way and the friendships have dwindled to a handful of those considered as family, the great silence has gotten louder. Trying to embrace this new normal can become a challenge when all I have known is loud, dramatic screams of my voice crying, "I don't understand!" I've learned that I am not meant to always have the answer, so this is where my faith and trust in God and myself is—in the quiet heartbeat of my life.

WITHIN

Within us, we have the capacity to love. This brings compassion, empathy, and respect to the forefront of relationships. Having a deep-seated core within, we move into relationships, and this is where confusion begins, when our within-ness that is being shared gets clouded with our connections. We start seeking from others what we think we are lacking in ourselves, thus giving away our control. Our light, love, wisdom, truth, and understanding become enmeshed; and we forget where we begin and where they end. So once again, I become still and silent, and I listen to the beating of my own heart and reconnect within so that tomorrow, I can try again. I carry me and let go of carrying you. We can be separate and journey together.

ADD ANOTHER CUP TO ME

After being ignored, dismissed, and deemed invisible, I've learned to see the reflection in the mirror. I see me, I hear me, and I feel me. Living in situations of depletion left a hunger that could only be filled with positive love and light, yet so many times, I settled and assimilated myself. I lost my voice, my reflection, and myself for a temporary fix that only left me more depleted and empty. So as I continue on my journey and deal with these triggers, I will be still and know that I am grateful. Although I may be alone, I am learning to sing with my voice and dance to my song, and I know I am a true gift and have a purpose. Displacing my emptiness onto another and asking them to fill it with them to complete me is an old behavior. Instead, I add one more cup to me, a cup of love, light, faith, and peace.

WHEN THE VOICES GO SILENT

When one develops language, opinions start to assimilate themselves into creating and molding us. But when the voices get louder and the message is not positive, more of God's creation begins to change form. When I became aware of this, I had to choose to dismiss influences and sift through others' opinions to make my own decisions. Even with all the blessings I had, I still had an unrest that kept me holding on to their definition of me. I still struggled with the negative voice that held me hostage. What part of them belonged with me? How did our destiny lead us in the same direction?

I know I am able to live in the silence of joy and happiness, not needing the dramatic, spectacular bells and whistles of another's drama to feel joy and purpose. I no longer need to plan a conversation that will not take my voice or have to be concerned with another's acceptance and approval. When the voices go silent, I can hear the only message that matters: that I am loved, I am cherished, I am worthy, and I do matter. I listen to the voice of truth, love, compassion, and faith—God's voice.

ALLOWING PEACE

I used to think I needed drama to feel alive or to be a part of something special. When the silence got too loud, I made some noise. Now I am accepting what my drama is and what is not. I am accepting that my past is done, that I cannot change anything I've said or done or how I've reacted and hurt others and myself. I am accepting my life's journey and how I've serviced others and where I've landed. I've accepted all that I can control and those I have to let go because they're not mine. I've accepted how I've learned to breathe and how I've found a life without them, only for them to return. I've accepted myself as whole and my life as filled with positive love, light, fear, and darkness. I am now seeing myself, and I am allowing myself to feel peace.

In My Aloneness

I used to fear being alone, as if I wasn't lovable enough to be in someone's company. When I chose to be alone, it was because it was my downtime, my chance to figure things out. Remaining in the drama made it seem less painful because I was trying to fix things to my satisfaction, and this numbed the pain of loneliness. What I came to understand was that I was the only one showing up to fix things, because the others were okay with that status quo. This was when I started searching for my solutions and became reacquainted with my own truth. In my aloneness, I started to hear my voice speak that truth.

Keep Living during the Waiting Time

When anxious about a vacation or a special event, all my energy may seem to flow into the future. When I do this, I miss living today. As I am living today, I am learning that the waiting will eventually turn into today. To hurry it along by choosing to control it, I will miss opportunities that are presented in my now. In my stillness, silence, and emptiness, I still am in this very moment, making my now into yesterday, while I wait for my tomorrow to be my now. My own approval is all that I need, because I know what best defines me. Others may have their opinions, as do I, but I know my heart, my truth, and my soul. I will live while in the wait of what is meant to be.

All Gets Done

Slow down, smell the roses, watch the sunset, smell the air when it rains, watch the snow fall, and take a walk. All these things bring me joy in an anxious world. What will happen if I awake every day, make my to-do list, and accomplish all that needs to get done without interference, fear, judgment, disappointment, resentment, or failure? What then? The things on the to-do list are things I do out of need or obligation. That list does not define who I am, yet my worth and success ride on completing one more thing from that list. Interestingly, the list disappears when a child cries or a loved one turns ill or I don't smile. I am not a to-do list, so I'll smell a rose and take a walk!

A Step Back

At times, we are required to step aside if we are in another's way as we step forward. And sometimes, we need to step back while confronted with a feeling or another's drama. This step back is not a regression and should not be confused with not making progress. This step back is a step away from potential harm or discomfort. Yet in the feeling of discomfort, there may be a lesson to experience and learn. A step back from myself is very useful when I am angered by a situation that I cannot control. Instead of lashing out at that which has passed or when it is not in my power to control a desirable outcome, I can step back and remove myself enough to assess why I do indeed need to step back.

In the Silence and Emptiness

Life can be filled with clutter—the clutter of responsibilities to others and to our own checklist, the clutter of noise, the clutter of being in a crowd, or the clutter of noise in our own head. Silencing the noise of the world and the voices in my head requires me to stand still and breathe. The heaviness of carrying another's burden or living in their drama requires me to empty all that which is not mine and to venture into my own stillness. Finally, when all becomes still and I am empty, I find my own reflection in the calm pond of life. When another's pebble falls into my pond and their ripple disappears, I'll still see myself and still see the world waiting for me to fill myself up with positive love and light.

Stillness in Change

Trying to rectify a wrong requires humbleness against undesirable behaviors that are against my soul's purpose. Saying, "I'm sorry. Please forgive me," requires an understanding of how my choice has hurt another or myself. How many times have I wished I were someone else or somewhere else, only to squander away the precious, delicate moments that I can never get back? I gave away so much of me, neglecting to look at the amazing treasure in the mirror. Today, I am given another blessing and the chance to be in my silence to reflect where I am meant to be and who I am meant to be, so I'll remain in the stillness as I watch myself shed the skins of my past transgressions so that I change into the light beneath the burdens that have dulled my light. In my own stillness, I change.

Juggle

We can put all our energy into something and act as if it is all that matters. Sometimes, we have a to-do list a mile long. Sometimes, our to-do list includes relationships that take up most of our time and energy if we are trying to be the rescuer. Our responsibilities may control us instead of us controlling our responsibilities, and this is a lesson we all need to learn. Our journey is lost in the "Get it done" mentality when we only see a destination. We miss out on the opportunity to enjoy the adventure, to look for a life lesson, or to just breathe. It all stops in a heartbeat when one of the balls we are juggling drops. Then what? What really matters? All will be accomplished, and all gets done. Time will pass, and situations are fluid, so things come and go. So watch the snowfall, listen to the rain, smell the flower, and give thanks that you are blessed. I know I am.

Turn the Page

I have always had to reread information to comprehend; this skill enables my understanding from the writer. When I realized that we were all authors of our own lives, I spent decades rereading and reliving the words on the pages of my life, which I authored. Rereading and reliving but not really comprehending my life lesson was the deep-seated message of the words on the pages of my life. I thought that if I relived it, the outcome would be different or that if I heard the accountability of another's behavior, it would heal my pain. Now I know I lived the words on the pages of my life, and now that I'm turning the page, I see, read, and live the life lesson. I am living all the words on the pages of my life.

Look for the Message

In nature, wildlife has been given the gift of camouflage, which gives them the advantage of control. Hidden in that gift, there is a message. When I am confronted with a situation, I need to step back if I feel I may react out of domination or to look for the message that may teach me something. These times are my most difficult, for I fear that if I don't blend in, then I may look for a conflict, and this distracts me from any positive outcome. When I find that my peace is distracted by another's drama, I may find the need to jump in and rescue or add fuel to the fire. This old behavior no longer serves my evolutionary needs. I can choose to be here in peace without them or engage in their conflict. I am learning to look for the message before I am willing to enter a conflict, and if I do, I look for the opportunity for growth and leave the influence of the past in the past.

Reaction toward the Negative

When I am in the presence of drama, I may feel alive and stimulated, but it's actually negative energy that is seeping into my soul. I then react toward the negative in defensive justification and just add more turmoil to what may only be a fleeting moment. Having been the caretaker of many, whether required or due to my own choice, I felt the way they felt. Having learned this behavior, I am now taking steps to watch my reaction very closely; and if I allow it to affect me in a negative way, I will immediately shut it down. I send out a prayer for them and myself that the conflict will be resolved. It is when I become a participant that I find that my armor is in place so I can fight in the battle, whether it's theirs or mine, but I now walk away from the negative.

Noise in the Silence

There is a thing called white noise, such as the soft humming of the earth, the still small noise indicating that life exists. There is also the silence in a heartbeat and a breath and the silence in the calmness when all seems well in my world, but then the noise of a knock on the door or the noise of a text or a phone call has the capability to interrupt the silence. It's easy to silence the world's drama by not listening to the TV or the radio. It's easy to listen to the dramatic details of someone's life imploding, but it is not easy to escape the noise that I allow to disrupt my silence: my own negative voices. The noise in my ears can be muted, but the noise that is self-inflicted can only be silenced with the kind, soft, gentle whisper that says, "All is well." What can the message in the noise teach me?

Stay Focused in the Moment

So much of my day is in my head and heart. I am forever thinking, planning, meditating, and praying. When I am in my moment, nothing can distract me from my task; yet if I have plans for the day, I can be detoured into thinking about what to wear, where to go, what to eat, and what to buy. This distracts me from staying focused on the journey. I sometimes miss the opportunity to see the sights on the journey, and I forgo opportunities to bond with my traveling companions because I'm busy reflecting on the destination. When thinking about how to resolve a conflict or where to find my answers to deep-seated questions, if I don't remain in the moment, focused on the task, then life lessons and the journey can be detoured into the destination. I would miss my opportunity, and I would feel like I've wasted my time, so I'll continue to try to stay focused in the moment and enjoy the journey and each moment it brings.

Listen to Hear

Sometimes, I get so caught up in the noise of the world or the noise in my head that I just don't hear. Trying to silence the excess noise can sometimes be so difficult. My contradicting thoughts leave me, at times, deaf to what I need to hear; listening can be sabotaged by loud noises that I cannot silence. I try to decode what the noises are about, and it usually takes me away from what my focus should be. I have to stop, breathe, and be in the moment so that I can listen to what I'm supposed to hear. I also know that when I burden myself with others' drama, I tend to lose focus, so I will listen to hear.

Purposeful Opportunities

When confronted with difficult situations, I have learned to advocate for myself. I appreciate the journey I am on and validate my growth and recovery. At times, I feel as if I am wondering about the outcome as I wander through the different scenarios that intersect in my path. Knowing that all my life experiences hold a purposeful opportunity to enhance my journey, I do, at times, feel as though I get lost in my own silence since I have decided to mute the drama. It may continue around me and may even seep into my peace, but at the end of my day, I validate my success as I advocate for my journey. Appreciating the life lessons, experiences, and opportunities, I have decided to live my truth, use my voice, and live in peace.

Just to Be Content

Strip away the noise of the big city and I'll be content. Silence the negative voices and I'll be content. Appreciate what I have after seeing another's life and I'll be content. Sometimes, it takes a step away to take a step toward. When the predictable happens or the routine of the day gets in the way of true happiness and the blessings in my life, I just stop and move into the joy, and I am content. This is not settling but is an appreciation and celebration that what becomes an obstacle when remaining stagnant can become a grateful acknowledgment by taking a moment to step away and be grateful that my energy rejuvenates me as I say thank you. I am content.

LISTEN TO THE BIRDS SING

In this hurried world filled with what one desires and what one attains, it's in the subtle, quiet, still moments that the wonder of life unfolds. Yet we tend to be so busy gathering more than we need to stay quiet enough to enjoy. In my hurry to grow up, always having my eye on the future, I robbed myself of the quiet, special moments. I rarely took the time that a child was given to stop and listen to a bird sing or watch the snow fall or see my own reflection in the mirror. Now that I am at the last chapters of my life, I am humbled to forgive others and myself and be grateful for my many comforts, blessings, life lessons, experiences, and opportunities to listen to the birds' song as I watch the snow fall.

JUST ONE MOMENT

I can wake with gratitude in my heart, sending a shout-out of thanks for all my comforts and blessings. But in just one moment, I can be robbed of all my joy. In that one moment, a text, a phone call, or an unexpected delay in plans can send me spiraling down into feelings of disappointment and judgment. I then spend more time feeling the pain and healing from it, and then my joy gets lost. I am learning to choose where my energy is to flow. In just one moment, I can decide what to feel and how to react. I am given just one moment to think about how I want to spend my one moment.

RESTING HEART RATE

I used to think that if there was no drama and there was only peace, then I was living a boring life. I thought I needed my heartbeat to race beyond its resting rate to feel alive. I never trusted the silence. To me, it meant that something was brewing and waiting to boil. I could not trust the stillness and silence. I always felt like

I always needed to be prepared for something. In my anxiousness, I would sometimes stir the pot and encourage it to boil so that I could breathe. As I exhaled, my resting heart rate would only allow me to stay there for a short time, just waiting for the next boiling point. I no longer watch the pot, waiting for it to boil. I now accept the stillness and silence. The peace in my heart allows my heart rate to rest. My heart beats in peace and faith.

Play It Again

As children, we learned most of our social skills from our elders, such as the correct protocol on how to interact. We then get to practice how to interact appropriately so that we gain friendships. In this playtime, we get to learn the rules and the hierarchy among those who have a stronger sense of who they are, and we grasp new information from these friends on how to play nice and be accepted. There comes a time when we relinquish our playtime to the dutiful responsibilities of adulthood. We then savor the day for a vacation, only to continue our adultness, never really learning how to play again. After an illness, a death, or retirement, there you have it, we learn how to play again. Take the time to embrace this time. Hopscotch or checkers, anyone?

I Am That Someone

The story of that boy picking up one starfish at a time from the many hundreds that have been washed ashore to throw them back to save their lives is a chilling tale. When I encounter a rude behavior or witness an unjust act, I used to play victim, walk away from the uncomfortable feelings of the situation, or give up my truth and voice, allowing it to continue for fear of the repercussions: being abandoned and unloved. But no more choosing to be silent or accepting inappropriate acting out. I can now hear the saying, "Evil prevails when good men do nothing." I wondered why someone didn't help or say something, and then I realized I was that someone. We all are that someone.

Sometimes

Sometimes, the silence gets so loud that I feel the need to drum up some noise. Sometimes, I feel so lonely that I feel the need to put on a mask to belong. Sometimes, I feel that the destination is so far off that I forget to look at the blessings of the journey. Sometimes, I get so angry, hurt, impatient, and frustrated that I forget that we are all souls on a journey. In these moments, I stand still when I want to move, I smile when I want to cry, I send out a prayer and a blessing when I want to scream, and I remind myself of my blessings when I take all for granted. I treat this moment as my last as my "sometimes" continue.

Influences

If no one told me who I should be, who would I be? If no one told me how to act, how would I act? If no one's words crossed my tongue, what would I say? Watching the news and basing my opinion on what others report is like being held captive by the assimilation process that will make us all the same. If judged, it is the opinions or perceptions that cause harm, wreak havoc, and destroy relationships. No matter who I choose to be, how I choose to act, or what I choose to say and share, I will show up in love. I do not have to shame you or judge you into believing my truth. We just have to honor one another's stories enough to listen and hear. So tell me about your day.

Find Silence in the Noise

When the noise gets too loud, find the silence. The noise can drown out my heartbeat and can make me agitated, so my light gets dim. When I get immersed in too much noise, I find the silence. One thing I have learned when I find myself in a negative situation, whether it's self-sabotage or a need to be seen and heard, is that I become silent to find my inner peace and to find silence in the noise. If too much energy is put into trying to control a situation that cannot be controlled, I will find silence in the noise. As I retreat into my soul to reconnect with my life, I find silence in the noise.

STEP AWAY

When the noise of the world and the chaos of the day become too overwhelming, I have learned to step away. Much too often, I have found myself involved in drama that I only fuel when I see an injustice being done or a word not being honored, or I react to a situation that is not about me. I find that in my frustration from watching negative energy engulf those I love, I need to step away. I am still practicing this behavior, so I might jump in, try to right a wrong, or push a situation into an outcome I deem right. But then it clicks, and I can just control what I can, which are my choices. So I will send a prayer and a blessing and step away.

A THOUGHT

The brain, like all organs, has amazing capabilities and gifts. The mind can process anything it understands and find meaning, yet put emotions and feelings into that process, and that is where the conflict can begin. When I am content, I can find joy and peace in everyone and everything around me. Yet with one mean glance or one unkind word, I can be sent on a journey of recalling memories and set off a series of triggers that keeps my positive soul hostage.

A thought is a powerful tool, and at times, I am not even aware of the message that each fleeting bit of information is making me feel. I am not even aware that a fragrance or a sound kicks me into a tailspin. It is only through awareness and stillness that I can decipher if I am having a positive thought that is moving me into joy and more opportunities. When I become aware, I can choose what I want to think and how I want to feel. If it's in the past and brings sadness, I bless the thought for the life lesson, and I become grateful for who I am and where I am now.

Quiet

How often do I take the time to hear the wind blow through the trees as I watch them dance? How often do I stand still and watch the birds make their nest as they sing songs? How often do I watch a child sleep and embrace the inhale and exhale of his or her peace within? How often do I embrace the sound of my heartbeat? To remain still and silent takes as much effort as becoming stressed with threading a needle. Yet anxiousness and impatience have a tendency to snuff out all that the sunshine can harness as I awaken for my day, so I become diligent in embracing the stillness and quietness that become available when I choose to accept the choice I make. The best part about the entire journey is, I get to choose, as do you.

Right at This Moment

If I ask myself how I am at this very moment, I will know that all is well. When the day's worries set in and something goes awry or if I allow my past to come for a visit and it decides to overstay its welcome, then I may need to evaluate why I am allowing what was or what will be to rob me from this moment. Sometimes, if I'm not feeling anxious about something, I may question my convictions to relationships or projects. My old fear kicks in, and I have to remind myself that nowhere in my history has anxiousness ever paid off with a positive result. Right at this moment, all is well. I no longer need to look for clarity in every situation. I now have my faith, so I will stop, listen, look, and smell the fragrances of life and know right at this moment that all is as it should be and that all is well.

Watching Myself and Others

As I go along with my day, the experiences I encounter become a mirror for my life. Although the circumstances may differ or the reflection in the mirror is not identical to mine, we are all creatures of thought and reaction. I may be listening to a friend or relative tell me their story, and all the while, it is parroting the experiences of my life. My automatic need to respond with my story can cause turmoil; how I think and react may not be exactly what the other person wants to hear. It's not my responsibility to stop another's pain. I have a compassionate, empathetic kindness that I can share without adding my ingredient to the mix. I have chosen to listen, give words of encouragement, say a prayer, and offer to bless them so they will find their way out of the darkness. God is the light that can be seen at the end of my own tunnel.

A Lightning Bolt

"Today I will stop straining to know what I don't know, to see what I can see, to understand what I don't understand and I will trust that being is sufficient and I will let go and have faith that my need to figure things will be understood." With a clap of thunder and a lightning bolt, all can change in a moment. I may never understand everything that I don't understand unless I need to understand. Then in time, I will. In these fleeting heartbeats in life, just as a lightning bolt can change everything, so can how I choose to think, feel, and react. A moment in laughter can flip into a moment of tears. Reflections into the past can be visited to find the origin for healing, but if I stay there too long, I will lose moments from lessons I've learned from the past that will help make better todays. Visit, but don't stay, don't question, and don't wait for the answer. All will be revealed, as all is meant to be as it is.

My Focus

Each day is a clean slate in which to script the events that may cross my path. There are no guarantees for a pain-free life, so by showing up each day, I take the risk of knowing that some things may or may not be pleasant. I just wonder at the end of the day what I can recall that has made the day so memorable and what exactly I choose to script that has impacted my journey. Do I recall the laughter of the child at the park, the dog enjoying his car ride as the wind combed through his fur, or the majestic clouds that danced across the sky as the storm spoke? What I choose to focus on are moments that have been gifted today. Sometimes, the life lesson, although pain-less, has something to share; and sometimes, the pain helps me grow. What is my focus? How much of my past is present in my today? I will be still and silent to hear the answers.

When the Silence Got Too Loud, I Needed Noise

I have lived my life in the love of God. I have lived my life in the depths of pain. In this contradiction, I venture toward that which I could be filled. In the drama, I felt alive and connected. It was this very drama that I allowed to dim my light. When the silence got too loud, I needed noise. When the contentment got too comfortable, I stirred up drama. And if the threat of past drama crossed my path, I drummed up enough so I could put on my armor, ready for battle.

Now I am living my life in peace, having conquered the fear of not knowing and the emptiness of just being. It is this turmoil that I call aliveness that prevents God's light to shine in me. In the stillness of my soul and in my coming home to me, I am now void of the drama. I have now let go, and I live my life in peace. In this emptiness, I am once again filled with God's love and light. I no longer need drama to feel alive or to feel that I belong to someone or somewhere. In the stillness, I find peace, joy, and contentment, and in the silence is the entire joy of being.

The Formula

When all is well in my world, I can feel an inner peace; and with a mighty exhale, I know. If I find myself reacting to a phone call, text, email, or the news in a negative way, I need to explore the fear within to understand why I am allowing this to disturb my peace. This can be a momentary task to find a trigger and assure myself that all is well. I can live in it or address it to let it go. This is my formula to inner peace and to the restoration of faith.

Heal the Need

When recovering from a trauma, whether it is physical or emotional, the body, mind, and soul know what needs to be healed. When I act as if everything is fine and I stuff what needs to be addressed and healed, it only prolongs the inevitable. It will come out in a physical, emotional, or spiritual illness; so I have learned to listen to my body, mind, and soul for what it needs, and I give myself permission to take a sick day to get better. When I honor myself to know what's in my own best interest, I can heal what needs to be healed and continue on my way.

Accepting Opportunities

Having lived bound by my own fear of not being loved, I strove to assimilate you into me and me into you. I thought that if I had a request, you would fulfill it, because I did the same for you. But we can only give that which we are willing to give. If we allow ourselves to let anyone into our hearts, it's of our own doing—to love deeply into our soul or to love on the surface of our skin? Whatever the decision, it is in the accepting, receiving, and giving that we love with the best intentions based on what we know. Opportunities!

Ouch

I recall from when I was a child how when I was immunized, my arm would hurt when I moved it, so I kept it close to my body as if I was protecting a treasure. So it is with the heart. We keep it close and closed so as not to be hurt. Society may expect us to wear our mask, which shows others that everything is fine when we are crying for one touch of kindness. All the while, we know that in the movement, the arm heals and that in the openness of asking for a hug, the heart beats with joy. So even when the pain gets so deep into my core, I know that the only way out is through feeling the sadness and disappointment and sharing my story. Acknowledging and feeling the pain are necessary to heal and move on. In one moment, I say ouch!

React

When a relationship is damaged, the lack of communication can only add fuel to the existing turmoil. As I begin to heal and let go, I ask myself if I am suffering over my suffering or trying to dominate another or looking for some semblance of reaction that may bring us to the point of brokenness. I no longer feel the need to defend my honor if someone chooses to believe another's words instead of searching their own heart. This form of judgment only adds to the already existing separation. I can listen with an open mind, see with opened eyes, and keep my heart open with compassion rather than retribution.

Honor Myself

Sending blessing to others is my way of being my best, true self and of not allowing any of my pain to be inflicted into a relationship. Even if I have endured pain from another, I will not act with revenge or seek retribution, because that is not the person I want to be. Turning the other cheek can help me remain in peace. I can respect others by setting boundaries between them and myself. I honor myself and owe myself that much!

Live in Peace

It's interesting that when someone dies, we pray his or her soul will rest in peace. I am an advocate of this. Confrontations and miscommunications are components that can steal our joy or heal relationships. If we don't talk, we can't resolve our differences, so talk and share and express your feelings in the same way you would like someone to express their feelings to you. If we do unto others as we would have them do unto us, then all our souls can live in peace.

SELF-MONITOR

Life is not a drive-through window where my request is ordered and I get it as desired at the pickup window. Thinking I know better for me or for anyone else has been a prideful struggle, as well as thinking that my worth is in being right. Each experience is a life lesson for me or for someone else. Being a wife, mother, and teacher has led me down a road where I consistently have to monitor someone else, so consequently, I can lose sight of what I need to monitor myself. I can offer solicited advice as I make my own decisions.

MELT INTO PEACE

The automaticity of thoughts can be so random that I can lose track of one thought as it melts into another without realizing that it is or it's not in my best interest. When I can finally distinguish the negative thoughts from the positive thoughts, I can exhale and move forward. It's in the quiet stillness of my own turmoil that I can inhale, become aware, shift my thinking, and exhale into peace. I am in control of how I think, feel, and act. I am the keeper of my own happiness and contentment. I can or can't; either way, I eventually will as I melt my thoughts into peace.

IF THE LABEL FITS

A daughter, a sister, a mother, a wife, a teacher, a student, a writer, a reader, a hiker, a gardener, and a spiritual being of God on a soul journey—these are the chosen, specific labels given from life experiences and opportunities that define me and evolve my soul. What are the other labels that cause a soul to crack and to repress into the catacombs of darkness? Why have I given so much power to those other labels that have been casted upon me by others who are in pain? Why did I choose to listen to their definition? Now I listen to my definition, my label, my choices, and my life to become purposeful and productive.

Let Me Love You

When I meet someone for the first time, I exchange pleasantries and salutations. When the relationship begins to blossom, I want to be accepted and reassured that I am being seen. Yet the minute I encounter disapproval or a difference in opinion, I may take myself into the crossroad of authenticity and being masked. I have the willingness to give voice to whatever is happening, yet if I silence myself, I then become so muted that the other person begins to speak for me and through me, and their truth becomes mine.

If I remain voiceless, then the other person will unconsciously live out whatever inequity or misperception they have been led to be true. If I remain silent, then my participation may allow someone to continue to speak for me. If I allow this, then when will my pain be noticed? While I dread voicing my fears and hurts, not wanting to be judged or abandoned and dreading to be seen as vulnerable, the only way to resolve this is to voice my fears. Love has no other way of being acted on without something truthful to respond to, so when ready, take the risk and tell me who I am looking at so that I may love you.

Manage

At times, I have so much I want to do that I find myself managing my time so that I can get it all completed. I do this to feel successful and productive, but in my haste, I can forget the journey. The lessons and happiness can be lost along the way if I forgo my blessings as I forge toward my destination. Remaining in the moments of my life can help me see my growth and abundance. It can help me celebrate and appreciate what is in my control. If I find I am rearing off my path and onto another's, I can lose sight of what is mine. If I try to control more than me, I can become agitated and resentful if things don't go my way. This is when I need to detach and journey back onto my own path. I can manage what is mine.

After the Storm

I have watched footage of a tsunami devastating a small village or the eruption of a volcano, spewing its ash into the air. After the waves and ash have settled, all that is left to be done is to assess the debris left behind to clean up and start anew. I watch my reaction to situations that are presented to me. As I walk among what is left behind after the storm settles, I need to figure out what is left for me to rebuild my new normal. Not willing to replace the old with my new, I sit and wait for the new to arrive. In this waiting time, I am presented with what I can welcome in and what I will discard that no longer fits. After the storm, I get to rebuild a stronger foundation.

Standing Still as My Heart Continues to Beat

There may come a time in a relationship when stagnation may cause us to stand still as we reassess what it is that we want from each other and what our next steps are. These in-between times when we either stand still or move on can cause anxiousness toward resolution. It may not be the time for resolution, but this does not mean I can't engage in my life. It merely means that something needs to be resolved in my heart or in the other person. Waiting for an answer can be paralyzing, but I have a choice. I can still have a life in the in-between times, as my heart continues to beat.

Thank You

Sometimes, even when all is well and the stillness sets in, I may still feel a bit uncomfortable with the river of peace flowing over me. This is when I need to be totally aware of my feelings and thoughts as I attempt to silence the peace. I am learning to give myself permission to trust my word, to believe in my worth, and to accept the abundance of joy and peace that has been bestowed upon me. I can exhale and just say, "Thank you."

Living from the Core

The center of the universe is where we are all connected to the greatest of the glory of all that is. We are loved equally and are all given the same blank slate of opportunities to fulfill our purpose. We can all ask ourselves what our purpose is. When I sit quietly enough in my stillness, I know that I am meant to serve others. In my heart, my voice has always been my tool. I have used it to encourage a broken soul to heal and for a happy soul to dance.

Give Us This Day

When I was a child, I couldn't wait to become an adult so that I could make adult decisions for myself. When I was in pain, I couldn't wait for it to stop because I did not want to hear what it had to teach me. Hurrying up to get to the next thing has been a common practice for me, getting rid of the pain so I can enjoy the happy times, yet it was in my childhood that I learned vital lessons about integrity. In the pain, I learned how strong I really was so that I could endure to face another day. "Give us this day our daily bread"—this is all I truly am meant to have. Tomorrow may never come; so I will live in this day, learn from the pain, and enjoy the quietness of just being where I am, who I am meant to be, and who I have become.

Humbling Myself

I am humbled as I stand in front of my ancestors who have passed on. I am humbled to rekindle relationships of my origin and have my behavior mirror them. I am humbled by owning the behavior I witness in those who make me feel uncomfortable. Do I react in fear by needing to build a wall of anger or to justify and defend my actions in aggression? Although this is a painstaking experience, it is one more layer I can peel away toward reaching my destination. I am humbled by the life lessons that have stood before, and I bow and give thanks. It's time for a change!

To-Do List

In hurrying through life, our experiences can be lost in to-do lists. Often, I itemize my day, and my success is contingent on what is crossed off from that list. How many times has my goal been to draw a line through words on a list rather than to experience the fullness of the task at hand? How many times have I given worth to a completed list rather than walk away feeling that I have experienced the life of my day? Every day, I will put gratitude on my to-do list.

The Journey's End

When we are young, we can't wait to become an adult so we can do what we want whenever we want. In this young mindset, we don't take into account that having our own will comes with responsibilities to others. We have bills to pay, we will deal with unkind people with personal agendas, and we will have more responsibilities in our home and at work. Rushing to the next part of the journey can make us blind to the many blessings along the way. It's not until most of the journey is behind us that we realize what we've missed out on in the frenzy of our busy life.

Take care, be healthy, make wise decisions, be kind, enjoy the rose that blooms on a warm spring day, laugh at the wind, taste the rain, and slow down to enjoy the journey home at the end of your days. We can now be that child again, able to accept and appreciate the many comforts and blessings that we have to enjoy on our journey toward the end of our days.

I Do Know

The words "I don't know" get a bad rap because the answer is usually, "You're not supposed to know everything." This may be a true answer to some questions, but when the soul is involved, the best answer to "I don't know" is, "Yes, you do. You pray for clarity." I may not understand why I receive certain treatment from those I love, but I do know that they are exercising their free will to explore their possibilities without my influence. It is in these humbling moments that my heart breaks for their love. I have to honor their request because I know what to do. I pray.

New Year's Eve

The end of a year brings pause to what has been accomplished and what needs to be finished. It can prove growth and encouragement as a New Year begins. Nothing can be undone, but the prospect of new things can bring enlightenment. When I keep reminding myself that we are all souls on a journey, I can continue to seek blessings and grace for us all. I pray this for everyone, and I continue to pray for inner peace and joy.

Soul Sick

There are many illnesses that can cause life to pause, such as mental illnesses and specific body illnesses that may or may not be treated with drugs. Yet when the soul is sick, there are no drugs to cure this but prayer, meditation, blessings, grace, and mercy. So just as I nurture my mind and body, so I should nurture my soul. Taking a pill for a headache is effortless, but when the mind and soul are ill, I have to seek divine interventions. I will ask for help and then listen in peace.

Meeting between the Darkness and Light

When I am confronted by an agitated thought, I can allow it to grind into my happiness, or I can allow it to have a voice so I can address the issue and heal it. Usually, I can move forward if I understand its origin; but if I sit too long without any information, it can consume me into darkness. Staying in the darkness only leaves me scared and alone and full of fear. When I meet the issue between the darkness and the light, I choose to address what's eating at me so I can heal and move forward.

How I Live My Days

Often, I spend my time just going through the motions of life. I brush my teeth, I eat my meals, and I do the laundry. But when I become aware of my breathing and stop to watch a flock of geese fly in perfect formation or watch the waves of the river crash against the rocks or experience the joy in a dog's wagging tail, I live. How much more do I get to do? How much more do I get to be? How many more people do I get to bless and receive blessings from merely by our existence? What will I do with this moment? How will I seize this moment? How will I live my days?

Safety Net

Letting go is essential in the midst of change. It requires hope, faith, prayer, and trust that all will be as intended. But not making room for the new will make it too crowded, so a release is needed. Before the discard is underway, an examination of what may be saved is required. This may cause grief and sadness as the purging is underway. You will want to hold on to the familiar that are no longer required. There is a new safety net waiting, but the old must be discarded first. Saying goodbye can be sad and uncertain, but looking forward to new hellos can be exciting. I take time to say goodbye to what is no longer applicable and thank it for helping me as I make room for the new that will only enhance the journey.

Listen and Rest

Sometimes, I just have to rest. This simple statement holds a lot of weight when I push myself too far or I am not feeling my best. I can be combative with the voices that tell me to push on or to suck it up and deal with the pain. This self-sabotaging behavior can set me back further than if I just listen to my intuition and rest. I have an internal doctor on call 24-7 to assure self-care mentally, physically, emotionally, and spiritually. This gift is given to all of us, so when I ignore the gift, I suffer. It's time to listen.

The Small Things

When my mind is filled with thoughts of unrest, I can become agitated and anxious as I try to calm myself. The self-inflicted list of things I want to accomplish can overwhelm me to the point where I don't look forward to anything I need to get done anymore, and it becomes a burden instead of a blessing. I will approach everything with love, care, and responsibility and will do my best. The small things are important, just as much as the huge undertakings that cross my path.

Wait on God

Waiting for something to come to fruition, as per a prayer, can be a painstaking pull on my patience. I will try to assist the journey along to ease the pain by making the phone call or writing the letter or texting or tweeting, but this untimely, impatient response will only set me back into disappointment and despair. If I do this too often without learning to wait for God's time, my heart can harden, and I can become resentful as I visit similar hurts from my past. So in the silence, I will hear the voice. In the darkness, I will see the light in your eyes. In the stillness, I will move on and live.

My Offer

If someone was in pain or unhappy, I used to feel that it was my responsibility to cheer them up or make them well again. When asked, I offered advice or a helping hand. If not asked, I prayed and blessed them that they sought and received peace.

Proactive

When I find myself not feeling well, I will seek the origin of my discomfort. If my soul feels out of alignment, I need to find what is burdening me and how I can give it a voice so I know how to heal it. I can do this by remaining still and quiet enough to listen to the voice of reason. It's better not to react to it and to be proactive for it.

LIFE CONTINUES

As I sit alone in my sunroom, I hear the sounds of life outside. I can hear the bells of the churches, the whistle of the train, and the birds' song. It's the sounds outside my window that give me hope and assure me that life goes on. In my isolation, I am not alone and can feel God.

JUST ANOTHER DAY

With all the amazing possibilities that are ahead, it is just another day. It is just another day to celebrate life by feeling the warmth of the sun and the song of a bird and the quiet of the stillness that echoes as life is halted. It is just another day for opportunities to play like a child with no worries or to read a book that is calling my name or to speak to a friend who lives in my heart. It is just another day to be grateful for the opportunities to be still and silent and to remember the simplicity of what truly matters. Enjoy the day!

PRAY IN THE MOMENT

When I am asked to remain quiet, still, and patient, I may agree if I know how long I am required to display this behavior. I can become agitated if my request exceeds my comfort zone. I can step out of my agreement and continue to ask to have my prayers answered. This only prolongs my request, and I become more anxious as I wait. In this time, I miss many opportunities that are presented—a bird's song, a child's laughter, or a rainbow after a refreshing rain. So after I sabotage my waiting time by reacting and giving my anxiousness a voice, I have to go back to the initial request to remain quiet, still, and patient. This is when I humble myself, apologize, and restart. I pray that I believe and have faith and that in my waiting time, God's working to answer my prayers.

Exist where I Am

"If you spend your time longing for things you don't have, you are likely to miss the treasure you carry." This speaks to me because if I get what I want or even need, I celebrate it for a second, then I go after the next best thing. I never truly appreciate the blessing and am never truly satisfied with what I have. This leads me down the road of depletion, deprivation, and bitterness. Living with the "If only I had…, then I would be…" mentality is wasted effort. It overlooks any appreciation or gratitude. Now I have learned that I am meant to have what I have, where I am is where I am meant to be, and who I am with is who I am meant to be with. This is a comfort and a blessing. All is well. In my stillness and gratitude, I can allow myself to exist and enjoy what I've been given.

Already Here

I don't have to wait for God. He's already here, waiting for me to arrive. When I find myself being so impatient because I have placed my energy in the resolution rather than in the journey, this is when I need God the most to be present in my mind to sway me toward Him and away from what I think I need to soften the pain. When I find myself focused on someone showing up for me, this is when I need to seek God, for He's already here, waiting for me to arrive. My world may come to a halt in an uncomfortable time, but He sees an outcome that is not yet in my view. He sees the whole picture, and all I see is the present view of my pain. So knowing I am in the best of hands, I can trust and have faith that whatever the outcome, it will be better than I could ever imagine. So in faith, I just have to stop waiting for God to show up, because He's already here!

His Promise

When a thought comes to mind, it is the birth of a new experience waiting to happen. We breathe life into it by designing it for a specific purpose. God's purpose for us is the same. He has in store a specific experience, and He is just waiting for us to be prepared to accept it. We may think we are already prepared, and when anxiousness arrives, it may prolong our receiving His blessing because we think we're ready when we're not. I can get myself prepared to receive His gift with forgiveness, removing resentment to make room for hope and with compassion and seeing myself in another's pain. Stay still and silent. When we're ready, He'll know, and He'll deliver what is promised.

You Showed Up

I awoke feeling alone, and You told me You were there with me. I felt as though my needs were not being met, and You told me I had what I needed. I told You I wanted the restoration of my broken relationships, and You told me that I didn't need drama in my life. I asked for a friend to talk to, and You told me you were listening and asked me what was on my mind. I asked, and You showed up. Thank you for loving me.

The Memories of My Days

Having a to-do list or an agenda can give direction to how I spend my day. I am not advocating for being irresponsible. I am offering another vantage point on how I should spend my day. I know I have to pay my bills and walk my puppies and do the laundry, but I also need to take in the precious moments when I actually do what needs to be done. Although the tasks may be tedious, I can enjoy the journey and not dwell so much on the destination. I know for sure that once I arrive, there will be another road ahead, another chore to do, and another beautiful moment to embrace as my life unfolds into the memories of my days.

Stillness

Sometimes, while I'm waiting for something to happen or waiting for a prayer to be answered, I can become numb toward any kind of hope. I send out my prayer and try to do what I am responsible for, and then I wait. As I go on with my life, the desperate need for an answered prayer may fade. It's not that it's not important; it's that I've learned to move on and live without it. I have learned to find joy and peace as my life moves forward.

Be Still and Silent for the Answer

Sometimes, no matter how hard I try to pray myself out of my despair, I still feel sad. This makes me vulnerable to a word or a sound that may sway me if I am not disciplined enough to keep my mouth closed while my heart aches to remain open. Looking for an immediate behavior to elevate my sadness is a setup for me to revert to my old ways of looking for someone else or something else to stop the ache. It is when I learn to remain still and silent enough to hear the answer that I ask for help. Then I submit myself to peace to remember that all is temporary and all is fluid but that the one thing that will never change is that I am loved; He never changes.

Be Still

Some days, I feel so much unrest as if I'm a ping-pong ball bouncing from one thought to another. As I flitter in and out of a task, this behavior denies to me accomplishment of anything with depth. Waiting for something to arrive can paralyze me into sitting in a chair as life passes me by. Life will go on around me as I continue to gaze out the window, just waiting, just waiting. Where is the quality of life in just waiting? Then I have to take a deep breath and settle myself. With the exhale of stillness and silence, I can connect and hear what is preventing me from success. When God tells me something and I ignore it, I miss the opportunity to do His work, so I pray, "Please, God, help me hear You and listen to You and do what You want me to do." Sometimes, all it takes is to just sit and watch a bird in flight or a snowflake land on a leaf. I am still.

Waiting Time

When I think about something I want and the results include someone else, I may tend to become impatient while waiting for them to make a decision. Although I have the capability to become manipulative and controlling, I know how that feels when it's done to me, so I choose not to engage in that behavior. I will wait for the decision and move forward from there. In my waiting time, I will enjoy my life!

Check In with God

When I am confronted with a desire from another, I first check my physical and emotional availability to decide whether I will engage. I have been known to enable if I am insecure about a reaction. Before I make a decision to engage, I will seek my will and seek God's will. My spiritual availability drives my decisions to my core. I check in with God first, then I decide.

Stop, Look, and Listen

Hurrying through a painful situation to stop the pain will ultimately cause more harm and will bring on more issues for me to deal with if I don't stay in peace; so I will silence my pain with self-love, self-talk, and prayer. It usually results in having to take a look at my own behavior, which is painful in itself. If I remain peaceful, then I can have a conversation with God, and He will guide me through the pain. I can stop, look, and listen.

Role Model

Being rejected by someone who lives in my heart is one of the most painful aches that cannot heal, and God knows this heartache all too well because He has been rejected too. He knows how I feel because He has experienced the pain of being rejected by those He came to love and save. The one saving grace is that God has never stopped loving those who reject Him. He has never stopped long-ing for a relationship with those who refuse to recognize Him. How many times have I turned away from God to do my will and refuse His? How many times have I apologized for my indiscretions because of my own arrogance? And how many times has He waited for me to come back to Him? He promised He would never leave, and He has kept His promise. He is always waiting for us to come back to Him. He will forgive, and He will love, and He will continue to seek a rela-tionship with us. He will never abandon or mistreat those He love. This is a good lesson to learn; He is the perfect role model to follow.

Union Prayer Book

They have only given me knowledge where-with to grasp my problems more firmly and that during the pause of the night, thou hast granted me wisdom and strength. Create me in a stron-ger yearning for thy presence, so that chance what will I shall draw closer unto thee learning to know thee with a fuller knowledge and to love thee with a deeper love.

CHAPTER 15

Wandering, Wondering

THE LIFE LESSON IN THE PAIN

When it's time to say goodbye, the handshake of gratitude can hold a heaviness. Although all life is fluid, there are moments when I want to remain in the peace and joy that I am experiencing in that one very special moment. But as the saying goes, "Life must go on." Making closure with a particular situation can release the anxiety that has been held before the encounter. This healing process is vital to the relationship that has been estranged, but it is also freeing and validating, because staying true to myself is more important than the person I am missing in my life. When all is said and done and apologies have been exchanged, as I move forward in my truth and remain steadfast in the convictions of my faith and myself, I can say, "Thank you, God, for revealing what my life lesson was within the pain."

THE TIME IS NOW

After years of estrangement, meeting a loved once again can be bittersweet. Even knowing that the separation is a necessary part of the journey, it can still carry a heaviness from the memories. Even though I have healed from many issues that may have never been healed if the relationship had been sustained, it still makes me wonder, "What did I miss in your life as mine was progressing? What memories did we miss by not staying together? What issues would not have been healed if we had stayed in each other's lives?" Either way, we are where we are in this moment in time, so let's start making new memories now. No what-ifs or should-haves or sadness. Let's saunter on and live, for the time is now.

TEMPORARY

When I used to wait for something to happen, it would seem like forever for it to arrive. It reminds me of a long road trip, waiting for the destination to appear on the horizon, all the while chanting, "Are we there yet?" I've missed many opportunities by waiting to be there while ignoring where I am. Knowing the hard knocks of my life, I've also learned how fluid and temporary moments are. What seems like forever is just a blink of an eye in the rearview mirror of my life. So the next time I hear the chanting of my childhood, immersed in uncertainty and anxiousness, I will replace that chant with this: "I am where I am meant to be at this moment, so enjoy it. All is temporary."

DOUBT BEFORE RESOLUTION

I have been known to make a decision or to not make a decision and then doubt myself. This self-doubt can cause insecurity about my worthiness for goodness and a joyful life, so I am learning to stop and think about what my goal is before I make a decision. If the decision is to control another or a situation, then I know the resolution will not be in the best interest of my soul's journey. If I am acting in my own best interest to regain the power that I have given away to be loved, then that is quite a different scenario. Sacrificing myself to be loved is an old behavior that has left me feeling worthless and invisible. Setting healthy, reasonable boundaries toward the goal of resolution will help melt doubts into reassurance that I am feeling my worth, living in my truth, and using my voice to advocate for myself. I will walk with you, not behind you.

When I Finally Realized

When I finally realized that I could eat whatever I wanted in moderation and exercise on a daily basis to keep my body strong, I ate what I wanted in moderation and exercised to keep my body strong. When I finally realized that if I felt my feelings, I wouldn't die but that I could heal my pain to begin to live in peace, I felt my feelings to heal my pain so I could live in peace. When I finally realized that I was worthy of love and kindness and I was meant to live my purposeful life, I finally began to show myself love and kindness and decided to love my life to fulfill my purpose. When I finally realized that I was not seeing my own reflection in the mirror but saw those I was allowing to define me, I got a new mirror and saw myself. When I finally realized that the adults in my life lied and I was allowing their lie to be my truth, I began my quest to empty myself of their lie to find my truth. When I finally realized that I deserved the blessing, love, and goodness of life, I started living that life. I found my when and knew I was blessed.

Explore New Possibilities

When I run away from problems, it only prolongs the inevitable. They must be dealt with so that I can heal. Fear is the biggest factor for why I do not face my problems. Whatever the origin of the fear may be, it is the pain that has to be explored so that I can come home. So many times, I lived in denial, thinking that if I acted as if the pain was no big deal, I could cope long enough to manage or to get through.

Holding on to a painful situation may sound insane, but in the predictability of its outcome, it seemed to be more acceptable and comfortable than actually dealing with the pain I feared the outcome, that it would leave me feeling unloved, unworthy, and alone. This was no way to live a life, and having made that choice, I am now dealing with the residue of all my unfinished pain. Even though my biggest fears did come to pass, I survived and became the me I was destined to be. I am worthy, I am lovable, and I am surrounded by God's love. I can now say I have come home.

Sharp Needles from the Rain

When caught in a storm, the rain may pound against me like sharp needles penetrating my skin. At these times, I will seek shelter to feel protected. This is the same behavior I choose when I am confronted with a situation that is not in my control. Behavior choices of another may sting like the sharp needles of a rain from a storm. It is then that I seek shelter within my own heart and with God knowing that their behavior is not in my control. I do look for the life lesson from the encounter, yet I can walk away from the hurtful behavior that has pieced my heart. Although I will walk away from the storm, into the light, I will continue to pray for a resolution knowing that all is well and that His will, will be done.

Visit With but Not Be a Part Of

How many times have the words, "Let it go!" been spoken? There is a great lesson in holding on to that which needs to be healed, and letting it go before the right time can cause more harm. The healing process is a deep, delicate visit with the pain; the pain has a very specific message for our growth. Not being in the pain but with the pain gives an opportunity to revisit its origin and the specific messages it has left in our hearts and in our minds. Many questions can be answered, and many questions can develop while visiting with a memory. So visit with but not be a part of, and help heal the years of anguish by just hearing, feeling, and acknowledging. You have already survived the trauma. Now it's time to revisit it, thank it for its vital lesson, and say goodbye.

A Closed Door

I believe that there is a door in the heart to the soul. When opened to the possibilities of life, joy and sorrow will enter. Yet if the door remains closed, nothing can penetrate it; it's through the cracks that God enters. How many years did I spend knocking on a closed door? If I had only prayed enough, waited long enough, or gave them what they wanted, then the door would have opened. Yet my door would be closed. So as I continue to move forward on my journey, I no longer knock and wait for doors to open. I focus my energy in keeping my door open to opportunities, possibilities, and experiences that carry joy and sorrow so I can know the richness of life. An open door will let the light in.

APPLICATION

It's time to apply what I've learned. My biggest asset has been my need to find out the whys. When I don't understand, I drill down until I find the answer to my questions and find peace. Yet sometimes, my answer will have to be, "Have faith!" This means I have to keep going within, to my core, to strive to be my best knowing that others are struggling to find and see themselves too. Now after years and years of gathering information and learning and filling myself with knowledge, I am sifting through to find the deepest truth. What I've learned so far is, God is, love is, and I am.

INNOCENCE

When a child is born, he/she is pure in mind, body, and soul. The navel is not only the lifeline to the mother but also the eternal scar that, once attached to God, is forever housed on our body. As this young soul evolves, he/she explores the wondrous simplicity of nature—the birds' song, the clouds' various formations, or the trees' dance. When a young soul is clouded with the shadow of doubt, it can take a lifetime of wondering and wandering, only to return to the simplicity of the innocence he/she is born with. So in my innocence, I will listen to the birds' song, look at the cloud formations, and watch the trees dance; and I will just be.

FORK

At times, while traveling on my life's journey, I may encounter potholes, detours, boulders, and landslides or just a fork in the road. At times like this, my competitiveness will not be my best advocate. I just need to stop, access the situation, and perhaps just be in the moment. I know what my purpose is, and I know what I am meant to do, so when someone or something gets in my journey's path, I can choose which way to travel. Life goes on despite the potholes, detours, landslides, or forks. I am moving on. There will always be something that may get in my way, so I bless my entire journey.

HOLES VERSUS WHOLE

We are all born whole in God's love and light, yet after being given one opportunity for another's words to define us, we end up in a hole. After dragging myself out of my hole for most of my life, I have found that how I choose to react and what I know to be true can keep me out of that hole. Yet I allow myself to teeter on the edge, waiting for one moment to remain in or crawl out. I have struggled with my wholeness. I have allowed words and actions to chisel away piece by piece, only to frantically hold on to my brokenness. Now I choose to remain whole knowing my truth. I am a light of positive energy and filled with love, passion, joy, kindness, compassion, and God.

I AM HERE

How long have I chased after the results, the destination, the "Only if…, then I'll be"? For so many decades, I put all my energy into destinations while, all along, giving it all my energy. I failed to see that this destination was, in fact, the journey to the destination. Now as I reflect on all my experiences and the life lessons they carry, I see that I know and that I am already here. All does work out to God's greater good; God does guide me and answers my prayers. All I have to do is be aware, be empty, be present, be grateful, and have faith. When all my suspicions have been affirmed, where do I go from here? Not wanting to be right but to be happy leaves me disappointed that what I want has been washed away. Since the only thing in my control is how I react to this disappointment, I will move on in faith and know that things will work out for my benefit, and I will let life happen.

Focus—Squirrel

The movie *Up* depicts how easily a dog can lose focus and become distracted, yet when I allow myself to truly read or hear my thoughts, my focus almost always wanders away; hence, I lose focus—"Squirrel." It does amaze me that in wandering away from my positive, pure thoughts, I get caught up in the negative, in the sabotage of fear. I used to live in that negative abyss, always wandering into the worst what-if. Now at least I am aware of my focus when I stray and how to get back home again. Judgment, resentment, and disappointment live in that abyss; I choose to focus on the light.

Back Home

When the summer vacations are over and the traveling is done, back home is where I go. The hiatus from daily life can bring new joy and wonder to all the possibilities of the newness, but when it's time to go home, there is sadness in the goodbyes. However, after being away from the daily rituals, a spark flies when coming back to the familiar. Settling into what is predictable can bring a new flavor from my travels. Relationships are like this. Some journey with me for a lifetime while others are like a vacation—they come, and they leave. I am blessed to be able to have such amazing opportunities and to come back home to me.

The Journey

Looking at the journey of my life and remembering all the joy and sorrow in my life lessons, one thing I know for sure, in the fluid existence of my evolution, is that I was never alone. I am a soul who feels deeply into my core, so when I was hurt, I bellowed as if I was a wolf caught in a trap. And when I found joy, I laughed until my jaw and gut ached with elation. All the while, when I was up or down, I always found home with God. I was never alone. I was always with God. I am a soul on an evolutionary journey to learn, to laugh, to love, and to be the blessing that I am for God.

What If?

What if all the what-ifs were answered? The what-ifs can lead me down a dark road, paralyzing me into giving all of me away to be loved and included. What if all my family were restored, my marriage were filled with intimacy and romance, I were a successful author, loved and admired by all, or I had more money than I could ever spend? But as I review my life, I see that I have been such a blessing to others by loving God's children, I have enough financial security to live one day at a time, I am in good health from eating well and exercising, and I am already famous in my own right, having touched others and having learned from them. What I've learned is that when it's all said and done, the what-ifs have already been answered.

Unfinished

I used to take on a task and hurry through the journey of doing it to the destination, it being finished, only to wait for the next opportunity toward doing and finishing. Yet how many chances was I given to see the mere splendor of the journey, only to sacrifice all that it held to finish? My fear drove most of my decisions; I needed to be in control since I had given all that away to be controlled. So in my innocence and ignorance, thinking that I knew more than I needed to learn, I was unable to see the simplicity of an unfinished journey. Because of forgetting my worth and not trusting enough, I was never going to find my joy and passions. Now I accept that my being unfinished just means there is more to learn and there is more coming my way. God's not finished with me.

The Road Back

When we travel down the road of life with all its roadblocks, detours, potholes, and dead ends, the road back is usually the road less traveled. Yet to expect a journey without obstacles is futile, because how else will I know where to go if where I've been is not where I belong? I allowed them to make all my decisions. I gave my power and energy to someone else. I believed all their broken promises, and I allowed myself to be defined by their perceptions, believing that they knew better for me than I knew for myself. So I got back on the road to take me home to God. This road less traveled now has my footprints.

Still Standing

Sometimes, there is no one to talk to, no place to go, nothing that needs to be done, or no need or want; so I stand still, wandering and wondering, "Is this okay?" And then the light shines on a snowflake falling to its new home and a squirrel scurries around and becomes an acrobat on the high wire, and life just is. The contemplation begins, rewinding my life's journey and how I have arrived to this moment, still healing, still healthy, still financially secure, still emotionally stable, and still just being who I am. With one deep breath and one exhale, I give one more praise and a thank-you to God.

What's Best, and Who Knows It?

As babies, we depend on our parents to know what is best for our well-being. At times, we may question this authority if it doesn't align with our greatest good. Not all lessons are attached to a positive message, yet our authentic self knows deep into our soul's core what is best. On the detours, we may stop looking at who knows what's best for us and start making those decisions for ourselves. The outcomes may not always be favorable, yet it is in the coming home to the core of our being that we know who knows.

Arrival

After decades on my journey of wondering and wandering away from who I truly am, I have come back to the core of what is real: God's truth! After toying with the contradictions of life, coming home merely complements learning and knowing that my truth is in the light. I lived life in the past with what-ifs and by projecting life into the past and future, but I am now at home with what is, knowing it is all meant to be. I can live in peace and joy with contentment. Whatever happens, not knowing will never change my core. I have faith, and I have always been and will remain to be God's child.

LPs and 45 Records

In the fifties and sixties, before the CD or the iPod, music was played and heard on a turntable with a fine needle. It played our hearts' songs. If scratched, the music would skip, like I would when I detoured off my path. At times, the needle would get stuck in one of the grooves of the records, replaying the same stanzas over and over again, somewhat like a life lesson reoccurring in my life if I had not dealt with and healed from the issue. In the playing of and listening to the music of my life and dealing with, at times, a dull needle or a scratched area on my LP or 45, God always lifted the needle and slowed down the music so that I would see that where I thought I was stuck was a mere pause for me to reflect on my purpose, my journey, and my life lessons so that I could deal and heal enough to play the songs of my life.

Where I Am

Sometimes, I wonder why I have been where I am for so long. After revisiting my journals, I realize that the same distractions and issues have been on the forefront of my journey for as long as I have been awake. I reread the same messages again and again, wandering through the years, wondering if I will ever arrive. Then the still, quiet voice tells me I am exactly where I am meant to be. I am moving forward and evolving because what I am supposed to learn and who I am to become is where I am.

LEFT TURN, RIGHT TURN, THEN DECIDE

How many decisions have I made or have allowed to be made for me? God's decision is that our body functions so that it may house our soul to evolve on this human experience. With my first utterance of the word *no*, I began my life journey—left turn, right turn, then decide. With free will, the amazing power and gift from God, what I choose to make of my life to fulfill my soul's need to learn, grow, and continue my journey is mine to decide. Reflecting on my life choices and experiences, I realize I have lived my life through someone else's words. Now that I know, I see myself in my own emptying of them, and I hear myself in the silencing of them, and I now decide whether to choose left turn or right turn. I let go of any doubt and fear, and I know that I am fulfilling my purpose at every turn I decide to take.

WANDER

How many times have I started on one path of my journey only to get sidetracked by a detour, beneficial or just an interruption, and I begin to wander? When I am focused on one task and pulled out of that thought and into another, the question then becomes, "Am I avoiding what is best for me?" The contradictions of my life have not always brought favorable results as far as feeling that I am on the right path for my soul's evolution is concerned. Yet it is in this wandering that I am awakened into wondering what it is I am avoiding and what the life lesson is. I used to deny my journey by making excuses, blame-shifting, and being a prisoner of my own ghosts. Now able to see my path and my own reflection, I wander into the light of my soul's existence.

And so I Wait

We wait all these years to find someone who understands us, someone who accepts us as we are, someone with a wizard's power to melt stone into sunlight, who can bring us happiness in spite of our trials, who can face our dragons in the night, who can transform us into the souls who we are chosen to become…and so I waited! Then I looked in the mirror and I saw that face in the mirror and that 'someone' was God in my eyes.

And He Answered

"Disappointments are inevitable. Misery is optional." Why am I estranged from those I love the most? He answered, "You have lived long enough in the pain of the drama. You have wandered long enough in the darkness, wearing the masks that others deemed yours to wear. You have defined yourself for them long enough. Now it's your time, my dear, sweet child. It's your time to evolve. It's your time for peace, joy, contentment, self-love, acceptance, and approval to be exactly who I intended you to be." Who am I to argue with God's answer?

Explore

Total acceptance has been a difficult concept for me. I put a lot of energy into thinking, wishing, and hoping for if-onlys, could-haves, or should-haves. But life has been kind to me. I've learned that I am loved. Giving up the illusion of could-haves, should-haves, and what-ifs toward acceptance put faith and trust in God's plan rather than on what I think it will be or should be.

In my early years, I depended on others' behavior and on them showing up and being what I wanted. I found myself looking outside of myself instead of within. I overlooked my abundance of love, happiness, contentment, worth, blessings, comforts, and achievements, thinking there was more than I was getting. When I was lonely, I looked to others to keep me company. When I was confused, I looked for clarity from others. When I needed respect, I looked to accomplish a task to receive affirmations. I was always looking outside of myself to feel worthy. In the end, seeking only brought me to the edge of knowing myself. If I had never looked inward, I would have become an expert in living life on the edge of knowing myself.

While seldom unlocking what seeking me meant, I became a master at climbing mountains instead of breaking trails to the center of my soul. I blame-shifted my anxiousness, only pushing others to hurry up and take this journey of inner exploration with me. But now I know! This journey of inner exploration has to be taken alone. My inner exploration, my becoming a diver, and my breaking trail to my center are between me and God. I can share my experiences and support others' quests, but no one is responsible for me but me.

THE BEST TIME

I couldn't wait to get to the other side of a crisis. I used to pray away the pain. I used to bargain with promises that I might never have been able to fulfill. My intention was to stop the pain at any cost. I used to give all my energy to wandering away from where I was at that moment. Then I began to let go and have faith, believing that God could do anything, including helping me manage through my pain. I began to look for the message the pain was whispering and the meaning or the lesson I was supposed to learn. Now I know that the best time in my life is where I am in that moment. I can rewind my memories, and the only sadness that comes to mind is my thoughts of hurrying through the journey to the final destination, where the pain is gone. I have learned to live with the pain and not in the pain. Now in this moment, where my heart beats and the sun rises, my deep inhale is the best time.

WHERE ENERGY FLOWS

At any given moment, a smile can turn into a frown, joy into sorrow, or lost hope into faith. Where does my energy flow? I've found myself spending more time in the negative than in the positive, trying to turn the former into the latter, and this is where my energy flows. Giving all my energy into a negative, trying to turn it into a positive, is wasted energy. It's like turning on a light switch, waiting for the light to illuminate, and then realizing the bulb is burned out. How much energy have I given to burned-out bulbs, relationships that have ended, waiting for a loved one to return, or the restoration of a lost wish? So my question is, where do I want my energy to flow?

THE FLOWER IN THE SEED

At times, trying to find the positive in a negative situation can be a challenge to a lifelong victim. It is only when positive energy force flows into and through the experience that the seed then becomes a flower. Surviving and seeing the positive results in my life experiences have assisted me in remembering compassion, empathy, patience, and forgiveness toward those who still struggle, like myself, to become their best, true self. It is when I look into the eyes of another that I can see myself. Their story is also, like mine, a seed waiting to flower. As I continue on this purposeful journey, I remain steadfast to weather the winter of my life, awaiting the flower of spring.

WHERE I DWELL

Something happens, and I react. A simple moment of pleasure can be flipped in a heartbeat. Do I choose to dwell in the pleasure or in the reaction to another's behavior? Once the trigger has been felt and acknowledged, where do I choose to dwell? If I turn my attention back to that moment of pleasure, I realize the pain and worry are only in my mind. I miss a great deal of joy by dwelling in my reaction to another's behavior. I deprive myself of the simplicity and the silence of a moment when I choose the bells and whistles of another's drama, which then become mine. Where I choose to dwell is a conscious choice of reactions. So I detach, look for that pleasurable moment, and reflect on the positive. This is where I choose to dwell.

Live On

When an obstacle crosses my path, I have a choice to sit there and wait for the obstacle to be removed, or I can move around it or through it and live on. When I encounter my own issues, I seek knowledge and assistance to heal. When I see another struggling, I offer my assistance; but if the answer is no, I choose to move around it or through it and live on. I've learned that getting stuck in another's life story does not allow my own life story to unfold. If we are meant to journey together and your life story should be a part of mine, then we live on together. Complementing one another or contradicting one another can be powerful experiences to help me sift through and live on. I have a life.

I've Always Been

I do not need to prove anything to anyone anymore. I've come home to me. The truth is, I was there all along, only I forgot to look for myself. Instead, I searched for me in other people's meaning of me and became lost in their stories. Agreeing with someone used to mean giving away my truth and voice. One of my life's deepest opportunities is not only getting to know my true self to hear my voice and to live my truth but also learning how to live in this world as me. Now that the masks are off and my cloak from being a chameleon have been discarded, I show up as me. I will engage but not become a part of their drama. I will show up as a beacon of light even if there is darkness. I've always been this way, and now I truly am. Are you?

Solitude

Living my life based on the word of another led to disappointments when they did not walk their talk. Making decisions based on the experiences of another left me wandering from my own path. Believing my worth based on the defined adjectives of another left me hopeless, fearful, and lost. When I began to say no and find my truth, I was tested to see if I could walk my talk. When I started to trust my own word, I was enlightened, not disappointed. When I started making my own decisions, void of input, I found my voice. When I started believing myself worthy of love, saw my own light, and spoke my own truth, I traveled on my own path, and I saw myself. In my solitude, void of others' drama and noise, I see me, I hear me, and I am who God wants me to be. Now care to join me?

Same Journey, Different Path

I have walked many paths on my journey toward fulfilling my destiny. I have worn many masks and have been a chameleon on most of these paths to find love and acceptance and to fill my emptiness. Yet although my journey remained intact, my path had a repetitive theme, resulting in the same. I always strove to unmask my true self and to be accepted for my differences and special gifts. I kept taking the same paths, always looking for a more fulfilling ending. Now I am no longer taking the same paths, for they do not align with my journey. My destination is clear, and my past has been cleaned of undesirable control and manipulation. I continue my journey on the path of love and truth for others and myself. This house is clean.

Rearview Mirror

It's been said that the windshield in a car is larger than the rearview mirror because seeing what lies ahead is more important than what has been left behind. This is not to dismiss or diminish my past, yet it is true that watching constant reruns or looking in my rearview mirror can only sidetrack me from what lies on my immediate path. Needing to occasionally look into the rearview mirror or watch a rerun can be helpful as a reference if I am confronted with a similar situation that triggers my fears, but it is not helpful to dwell in that image for too long, for I will find myself off my path and back to reliving that rerun that I see myself in. So with diligence, discipline, faith, trust, and love for myself, I forge forward, glancing occasionally to wave goodbye and say thanks for the visit.

Stay within Me

"Just breathe, find your core, and feel the center of your being" are words of encouragement and wisdom that I have learned to remember when I find myself straying away from me and into you so I am reminded to stay within me. Walking within myself, I encounter the many others whom I allow to draw on my energy. I may even displace a fear of mine onto you so that I don't have to stay within me. But blame-shifting is an escape and only allows me to journey so far. I get sucked back into myself, inevitably having to face the very obstacle I fear, so I will stay within me to celebrate us.

Who Speaks My Truth

When giving the accounts of an accident, all bystanders will have a different interpretation of the event, all believing the truth. As we mature, we take bits and pieces of information from all we meet. As babies, we learn from our families; and as adolescents, we learn from our peers and teachers until we are a culmination of who we meet. Put all that information and ingredients into a bowl and mix it and we are who we are supposed to be. But if adults' lie becomes a child's truth or an assimilation of another has warped our being, then who will speak our truth? It takes a life's journey to gather and purge that which does or does not complement our truth. The still small whisper within knows who I truly am. Who are you? Let's share ourselves.

Change in a Destination

In a lifetime, change is inevitable. We will grow in height, gain weight, our bodies will learn to function at a desired request, and we will and do change. One thing does remain unchanged, and that is the love and light of God in our souls. It does and will remain intact no matter how many challenges we face, and no matter how much we try to change the unchangeable, we will still remain who we truly and deeply are, and that is the love and light of our souls. So as we travel on this journey, our destination, which is to change our human form, is inevitable. Like a clock, we reach maturity and then revert toward our destination. Yet during our journey toward our destination, we are ever changing, ever evolving, and ever and simply just being. No one can avoid the inevitable destination, but the journey, ah, enjoy the changing scenery.

Leave Home to Go Home

At times, we are meant to escape from our everyday living and go on vacation. This ritual allows us to rejuvenate ourselves when we become too predictable. They are not permanent days away from home but simply the need to get a balcony view of our many comforts and blessings, which we tend to take for granted. Taking our comforts and blessings for granted is not intentional, yet they do creep into our lives, causing a bit of discomfort. A vacation allows us to leave home for a while to appreciate the miles that separate us it. In the absence of our everyday life, we can then return with the fresh view that there is no place like home.

Running Back to Me

As soon as we learn to walk and then run, our legs, hearts, souls, and minds take us on an adventure. We may be led to a foreign land beyond our seas or a foreign thought beyond our minds. Whatever the case may be, we will always need to come back home. I've spent decades as a wanderer, wondering what might lie in someone else's backyard or what it would be like to walk in another's shoes. I've spent decades dressed in the outfits of another's world, only to realize that I can only wear my own shoes, dress in my own outfits, and live in my own backyard. So as I continue my adventures and live life to fulfill my purpose, I know I will always be running back to me.

Remain or Remove

Things that are predictable cause comfort and may border on being taken for granted, such as the sunrise or the bloom of a flower in the spring. Things that are predictable can also cause discomfort, such as a bully's put-down or a siren screaming down the highway. We get to choose whether to remain comfortable in our discomfort or remove ourselves into an emptiness of new wonder. Saying it's predictable does not mean we have to settle. It's the discomfort that stirs the change. If we remain, we get more of the same; but if we remove ourselves, then this new discomfort of not knowing will strengthen faith and help us settle into a positive new journey. Where do you choose to be?

Growth

During the winter months, when everything lies dormant and asleep, we cannot see growth. When a baby becomes a toddler, we cannot conceive how fast time flies, but just look at a childhood picture or a wedding album from twenty-five years ago and you'll see that time does move forward and growth does take place. Sometimes, I find myself stuck thinking about how I left a broken dream on the side of the road of my journey. Then when I connect with a childhood friend or see a relative whom I haven't seen in a while, the growth shines through like the sun's rays dancing through a prism. I may not always see my growth, but when I can take a deep breath, not feeling the pain, I know I have moved forward, and I bless the past.

Memories

The blessing of overlapping old and new are experiences with getting reacquainted with family and friends. It is a bittersweet experience when I look into the eyes of those I knew as a child, only to see the reflection of a life that has passed. The years have worn us down. We walk slower and remember less, yet there is still a deep-seated connection through the eyes of our souls so that we may still say, "I see you." Making new memories that align with the old only adds layers to a deep love that, over time, has strengthened. Time away from loved ones restores an appreciation for what is truly important.

The connections I've made in my lifetime have endured the test of time. Seeing a familiar face or seeing the ocean again restores me and affirms that all is well and that I am who I should be and where I should be with my new memories.

The Right Path

At times, a detour off the direct path may have given me immediate gratification and temporary joy, but now I know that the only road is the one that is direct. That is the road of peace, true joy, and pure love. The other road causes pain, loneliness, and sadness. Although different roads may have potholes or detours, I have learned to choose the straight path. If my road crosses with another, I may ask them to join me; but if not, with or without a passenger, I am on the right road for me. Never needing directions, the one road I travel that I never lose my way on is God's path. There is only one road: the road of truth, love, and the all-encompassing light in God's love.

Turn the Page

Sometimes, in the quiet, a flood of memories may wash over me. Some memories are joyful while others suffocate me. I used to pitch a tent in the painful moments of my life, only to realize that the more I healed, the more that the pain of my past continued to try to drag me back. This would cause me to feel that the joy and peace that awaited me became so untouchable that I felt like giving in and giving up, but in those moments, my light shone through and burned off all that used to hold me hostage. My path may have detoured from my destiny, but with regrouping, I came back to who I had become and accepted that all that I did and all that was done to me allowed me to script words of hope, love, joy, and faith. I now turn the page to write my happy ending.

Redo

"Tragedy stays alive by feeling what's been done to us, while peace comes alive by living with the results." Triggers are gentle reminders of what happened and how I survived. Many times, I have found myself immersed in the trigger while giving pause to how I survived the trespass. Sometimes, the trigger is an affirmation of that survival, and the life lesson it brings to light is not about me. How I choose to react may be one more opportunity for me to celebrate my growth, so if I find myself in situations in which I feel I have grown, maybe it's there for me to pay forward the light that follows the darkness.

Invest in the Moment

As the productive members of society that we are and that we hope our children will become, we are responsible for fulfilling our requirements, pay our bills, obey the law, and do unto others. Yet in the hectic pace of things that we need to complete, we endlessly strive to check off one more thing on our list to feel productive or successful. But when we are put in unwanted or unexpected situations, that checklist becomes obsolete. Weeding the garden will take a back seat to a person in crisis who needs a soft place to land. How many times in the busyness of the day do we miss opportunities to sit and have a cup of coffee and allow ourselves to invest in that one moment? The memories may fade, but the opportunity for inner peace will last a lifetime. Come, sit. Let's talk and share our stories.

Move On

After living my life with predictable reactions, I am now choosing to move on. After allowing myself to be dismissed, asking to present myself with a mask of deceit, and choosing to give even when I feel depleted, I have now chosen to move on. Some may view this as running away, yet what I've learned is that what is not addressed and healed will move on with me. Now that I am in the latter season of my life, I no longer run from that which no longer serves me, but I am healing and choosing to move on. I still encounter that which has not healed, either from my soul or another's, so I am choosing to move away to move on. I may be alone, but living in peace is better for me than living in another's drama. I pray we all heal.

WHERE I AM IS NOT OVER THERE

Always thinking life and love were somewhere over there, not where I was, I put all my energy into getting over there. Yet when I got there, I was not allowed in. I continued to try to get inside where they were. I assimilated myself so I would blend into their world. I blended so deeply that I didn't even recognize my reflection. After decades of bloody knuckles from knocking on the doors of others, I finally decided that my door was the door I should enter. It took me years to realize that no matter the pain, life is always where I am. No more giving of my energy for another's lies to become my truth. I stepped into my door and decided to start living my life where I am, not over there. Although at times I will grieve over broken dreams, I will remain hopeful that we will all find our truth and live in that truth. No longer living over there, I am planting my new garden where I am, always willing to share the fragrances of the flowers of my life.

ABOUT ME, ABOUT YOU

There is a very fine line between what is about me and what is about you. The universe has an amazing gift for us on our journey: So that we do not journey alone, we are connected with others who have similar life lessons to experience. We may sometimes feel that this can be a burden, a feeling, or a need to take care of another while we are learning to take care of ourselves. At times, more than not, I lost myself in another's drama, so much so that when I stood in the sunlight, there was only one shadow.

I am not here to heal you, only to join hands with you to enhance your journey, as you do mine, and what is about me and what is about you is about us. Not meant to travel alone but separate, we can all learn to live with compassion without caretaking. We can all learn to support without sacrifice. We can all learn to make it about us—together, apart, as two, as one. Walk by my side, not behind or in front of me, so that we can join hands and walk together on our life's journey, never alone but separate.

The Voice in a Feeling

It's very transparent to me why I feel joy—a child's laughter, a beautiful sunrise, or a song to dance to. Yet to truly understand the meaning behind the feeling, we have to unravel the pain's so many layers and roots. I laugh, and then I can immediately know why, yet when I cry, I spend countless moments drilling down to its origin in order to heal it or learn its life lesson.

When in pain, it may seem so endless when compared to the fleeting elements of joy. If that is where I grow and evolve, I will learn how to deal with what I feel, yet it's still so reactionary to defend my feelings, so that puts one more layer that I have to drill through to find the message. I will feel the feeling, I will refine my reactions, I will learn the lessons, and I will continue on my evolutionary journey. With one more opportunity, I will explore why I feel as though I need to react to a painful situation with pain. I will look for my joy.

Focus on Me

Being preoccupied with what I cannot mend or fix or what I left behind is robbing me of my today. I know my truth and I have my voice. Spending my precious time on trying to convince someone of my truth is a waste. I am now spending as much time loving and living my life as the time I have wasted on them. I am not in their thoughts and I have chosen to let them go. I live my own life in my own world with God.

Living in My Now

If I had waited for all of my prayers to be answered on my time, then I would have not lived. Having a life in spite of all of my disappointments, gives power to the life I have chosen to live. If I continue to sacrifice my journey in order to have what I want, then I will miss my many opportunities to see how blessed I am in my experiences in mind now. Focusing on my disappointments has taught me that God's timing is perfection. What I thought I wanted has been replaced with what I need. If I standstill at the crossroads, then I miss any and all opportunities to adventure into my journey of my life. I am now giving myself the gift of living in my 'now' instead of mourning over past transgressions or hoping for a better tomorrow. My 'now' is where I belong and is assisting me to fulfill my purpose on this journey. I will always have what I need and get what God wants me to have.

In the End

A childhood dream can come with many expectations and disappointments. Friendships may come and go, life lessons and experiences can bring joy or sorrow. A relationship that was meant to last a lifetime can dwindle away like the last flower of spring loses its petals. In the deepest, most sacred places of all, the heart keeps on beating. The soul keeps on exploring and questioning for the just right answered to the questions; where do I belong, what is my destiny and where is my path to lead me to fulfill my childhood dream and to take me to a place of peace? Either way in the end, we can sit down, with a cup coffee and ask, "How was your day? Tell me your story."

I Get to Choose

There are so many choices in the world, and I get to choose which option favors me. I get to choose the food that is pleasant to my pallet. I get to choose the clothes and jewelry I feel fit me best. I get to choose where I live, and I get to choose my friends. I get to choose how I spend my days and the books I read and the places I visit. If all this is in my power because of the amazing gift of free will and choice, why would I ever choose to think ill of myself or judge my neighbor or be with people who are abusive and controlling? Why would I focus on the negative instead of the positive? Why would I ever choose to believe that I am not as worthy as anyone else to receive God's blessings, love, amazing gifts, and opportunities? I get to choose what I believe.

My Quest

Having spent my life becoming a product of all the parts I took from others, I became a productive member of society, took care of my body, and became financially responsible. My soul hungered for my own truth. Even though I received misinformation about finances and health, the one thing I did know was true was that there was a god. I had been raised with misguided ideals and ideas, so I began to question and uncover all that had been done and said in the name of God. I was given the gift of curiosity and inquiry, so I began my quest for my own truth. I knew there was a god, but I wanted to explore what I believed about who He was. I prayed I would find my answers and became selective in what I believed to be true.

It occurs to me that we have it when we are born, yet we lose our way due to our free will and the messages we receive from those who want to control and impose their views on us. We try on many outfits thinking society knows what is best for us. We lose our voice by listening to others as they speak for us. We misplace our truth, thinking others know what is best for us. After all, our elders are sup-posed to love and cherish us. We then must decide what is best for us with God's hand guiding us. We must listen to the voice of God as He guides us. Sometimes, this takes one's lifetime.

This has been my journey, which has brought me back to me. I am living out my years by healing from my painful past, whether it is from the abuse of others or my own. My task in recovery is to return myself to the physically, emotionally, and spiritually healthy point where I don't blame others. When I am healed inside and live with my own truth and keep my voice, I will not run anymore. My inner fear and darkness have kept me stuck, so I am bringing me into the light. I am finding that voice that helps me be my best, true self. Where the pain came from is no longer an issue. What matters is my journey today and keeping my connection with God and myself. This is my quest.

Look and See

I am learning not only to look but also to see. For many years, I blame-shifted my pain onto others, as I was accused of causing their pain. Knowing what I do own as mine has allowed me to unload the burden of carrying what is not mine. After sifting through and looking at the debris that has been left behind, I can now say, I do see what is mine. Although this painful experience is one we can label as humbling, I am now moving forward and into my journey of knowing.

Place of Origin

It is said that if lost, one must retrace their steps back to their original place. It is said that if one needs to know the depth of their joy and pain, they need to find the depths of the passions that define who they are. It is said that we can return by facing ourselves, and we need to look deep into the eyes of the reflection in the mirror to see who we really are. If you look at the center of your body, there is a scar that we all have, our first indication that we are attached to something greater than what we can ever comprehend or imagine. Our navel is our one true connection to ourselves and to one another. We are all from the same place of origin. We are God's children.

Distractions

Sometimes, it's most difficult to just accept and be. Finding faults or drama may make me feel alive. It's sometimes too easy to want to fight or to think that things are against me. But fighting will only separate me, and this will distract me from feeling loved.

If I have unkind things to say, it's only because I experienced unkind behavior. My only guide in this witnessing is to be accurate and honest. While I am not a victim, I didn't ask for certain shaping experiences to happen to me. If I had experienced different behaviors, I would have different things to say. What is most healing about bearing witness to things exactly as they are including my own part in the pain is that when the voice of the pain, fits the pain there is no room for distortion or illusion. Truth becomes a clean bandage that heals, keeping dirt out of the wound.

I can't change the past, only heal it with truth and love, so now I look at my distractions and give energy to that which will heal and bring love, joy, and peace.

THE BRIDGE

A bridge's sole purpose is connection from one point to another. It is in this connection that trust evolves in order to move toward a specific destination once the bridge is crossed. Sometimes, the bridge may need maintenance; other times, it may be secure. When crossing the bridge, there are many things that will be left behind due to the fact that the weight is too intense to make the journey or that the purpose has been addressed and is no longer needed to be brought along on the journey. Invitations toward another may cause a lonely journey, for in our own times, we do, in fact, cross a bridge. When crossing the bridge, looking back at what's left behind and moving toward what's better will enhance the journey.

What Is Needed?

If I were to release all that no longer fits, what would I be able to give up? What can I truly live without? What do I really need to sustain my life and to find joy in each moment?

Slow Down

At times, my to-do list becomes so overwhelming that I push myself to complete a task; and sometimes, I do not give it my best. During my anxious times, I can become so disengaged that it becomes a chore, not a journey. This does not give me the results I want, so inevitability, I have to redo in order to get the results I want. I am learning to look for the blessings in the moments and the experiences that are held in the journey. Learning and experiences are so much more important to me than arriving. It doesn't matter when I get there but how I enjoy what I am learning along the way. If I slow down, then I will have all that I am meant to have when I am meant to have it. I will eventually arrive!

Wondering as I Wander

Knowing what's true and filtering through the information to find the truth is a process that I find myself engaged in every time I search for more truth. Having learned to refine my dulled filter, I find myself questioning deeper, as I used to accept what was offered. This may be viewed as being indecisive or difficult, but I have lived with another's word for so long that I need to purge myself of their lies in order to find my truth. I am continuing to wonder as I wander.

Destination Known

When the dust settles into the days of my life, I will have a true testament of survival and knowledge to sift through in order to find my truth. No longer living in fear of judgment, retribution, abuse, or abandonment, I can uncover and unravel the truth of my being. As it has taken a lifetime to accumulate, I am being gentle with myself as I assess what I believe. I'm in no hurry through this part of my journey. I already know my destination.

Time to Figure It Out

If I feel as though I am stuck in a rut, what is holding me there? Have I forgiven my trespasses and the trespasses of others? Am I still harboring resentment for what others have done? Am I still feeling disappointment from unmet dreams? Am I still angry and waiting for another's apology to give me permission to let things go? Am I still carrying the burdens of others? Am I still waiting for someone to show up and walk their talk? Am I still allowing their reactions to dictate how I feel? Am I still sacrificing my boundaries to please them? What is stealing my joy and preventing me to live in peace? It's time to figure this out!

Time to Release

Nelson Mandela said, "Resentment is like drinking poison and then hoping it will kill your enemies." I used to think that if I held on to my anger long enough, I would receive the apology that would melt into happiness. I used to think that if I harbored enough resentment, then the person who hurt me would also feel my pain. I used to think that if I remained in my pain, then I would be justified for being angry, resentful, disappointed, and unhappy at the cost of someone else's actions. What am I still holding on to that I don't need anymore? What am I holding on to that no longer serves the person that I am? What am I holding on to that is keeping me from my joy, peace, love, and truth? If I don't need it anymore, why am I still holding on to it? It's time to release and let go.

Not Giving Up but Letting Go

I have learned that when I have a desire in my heart, I am given the tools and opportunities to pursue that experience. I have also learned that obstacles along the way may detour my desire in a different direction, either bringing in new opportunities or delaying my destination. I can filter through that which will benefit or deter my destiny. When I try to manipulate the experience into what I want it to be, I engage in combat and unrest. It's easier when I give up my need and let it go, following the road that I am destined to travel. Either way, with or without the pain, I will arrive.

Enjoy the Journey

Impatience is aspiring to reach the destination by hurrying through and not appreciating the blessing of the journey. After I have silenced the noise of distress, I can refocus on appreciation and finding gratitude in all my experiences. After I have found my calmness in the midst of my reactions, I say a prayer and find peace and serenity in knowing that all is and we all are. In these simple moments, I find my peace. I'm blessed to have found peace with God and myself, and I'm learning to visit this place more often. Enjoy the journey.

Come Home

I am letting go of attempting to change what is. I am learning to live my life in the peace of having conquered the fear of not knowing. I believe in a future that I do not see. This is faith. I am learning to celebrate having come home to myself and experiencing great contentment and satisfaction. Having come home to myself, I am experiencing greater joy than I've ever expected. I now know who God is! I've stopped chasing what is not and becoming more comfortable with what is. I am learning to accept God's plan for me as I learn to let go of what I think I need to be happy and accepting what God thinks I need.

My Road

When I find myself holding on too tightly to an outcome, I can lose sight of the destination and the many life lessons within that journey. I have heard the words "Hurry up" and "Get over it" many times, and this has caused self-doubt and much anxiousness, making me feel as if I am inferior to another person. I know that we all have many experiences, some common and some foreign, so that sharing our stories can become our common ground without us becoming a part of their drama or even abandoning our life to engage in theirs. So I will continue on my road, embracing all the experiences and people I meet along the way as I move toward my destination at my own pace. I will also honor others in this fashion.

ALL MY PIECES

I'm wondering how strange it is that when I finally receive something that I have prayed for, it no longer has the power I used to give it when I was praying for it. This letting go and seeking refuge in God has strengthened my faith that I am really whole without their pieces, which I thought I lacked. Taking time to find my own missing pieces has brought me to my own knowledge that only my pieces complete me. Although we are all a part of a greater picture, I know I have to be complete in order to bring my wholeness to the picture of life. I still explore what pieces do fit, but I no longer force them to be a part of me if they don't. I am complete in my own picture.

READY TO JUMP

Too many times, I jumped before I was ready. Faking it until you make it will only work if the desired outcome is known, but when doubt and trust are still in the forefront, driving decisions, I know it is better to wait than to regret my decision. Even if there is another person waiting for me, I have to honor myself first so that I will show up complete, whole, and authentic instead of what they want me to be. So when I'm ready, I will jump.

TOO MANY TIMES

I wonder how many times I experienced someone dismissing me and I took it personally as if I was the root cause of their unhappiness. I wonder how many times I allowed this behavior to flip my happiness into sadness and affirm my self-doubt. I wonder how many times I looked into another's eyes and hung on every word that they spoke and made it my truth and made it define my mindset and fill my worth. If I did it once, that was one too many times!

Be like a Child

Have you ever watched a child giggle at their own little feet as they devoured them into a yummy meal? Have you ever watched a child on a merry-go-round laugh so hard that their happiness echoed into the sky or smile at an elderly person who was a stranger and hugged them with their glance? I can recall times when I squinted to see formations in clouds or made a wish on a dandelion's flower and watched it sail into the sky or dance to a rhythm that made me so happy that I laughed out loud. These were times when I lived in joy. Every day, I can see the blessings and gifts, and I can be like a child again.

Replant My Garden

It's spring, and the world is awakening and blooming again. It begins the promise of a new cycle of joy and flowers and rejuvenation. Old growth may need some attention by removing weeds and replanting. Repotting a plant that is root bound is giving it an opportunity to grow stronger and thrive. So it is with my walk with God. I have to be removed from my old planter, and the dead old roots must be cut away, which depicts the life I am embedded in, suffocating in the old planter of my life. I have to be placed in a new planter with a more sturdy foundation so that the existing strong, purposeful roots will thrive and grow. Discarding the old to make room for the new is the cycle of life. It's time to replant my garden.

Journey

A journey with another may take us on different paths. The things that connect us may no longer be viable, so it may look as if the journey has ended. What is meant to be will be. If we part ways, I wish you well; and if we meet again, I'll welcome you back. I hope you find what you're searching for, and whether we are together or apart, I bless you on your journey.

FIND THE FACTS

I am caught in a world of miscommunication, polarized kindness, and illness of the soul and body. When I seek the truth, I have to filter the lies from my past while I sift through the information from my present. I may find myself swaying toward the loudest voice or the one who speaks the language of my metacognition. Neither my happiness nor my truth can be contingent on other people's word or deed. It's not that I think I know more than anyone else or that I am better than anyone else. It is about me wanting to be better than who I was. It is about seeking the truth through the endless opinions, judgments, biases, and prejudices toward finding the facts.

AUTHENTIC

When I was a teacher, I knew I had to be smarter than the book that was teaching me to teach, which meant I had to seek more knowledge than what was being offered. So is my journey to seek the truth about who I am and who God is. If I take the word as merely print on the page or I trust another's words that are spoken based on their knowledge and experience, then I become a carbon copy without a soul. I have been labeled difficult for asking my deep-seated questions. All the while, I was merely a lifelong student looking for answers. I will continue to seek the truth so that I will evolve into who I am meant to be and so that we can journey together as our authentic selves.

PLEASE EXPLAIN

There comes a time when a voice that has been silenced must be heard. Please explain to me how someone can claim to love his neighbor but gossip about them behind their back. Please explain to me why if the other person's story has not been told, they are judged because they do not align with the masses. Please explain to me how the color of a race matters more than another. Please explain how someone can advocate for peace yet cause harm or curse someone else who has a different political affiliation or a different skin color or a different belief system. Please explain how your view is more important than my view and your voice should be heard and mine should be silenced? Please explain it to me as if I were a child. I'm no better or worse than anyone else. I just want to be better than who I was. Please help me to understand why!

Choose Wisely

When I am searching for answers to my questions, what choices do I have? I can believe what others are speaking rather than look for the valid truth. When I am looking for a resolution for my problem, what choices do I have? I can force my hand toward the situation for my benefit, but how will that leave me knowing that there could be a different resolution than what I force it to be. I seek wisdom, seek guidance, and seek truth so that I can choose wisely!

To Wait

I find it interesting that we act as if we have all the time in the world to get things accomplished. How long must I wait for an apology or to wait to resolve a conflict or to wait for the honor of a rite of passage or to wait for the pain to stop? It is in my experience that life goes on, and I have moved forward despite not receiving the apology or getting everything accomplished to resolve a conflict or to be honored with the rite of passage or for the pain to stop. I have moved forward with my life and have learned to live with the pain of the deprivation. All I want may never come to pass, but I am hopeful in my faith that someday, I will see me in your eyes.

Answers

What are the obstacles to my growth that are hindering my evolution? Is it my old belief system, that I am unworthy, that still wreaks havoc on my peace? Is it my uneducated mindset, that I am not learned enough to move forward, that there's something more I need to learn to solidify my foundation? What don't I understand, and what questions do I need to ask? Am I still reacting in a defensive manner to keep my voice?

Have I given up hope for and faith in my family situation? Have I resigned myself to the fact that my disappointments will never be healed and that I hold bitterness in my heart? Am I still resentful for what I didn't receive and not grateful for what I have? Do I not yet fully believe that I am loved, cherished, saved, forgiven, and redeemed and that I have been given salvation, grace, and mercy? It's time to seek my answers!

Wise

The definition of *wise* is "to be graced, not only with experience of age but also with the honored skills of watchfulness, awareness and thoughtfulness." Becoming who I am from all the experiences I have encountered and all the knowledge I have gathered does not make me wise unless I sift through all of it to find the truth. "Borrowed wisdom is not wisdom at all." I must seek my own wisdom through my own experiences and seek the truth.

Who Will You Follow?

When confronted with a situation, there are always choices—pick a behavior that will benefit a few and will hurt others, pick an outcome for the greater good, pick an outcome that will bring joy and peace, or pick an outcome that will wreak havoc. There are always choices, and they require an awareness of compassion and empathy, communication, patience, forgiveness, and kindness. If asked to follow a joyful, peaceful road or to err on the side of pain and sorrow, what will you follow?

Open Ears

This morning, I awoke early and walked into my sunroom to watch the sunrise. My Christmas lights were still on since they were set on a timer from dusk to dawn. My thoughts started to wander into my to-do list for the day, and as I began to walk away, I stopped and asked myself, "If this were my last moment on earth, how would I want to spend it?" The answer was obviously clear as the sky burst into the flames of a new day. I remained at my window as the Christmas lights closed their eyes until dusk, and I thanked God for where He placed me and thought that if this was my last moment on earth, He did me well. I'm glad I'm beginning to listen.

Shadow

When someone was seen walking in the sunlight, their shadow would be on the ground; in their shadow was where I used to dwell. I would do exactly what I was told to do even if I knew it was not in my best interest. But now I walk in the sunlight with my own shadow, and I make my own decisions in the best interest of my own soul even if it may differ from another's. In the combative nature of another who is trying to force me back into living in their shadow is where I voice my truth and stand firm in my convictions. Even though it may cause them to leave, I know that I am always safer in God's hands than in someone else's shadow.

The Day Goes By

There isn't a day that goes by that I don't miss them. There isn't a day that goes by that I don't reflect on what was said and the results of the actions that were chosen. There isn't a day that goes by that I don't think, "If things were said and done differently, what would my life be now?" There isn't a day that goes by that I don't bless them and pray for their health and welfare. There isn't a day that goes by that I don't pray for resolution and restitution before I leave this earth. And then the day goes by.

HOME

"I never need to look further than my own backyard" were the words Dorothy spoke in *The Wizard of Oz*. After searching for something she already had within her, she realized that there was "no place like home." A life's journey takes us on many roads. We may choose to detour from our designated path, or we may hit a dead end and have to turn around, or the road may need repair due to the potholes of our pain. Whatever road we choose to travel, it always leads home. So I've reviewed my journey and the roads I've traveled on, and indeed, I found dead ends, potholes, and detours. But the lessons I learned along the way and the people I encountered became my compass that always pointed me home. I will be forever grateful for this journey. There's no place like home.

JUST ASK

If I were asked when I finally began to heal, I would tell them this: My peace of mind started to unfold when I stopped filling myself with the lies of others and began seeking the truth. It started when I stopped letting others' opinions and judgments of me define my worth. It started when I stopped blaming others for my self-inflicted prison of bitterness, resentment, and hopelessness. It started when I emptied myself of the toxins that lived within me and began accepting God's love, which is available to all of us. It started when I became a believer that I was worthy of His love and when I asked to be forgiven. It starts with a quest, and all anyone needs to do is ask.

INCOMPREHENSIBLE

I will never understand unkindness, meanness, spitefulness, and hate. I know how it originates and how it festers and how it takes on a life of its own, but if given the opportunity to turn away from all that negativity, I don't understand why one would choose to stay there. Perhaps it's good that I don't understand, but I can show compassion and pray for the light.

UNCOVERED

Being ridiculed and mocked for my beliefs can be an exhausting undertaking if I choose to engage in the act of assimilation. I've watched people plead their case for a political party or for a new age product or to follow a specific belief in God. So many opinions and judgments toward forming a following can lead to deceit and manipulation and warp into bullying. I used to engage in these systems, where if I did not comply or align myself with a certain task-oriented outcome, I would be shamed and banished. I felt as if my life's breath was held within their approval. I was smothered in my own self-inflicted shame to be seen and heard. Once I was able to silence myself away from that system and uncover the truth, I found peace in my own heart as I uncovered my smothering life into the light of truth, love, peace, and joy. I know where my true nourishment lies.

MY SIDE OF THE ROAD

How easy it is for me to fall prey to a special word or a twinkle in an eye or a pleasant smile. How easy it is to fall off course just by receiving a kindness. I need to always be aware of how I am willing to cross the road into a situation that will only cause me heartache because I give my worth away to the hopes that my prayers will be answered by that special word or twinkling eye or pleasant smile. Where does my true nourishment lie? So I once again cross back to my side of the road with hope and faith that I remain with who truly fills me.

Distractions

When waiting for a cool breeze on a hot summer's day, I can seek refuge in the shade. When waiting for a prayer to be answered with an anxious, impatient heart, I can be reminded of all the prayers that have not been answered for my own well-being and the prayers that have been worth waiting for, because in that wait time, I grew! I'm grateful for the distractions while I wait—a snowfall, rainbows, a flowing river, a child's giggle, and your smile. Thanks for helping me through my impatient times as I wait.

Return

What are the obstacles in my way? Is it the behavior of another's unfulfilled words, or is it my expectation that that person's word will fulfill me? Am I relying on the kindness of others for my worth, or am I looking toward where my true nourishment lies? Where and on whom am I focusing my energy? Time to come home again!

Precious Seconds

I find it interesting how time is taken for granted. We allow seconds to tick by without a thought about how precious that second is. Such as with a word or an action, we act as if spewing venomous words or striking an abusive blow will flow by without any regard for how precious those moments that are squandered are. When did we get to the point in our lives when words and actions stopped mattering and how we react to another lays the groundwork for a future foundation being restored or crumbling? When did we stop caring about our family, friends, and neighbors to the point of self-gratification, judgment, and assimilation? When did the precious seconds of our lives stop mattering?

CHAPTER 16

A Few Thoughts
Just Another Thought
and
A Few Notable Quotables of Inspiration

Recreation

When we engage in a recreation of our choice, we are allowing ourselves the downtime that is needed to recreate ourselves. This is not to say that we do an entire makeover, but it is allowing ourselves to reexplore a passion, reaffirm a decision, or recommit to a relationship or project. Recreation has always been given a label of play, allowing ourselves to just be can bring a new light to a darkness that has us hostage. The next time you need to take a break, go out and play and recreate yourself into a child who has wonder, joy, passion, and love to share.

Make New Memories

When the new day dawns, there is a feeling of peace and a cleansing from yesterday's fears. In the early hours of dawn, calmness and security surround me like a warm hug. Attempting to carry this feeling throughout the day can become challenging if a situation that does not align with peace occurs, so in the reaction that may or may not disrupt this peace, I seek guidance and the knowledge that all is well. I used to think that if only I could, then all would be, but it is not living without but learning to live within, to deal and cope with all that is or isn't meant to be. So I will continue to embrace the new day's dawn and that feeling of peace and a cleansing from yesterday's fears and make new memories of joy and love.

New Year Blessing

After the snow has fallen and the clouds have cleared, this is the quiet, peaceful time to feel the peace within my soul. It's before the snow has been disturbed that the silence within helps me appreciate my abundance of blessings. Although life has turned out a bit different from what I anticipated, I know all is well and as it should be. In this New Year, may I continue my spiritual journey to fulfill my destiny and accept all that is and let go of all that is not. May we all be blessed with God's grace, mercy, and unconditional love. May we all have financial security and good health and find emotional peace within.

Let Go

Let go of attempting to change what is. At most, all that you will change is the appearance of things. You can make the crooked line straight and the heat cold, but if you want to change the nature of things, you will never succeed.

Finished

My pain comes from my memories, from holding on to all the indiscretions of others and my own. I can forgive, and I do not need to seek restitution. I do not need to retaliate. I can be cautious and hopeful. I can wait for behaviors to change. I can move forward; it is finished. When I can forgive these indiscretions and release the hopes that it will change, then I can give these burdens to God. "Forgive them for they know not what they do."

Missed Opportunities

Her name was Vivian. A while back, I was going to try to reconnect with her, but she decided to say goodbye. I started to call, but my fear set in, thinking she won't accept me, she will judge me, and she will dismiss me again. *Why am I setting myself up for another disappointment and rejection?* I thought. So what I've learned is that if my thoughts are coming from a place of love, then I should act on them! It was another missed opportunity. She died. I should have called. Next time, I will follow my love thoughts!

Adversity

Adversity is such a strong word that takes on a personal meaning. This is how I have incorporated adversity into my life: Learning to live with the pain and not in the pain is a sign of adversity. Showing up as my best, true child of God is a sign of adversity. When I know better, when I choose to do better, is a sign of adversity. Doing what's ethically and morally sound even if no one is watching is a sign of adversity. Taking the risk to stand beside the truth, even when knowing it may result in standing alone, is a sign of adversity. Honoring my own word and truth is a sign of adversity. Tell me, how do you deal with conflict?

Displace

When sleep-deprived or hunger sets in or I feel depleted, I can become agitated by anything that tries to get my attention. In the past, if my temper was short, my sons would ask me if they did something to offend me; and of course, my reply was no. I gave them permission to guide me by saying, "Please don't take it out on me." This humble request would help me refocus on what was really important. I am now aware, by my sons' gift, that when I am hungry, I will eat; and when I am tired, I will rest; and if I feel depleted, I will take time for myself to replenish that which I have shared. There is no need to displace my stuff on anyone else.

Be Content

Be content with doing things well. Let the world take care of itself. Live your life in the peace of having conquered the fear of not knowing. Having come home to yourself, you will experience great contentment and satisfaction. Having come home to yourself, you will experience a greater joy than you've ever expected. Stop chasing after what is not. Become more comfortable with what is. This is the key to satisfaction.

Satisfaction in What Is

Satisfaction is letting go of attempting to change what is. I will live my life in the peace of having conquered the fear of not knowing. This is what faith is. I will believe in the future that I do not see. Celebrating having come home to myself, I will experience great contentment and satisfaction. Having come home to me will help me experience a joy greater than I've ever expected.

Stop chasing what is not and become more comfortable with what is. It eludes us because we are trying to fill an empty hole whose very nature is to be empty. We try and try and try, but the empty hole cannot be filled. We spend so much energy in trying that we completely forget that there is nothing to do. Satisfaction eludes us because all effort is in vain.

*****

A child who is never told no will never learn to say no. Happiness isn't getting what you want but experiencing who you are. Discover the difference between doing and becoming. Consider the source of who is attacking you before you react. It may be their issue. Do I really need to convince the other person of what I see? I will just escape the situation with my own peace of mind intact.

Before I waste it on anger, resentment, spite, or envy, I should think of how precious and irreplaceable my time is; positive reactions pay off. Trying excessively to make a point with another may be an indication that I have not yet made that point with myself. It's about taking myself seriously and walking my talk. Do I struggle with an unending darkness, briefly looking for a glimpse of light?

I don't need to remember the pain of every experience that has taught me a lesson, only the lessons themselves. Forgiveness is giving up and letting go of the hope that the past could have been different. The outcome will never change, only how I react to it.

So often, through my compassion and forgiveness for others, I lose myself or cut others off to preserve myself. But compassion is a deeper feeling that waits beyond the tension of choosing sides. Compassion, in practice, does not require me to give up the truth of what I feel or the truth of my reality, nor does it allow me to minimize the humanity of those who have hurt me.

Rather, I ask myself enough that I can stay open to the truth of others, even when their truth or their inability to live up to their own truth has hurt me. I need to tap into me and remain God centered. I am not a pebble on anyone's shoes. I need to break things down in order to get them out. I need to let the cold thaw and to let the warmth in and break and crack the hardness so the light may enter.

My truth is when I know something from within, and nothing or no one from without can shake it. It is something so real to me that it won't matter if the whole world goes against me, telling me I am wrong. This is the joy of my inner knowing. I will go within to seek my truth and live life in peace and confidence.

Revenge is the weak pleasure of a narrow mind. Resentment is like swallowing poison in hopes that your enemy will die.

I will work with the shadow and examine what inside me magnifies misfortune into my life. I recognize the troubles, denials, and setbacks of life as teachers, guides, and allies. There is work to be done on me. At the point of great darkness, I become aware of my light, my creative power, of who I am. Though I walk through the valley of the shadow of death, I will fear no evil. God is with me.

Love like you'll never get hurt, dance like no one is watching, and sing like no one is listening. Life is not waiting for the storm to pass; it's learning to dance in the rain. All human actions are motivated at their deepest level by one of two emotions: love or fear. As you think, so you are. Don't die a failure because you don't try. Don't be afraid of death; be afraid of a life that is not fulfilled. I have to try, because if I don't try, I haven't lived.

The danger is that through hasty or ill-timed action, life force leaks out or is spelled away. If an association is short-lived, do not grieve, but

know that it has fulfilled its span. Matters of trust and confidence are at issue here and, with them, the authenticity of your way of being in the world. Examine your motives and ask if it is self-conquest of which you are concerned, or are you trying to dominate another? Are you lusting after outcomes, or are you focused on the task?

Owning my own power, relinquishing control to another, and trying to manipulate outcomes are heavy issues for me. In owning my own power is where I am secure and confident. Relinquishing my power to others comes from my fears and insecurities of being unloved and abandoned. Trying to control others is my reaction to losing focus and power. Side steps are when I lose my focus and power. It's when it's time to regroup and get back to me. These are hard lessons, but they are very welcome. They cause growth and pain.

If we spot a problem, we must be honest about it. If something isn't working now, accept reality. Let us not dwell on the negative parts of our experiences. There is magic in the empowering of good, because whatever we empower grows bigger. Some ways to empower the good are through affirmations, positive reactions, and simple, positive statements that we can make to ourselves. Our choice for recovery is in finding the answers within ourselves, not in outside advice. Let us consult ourselves and the actions proper to ourselves. The need for someone's love to feel validated is a contradiction to letting it begin with us.

I have come to expect only what I have already decided is there, and I've missed the moment-to-moment experience. My fantasies also limit me, because I've boxed myself in a predictable pattern. No matter how rich my thoughts are, I become rigid and binding when they are fixed rather than spontaneous; and in so being, they lose their life and their beauty. Live each day as if it's the last, and seize the moment.

Many of us lived in systems with people who refused to tolerate our emotions. We were shamed or reprimanded for expressing feelings, usually by people who were taught to repress their own. It's okay for us to acknowledge and accept our emotions. We don't need to allow our emotions to control us, but we have to be aware that there is something that needs our attention. It's okay to feel without punishing the source of the pain. Dealing with feelings prevents anger from turning into resentment.

I don't use recovery as an excuse to harden my heart and shut down my emotions. I can still feel and listen, and I stay with my feelings until it's time to release them appropriately. So feel, be aware, act when it's time, and choose appropriate behavior. Release and move to the next life lesson, because all is temporary and all causes growth. Obstacles of my past can become the gateways that will lead to new beginnings.

It is unreasonable to expect anyone to be able or willing to meet our every request. We are responsible for asking for what we want and need, and it is the other person's responsibility to freely choose whether to respond to our request.

If we try to coerce or force another to be there for us, that's controlling.

There is a difference between demanding and asking. It's unreasonable and unhealthy to expect one person to be this source for meeting all our needs. Ultimately, we will become angry and resentful and may even be punishing toward that person for not supporting us as we expect. If a person cannot or will not be there for us, then we need to take responsibility for ourselves in that relationship.

*****

The Cycle of Abundance
Rabbi Rav Brandwein

Once a person begins on her spiritual path of knowledge, she will only look inward, learning how to fix herself, instead of trying to fix others. Attract, receive, gratefulness, generosity, giving and align with God.

Hidden Lessons That Teach
Jackson Kiddard

Anything that annoys, teaches patience.
Anything that angers, teaches forgiveness and compassion.
Anyone who abandons, teaches self-reliance.
Anything that holds my power, teaches me to take it back.
Anything I hate, teaches unconditional love.
Anything I fear, teaches courage and bravery to overcome fear.

Anything I can't control, teaches me to let it go.

*****

I realize that all of us were mistaken in thinking we were supposed to be who they thought we should be and us agreeing with them.

Being who I am doesn't let others down, but not being who I am lets God down.

"Do unto others…" It should be, "Do unto myself as I would do unto others and as I want them to do unto me."

Forgiveness doesn't build walls. It builds boundaries. I don't have to keep the pain alive to keep the truth alive. The pain has a message.

Self-acceptance is releasing others' opinions.

Loving myself requires courage unlike any other so I can define my own self-worth. It requires me to believe and stay loyal to something no one else can see, and it keeps me in the world.

Dreams are questions we haven't figured out how to ask.

To bring anything into my life, I imagine it's already there.

I don't need to be better than anyone else. I want to be better than I used to be, not bitter.

It was never truly about convincing them that I was lovable, worthy, trusting, kind, compassionate, empathetic, patient, forgiving, and a blessing. It was about believing it myself.

Always, what is rising up replaces what is falling away as I begin to fall back into myself.

And when they came back, I had filled myself with me so that the void that was left when they left was already replaced.

Accepting rather than expecting brings me peace.

In the movie *Hugo*, the title character said, "The whole world is one big machine. Machines don't come with extra parts. They always come up with the exact amount they need. If the entire Universe was one big machine, I couldn't be an extra part. I had to be here for some reason."

I have a purposeful life that I am to fulfill to my highest potential. I have a voice. I have a truth. I see me. I hear me. I am!

I will treat myself the way I treat others. I deserve the best!

I will act rather than react on my behalf. Only I know what's best for me.

I can define me! What others think are just suggestions. I don't need to be right. I just want to be happy.

We always benefit from our ancestors' struggles. I thank them for the foundation they laid so that I could build my life upon their sacrifice.

"I am not willing at this time" means no. "I am willing at this time" means yes. These are divine opportunities toward problem-solving.

If you don't have a test, you won't have a testimonial.

"I am temporarily out of money" means there is more to come.

When I come to a crossroad and I say to myself, "I don't know," I close my eyes, take a deep breath, and listen to myself, and then I listen for the answer.

I've got to be willing to be wrong.

God has a plan, and the problems come with solutions.

If you want to know the end of the situation, take a look at the beginning.

Nothing can penetrate solid. It is through the cracks that the light of God can enter.

An adult's lie becomes a child's truth.

When I am still and listen, I can hear me, I can see me, and I can feel God in me. My truth and my voice come from God.

I will confront the darkest parts of myself. I will work to banish the darkness with illumination and forgiveness. My willingness to wrestle with my demons will cause my angels to sing.

Faith is making it across the dark from the point of light to the point of light. God is there, even in the darkness.

Faith is the substance of things hoped for and the evidence of things not yet seen. How important is it that I can't wait for God's timing?

Fear is the opposite of faith, God is the opposite of Satan, and dark is the opposite of light. When I turn my problems into opportunities and goals, I turn my fear into faith.

That, that is seen as temporary. That, that is not seen as eternal.

Where I am is better than where I was before. New beginnings have new endings.

Disappointment comes with expectations and judgments. Disappointment is inevitable, but misery is optional.

"We do not lead others into the light by stepping into the darkness with them." (Melody Beattie)

Simplicity means returning to the source. Patience leads to understanding, and compassion brings love.

We always benefit from our ancestors' struggles, so thank them.

Not about me, yet all about me.

The new seed in the old shell, I guess it's time to crack it open and see what's inside.

We are all souls on a spiritual, evolutionary journey. We are all here to learn from and teach to one another. We are all here in this very moment that is not defined by our past, but we know we've learned from it. Our future is nothing more than a welcome experience of joy, love, and blessings. We get to decide what to do and how to feel in any given moment knowing nothing is done to us, only for us.

It's a journey, not a destination, so wait for a moment and ask, "Did I see that?"

Whispering ever so softly, God speaks to me and says, "I have what you need for the day, so pack light."

Guns don't kill a soul, and pills don't kill a soul. What kills a soul are words and lack of faith.

Fear is perhaps the greatest enemy, and what is it but ignorance? Ignorance is the unwillingness to accept the nature of things. It is a forgetfulness or thoughtlessness. Fear is not an obstacle to a person who pays attention.

A blessing is invoking divine favor and conferring well-being or prosperity.

I choose happiness, peace, and joy by acting on my own behalf rather than reacting to others. I respond to misunderstandings by being who I am completely. Otherwise, I am reacting, countering, and never being. I would rather be proactive than reactive.

The approval I get is never truly satisfying when I have given away myself to get it. God shows His approval through my peace of mind. Self-love is believing we are worthy of being loved and of accepting God's love.

A walk with God means being untouched by selfishness, being unmoved by passion, and being impervious to strife and dissension by keeping an open heart and open mind and choosing words with love.

I must examine my motives. Is it self-conquest about which I am concerned, or am I trying to dominate another? Compassion or condemnation? What is the clarity of my intentions? I must be certain that I am not suffering over my suffering. Contemplate, be still, and wait for God.

Expectations lead to a detour of my faith and cause judgment, resentment, despair, bitterness, and disappointment. Anticipation is done in faith and in waiting for the truth of God's will. I am grateful when I forgive trespasses and when I remain connected to my faith, which dissolves resentments, judgments, and disappointments from unmet expectations.

The virtues seriousness, sincerity, and emptiness—to possess them is to have tranquility, which is the ground for clarity, patience, and perseverance.

Fame or peace? Being a celebrity, or celebrating being? Walk to be seen, or devote to see? Build an identity on attention I get, or find my place in the beauty of things by the attention I give? Great power, or clear and true?

Impatience is aspiring to reach the destination by hurrying through and not appreciating the blessing of the journey. Where I commune, God is in my soul.

I'm no better or worse than anyone else. I just want to be better than who I was.

Thy will, not mine, be done!

Let God do the work, and ask Him how you can serve Him. Think before you speak, act, and react. Let Him love you and guide you, and accept His love.

Feel deserving of His love, and love yourself, and then in turn, love others.

Flip the negative into a positive. Contradictions—God is love and light, and Satan is hate and dark.

CHAPTER 17

My Testimony

When making a decision, I tend to weigh the pros and cons of the results, and then I have to deal with the combative voice in my head that tells me I will fail or it's the wrong thing to do. Once I silence that voice from my thoughts, I can clearly determine if I can live with the consequences of my decision. So I stop and retreat from the combat within me and listen to hear what wisdom and guidance I've been given to live with what decision I choose.

After spending decades listening to opinions, judgments, and interpretations, I was guided to seek the truth. I became a truth seeker. I asked questions, researched references, and read the Bible. This was not an easy task, because I had to question what I believed was my truth and who I trusted to deliver the truth. I asked how I would really know what the truth was. I lived my life in the shadow of another's interpretation of the truth.

I always feared doubting their word, because when I sought an alternative to what they offered, I was threatened with banishment, so consequently, to my own detriment, I stayed in bondage in my own self-inflicted prison. I knew that love was the opposite of fear, light the opposite of darkness, and truth the opposite of a lie. I knew a lie was still a lie even if one hundred people said it was the truth. I just wanted to know the truth so I could continue to live in the light and love and have faith that when I asked for the truth, I would get it.

I know I can share what I know about someone, but does that characterize a relationship? I can say I know about God and believe there's a God, but does that mean I know Him, trust Him, and have faith in Him? Does this mean I have a relationship with Him? He's made seven promises: "I am your strength," "I will never leave you," "I have plans for you to prosper," "I hear your prayers," "I fight for you," "I will give you peace," and "I always love you." Now why wouldn't anyone want to have a relationship with someone who offers these promises?

In my truth-seeking quest—asking questions, researching references, and reading the Bible—I read Isaiah 53 in the Old Testament and started to align my prior background knowledge to what I was learning. I discovered this truth: Sin separated us from God. Jesus, being God in the flesh, loved us so much that He was willing to separate Himself from His spiritual God self, to take on our sins as the human self-sacrifice. By this act of grace, He washed away our sins and became the last sacrifice. "My God, My God, why have You forsaken Me?" were the words Jesus cried as He lay dying on the cross. This was His human self, separated from His God self due to taking on our sin so that we would no longer be separated from God due to sin.

I also learned that He never left me, that I left Him. I know what separates me from God; it's me. So I will repent and change my behavior and try to sin no more. With God's guidance, I can decide what's best for me. With one more promise fulfilled, the sun rises. With one more promise fulfilled, the birds sing. With one more promise fulfilled, the flower blooms. With one more promise, I awake to a new dawn, take a deep breath, and thank God for one more promise that He has fulfilled. How do I know this? Because He promised! Now who wouldn't want this?

So if you'll reread the first paragraph about making decisions, you'll notice I've made one of the most important decisions of my life. This weekend was the beginning of my High Holy Days, and Friday night through Sunday was Rosh Hashanah, my New Year. My Israel trip in February may be canceled, where I plan to be baptized in the Jordan River, so I decided to be baptized this past Sunday, September 20, 2020, year 5781, in the Arkansas River at 11:45 a.m.

After living most of my life in the shadows, I can now come into the light knowing that I am safe and secure and that I am loved, cherished, wanted, and purposeful. I know Jesus is my Messiah and my Lord and Savior. In this humble self-proclamation is the knowledge that God's love for me far outweighs the bitterness and despair that dwelled in my heart. Knowing where my true nourishment lies, I can move forward. I know that for the rest of my life, God, Jesus, and the Holy Spirit will love me, and that's the truth!

May God bless you and keep you in His care. May God bless your journey, and may you find joy and peace and love, as I have.

BIBLIOGRAPHY

Andrews, Andy. *The Traveler's Gift*. Nashville, TN: W Publishing Group, 2002.

Beattie, Melody. *Codependent No More*. New York, NY: Hazelden Foundation / Harper Collins Publishers, 1986.

———. *Beyond Codependency and Getting Better All the Time*. New York, NY: Hazelden Foundation / Harper Collins Publishers, 1989.

———. *The Language of Letting Go*. New York, NY: Hazelden Foundation / Harper Collins Publishers, 1990.

———. *Finding Your Way Home*. New York, NY: Hazelden Foundation / Harper Collins Publishers, 1998.

———. *Playing It by Heart*. New York, NY: Hazelden Foundation / Harper Collins Publishers, 1999.

Blum, Ralph. *Book of Runes*. New York, NY: St. Martin's Press, 1982.

Caddy, Eileen. *Opening Doors Within*. Scotland: The Findhorn Press, 1987.

Central Conference of American Rabbis. *Union Home Prayer Book*. Philadelphia, PA: Press of Maurice Jacobs Inc., 1951.

Dayton, Tian, MA, AMS. *Daily Affirmations for Forgiving and Moving On*. New York, NY: Innerlook Inc., 1992.

Hayes, Louise. *You Can Heal Your Life*. New York City, NY: Hat House Inc., 1999.

Nepo, Mark. *The Book of Awakening*. San Francisco, CA: Conari Press, 2000.

Osteen, Joel. *Your Best Life Begins Each Morning*. New York, NY: Faith Words / Hachette Book Group, 2008.

Wisdom of Tao. Vancouver, Canada: The Book Laboratory / Raincoast Books, 2002.

Young, William Paul. *The Shack*. Newbury Park, CA: Windblown Media, 2007.

BIBLES

Life Application Study Bible, Third Edition, NIV. Grand Rapids, MI: Tyndale / Zondervan Publishing House, 2019.
Recovery Devotional Bible, NIV. Grand Rapids, MI: Zondervan Publishing House, 1993.

ABOUT THE AUTHOR

Robin Beth Saget describes herself as a completed Jew. She just recently started her relationship with Jesus as her Messiah, Lord, and Savior. She was baptized on September 20, 2020. She is a retired elementary school teacher/lead instructional teacher, having served for over twenty-five years. She grew up in Philadelphia, Pennsylvania, and attended Temple University, receiving her bachelor's degree in education.

After relocating to New Mexico, she furthered her education at the University of New Mexico, receiving her master's and EdS in education with an emphasis in administration and reading, where she was published in a reading journal and a book about character education. She is the mother of four, grandmother to nine, and wife to Washington Barrow IV for thirty-one years. She and her husband have retired to Colorado, where they enjoy their three Airedales in God's backyard.